S

R

THE STATE OF TEXAS:
Government, Politics, and Policy

THE STATE OF TEXAS:
Government, Politics, and Policy

SECOND EDITION

Sherri Mora
Texas State University

William Ruger
Texas State University

Mc
Graw
Hill
Education

THE STATE OF TEXAS: GOVERNMENT, POLITICS, AND POLICY, SECOND EDITION

Published by McGraw-Hill Education, 2 Penn Plaza, New York, NY 10121. Copyright 2015 by McGraw-Hill Education. All rights reserved. Printed in the United States of America. Previous editions © 2014. No part of this publication may be reproduced or distributed in any form or by any means, or stored in a database or retrieval system, without the prior written consent of McGraw-Hill Education, including, but not limited to, in any network or other electronic storage or transmission, or broadcast for distance learning.

Some ancillaries, including electronic and print components, may not be available to customers outside the United States.

This book is printed on acid-free paper.

1 2 3 4 5 6 7 8 9 0 DOW/DOW 1 0 9 8 7 6 5 4

ISBN 978-1-259-18701-8
MHID 1-259-18701-2

Senior Vice President, Products & Markets: *Kurt L. Strand*
Vice President, General Manager, Products & Markets: *Michael J. Ryan*
Vice President, Content Design & Delivery: *Kimberly Meriwether David*
Managing Director: *Gina Boedeker*
Brand Manager: *Laura Wilk*
Lead Product Developer: *Dawn Groundwater*
Digital Product Analyst: *John Brady*
Product Developer: *Denise Wright*
Marketing Manager: *April Cole*
Content Project Manager: *Rick Hecker*
Senior Buyer: *Michael R. McCormick*
Designer: *Matt Diamond*
Senior Content Licensing Specialists: *John C. Leland/Ann Marie Jannette*
Media Project Manager: *Emily Kline*
Typeface: *10/12 Kepler STD Regular*
Compositor: *Laserwords Private Limited*
Printer: *R. R. Donnelley*

All credits appearing on page or at the end of the book are considered to be an extension of the copyright page.

Library of Congress Cataloging-in-Publication Data

Mora, Sherri.
   The state of Texas : government, politics, and policy/Sherri Mora, Texas State University, William Ruger, Texas State University. — Second edition.
      pages cm
      ISBN 978-1-259-18701-8 (alk. paper)
      1. Texas—Politics and government. I. Ruger, William. II. Title.
   JK4816.M67 2015
   320.4764—dc23
                                                                          2014019400

www.mhhe.com

The State of Texas: Government, Politics, and Policy is designed around the Learning Outcomes and Core Objectives for GOVT 2306 as defined by the Texas Higher Education Coordinating Board. With a comprehensive content program, a revision that was informed by student data, and numerous assignable activities in Connect Texas Government®, *The State of Texas* includes ample material for a full semester course on Texas government. Connect Texas Government with LearnSmart and Smartbook is organized around the Texas Learning Outcomes and provides the ability to assess directly on those outcomes.

The State of Texas offers the best coverage, assessment, and learning resources on the market. It's an easy choice.

Coverage Made Easy

The State of Texas not only covers the new Learning Outcomes and Core Objectives for GOVT 2306, but also does so in a way that makes the program SACS-compliant. Although it is important to meet the legislative mandates and the requirements of external accrediting bodies, we should strive to assess and evaluate outcomes in the spirit of "institutional curiosity" (Maki, 2002).[1] *The State of Texas* hits the mark, drawing from SACS best practices in assessment. Each learning outcome is mapped to core objectives using two measures within two domains, thereby providing a comprehensive view of student learning.

Learning Outcomes and Core Objectives

GOVT 2306 is one of the foundational component areas within the Core Curriculum identified by the Undergraduate Education Advisory Committee (UEAC) of the Texas Higher Education Coordinating Board (THECB). The UEAC has identified six core objectives, of which four—critical thinking skills, communication skills, social responsibility, and personal responsibility—must be mapped to content in GOVT 2306. Those four core objectives are mapped to specific *The State of Texas* content here and throughout each chapter.

Institutions must assess learning outcomes (provided in the *UEAC's Academic Course Guide Manual*); for example, the student's demonstrated ability to explain the origin and development of the Texas constitution, consistent with assessment practices required by the Commission on Colleges of the Southern Association of Colleges and Schools (SACS-COC).

These requirements include an explanation of measures, methodology, frequency, and timeline of assessment; an explanation of targets and benchmarks of "Core Objective" attainment; evidence of attainment of the required core objectives; interpretation of assessment information; and the use of results for improving student learning. SACS principles of accreditation 3.3.1.1 requires institutions to identify expected learning outcomes, assess the extent to which it achieves these outcomes, and provide evidence of improvement based on analysis of the results.

Adopting *The State of Texas* and using the provided assessment tools makes SACS compliance easy while meeting the purpose of the Core Curriculum.

[1]Maki, Peggy L. "Developing an assessment plan to learn about student learning." *The Journal of Academic Librarianship* 28.1 (2002): 8–13.

Learning Outcomes and Core Objectives Correlation Table

CHAPTER 1	**Learning Outcome:** Analyze the political culture of Texas.	Thinking Critically	How have settlement patterns impacted Texas? Give current examples.
	Learning Outcome: Analyze the political culture of Texas.	Communicating Effectively	Write a short synopsis of Texas's changing economy and its role in international trade.
	Learning Outcome: Analyze the political culture of Texas.	Taking Personal Responsibility	What can you do to become well informed about political issues so that you can make good decisions at election time?
	Learning Outcome: Analyze the political culture of Texas.	Being Socially Responsible	Understanding the relationship between religious affiliations and politics can improve civic knowledge. How would you use this knowledge to engage effectively in your community?
CHAPTER 2	**Learning Outcome:** Describe separation of powers and checks and balances in both theory and practice in Texas.	Communicating Effectively	Analyze the diagram in Figure 2.1 and the division of powers in Table 2.1 to describe the separation of powers and checks and balances in both theory and practice in Texas.
	Learning Outcome: Explain the origin and development of the Texas Constitution.	Thinking Critically	What is the impact of a constitutional convention dominated by one party? What were the consequences of the 1875 constitutional convention in the development of the Texas Constitution?
	Learning Outcome: Describe state and local political systems and their relationship with the federal government.	Being Socially Responsible	Considering the argument that the national government has eroded state power, to what extent should the government "promote general welfare?" What does promoting general welfare mean to you? In developing an understanding of state and local political systems and their relationship with the federal government, who do you think should play a greater role—the states or the federal government?
	Learning Outcome: Describe state and local political systems and their relationship with the federal government.	Taking Personal Responsibility	As a resident of Texas and a citizen of the United States, can you identify and discuss examples that reinforce the Full Faith and Credit Clause and the Privileges and Immunities Clause of the U.S. Constitution? Can you identify examples that, in your opinion, violate these principles?
CHAPTER 3	**Learning Outcome:** Demonstrate knowledge of the legislative, executive, and judicial branches of Texas government.	Communicating Effectively	In the preceding paragraph, an argument is made that smaller constituencies might allow a wider array of people to participate in state politics, rather than just the "rich" or "well born." How would you argue in favor of or against this statement?
	Learning Outcome: Demonstrate knowledge of the legislative, executive, and judicial branches of Texas government.	Being Socially Responsible	To what extent should legislators use race when redistricting? Do you think redistricting is an appropriate tool to increase intercultural competency? Why or why not?
	Learning Outcome: Demonstrate knowledge of the legislative, executive, and judicial branches of Texas government.	Thinking Critically	As we have discussed, both the demographics and the voting patterns have changed in Texas, and some districts have become more competitive, especially for Democrats in South Texas and in inner-city districts. Referring to the previous discussion and Table 3.6, discuss what these shifts mean for future elections and the composition of the Texas House and Senate.
	Learning Outcome: Demonstrate knowledge of the legislative, executive, and judicial branches of Texas government.	Taking Personal Responsibility	It has been stated that the success of legislation depends largely on a relative few individuals who make up the leadership in the Texas House and Senate. Do you think the speaker of the house and the lieutenant governor have too much control over the passage of bills? How can you influence legislation? What can individuals do to affect legislation?

CHAPTER 4	**Learning Outcome:** Demonstrate knowledge of the executive branch of Texas government.	Communicating Effectively	Analyze Map 4.1. What inferences can be drawn from the data?
	Learning Outcome: Demonstrate knowledge of the executive branch of Texas government.	Being Socially Responsible	How does the comptroller promote effective involvement in regional, national, and global communities?
	Learning Outcome: Demonstrate knowledge of the executive branch of Texas government.	Taking Personal Responsibility	What can you do to become more actively engaged in the civic discourse about the role of the State Board of Education?
	Learning Outcome: Demonstrate knowledge of the executive branch of Texas government.	Thinking Critically	We discussed six factors that influence the strength of the power of the governor. Those six factors are the number of elected statewide executives; tenure of office; the governor's appointive powers; the governor's budgetary powers; the governor's veto powers; and the extent to which the governor controls his or her political party. What can you conclude about the powers of the governor?
CHAPTER 5	**Learning Outcome:** Demonstrate knowledge of the judicial branch of Texas government.	Communicating Effectively	Analyze Figure 5.1. Describe the appeals process for a civil case filed in county court.
	Learning Outcome: Demonstrate knowledge of the judicial branch of Texas government.	Being Socially Responsible	What impact, if any, do you think partisan election of judges has on judicial outcomes?
	Learning Outcome: Demonstrate knowledge of the judicial branch of Texas government.	Thinking Critically	As you learned from the discussion on minority representation in the Texas judicial system, African Americans represent 12.3 percent of the population of Texas, but only 4.1 percent of all judges in Texas are black. Compare these facts with Figure 5.3. What do you think accounts for the disproportionate number of African Americans incarcerated in Texas?
	Learning Outcome: Demonstrate knowledge of the judicial branch of Texas government.	Taking Personal Responsibility	Currently, at what age does the State of Texas consider a person an adult in criminal and civil proceedings? At what age do you think the state should require individuals to take personal responsibility?
CHAPTER 6	**Learning Outcome:** Describe local political systems in Texas.	Communicating Effectively	Compare Figures 6.1, 6.3, and 6.4 with Table 6.2. Discuss the fundamental differences between weak mayor, strong mayor, and council-manager forms of government. Which do you prefer and why?
	Learning Outcome: Describe local political systems in Texas.	Being Socially Responsible	Compare at-large election systems and single-member district systems. An argument in favor of single-member district systems is that they increase minority representation in local government. In your opinion, does increased minority representation increase intercultural competency? Why?
	Learning Outcome: Describe local political systems in Texas.	Taking Personal Responsibility	Local government directly impacts people in their daily lives. What can you do to improve local governance?
	Learning Outcome: Describe local political systems in Texas.	Thinking Critically	Identify some of the problems facing county governments. What solutions would you propose?

Learning Outcomes and Core Objectives Correlation Table continued

	Learning Outcome	Core Objective	Question
CHAPTER 7	**Learning Outcome:** Identify the rights and responsibilities of citizens.	Taking Personal Responsibility	What activities do you engage in that are related to governance? Which forms of political participation do you think are the most effective?
	Learning Outcome: Identify the rights and responsibilities of citizens.	Thinking Critically	How do you think the Texas voter ID law will impact voter turnout in Texas? Where do you stand on the issue? Explain why you favor or oppose voter ID laws.
	Learning Outcome: Identify the rights and responsibilities of citizens.	Being Socially Responsible	Considering the discussion on the socioeconomic factors that affect voter turnout, identify effective ways to increase civic knowledge in culturally diverse communities.
	Learning Outcome: Identify the rights and responsibilities of citizens.	Communicating Effectively	Write a one-page summary of the rationalist explanations for low voter turnout.
CHAPTER 8	**Learning Outcome:** Analyze the state and local election process in Texas.	Thinking Critically	Explain the challenges that hinder minor party candidates from succeeding in statewide elections.
	Learning Outcome: Analyze the state and local election process in Texas.	Communicating Effectively	Do you think the Voting Rights Act requirement that Texas provide a bilingual ballot in counties with more than 20 percent Spanish speakers increases voter turnout? Construct an argument in favor or against this provision of the Voting Rights Act.
	Learning Outcome: Analyze the state and local election process in Texas.	Being Socially Responsible	What responsibility do you think the media have in covering campaigns and elections? Are the media living up to your expectations?
	Learning Outcome: Analyze the state and local election process in Texas.	Taking Personal Responsibility	If you choose to contribute to a candidate's campaign, to what extent is the candidate obligated to you as a contributor? Should your contribution influence public policy? What about corporate contributions?
CHAPTER 9	**Learning Outcome:** Evaluate the role of political parties in Texas.	Taking Personal Responsibility	Examine your political values and compare them to the expressed values of both parties. Do your ideas about the role of government, politics, and policy align with one particular party?
	Learning Outcome: Evaluate the role of political parties in Texas.	Being Socially Responsible	What impact, if any, do factions have on enhancing or diminishing civic engagement? In your opinion, do factions promote acceptance of diverse opinions?
	Learning Outcome: Evaluate the role of political parties in Texas.	Communicating Effectively	Explain how political reforms have weakened political parties.
	Learning Outcome: Evaluate the role of political parties in Texas.	Thinking Critically	On average, about 1 in 3 Texans identify themselves as independents, suggesting that they do not align with either the Republicans or the Democrats. What measures might be taken to level the playing field for third parties and improve their competitiveness in elections?

CHAPTER 10	**Learning Outcome:** Evaluate the role of interest groups in Texas.	Thinking Critically	Review Table 10.1. Are you a participant in a membership organization? If so, how does the organization represent your interests? If not, how are your interests represented at the state and federal levels of government?
	Learning Outcome: Evaluate the role of interest groups in Texas.	Taking Personal Responsibility	Socrates suggested, "know thyself," and Shakespeare's Hamlet admonished "to thine own self be true." It is important to know what your interests are and how they are represented in government. Consider what you have read in this chapter and determine how interest group efforts align with your personal interests. If they do not, what can you do to ensure that government addresses your interests or the interests of those who share similar values?
	Learning Outcome: Evaluate the role of interest groups in Texas.	Communicating Effectively	Review the data presented in Table 10.4. Identify the interest group category that spent the most money in 2012. Discuss the impact that PAC spending has on government.
	Learning Outcome: Evaluate the role of interest groups in Texas.	Being Socially Responsible	How can geographic distribution of interest groups improve political awareness between culturally diverse populations?
CHAPTER 11	**Learning Outcome:** Analyze issues and policies of Texas.	Taking Personal Responsibility	How can you impact public policy decisions? At what point in the policy cycle could you voice your preferences?
	Learning Outcome: Analyze issues and policies of Texas.	Being Socially Responsible	To what extent should Texas be responsible for ensuring equal funding for wealthy school districts and poor school districts?
	Learning Outcome: Analyze issues and policies of Texas.	Communicating Effectively	Summarize the legislation that Texas has passed on abortion. Discuss the advantages and disadvantages of state involvement in this policy issue.
	Learning Outcome: Analyze issues and policies of Texas.	Thinking Critically	Given the water-related challenges facing Texas, what measures would you recommend to ensure all Texans have access to water? What might be some negative or unintended consequences of your recommendations?
CHAPTER 12	**Learning Outcome:** Analyze issues and policies of Texas.	Thinking Critically	What goods and services do you think state government should provide? Consider the consequences of your answer. What would the possible impact to society be, given your position?
	Learning Outcome: Analyze issues and policies of Texas.	Being Socially Responsible	Texas taxes prepared food items, but does not tax unprepared food items (e.g., raw meats and fresh produce). If, as it was noted earlier in this chapter, individuals can be excluded from receiving services, such as electricity, because of the inability to pay, how does taxing prepared food impact our state's poorest citizens?
	Learning Outcome: Analyze issues and policies of Texas.	Communicating Effectively	Consider Table 12.6, which illustrates how specific appropriations are restricted. What percentage of funds is not restricted? How does restricting funds impact budget flexibility?
	Learning Outcome: Analyze issues and policies of Texas.	Taking Personal Responsibility	Although few individuals would express a preference for higher taxes, given the information in this chapter about the goods and services the state provides and the revenue data presented in Figure 12.8 and Table 12.7, should Texans advocate for a personal income tax? Why or why not?

Assessment Made Easy

▤|SMARTBOOK˚

S tudents study more effectively with LearnSmart® and SmartBook®.
LearnSmart is an adaptive learning program designed to help students
learn faster, study smarter, and retain more knowledge for greater success.
Distinguishing what students know from what they don't, and focusing on concepts they are most likely to forget, LearnSmart continuously adapts to each student's needs by building an individual learning path. Millions of students have
answered more than a billion questions in LearnSmart since 2009, making it the
most widely used and intelligent adaptive study tool that's proven to strengthen
memory recall, keep students in class, and boost grades.

Fueled by LearnSmart, SmartBook is the first and only adaptive reading experience currently available.

- **Make It Effective.** SmartBook creates a personalized reading experience by
  highlighting the most impactful concepts a student needs to learn at that
  moment in time. This ensures that every minute spent with SmartBook is
  returned to the student as the most value-added minute possible.
- **Make It Informed.** The reading experience continuously adapts by
  highlighting content based on what the student knows and doesn't know.
  Real-time reports quickly identify the concepts that require more attention
  from individual students—or the entire class. SmartBook detects the content
  a student is most likely to forget and brings it back to improve long-term
  knowledge retention.

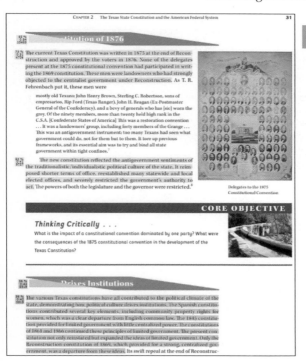

The Power of Student Data

Students helped inform the revision strategy:

STEP 1. Over the course of three years, data points
showing concepts that caused students the
most difficulty were anonymously collected
from the Connect Texas Government
LearnSmart product.

STEP 2. The data from LearnSmart was provided to
the authors in the form of a **Heat Map,** which
graphically illustrated "hot spots" in the text
that impacted student learning (see image to
left).

STEP 3. The authors used the Heat Map data to refine
the content and reinforce student comprehension
in the new edition. Additional quiz questions
and assignable activities were created for use in
Connect Texas Government to further support
student success.

RESULT: Because the **Heat Map** gave the authors empirically-based feedback at the paragraph and even sentence level, they were able to develop the new edition using precise student data that pinpointed concepts that caused students the most difficulty.

Real Time Reports, On the Go, Made Easier

Student performance reports shows you about their progress.

The first and only analytics tool of its kind, Connect Insight® is a series of visual data displays—each framed by an intuitive question—to provide at-a-glance information regarding how your class is doing.

- **Make It Intuitive.** You receive instant, at-a-glance view of student performance matched with student activity.
- **Make It Dynamic.** Connect Insight puts real-time analytics in your hands so you can take action early and keep struggling students from falling behind.
- **Make It Mobile.** Connect Insight travels from office to classroom, available on demand wherever and whenever it's needed.

BRIEF CONTENTS

CONTENTS

Sherri Mora is the Associate Chair and Undergraduate Program Coordinator for Political Science and Public Administration at Texas State University. She earned her Ph.D. in Adult, Professional, and Community Education, and an M.A. in Political Science and M.P.A. in Public Administration from Texas State University. She has published on teaching and learning in political science and has served as a vertical team member on College and Career Readiness Standards since 2004. As an active member of the assessment group, Mora is responsible for core curriculum assessment and programmatic review in the Department of Political Science at Texas State.

William Ruger is an Associate Professor of Political Science at Texas State University and an Adjunct Assistant Professor at the LBJ School of Public Affairs at the University of Texas-Austin. He earned his Ph.D. in Politics from Brandeis University and an A.B. from the College of William and Mary. Ruger's most recent scholarly articles include pieces in *State Politics and Policy Quarterly, Economics of Governance,* and the *Review of Political Economy.* He is also the co-author of *Freedom in the 50 States.* His research on state politics has been highlighted in many prominent news outlets, including ABC News, the Associated Press, *USA Today,* MSNBC, Fox News, the *New York Daily News,* the *Chicago Tribune,* and the *Atlanta Journal-Constitution.* Ruger is a veteran of the war in Afghanistan.

ACKNOWLEDGMENTS

We would like to thank Jennifer Ruger, Jamie Falconnier, and Mystery Cromwell for their exceptional research assistance for the second edition. We also want to thank the anonymous reviewers of the first edition, whose questions and comments made this a better edition. At McGraw-Hill Education and Southern Editorial, we are indebted to Denise Wright, Laura Wilk, Eliana White, April Cole, Michelle Greco, Dolly Womack, Tamara Newlin, Will Walter, and Rick Hecker. For their help on the first edition, our gratitude to the following individuals: Tracy Cook at Central Texas College for her thoughtful comments on the manuscript; Christopher Brown at Texas State University, Sandra Geiseler at Alamo Colleges, David McClendon at Tyler Junior College, Jerod Patterson at the University of Texas-Austin, Cindy Pressley at Austin State University, and Jason Sorens at Dartmouth College for their helpful contributions; and Meredith Grant for helping make this all happen in the first place.

Additional thanks goes to the following reviewers:

Lindsey B. McLennan, Kilgore College

Eric Miller, Blinn College, Bryan

Martha Musgrove, Tarrant County College, South

Paul Philips, Navarro College

John M. Osterman Jr., San Jacinto College, Pasadena

Blayne J. Primozich, El Paso Community College, Verde

Wesley Riddle, Central Texas College, Killeen

Jeff Stanglin, Kilgore College

CHAPTER 1

Introduction to Texas History and Politics

Upon completing this chapter, you will be able to . . .

- **Demonstrate knowledge of the history, economics, demographics, and political culture of Texas.**

History and politics are inevitably intertwined, and this is also the case in Texas. Today's Texas is the product of a variety of factors: multicultural influences, a unique geography including a vast amount of land that borders a foreign nation and has thriving ports, complicated historical relations with European powers, a unique experience with the U.S. Civil War and Reconstruction, economic shifts from agriculture to industry, shifts in political dominance from one party to the other, and changing demographics due to waves of opportunity. The current challenges Texas faces are also tied to national events. To gain a full appreciation for Texas government, we must examine the Texas of the past as well as today's Texas and put them in a framework within which we can understand them—the framework of political culture. By doing this, we can begin to appreciate the unique position Texas occupies within the United States, the ways in which it is very much "American," and the ways in which it is uniquely Texan.

The Six Flags of Texas: From Spain to Statehood

Settlement of the territory known as Texas began with north Asian tribal groups migrating down from the Bering land bridge into the Americas. These groups spread out throughout the Americas, and several eventually occupied the plains, grasslands, and coastal woodlands that are now called Texas. The Caddo Indians settled primarily in the eastern parts of Texas. The Wichita Indians claimed much of the Red River Valley and the lowland grass plains. The Karankawas made their home along the coastal plains, and the western parts of the state were settled by those tribes that eventually became part of the great horse cultures in North America: the Comanches, Apaches, Kiowas, and Tonkawas. Each of these groups would have an impact on later European settlers.

1

Spain

Spain was the first of the modern European nations to lay claim to the territory of Texas, although Spanish Texas included only a small part of today's state. Alonso Alvarez de Pineda explored and mapped the Texas coastline as early as 1519, more than 100 years before the Pilgrims landed at Plymouth Rock. However, it was not until 1540 that Francisco Vasquez de Coronado intentionally surveyed the interior of Texas. After Coronado reported back that rumors of a land filled with treasures were unfounded, Spain all but abandoned Texas for almost a century and a half. Still, Spain had raised the first of the six flags that would eventually fly over Texas.

France, Briefly

France was the second nation to lay claim and bring its flag, briefly, to the territory of Texas. After the European discovery of North America, France laid claim to all the territory encompassing the Mississippi River system (bordering much of the territory of Texas in the east and north along the Red River) as well as parts of the Spanish claims in the northwestern territories of Mexico. One settlement attempt, led by René-Robert Cavelier, Sieur de La Salle, began in 1685 (mostly by accident) when his expedition overshot New Orleans and landed on the Texas coast near Matagorda Bay. Fort Saint Louis, however, was a dismal failure because the expedition was inadequately supplied and La Salle was a poor leader. When La Salle left in 1687, taking an overland route to seek assistance from New Orleans, he was killed by his own men. The next year, Karankawa Indians destroyed the fort and either killed or captured the remaining settlers.

Spain Returns

After the remains of Fort Saint Louis were discovered in 1689, the Spanish crown decided to increase settlement efforts by establishing missions and presidios (fortified settlements) in the eastern part of its territory. The goal was to fend off future French claims by bringing Spanish settlers from Mexico into Texas territory. These Spanish settlers were known as Tejanos, and the first area they settled was the Rio Grande Valley. They established settlements along the Rio Grande and as far north and east as San Antonio. (Spanish settlements in other parts of the state lasted for only a few years, with the exception of Nacogdoches.) Although permanent Spanish settlement did not penetrate much beyond San Antonio, Spanish influence permeated the entire state. For example, most of the major rivers in Texas have Spanish names, as do other geographic features and a number of cities and counties. Spanish legal systems also left their legacy on state laws, especially those regarding land ownership and rights. For example, current laws regarding community property and those preventing the forced sale of property (ordered by a court to pay off a debt) have their origins in Spanish law.[1] The homestead exemption is another such legacy.[2]

When the United States purchased the Louisiana Territory from France in 1803, new settlement and immigration patterns emerged in East Texas. As Anglos encroached through Louisiana, Spain continued to promote settlement. But Spanish-Mexican relations were deteriorating, and Mexico declared its independence from Spain in 1821.

The Republic of Mexico

The third flag to fly over Texas was that of the Republic of Mexico, which included what had been Spanish Texas. By 1824 Texas, the northeastern-most territory of the new nation, had been combined with another province to form the new,

Gonzales flag

Mexican state of Coahuila and Texas.[3] The empresario land-grant system that had begun under the Spanish continued. (Stephen Austin renegotiated his father's Spanish grant with the new Mexican government.) Mexico continued to attract settlers into East Texas. Southern U.S. Anglos and the African American slaves they brought with them began settling there in the 1820s. These southern white Protestants were decidedly different from the Spanish Catholic settlers who already occupied Texas. Because of Mexico's own history of ethnic diversification, a strong antislavery movement was brewing. When President Santa Anna effectively declared himself dictator of Mexico and issued decrees limiting property rights and economic freedom for Anglos, the simmering conflict led to increased Anglo-Texan calls for rebellion.

Open revolt began in late 1835 when Texan and Mexican forces fought over a small six-pound cannon in Gonzales, Texas. Famously, the defenders of the cannon at Gonzales raised a flag with the words "Come and Take It" underneath a lone star and cannon. A Texan victory fed the fever of revolt, and political leaders began planning for rebellion against Mexico. Internal conflicts in Texas complicated matters. Many of the Catholic Spanish remained loyal to Mexico, while the more recently arrived Protestant Anglos generally favored independence.

Santa Anna himself took command of the Mexican forces and marched north into Texas for the stated purpose of suppressing the rebellion and expelling the Anglos. His first battle was the siege of the Alamo in February 1836. Texan forces under the command of William B. Travis were hopelessly outnumbered and had no real chance to be reinforced. The siege lasted two weeks, ending with the death of all 187 Alamo defenders on March 6, 1836. The brave resistance by the Alamo's defenders provided additional motivation for the independence movement and is today seen as the Texan equivalent of the famous Battle of Thermopylae between the Greek forces led by the Spartan 300 and the Persians. Just before the Alamo's fall, on March 2, 1836, the provisional government of Texas declared its independence from Mexico.

The Republic of Texas

The Republic of Texas flew the fourth national flag. The immediate problem for the new republic was surviving the war with Mexico. The republic did not have an organized army, and the one being assembled had little to no experience.

The Battle of the Alamo, Percy Moran, 1912

Sam Houston, the general of the Texan army, knew that he needed time to orga-nize and train if Texas was to have a chance at victory. Meanwhile, Santa Anna continued his march north and captured and killed all 350 of James Fannin's troops at what is now called the Goliad Massacre. It was becoming increasingly clear that Santa Anna intended to wipe out the Anglo-American presence in Texas permanently. In what came to be known as the "Runaway Scrape," Texans and Texas forces retreated for several weeks, moving in front of Santa Anna's army toward Louisiana. Finally, on the banks of the San Jacinto River on April 21, 1836, Houston found himself with a tactical advantage; he attacked and defeated Santa Anna's army. Santa Anna was captured and forced to sign the Treaty of Velasco, recognizing Texas's independence from Mexico.

In the aftermath of the revolution, Texas found itself a new nation with no real desire to *be* a nation. With limited resources and infrastructure, the new govern-ment was quickly bound by debt and struggled to meet its minimum obligations to its citizens. Houston had been elected the first president of Texas, and as one of the first acts of the new republic, he petitioned the government of the United States for statehood. Because the vast majority of Anglo settlers considered them-selves Americans, it seemed fitting for Texas to become part of the United States. However, the petition for statehood was denied because of the intensely political and divisive issue of slavery. At that time, if Texas was admitted into the union as a slave state, a corresponding free state would need to be created. This balancing act was not possible then, and Texas was forced to stand on its own. The United States recognized Texas's independence and set up diplomatic relations.

From 1836 to 1845, the Republic of Texas struggled to survive. Poor relations and border disputes with Mexico to the south and open hostilities with Indians in the west made governing Texas difficult. Lack of revenue and poor infrastructure continued to plague the nascent republic and made economic development challenging. Nonetheless, Texas promoted settlement of its frontier to Americans and Anglo-Europeans by offering the one thing it did have: land. In the 1840s, an organization called the **Adelsverein Society** aided this appeal for settlers by actively promoting German immigration to Texas. By 1847 this society had brought more than 7,000 Germans to Texas, most of whom settled in the vicinity of Fredericksburg in what is now known as "Hill Country."[4] By 1850, German settlers composed 5.4 percent of the population.[5]

Adelsverein Society

An organization that promoted German immigration to Texas in the 1840s

CORE OBJECTIVE

Thinking Critically...

How have settlement patterns impacted Texas? Give current examples.

The Twenty-Eighth State of the Union

Meanwhile, the idea of Manifest Destiny was gaining popularity in the United States. Many in Washington wanted to ensure that Texas and all its lands would be part of this nation, one that would stretch from the Atlantic to the Pacific. Although the diplomatic efforts to bring Texas into the Union were complex, on December 29, 1845, President Polk signed the act making Texas the twenty-eighth state of the Union. When Texas entered the Union, it retained its public debt and its public lands, forcing the U.S. government to purchase all land that was to be designated as federal. During the Compromise of 1850 (see Map 1.1), when Texas's boundary lines were finally settled, the U.S. government purchased lands that were formerly the west and northwest parts of Texas (now much of present-day New Mexico and some of Colorado and Wyoming).[6]

Thus the U.S. flag became the fifth to fly over Texas. But Mexico did not give up easily. Still claiming all of Texas as its own, Mexico broke diplomatic relations with the United States. The resulting Mexican-American War lasted from 1846 to 1848, ending with a decisive victory for the United States. In the Treaty of Guadalupe Hidalgo (in conjunction with the Gadsden Purchase in 1853), the United States officially gained Texas, California, and all the land between them. However, Texas had entered the Union at a time when the very structure of that Union was becoming tenuous.

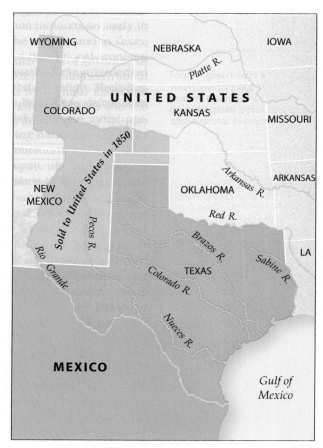

MAP 1.1   Compromise of 1850 Present state boundaries are shown along with territory transferred to the federal government as part of this agreement.

The Confederate State of Texas

From 1848 to 1860, settlement increased dramatically, with more and more immigrants coming from the southern United States and Europe. Increasingly, Texas's economy became tied to that of the southern states and the slave system. These ties were the primary reason Texas seceded from the Union in 1861 and joined the Confederacy. Texas was not among the first states to do so, because its constitutional requirements were more stringent than other southern states, but in the end, the Confederate flag was the sixth national flag to fly over Texas.

Civil War and Reconstruction: A Time of Transition

The Civil War was a costly and brutal conflict, but Texas was lucky compared to many Confederate states. Politics and geography combined to create that "luck." Oddly enough, the machinations of Napoleon III of France played a role in the war in Texas. Napoleon's goal was to set up a government in Mexico under a new emperor, Archduke Ferdinand Maximilian of Austria. Napoleon was openly pro-Confederate but did not want to risk warfare with the United States. Despite the Confederacy's desperate need for French funds and official recognition, events in Europe combined with U.S. threats to keep the French from fully committing to Confederate support. President Lincoln had ordered the Army of the Gulf, under the leadership of General Nathaniel P. Banks, to invade Texas as a show of force, to discourage French support of the Confederacy. Thanks to a complex series of events worthy of the most intrigue-laden novels, the campaign failed. Banks was relieved of field command, France did not throw her support behind the Confederacy, Maximilian became emperor (though only for a brief time), and Texas never faced the battles and physical devastation that affected much of the rest of the Confederacy.[7]

Geography also played a role in limiting Texas's exposure to the ravages of war. A line runs from the Red River to present-day Fort Worth and south through Waco and Austin to San Antonio, and the settlements of Anglo southerners did not extend west much beyond this line. (This line is a natural geological feature, known as the Balcones Escarpment, which separates the Coastal Plains and pine forest regions of Texas from the middle and High Plains regions of the state.) In fact, most areas west of this line were not settled by whites until after the Civil War, for two reasons. First, Native American tribes—Comanche, Lipan Apache, Kiowa, and Tonkawa Indians—already inhabited the region. In the 1850s, the U.S. Army tried to control this region by constructing a series of forts on the edge of the Cross Timbers area. Forts Belknap, Cooper, Phantom Hill, Chadborne, McKavett, and Terrett were part of this plan. During the Civil War, however, the U.S. government abandoned these forts, and the Indian presence in the region reemerged. Indian domination of the area continued until 1875, when Comanche Chief Quanah Parker was captured in Palo Duro Canyon, near present-day Amarillo. The second geography-related reason settlement was limited was that the dry, arid, treeless plains west of the Balcones Escarpment (Grande Prairie, Cross Timbers, lower plains, and High Plains) were not conducive to the wood, water, and plantation culture that southern Anglos brought with them.

Despite Texas's relative "luck" during the war years from 1861 to 1865, it was the home of some important Civil War events. Foremost among them were the

Battle of Galveston, Harper's Weekly, January 31, 1863.

Battle of Sabine Pass and the Battle of Galveston, both fought in 1863. In the former, a small Confederate force prevented a larger Union force from moving into Texas. In the latter, Confederate forces on land recaptured Galveston while its naval forces captured the USRC *Harriet Lane*, despite being heavily outnumbered and losing CS *Neptune*. Other noteworthy actions included the Union blockade of the Texas coast, General Henry Sibley's march to El Paso and attempt to take New Mexico and Arizona, and the ultimate stationing of nearly 50,000 U.S. troops in south Texas opposite Emperor Maximilian's Mexico during the French Intervention. It is also worth noting that roughly 90,000 Texans served in the war.[8] Overall, the lives lost in battle and the time and money lost to the conflict were devastating to both Texas and the nation.

In the immediate aftermath of the Civil War, Texas, like many other states of the former Confederacy, found itself deeply in debt and under the military control of the Union army. The era that began in 1865 and was known as Reconstruction had two primary political goals. First, the Union wanted to restore law and order to a society recovering from war. Second, the Union sought to finally dismantle the institution of slavery. As James M. McPherson and James K. Hogue stated, "No single generalization can encompass the variety of ways in which freedom came to the slaves."[9] In Texas, Union General Gordon Granger started the process of emancipation on his arrival at Galveston by issuing General Order Number 3 on June 19, 1865. This order informed Texans that "in accordance with a procla-mation from the Executive of the United States, all slaves are free." Importantly, it went on to note that "This involves an absolute equality of personal rights and rights of property between former masters and slaves, and the connection heretofore existing between them becomes that between employer and hired labor." This is the origin of the "Juneteenth" holiday in Texas and other states.[10]

By the time the Thirteenth Amendment became the law of the land in December 1865, U.S. slavery was outlawed. It would prove more difficult to reunite the country and truly protect the rights of African Americans in the former states of the Confederacy.

Reconstruction's goals created a culture clash between the two major ideological groups in Texas. One group was the dominant Confederate sympathizers (typically southern Democrats) who wanted to maintain the status quo of society as much as possible. The second group was composed of Union supporters, including Republican "carpetbaggers," a pejorative term used to describe Republicans who moved to the South to be appointed to political office during Reconstruction, and "scalawags," an equally derisive descriptor of Southerners who supported Reconstruction policies. During this time, being a Republican in the South essentially came to mean that you were an outsider and could not be trusted by "true" (meaning white) Southerners.

In 1866 Texas rejoined the Union after adopting a new constitution that abolished slavery, nullified the ordinances of secession, renounced the right of future secession, and repudiated the state's wartime debt. This constitution was short lived; it was replaced with another in 1869 as a result of the Reconstruction acts of the U.S. Congress and subsequent military rule imposed on Texas. This "carpetbagger's constitution" was a drastic departure from other Texas constitutions, past and future (see Chapter 2), and granted African Americans the right to vote while also disfranchising whites who had participated in the Civil War.

Southern Democrats were able to regain control of state government with the election of 1874. The new governor, Richard Coke, called for a convention to write yet another constitution. When Texas adopted its new constitution in 1876, the document demonstrated a strong distrust in the institutions of government and a heavy emphasis on the freedoms and liberties of its citizens. Although it has changed dramatically due to hundreds of amendments over the years, the 1876 constitution remains the outline of our fundamental law for the state of Texas. The Coke administration also marked the beginning of one-party Democratic politics in Texas that lasted about 100 years. Without the legal tools created by the policies of Reconstruction, or the broad political support necessary to win any public office, Republicans began to vanish from the political scene. Democrats were triumphant in Texas.

Post-Reconstruction Texas

land-based economy

An economic system in which most wealth is derived from the use of the land

A state's economy plays a role in its politics. For most of its history, the Lone Star State has had a **land-based economy**. However, that economy changed in the many decades since Reconstruction. Texas is no longer simply a rural state with an economy dominated by cattle, cotton, and oil, although these are still important elements.

Land

Early in Texas's history, many settlers were lured to the region by offers of free land. The Spanish and, later, Mexican governments provided generous land grants to any family willing to settle in the state. Each family could receive one *sitio* or *legua* (Spanish for "league"), the equivalent of about 4,428 acres of land, and a single person could receive 1,500 acres. By the 1820s it took generous incentives to convince people to settle in Texas, given the hardships of travel and simple survival there. "GTT" ("Gone to Texas") was a common sign left behind by those escaping debt or the long arm of the law. In a letter dated 1855 from Fort Clark, Texas, General P. H. Sheridan said, "If I owned Hell and Texas, I'd rent out Texas and live in Hell."[11]

Land issues also played a role in the Texas revolution in 1836 and subsequent annexation of Texas by the United States in 1845. The sheer vastness of Texas—all those acres of land—has played a role in Texas history for generations.

The Texas Economy: From Agriculture to Oil to the Service Sector

From the 1820s to 1860s, the primary use of that land was for cotton farming, which dominated the Texas economy. King Cotton was the state's major cash crop, helping Texas pay its bills from Independence through Reconstruction. The giant cattle ranches in south and west Texas also helped develop the cowboy culture and mystique of the frontier Texan. In the years following the Civil War, cattle became Texas's economic mainstay. In 1901, however, the Spindletop oil field was tapped near Beaumont, and the economy and politics of the state began to change dramatically.

Queen of Waco gusher. Spindletop, Beaumont, Port Arthur, and vicinity. Texas oil industry ca. 1901.

The discovery of oil transformed Texas in three major ways over the next century:

- Oil sparked the transition from an agricultural economy to an industrial economy. In addition to jobs directly related to the oil industry, high-tech peripheral jobs and industries developed to support or benefit from the oil industry.[12]

- Oil accelerated the growth of Texas's population and brought in new citizens from all over the United States and abroad, looking for work. These new citizens brought with them ideas about government and economics that challenged and diversified the ideas of Texas Democrats and Republicans.

- Oil accelerated the demographic shift from a rural society to an urban society. In 1900, less than 20 percent of Texans lived in urban areas. In 1950, about 60 percent lived in urban areas. By 2000, that number had increased to more than 80 percent.[13]

During the 1970s and early 1980s, the state economy experienced tremendous growth because of an increase in oil prices. But oil was not always reliable. In the mid-1980s, the price of oil declined, and with it the economy of the entire state. To many, the economic recession of the 1980s pointed to a need for more economic diversity. Perhaps the old land-based economy, which had been so important in Texas's history, could not carry the state into the twenty-first century. Passage of the North American Free Trade Agreement (NAFTA), which went into effect in 1994, offered the promise of significant economic growth because of increased trade with Mexico. Furthermore, new high-tech industries, especially in Austin, Dallas, and Houston, significantly bolstered the Texas economy. Texas Instruments helped turn the calculator into a common household item in the 1970s, and today's Texas boasts a thriving software, equipment, telecommunications, and semiconductor industry. To support this industry, Texas has become a leader in scientific and technological research and development.

A good indicator of technological innovation is the number of international patent applications filed under the Patent Cooperation Treaty. In 2008, Texas ranked fourth among the 50 states in the number of patents filed, trailing only California, New York, and Massachusetts. According to the U.S. Patent and Trademark Office, Texas was second among the 50 states in total patents in 2013 (although this ranking is not nearly as high when considered on a per capita basis).[14] When Texas entered the twenty-first century, the economy of the state was far more diverse than it was even 20 years earlier. Although energy and agriculture are still important elements in the state's economy, they are balanced today by many new elements.

Today, the service industry dominates the Texas economy. In 2012, service industries employed 76 percent of the private sector workforce. Moreover, those industries accounted for 56 percent of output.[15] The state's location, its proximity to Mexico, and its centrality within the continental United States has pushed this sector's growth. Trade has expanded rapidly owing to both NAFTA and globalization, and Texas has become a transportation hub. Increased trade has also fueled the growth of professional and business services in areas such as accounting and legal and computer services, as well as construction, engineering, and management. Meanwhile, population expansion has led to a marked increase in the need for health care and education services. Simultaneously, the rise in both trade and population has sparked the growth of the leisure and hospitality industry.

Texas has become a major trading power in its own right, leading the 50 U.S. states in exports. When Congress passed NAFTA in 1993, Texas anticipated significant economic growth because of increased trade, primarily with Mexico. But in reality, Texas has become a major center of international trade. From 2003 to 2013, it led all states in U.S. exports. In 2013, Texas exported nearly $280 billion in goods, whereas California, in second place, exported only $168 billion. Texas's major trading partners are Mexico and Canada, followed by countries in South America, Asia, and Europe. Mexico's importance is not to be underestimated, however; that nation alone accounted for more than 36 percent of Texas's exports in 2013 (see Figure 1.1 for major categories of exports).[16]

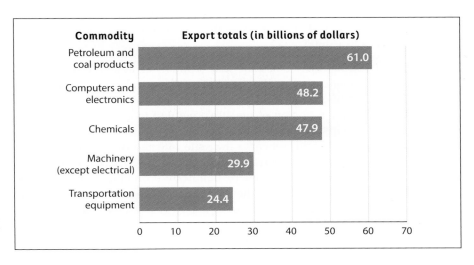

FIGURE 1.1   Top Five Exports (in billions)

CORE OBJECTIVE

Communicating Effectively...

Write a short synopsis of Texas's changing economy and its role in international trade.

Texas's Economic Regions

The state comptroller's office has divided Texas into 13 **economic regions** as a convenient way to talk about areas of the state.[17] To simplify discussion, this book merges these 13 regions into six, as shown in Figure 1.2. A basic knowledge of these regions will be useful in considering how Texas's economic diversity impacts its government.

The East Texas or Piney Woods region was traditionally dominated by agriculture, timber, and oil. Today, agriculture is less important and oil is declining, but

economic regions
Divisions of the state based on dominant economic activity

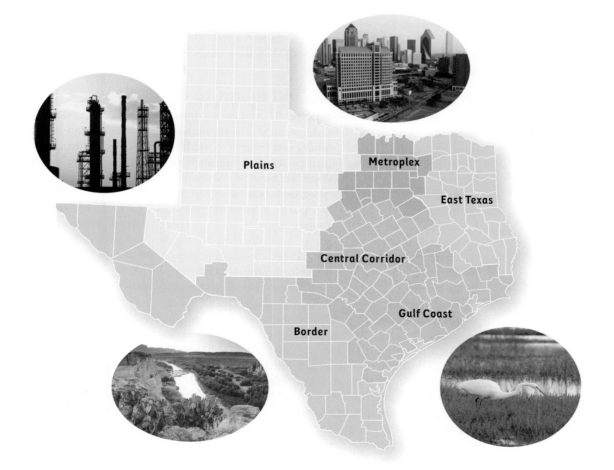

FIGURE 1.2   Economic Regions of Texas

timber is still important. Some diversification has occurred, with manufacturing becoming a more important element in the economy of this area.

The Plains region of the state, with Lubbock and Amarillo as its major cities, has historically been dominated by agriculture (especially cotton, wheat, and maize) and by ranching and cattle feedlots. In recent years, the economy of this region has become more diversified and less dominated by agriculture.

The Gulf Coast region, extending from Corpus Christi to Beaumont/Port Arthur/Orange and including Houston, is dominated by petrochemical industries, manufacturing, shipping, and fishing. In recent years, this area has further diversified with the addition of high-tech industries. It is also the area with the highest concentration of organized labor unions in the state.

The border area of South Texas and the Rio Grande Valley, stretching from Brownsville to El Paso, is noted primarily for its agricultural production of citrus fruits and vegetables. In recent years, trade with Mexican border cities has diversified the economy of this region, a process increased by the passage of NAFTA.

The Metroplex, or Dallas/Fort Worth area, is considered the financial center of the state. This region is the most economically diversified, with a combination of banking, manufacturing, high-tech, and aerospace industries.

The Central Corridor, or midstate region, is an area stretching roughly from College Station in the east to Waco in the north and Austin and San Antonio in the southwest. This area is dominated by two large state universities—Texas A&M University and the University of Texas at Austin—along with high-tech industries in Austin and San Antonio and major military bases in the Waco/Temple/Killeen and San Antonio areas.

Texas Politics: From Democrat to Republican

The Democratic Party dominated Texas politics from the end of Reconstruction until the mid-1970s. In the absence of a strong and viable Republican Party, third parties became the primary challengers to the Democratic Party during the "Progressive Era" of American politics. Groups such as the Greenback Party, the Farmers Alliance, and the Populists became known as progressives because they believed in the "doctrine of progress"—the concept that governing institutions can be improved by bringing science to bear on public problems.[18] Each of these groups had as their goal the use of government to try to positively impact the economy, by either increasing the value of agriculture or reining in the power of business and banking.[19] The Democratic Party successfully responded to these challenges by adopting many progressive reform proposals into its own platform. By the start of the twentieth century, Texas was effectively a one-party state with Progressive Democrats and Conservative Democrats contesting offices. In fact, a lack of meaningful competition from Republicans often led to straight-ticket party voting in elections. The term "Yellow Dog Democrat," coined to describe an individual who would vote only for Democratic candidates, aptly described the voting habits of many Texans (that is, "He would vote for a yellow dog if it ran as a Democrat").

From the 1920s through World War II, the oil industry helped shape state and local politics. The majority of Texas Democrats were conservative in their political ideology. Conservative business interests actually aligned more with the national Republican Party at times, and the state supported Hoover in 1928—one of only four instances from the end of Reconstruction to the mid-1970s in which a majority of Texas voters favored the Republican candidate in a presidential election.[20] The Great Depression, however, soured Texans on the Republican Party again, and the Democratic New Deal brought Texans back into the party fold. Progressive

Democrats supporting jobs programs and military development helped attract more liberal-minded citizens to the party.

The next time a majority of Texas voters supported the Republican candidate was in 1952, when Dwight Eisenhower was elected president. He was backed by the "Shivercrats," a faction of Texas Democrats who followed conservative Democratic Governor Allan Shivers. Texans supported Eisenhower again in 1956.

As the national Democratic Party increased the federal government's role in the lives of individuals and businesses through the New Deal, the Fair Deal, and Great Society programs, conservative Texas Democrats became disenchanted with the national party and chose not to support it in national races. This coincided with an increase in the number of liberal Democrats joining the party and achieving leadership positions. The Civil Rights movement of the late 1950s and 1960s also pushed socially conservative Democrats away from the Democratic Party and started pulling them toward the Republican Party. John Tower's 1961 election, the first time Texas had sent a Republican to the U.S. Senate since 1870, reflected the beginning of this shift.[21] A majority of Texas voters supported Richard Nixon, a Republican, for president in 1972.

This pattern of supporting Republicans for national political offices eventually evolved into supporting Republican candidates for state offices (for example, Bill Clements for Governor in 1978) and, eventually, supporting Republican candidates for local office. For example, beginning with the election of Ronald Reagan in 1980, a majority of Texans have voted Republican in every presidential election to date.[22] Texas fully transitioned from a predominately Democratic (conservative) majority to a fully Republican statewide majority by 2002. After the 1994 political party realignment, which swept away Democratic majorities in the U.S. House and Senate, Texas rapidly converted to the party in power/party ideology dynamic and voted a large sector of experienced, powerful Democratic officeholders out of public office. Anglo male voters, resentful of decades of affirmative action, as well as businesses and conservatives seeking big changes in the state's legal and regulatory system, found and supported Republican candidates at all levels. By 1998, all statewide elective officeholders were Republicans, and by 2002, the Texas House of Representatives had a Republican majority for the first time in its history, also a testament to the significance of redistricting. During the past two decades, the Republican Party has grown so much in Texas that the state is again virtually a one-party dominant state, but now the advantage goes to the Republicans.

There are other, non-ideological reasons for the shift toward a one-party, Republican state. Culturally, there are likely more individuals who would self-identify as Democrats or who would vote for Democratic candidates more than their opponents. Structurally, however, there are problems with making today's Democratic Party a competitive entity. Many likely Democratic voters either do not register or do not vote, and redistricting has virtually guaranteed Republican majorities in the state and federal representative races. Additionally, the Texas Democratic Party has not offered much in the way of dynamic candidates or organization.

Evidence from the 2008 election suggests that if these conditions changed, very different political outcomes could occur in Texas. In the 2008 presidential primary election in March, nearly 3 million Texans voted in the Democratic primary, compared to only 1.3 million in the Republican primary.[23] In the general election, 8 million Texans cast ballots, and although Republican John McCain won the state, Democrats made significant gains in the Texas House, closely missing a tie with 74 seats.

The situation, though, changed quickly and dramatically. Aggressive reaction to the Obama presidency in 2010 and 2012 prompted a tidal wave of small-government or social conservatives to run for office, and many succeeded in winning primaries, unseating a number of long-standing Democrats in both the state and U.S. House of Representatives. However, in 2013, Democratic operatives launched "Battleground Texas," an attempt to revitalize the Democratic Party in the state and ultimately "turn Texas blue."

It should be noted that although political party realignment has occurred in the past 50 years, the ideological landscape of Texas has not really changed. When public opinion polls ask about political ideology, a solid plurality of Texans continue to identify themselves as conservative (rather than moderate, independent, or liberal). One of the characteristics of Texas political culture has been its strong tendency toward conservative ideological principles in all areas of public policy. In fact, "ideology" has meant more to many Texas voters than political party labels. This strong ideological association helps explain why Texas voters realigned between the two major parties during the latter part of the twentieth century. For most Texas voters, whether a candidate was a Democrat or a Republican was not relevant; the most "conservative" candidate would likely win most elections.

CORE OBJECTIVE

Taking Personal Responsibility...

What can you do to become well informed about political issues so that you can make good decisions at election time?

Demographics: The Road to Majority-Minority

Demography refers to the statistical characteristics of a population. Typically, data used to develop and describe population statistics come from the United States Census, which is conducted every 10 years. Regardless of the best efforts, the census is subject to error, particularly in the form of an undercount. Nonetheless, census questions and the information derived from them provide a means of measuring meaningful features of a population. Population trends reflect much about the political, social, and cultural features of a given region and are very important indicators for government at all levels. Population data allow governments to plan well, and well in advance, in providing the vital needs for which they are responsible.

Of the 50 states, Texas ranks second not only in total land size but also in terms of population. In 2010, the U.S. Census Bureau calculated the state's official population at 25,145,561. The 2013 estimate jumped to 26,448,193, reflecting a rapid increase of 5.2 percent, or nearly one and a half million residents in three years. This compares to national growth of only 2.4 percent over the same period.[24] This is yet another segment of a continuing trend of explosive population growth for the Lone Star State (see Figure 1.3 for a comparison of Texas's population growth with other states). In 1970, the population was 11.2 million; by 1990 it had increased to almost 17 million; and in 2000 the population reached 20.9 million. Although birthrates account for part of this growth, it is also attributable to the arrival of newcomers from other states and countries.

This incredible growth has had an impact on Texas's standing in national politics. As a result of the 2010 Census, Texas was awarded four additional seats—the biggest gain of any state—in the U.S. House of Representatives.[25] The location of the four new districts highlights two very salient shifts in political power in the state: from rural to urban and suburban areas and increasing majority/minority demographics.

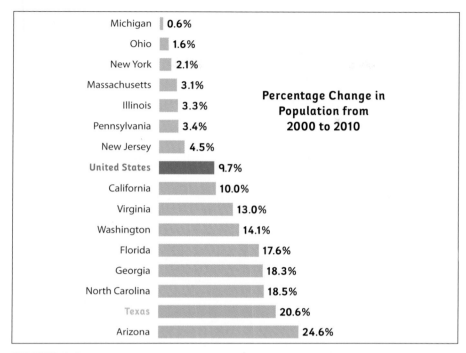

FIGURE 1.3 **Percentage Change in Population, 2000–2010**

SOURCE: U.S. Census Bureau.

Urban and Rural

As *The Economist* noted, "The imagery of Texas is rural—cattle, cotton, cowboys and, these days, wind turbines whirring against the endless sky. But the reality is increasingly urban."[26] Although definitions of rural and urban can vary, the U.S. Census Bureau uses the following distinction for densely populated areas: "Urbanized Areas (UAs) consist of 50,000 or more people; urban Clusters (UCs) comprise at least 2,500 but less than 50,000 people, and 'rural' encompasses all population, housing, and territory not included within an urban area."[27] When this definition is applied to 2010 census data, 21,298,039 Texans live in urban areas. This amounts to 84.7 percent of the state's population, leaving 15.3 percent of the population (or 3.8 million people) in rural areas.[28] By comparison, in 2000, 17.5 percent of Texans (or 3.6 million people) were considered "rural."[29] In other words, while the overall population of Texas has increased, the proportion of Texans living in rural areas is declining. The state comptroller's office projects that over the next 40 years, urban areas will continue to grow much more rapidly than rural areas.[30] In Map 1.2, the urban nature of today's Texas is apparent, with so many Texans living in a handful of populous counties.

As stated previously, Texas has added four new congressional districts: numbers 33, 34, 35, and 36. Several of these new districts have been established in urban centers and will capture a significant number of minority voters.[31] Minority groups are particularly concentrated in major cities because of minority migration to urban centers and higher birth rates for minorities, along with white migration to suburban areas. The role of minority groups is particularly important in Texas.

Majority-Minority

Since 2004, Texas has been a "**majority-minority**" state, meaning that all ethnic minority groups combined now form a majority of the population and outnumber the non-Hispanic white population.[32] As of 2012, white non-Hispanics made

majority-minority
Minority groups that make up a majority of the population of the state

Percentage of All Texas Voters in 2012, By County

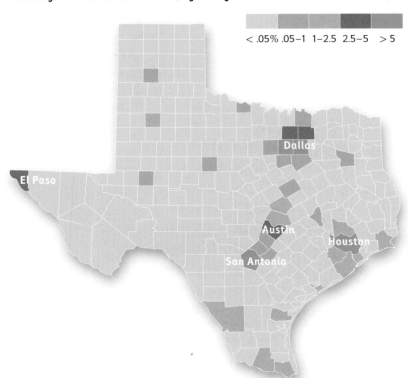

MAP 1.2   Population Density as Indicated by Percentage of Voters in Each County

up 44.5 percent of the total state population, making them a numerical, statistical minority.[33] Public school enrollments have been majority-minority for some time. According to the Texas Education Agency, 2001–2002 was the first school year in which Hispanic students outnumbered whites. By 2012, Hispanic enrollment was just over half of all students, and white enrollment had declined to 30.6 percent of the total school population.[34] These changes in majority and minority status have significant implications for state politics as well as public policy decisions.

Hispanic immigration from Mexico to Texas has steadily increased over the course of the past half-century and has become a major factor in state politics. In 1960, Hispanics represented 15 percent of the total population of Texas. That increased to 18 percent by 1970, 21 percent in 1980, and 25 percent in 1990. According to the U.S. Census Bureau, Hispanics or Latinos made up 38.2 percent of the state's total population in 2012.[35]

With the aid of liberalized voter registration procedures, Hispanics have begun to dominate politics in the border areas, in some sections of South Texas and the Gulf Coast, and in the San Antonio area. They have successfully elected local officials to city and county government and school boards, to the state legislature, and to Congress. The first Hispanic either appointed or elected to statewide office was Raul Gonzales, in 1984, to the Texas Supreme Court.[36] Dan Morales was subsequently elected state attorney general in 1990 and served until 1999. In 2002, Tony Sanchez was the first Hispanic to become a major-party candidate for governor. In 2012, Ted Cruz was elected to represent Texas in the U.S. Senate, the first time the state has sent a Hispanic to the upper chamber of Congress.[37] It is clear that Hispanic voters will continue to be a major force in Texas state politics in the future.

Whereas the Hispanic population has grown as a percentage of total state population since the 1960s, the African American population has remained fairly constant over that period. The 2012 estimate for African Americans was 12.3 percent of the population.[38] African Americans tend to be concentrated in three metropolitan areas: Houston, Dallas/Fort Worth, and Austin. African Americans have had some political success winning election to local offices (school boards, city councils, and county offices) and the state legislature, in addition to winning a few seats in the U.S. Congress. Only one African American, Morris Overstreet, has been elected to statewide office. From 1990 to 1999, Judge Overstreet served on the Texas Court of Criminal Appeals, the highest court for criminal matters in the state. In 2002, Ron Kirk, the popular African American mayor of Dallas, ran for a U.S. Senate seat. Although polls showed Kirk to be in a dead heat with Republican John Cornyn, Kirk lost the race by a margin of almost twelve percent (43 percent for Kirk compared to 55 percent for Cornyn).[39]

Asian Americans constituted less than 1 percent of the population of Texas in 1980 but composed 4.2 percent of the state population by 2012.[40] The state's Asian American population is projected to continue increasing in the years ahead. In fact, the State Demographer's Office argues that "the non-Hispanic Other group, consisting of mostly Asian Americans, will grow at the fastest rate, when compared to other racial/ethnic categories."[41] Most of Texas's Asian American population is concentrated in the Houston area. In fact, one section of Houston has such a large proportion of Chinese Americans that some of the street signs are in Chinese. However, there are also significant concentrations of Korean Americans in the Dallas/Fort Worth Metroplex and in Killeen. Asian Americans in the Houston area have had some success in electing local officials, including one city council member and a county court of law judge. In 2002, Martha Wong was elected to represent the Houston area in the Texas statehouse. Wong was only the second Asian American to serve in the Texas House and the first Republican of Asian descent. In 2004, Hubert Vo was the first Vietnamese American elected to serve as a state representative, and he continues to represent his Houston area district. The first Asian American elected to the Texas House was Tom Lee from San Antonio. As of 2014, there have been five Asian Americans in the Texas House, including three in the current legislature.[42]

Religion in Texas

Religion in Texas bears the Roman Catholic imprint of its Spanish and Mexican roots as well as the conservative Protestantism of its later Anglo settlers. According to a 2008 survey by the Pew Forum on Religion and Public Life, approximately

Evangelical	34%	Jewish	1%
Mainline Protestant	15%	Muslim	< 1%
Black Protestant	8%	Buddhist	1%
Roman Catholic	24%	Hindu	1%
Mormon	1%	Other World Religions	< 1%
Jehovah's Witness	1%	Other Faiths	1%
Orthodoxy	< 1%	Unaffiliated	12%
Other Christian	< 1%		

Source: U.S. Religious Landscape Survey, Pew Forum on Religion and Public Life, 2008.

88 percent of Texans affiliate with a religious tradition. About 8 in 10 Texans identify as Christians, with Protestants accounting for 57 percent of the population and Roman Catholics accounting for another 24 percent.[43]

Due in part to the state's large population of evangelical Protestants and also its large metropolitan areas, Texas is home to some of America's largest churches. The Houston area, for example, boasts the largest church in the United States: Joel Osteen's Lakewood Church has a weekly attendance in excess of 40,000. According to the Hartford Institute for Religion Research, 206 Protestant churches in Texas have an average weekly attendance of at least 2,000 persons, making them "megachurches."[44]

Religion is also an important feature of Texas politics, and Republican politics in particular. For example, shortly before Texas Governor Rick Perry launched his 2012 presidential primary campaign, he organized a national televised prayer meeting in Houston. A 2012 report by the Irma Rangel Public Policy Institute at the University of Texas at Austin on religion and the Texas electorate helped to underscore the relationship between religion and politics in Texas. The approximately one-third of Texans who are evangelical Protestants are overwhelmingly Republican, whereas Roman Catholics are fairly evenly split in party affiliation. Protestants of the black church tradition, those who identify as atheist or agnostic, and those who do not identify with an organized religion are overwhelmingly Democratic (see Figure 1.4).

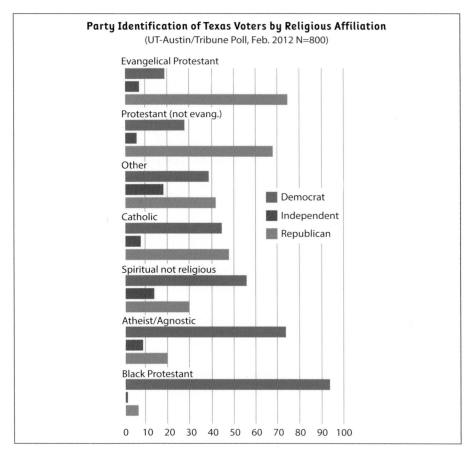

FIGURE 1.4   **Party Identification of Texas Voters by Religious Affiliation**

Being Socially Responsible...

Understanding the relationship between religious affiliations and politics can improve civic knowledge. How would you use this knowledge to engage effectively in your community?

Current Challenges: Texas Today

Today, Texas is confronted with national issues that affect all states to some degree, as well as issues specific to the state. The impact of these issues on Texas, and Texas's role in the nation, are crucial to understanding today's Texas government.

The Recent Recession

Texas's diverse and growth-oriented economy weathered the 2008 financial meltdown-turned-recession better than other large states. Texas had diversified and transitioned its economy to a combination of energy, agriculture, trade, and an array of professional and business services, utilities, and general services. Due in part to this diversification and its relatively business-friendly fiscal and regulatory policies, Texas both entered the recession later and emerged from it more quickly than other states.[45] The state's gross domestic product (GDP), a measure of economic growth and production and therefore an indicator of the state's economic health,[46] actually fell during 2009.[47] (This had not happened in Texas since the mid-1980s, the last phase of the state's boom-and-bust oil economy.) According to the U.S. Bureau of Economic Analysis, automotive manufacturing and mining sectors suffered the biggest percentage declines in Texas in 2009.[48] The state unemployment rate peaked at 8.2 percent in December 2009 and remained at that level for most of 2010.[49] The economic sector for state and local government services and layoffs for government employees added to the state's spike in 2010. Nonetheless, Texas unemployment was consistently lower than the national average for the period 2008 to 2012.[50] Despite a large number of mortgage foreclosures, home prices remained fairly stable in Texas throughout the recession, with housing demand propped up by the state's dramatic increase in population. Housing costs in the state were lower than the national average to begin with (and remain so), suggesting that not much of a bubble existed in Texas housing prices prior to the recession.[51] The state comptroller reported that for September 2012, the Texas foreclosure rate was "one in every 1,336 mortgages," lower than figures released for Florida, California, and Illinois.[52]

National Trends and Politics

National trends and politics, specifically the major domestic policies of the Bush administration (No Child Left Behind [NCLB] and tax reductions) and the Obama administration (the Federal Stimulus Plan and the Affordable Care Act), have impacted Texans in a variety of ways. NCLB has basically been abandoned in Texas, replaced by an emerging reform called STAAR (State of Texas Assessments of Academic Readiness). Texas continues to lag behind the national average in terms of its proportion of adults age 25 or older who have graduated from high school, completed a bachelor's degree, or earned an advanced degree of some kind.[53]

The average per capita income for the period 2006 to 2010 tracks with national trends; incomes did not increase relative to inflation. However, according to data from the U.S. Bureau of Economic Analysis, Texas's 2012 per capita income level of $41,471 fell below the national average of $42,693.[54] Poverty rates for that period are higher than the national figures, with 17.9 percent of Texas residents estimated to be below the poverty level in 2012, compared to 15.9 percent for the U.S. overall.[55] According to Steve Murdock, former census bureau chief during the Bush administration and former state demographer of Texas, "Poverty is typically a strong indicator of educational attainment."[56] This relationship is evident upon examination of the state's public school dropout numbers. According to the Texas Education Agency, 52.6 percent of twelfth-grade students who dropped out of Texas high schools in 2012 were considered "economically disadvantaged." Viewed from another perspective, economically disadvantaged students had a graduation rate of 85.1 percent in 2012, compared to the statewide graduation rate of 87.7 percent that year. Broken down by ethnicity, the dropout rate is higher among Hispanic and African American students than for Asian and White students.[57]

Immigration and In-Migration Today

Texas has been affected by two types of migration: movement of people into Texas from other U.S. states (often called in-migration) and from other countries (immigration). Both are important in terms of Texas's government and politics, but the former will be addressed first. Briefly, a look at population trends in the twenty-first century indicates that in-migration to Texas from other states is a reflection of both push and pull forces. In particular, economic, social, and political trends outside the state are pushing people to leave their home states and, in many cases, come to Texas. From 2000 to 2011, Texas had a net in-migration rate of 4.2 percent (meaning that Texas gained almost 900,000 more people who moved in from other states than it lost) and the second highest (to Florida) absolute gain of any state in the country.[58] From April 2010 to July 2013, Texas had net in-migration of more than 400,000 people.[59] This was the largest absolute jump of any state in the country during that period. One special push in the earlier period was the upheaval caused by Hurricane Katrina in Louisiana in 2005, which led to a significant flow of people to Texas. However, other Texas-specific factors have been pulling people here for some time now, such as the relatively inexpensive housing market and the attractive natural and business climate in the state.

Migration to Texas from other states over the past few decades has largely reflected well-established patterns of movement from the rust-belt states of Ohio, Michigan, and New York, and secondarily from California and Florida. More recently, California and Florida have generally outpaced the other states. In the period 2005 to 2009, the U.S. Census Bureau's American Community Survey (ACS) reported that 58,500 people moved to Texas from Louisiana. (Although 31,000 people moved to Louisiana from Texas during this period, it is difficult to estimate the accuracy of the inflow, especially because of the lack of routine record keeping, such as driver's licenses or housing data.) Other in-migration very clearly reflects economic upheaval from the home mortgage and banking implosion coupled with the appeal of Texas's fairly resilient and diverse economy and low cost of living. From 2005 to 2009, approximately 75,000 people moved to Texas from California, the most populous state in the United States. Approximately 38,000 people came from Florida, the fourth most populous state during that time.[60] High-tech workers, in particular, have been drawn to the Texas job market, and the devastation in Florida's housing market led to an exodus from that state.[61] The fourth-largest flow into Texas was from Oklahoma, a neighboring state and fellow energy state. In 2012, the latest date for which the U.S. Census Bureau has specific information on state-to-state migration flows, California and Florida continued to be the most likely states of origination for in-migrants to Texas. The U.S. Census Bureau estimates that almost 63,000 people moved from California, and more than 31,000 came from Florida. Louisiana followed with 29,500 pulling stakes for Texas; Oklahoma with 26,000; and 22,500 from North Carolina. New York and Illinois contributed another 20,000 individuals each.[62]

Push and pull factors also impact international migration to Texas. Texas continues to be an attractive location for immigrants both legal and illegal. Because of its long contiguous border with Mexico, Texas is a natural draw for Mexicans. Such migration will depend in part on political and economic conditions in Mexico. From 2006 to 2009, international migrants dropped below 100,000 and continued to decrease. This tracks with the general trend in illegal immigration. As of 2011, some 6.1 million unauthorized Mexican immigrants were living in the United States, down from a peak of nearly 7 million in 2007, according to Pew Hispanic Center estimates based on U.S. Census Bureau data. Over the same period, the population of authorized immigrants from Mexico rose modestly, from 5.6 million in 2007 to 5.8 million in 2011.[63]

Texas Political Culture

Sections of this chapter have covered historic settlement patterns, the changing makeup of the current population, and demographic characteristics of people in the state. The reason these factors are important in a study of Texas government is that they contribute to what is called **political culture**. Political culture consists of the attitudes, values, and beliefs that most people in a political community have about the proper role of government. This system of beliefs essentially defines the role of government and the role of citizens within that government. Although the average person might not possess much technical knowledge about government or how it works, most people do have views or opinions, even if poorly defined, about what government should and should not do and what their own personal responsibility should be.

political culture
A system of beliefs and values that define the role of government and the role of citizens in that government

In the mid-1960s, Daniel J. Elazar, in his book *American Federalism: A View from the States,* developed a system for classifying different types of political culture in the 50 states. That system is still relevant today. Elazar described three distinctive political subcultures in the United States: moralistic, individualistic, and traditionalistic. Map 1.3 shows his proposed distribution of political cultures across the nation.[64]

In the **moralistic subculture**, politics "is considered one of the great activities of [people in their] search for the good society . . . an effort to exercise power for the betterment of the commonwealth."[65] In other words, government is viewed as a positive instrument for change and a means of promoting the general welfare of all citizens. In the moralistic subculture, politics is regarded as the responsibility of all citizens, who have an obligation to participate in government. Individuals seek leadership roles in government not for personal gain, but out of a desire to serve the public. In addition, the government has a right and an obligation to intervene in the private affairs of citizens when deemed necessary for the "public good or the well-being of the community."[66]

moralistic subculture
Government viewed as a positive force to achieve a common good for all citizens

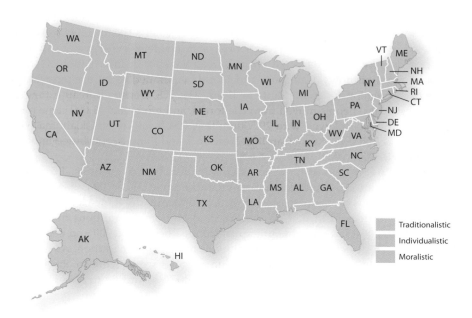

MAP 1.3   Political Culture in the States

individualistic subculture

Government that benefits the individual rather than society in general

traditionalistic subculture

Government that maintains existing political order for the benefit of a small elite

An **individualistic subculture** "emphasizes the conception of the democratic order as a marketplace. In its view, a government is created for strictly utilitarian reasons, to handle those functions demanded by the people it is created to serve."[67] That is, government is not concerned with the creation of a "good society," and government intervention in the private sector should be kept to a minimum. From this perspective, politics is not a profession of high calling, but rather something that should be left to those willing to dirty their hands. Participation is considered a necessary evil but not an obligation of every citizen.

The primary function of the **traditionalistic subculture** is maintenance of the existing political order, and participation is confined to a small, self-perpetuating elite. The public has only limited power and influence. Policies that benefit the public are enacted only when the elite allows them to be. In practice, most policies enacted by government benefit the ruling elite and not the public. Political participation by the public is discouraged. A class-based social structure helps to maintain the existing order.

As Map 1.3 shows, all the old Confederate states have traditionalistic political cultures, and many of the Midwestern states have individualistic political cultures. Southern Anglo settlers of East Texas brought a strong traditionalistic culture with them. This culture was a natural extension of the practice of slavery and persisted even after the Civil War. Conversely, German and Midwestern Anglo settlers in West Texas brought a strong individualistic culture with them. Few, if any, of these settlers were slave owners, and they came to Texas in search of individual opportunities. At the same time, Mexican immigrants brought a strongly traditionalistic culture. This culture had its origins in seventeenth- and eighteenth-century Spanish culture, which was characterized by a dominant, landed aristocracy and elite-controlled government. African American slaves in Texas were forced to adopt the traditionalistic culture of their Anglo slave owners.

The name of the party controlling the Texas governor's mansion, all statewide offices, and the state legislature has changed. However, the state's political culture has not. Texas has transitioned from a state dominated by the Democratic Party to a state dominated by the Republican Party but, crucially, there have been no significant changes in philosophy, ideology, or policy.

Examining political culture helps us understand the basic structure of state government, the nature of government policy, and the degree to which citizens are involved in government. The basic structure of state government in Texas fits the traditionalistic/individualistic model quite well. Government is limited. Power is divided among many elected officials. Executive authority—namely, the office of the governor—is weak, and most power rests with the state legislature. Few state regulations are placed on business, and many of those that do exist benefit specific businesses. Regulation of the environment is modest.

Yet the political culture of Texas is a reflection of a deeper ideological position for most Texans. Most Texans' ideology is a mix of elements from classical liberalism and social conservatism with some strains of populism woven through their political opinions as well. Classical liberalism, in general, has both political and economic components and is associated in the United States with the writings of John Locke, Adam Smith, Thomas Jefferson, and James Madison. Politically, classical liberalism focuses on the protection of individual rights, limited government, the rule of law, and a generally free market economy. Politically, classical liberals have often supported representative government and civil liberties (such as freedom of speech, press, assembly, and petition) as means by which citizens could control their government and secure their (natural) rights.

Just as classical liberalism rejects obtrusive government—whether monarchic or even democratic—it also rejected mercantilism in the economic realm. Mercantilism held that because a country's wealth and power were synonymous and war was inevitable, the government had a right and a duty to regulate the economy and foster economic development. Moreover, mercantilists believed the government could do so effectively. Under mercantilism, European monarchs granted trade and colonial monopolies, subsidized import industries, enacted strict trade and labor regulations, and imposed high tariffs. Classical liberalism viewed such intervention in the economy as a means by which governments and their cronies could buttress their power and influence in opposition to the interests of their people.

Adam Smith, in his *Wealth of Nations,* argued that the largely unregulated market would produce wealth on its own as long as government policies offered "peace, easy taxes, and a tolerable administration of justice." To Smith, "all the rest" would be "brought about by the natural course of things." Therefore, governmental intrusion into the economy would only "thwart" the efficient operation of the free market as well as support an overbearing government. Smith's metaphor for the self-regulating market was the "invisible hand." The American Revolution is an example of both the political and economic aspects of the classical liberal approach. Economic liberalism in the United States became dominant with Thomas Jefferson's inauguration. Jefferson favored strong state and local governments and a relatively weak federal government. The Jeffersonian ideal of limited government opposed governmental intervention in the economy; it did not support a role for the federal government in chartering banks—or in spending money on transportation infrastructure, or what would have been termed "internal improvements."

Texan opposition to taxes and government regulation of the economy is reminiscent of the distrust of the federal government that characterized the presidencies of Thomas Jefferson and Andrew Jackson. State government exists, in the view of these people, to provide a healthy business climate and keep taxes and regulations low. To facilitate commerce, the state may accept federal assistance for construction of roads and bridges. In general, classical liberals in the past—and many

Texans today—have held, at least rhetorically, that the government is best that governs least. This philosophy forms the basis of the modern Libertarian Party, as well as some of the planks of the Texas Republican Party. Except for a few periods of reform associated with James Hogg, James Ferguson, and the New Deal, Texas has frequently embraced the economic aspects of classical liberalism. However, many adherents have been willing to compromise this faith for political and personal advantage.

At the same time, many Texans also embrace social conservatism. Salient political issues for social conservatives include but are not limited to abortion, traditional family values, and school prayer. In general, they want *Roe v. Wade* overturned, are against gay marriage, want school-conducted prayer allowed, and would like to see alternatives to evolution (for example, creationism or intelligent design) taught in public schools. Many are uncompromising in their beliefs on each of these issues because they see their perspective as grounded in their religious faith.

Another facet of Texas political ideology and culture is populism. Populism is a difficult term to define, although most political analysts agree that it is an important part of U.S. and political history. Populism arose in the 1880s in the southern and western parts of the United States. Populists call for the federal and state government to help small businesses, farmers, and ranchers in the face of competition from large U.S. corporations and foreign businesses. Populists, historically, have wanted the federal government to regulate railroad rates and to ensure a money supply equal to the size of the economy. Populists also distrust banks and want the government to provide credit for industrial production and trade unions. They were, historically, also anti-immigrant. Populism, being primarily a rural and small town movement, supports more conservative religious values. It can also have an anti-intellectual strain, which is voiced as suspicion of experts. The rural anti-union, anti-immigrant, anti-intellectual strain of populism has survived and appears to have merged with social conservatism in Texas and other states.

It is also worth noting that a significant segment of Texans embrace a progressive or modern liberal understanding of the relationship between the people and the government. These contemporary liberals or progressives (like populists before them) are not as skeptical of government intervention in the economy and see the government as a potent force for good. Among other things, they favor a larger social welfare system and more regulation of business while opposing the agenda of social conservatives. Though a minority of Texans, they make up a large part of the modern Democratic Party in Texas and could be a growing force in the state. Indeed, as noted earlier, the "Battleground Texas" operation ultimately hopes to "turn Texas blue"—though its first steps, in the words of a *Texas Monthly* article on its efforts—are "to recruit and train volunteers, foster neighbor-to-neighbor contact about the issues, and enlist voter registrars."[68]

Conclusion

Texas government is complex. However, with a better appreciation of Texas history and the unique position the state occupies today within the larger United States, we can begin the journey to understand Texas government from within the framework of political culture. In the chapters that follow, the concepts of that framework will serve, repeatedly, as guideposts along the way.

Key Terms

Adelsverein Society
economic regions
individualistic subculture

land-based economy
majority-minority
moralistic subculture

political culture
traditionalistic subculture

Notes

[1] Texas General Land Office, History of Texas Public Lands, September 2010, accessed November 4, 2012. http://www.glo.texas.gov/what-we-do/history-and-archives/documents/history-of-texas-public-lands.pdf.

[2] Jean Stuntz, "Spanish Laws for Texas Women: The Development of Marital Property Law to 1850," *The Southwestern Historical Quarterly*, vol. 104 (4), April 2001, 542–559.

[3] "Coahuila and Texas," *Handbook of Texas Online*, published by the Texas State Historical Association, accessed November 04, 2012. http://www.tshaonline.org/handbook/online/articles/usc01.

[4] Terry G. Jordan, *German Seed in Texas Soil: Immigrant Farmers in Nineteenth Century Texas* (Austin: University of Texas Press, 1966).

[5] Robert A. Calvert and Arnold DeLeon, *The History of Texas* (Arlington Heights, Ill.: Harland Davidson, 1990), 99–100.

[6] T. R. Fehrendbach, *Lone Star: A History of Texas and the Texans* (New York: Collier, 1980), 276–277.

[7] James M. McPherson and James K. Hogue, *Ordeal by Fire: The Civil War and Reconstruction*, 4th edition (New York: McGraw-Hill Higher Education, 2009), 371; 446–447.

[8] Texas Historical Commission, Texas in the Civil War. http://www.thc.state.tx.us/public/upload/publications/tx-in-civil-war.pdf; Texas State Historical Association, Civil War. https://tshaonline.org/handbook/online/articles/qdc02.

[9] McPherson and Hogue, 428.

[10] Texas State Library and Archives Commission, Juneteenth. https: www.tsl.texas.gov/ref/abouttx/juneteenth.html.

[11] Roy Morris, *Sheridan: The Life and Wars of General Phil Sheridan* (New York: Crown, 1992).

[12] Robert A. Calvert et al., 363.

[13] http://www.laits.utexas.edu/txp_media/html/cult/features/0401_04/TXurbanchart.html.

[14] U.S. Patent and Trademark Office, Patent Counts by Origin and Type, Calendar Year 2013. http://www.uspto.gov/web/offices/ac/ido/oeip/taf/st_co_13.htm.

[15] U.S. Department of Labor, Bureau of Labor Statistics, Employment by major industry sector. http://www.bls.gov/emp/ep_table_201.htm; U.S. Department of Labor, Bureau of Labor Statistics, Output by major industry sector. http://www.bls.gov/emp/ep_table_202.htm.

[16] International Trade Administration, Texas: Expanding Exports and Creating Jobs through Trade Agreements, http://www.trade.gov/mas/ian/statereports/states/tx.pdf; U.S. Census Bureau, Foreign Trade, Top U.S. Exports by State. http://www.census.gov/foreign-trade/statistics/state/data/index.html.

[17] Susan Combs, "Texas Regional Outlook," *Window on State Government*–2012. http://www.window.state.tx.us/ecodata/regional/regions.html.

[18] Jay M. Shafritz, ed., *The Harper Collins Dictionary of American Government and Politics,* (New York: Harper Collins Publishers, Inc., 1992), 469.

[19] Robert A. Calvert et al., 228–241.

[20] Texas Secretary of State, Presidential Election Results. http://www.sos.state.tx.us/elections/historical/presidential.shtml.

[21] Texas State Historical Association, *Tower, John Goodwin.* http://www.tshaonline.org/handbook/online/articles/ftoss.

[22] Texas Secretary of State, Presidential Election Results. http://www.sos.state.tx.us/elections/historical/presidential.shtml.

[23] Though it should be noted that the Republican nominee was not in question at that point (and some Republicans may have shifted over to vote in the Democratic Party primary).

[24] U.S. Census Bureau, State & County QuickFacts. http://quickfacts.census.gov/qfd/states/48000.html.

[25] "Census shows Texas gains 4 seats in the U.S. House," *Houston Chronicle,* December 21, 2010–2012. http://www.chron.com/news/houston-texas/article/Census-shows-Texas-gains-4-seats-in-the-U-S-House-1700473.php.

[26] "The Trans-Texas Corridor: Miles to Go," *The Economist,* January 7, 2010–2012. http://www.economist.com/node/15213418.

[27] U.S. Census Bureau, 2010 Census Urban and Rural Classification and Urban Area Criteria. http://www.census.gov/geo/www/ua/2010urbanruralclass.html\#percent.

[28] U.S. Census Bureau, Lists of Population, Land Area, and Percent Urban and Rural in 2010 and Changes from 2000 to 2010. http://www.census.gov/geo/www/ua/2010urbanruralclass.html/#percent.

[29] U.S. Department of Agriculture, Rural Population Indicators for Texas, 2000–2012. http://www.ers.usda.gov/datafiles/Rural_Definitions/StateLevel_Maps/TX.pdf.

[30] Susan Combs, *Texas In Focus: A Statewide View of Opportunities*–2008. http://www.window.state.tx.us/specialrpt/tif/96-1286.pdf.

[31] Ross Ramsey, "Court Releases Congressional Maps," *Texas Tribune,* November 23, 2011–2012. http://www.texastribune.org/texas-redistricting/redistricting/court-releases-congressional-maps/.

[32] Susan Combs, *Texas In Focus: A Statewide View of Opportunities*–2008. http://www.window.state.tx.us/specialrpt/tif/population.html.

[33] U.S. Census Bureau, State & County QuickFacts. http://quickfacts.census.gov/qfd/states/48000.html.

[34] Texas Education Agency, *Enrollment in Texas Public Schools 2011-12* www.tea.state.tx.us/acctres/Enroll_2011-12.pdf.

[35] U.S. Census Bureau, State & County QuickFacts. http://quickfacts.census.gov/qfd/states/48000.html.

[36] http://www.texasbar.com/AM/Template.cfm?Section=Texas_Legal_Legends.

[37] Office of the Secretary of State, 2012 General Election, Election Night Returns. https://team1.sos.state.tx.us/enr/results/nov06_164_state.htm; Fox News Latino, "Election 2012: Ted Cruz Wins Senate Seat in Texas, Makes History," November 6, 2012, accessed November 8, 2012. http://latino.foxnews.com/latino/politics/2012/11/06/election-2012-ted-cruz-wins-senate-seat-in-texas/.

[38] U.S. Census Bureau, 2010 Demographic Profile Data. http://factfinder2.census.gov/bkmk/table/1.0/en/DEC/10_DP/DPDP1/0400000US48.

[39] Office of the Secretary of State, Race Summary Report. http://elections.sos.state.tx.us/elchist.exe.

[40] U.S. Census Bureau, 2010 Demographic Profile Data. http://factfinder2.census.gov/bkmk/table/1.0/en/DEC/10_DP/DPDP1/0400000US48.

[41] Office of the State Demographer, Texas Population Projections, 2010 to 2050. http://osd.state.tx.us/Publications/2013-01_ProjectionBrief.pdf

[42] Corrie Maclaggan, "A Race in One District Draws Focus to Asian Voters," *New York Times*, January 10, 2014. http://www.nytimes.com/2014/01/10/us/a-race-in-one-district-draws-focus-to-asian-voters.html.

[43] U.S. Religious Landscape Survey, Pew Forum on Religion and Public Life, 2008.

[44] Hartford Institute for Religion Research, Database of Megachurches in the U.S., accessed November 8, 2012. http://hirr.hartsem.edu/cgi-bin/mega/db.pl?db=default&uid=default&view_records=1&ID=*&sb=4&State=TX.

[45] Keith R. Phillips and Jesus Cañas, "Recession Arrives in Texas: A Rougher Ride in 2009," *Southwest Economy* (Federal Reserve Bank of Dallas), first quarter 2009, http://www.dallasfed.org/assets/documents/research/swe/2009/swe0901b.pdf; Susan Combs, "Comptroller's Weekly Economic Outlook," *The Texas Economy*, November 2, 2012, http://www.thetexaseconomy.org/economic-outlook/.

[46] Susan Combs, "Comptroller's Weekly Economic Outlook," *The Texas Economy*, November 2, 2012. http://www.thetexaseconomy.org/economic-outlook/.

[47] U.S. Department of Commerce, Bureau of Economic Analysis, Gross Domestic Product by State. http://www.bea.gov/iTable/iTable.cfm?ReqID570&step51&isuri51&acrdn51.

[48] U.S. Department of Commerce, Bureau of Economic Analysis, GDP by state. http://www.bea.gov/iTable/iTable.cfm?ReqID=70&step=1&isuri=1&acrdn=1.

[49] U.S. Department of Labor, Bureau of Labor Statistics, Local Area Unemployment Statistics. http://data.bls.gov/timeseries/LASST48000003; and see http://www.bls.gov/news.release/laus.nr0.htm.

[50] U.S. Department of Labor, Bureau of Labor Statistics, Labor Force Statistics from the Current Population Survey. http://data.bls.gov/timeseries/LNS14000000.

[51] Wenhua Di, "Residential Foreclosures in Texas Depart from National Trends," *e-Perspectives*, vol. 8(2), 2008. http://www.dallasfed.org/microsites/cd/epersp/2008/2_2.cfm.

[52] Susan Combs, "Comptroller's Weekly Economic Outlook," *The Texas Economy*, November 2, 2012. http://www.thetexaseconomy.org/economic-outlook/.

[53] U.S. Census Bureau, The 2012 Statistical Abstract, Educational Attainment by State. http://www.census.gov/compendia/statab/2012/tables/12s0233.pdf.

[54] U.S. Dept. of Commerce, Bureau of Economic Analysis, Per Capita Personal Income by State, 1990 to 2012. As cited in http://bber.unm.edu/econ/us-pci.htm.

[55] U.S. Census Bureau, Poverty Status in the Past 12 Months (2012 American Community Survey 1-Year Estimates). http://factfinder2.census.gov/faces/tableservices/jsf/pages/productview.xhtml?pid=ACS_12_1YR_S1701&prodType=table

[56] "Democrats say Texas graduation rate fell to 50th under Rick Perry," *Tampa Bay Times*, September 8, 2011. http://www.politifact.com/truth-o-meter/statements/2011/sep/08/new-hampshire-democratic-party/democrats-say-texas-graduation-rate-fell-50th-unde/.

[57] Texas Education Agency, Secondary School Completion and Dropouts in Texas Public Schools 2011-12, July 2011. www.tea.state.tx.us/acctres/DropComp_2011-12.pdf. Texas Education Agency, Texas high school graduation rate sets another all-time high, http://www.tea.state.tx.us/index4.aspx?id=25769806299.

[58] William P. Ruger and Jason Sorens, *Freedom in the 50 States: An Index of Personal and Economic Freedom* (Arlington, VA: Mercatus Center at George Mason University, 2013).

[59] U.S. Census Bureau, Estimates of the Components of Resident Population Change: April 1, 2010 to July 1, 2013, 2013 Population Estimates. http://factfinder2.census.gov/bkmk/table/1.0/en/PEP/2013/PEPTCOMP/0100000US%7C0100000US.04000%7C0200000US1%7C0200000US2%7C0200000US3%7C0200000US4.)

[60] U.S. Census Bureau, Geographical Mobility/Migration, State-to-State Migration Flows. https://www.census.gov/hhes/migration/data/acs/state-to-state.html.)

[61] U.S. Census Bureau, American Community Survey–2012. http://www.census.gov/acs/www/.

[62] William H. Frey, "A Rollercoaster Decade for Migration," The Brookings Institution, December 29, 2009. http://www.brookings.edu/research/opinions/2009/12/29-migration-frey.

[63] www.pewhispanic.org.

[64] Daniel J. Elazar, *American Federalism: A View from the States* (New York: HarperCollins, 1984; originally published 1966).

[65] Ibid., 90.

[66] Ibid.

[67] Ibid., 86.

[68] Robert Draper, "The Life and Death (and Life?) of the Party," *Texas Monthly*, August 2013. http://www.texasmonthly.com/story/life-and-death-and-life-party?fullpage=1 .

CHAPTER 2

The Texas State Constitution and the American Federal System

*Upon completing this chapter,
you will be able to...*

- Explain the origin and development of the Texas Constitution.

- Describe separation of powers and checks and balances in both theory and practice in Texas.

- Describe state and local political systems and their relationship with the federal government.

lthough we are familiar with the United States Constitution, it is important to remember that all 50 states have written constitutions, as well. A **constitution** establishes the fundamental rules by which states govern. Constitutions instruct, though not always explicitly, what a government can and cannot do. In the previous chapter, we discussed the political culture of Texas, and the Texas Constitution is very much an embodiment of both the traditionalistic and individualistic subcultures. Although Texas has operated under seven different constitutions, the current constitution of Texas, ratified in 1876, reflects the conservative nature of the state, the distrust of government, and the desire to limit the government's ability to act.

constitution
The basic document that provides a framework for government and limits what the government can do

Examining the several constitutions that have governed Texas since Anglo settlement began gives us a greater understanding of how political culture impacts the formal structure of government. In addition, this chapter examines how Texas and other states operate within a federal system of government.

Principles of Constitutional Government

History, culture, traditions basic principles, and ideas have an impact on constitutions. Later in this chapter, you will see how the individualistic and traditionalistic political culture of Texas influenced the current constitution. Fundamentally, several important principles specifically underpin the general idea of constitutional government. The first is the idea of **popular sovereignty**. This idea holds that, at root, power rests with the people[1] and, theoretically,

popular sovereignty
The idea that power granted in state constitutions rests with the people

legitimate constitutions should articulate the will of the people. Constitutions are written by a popularly elected convention of citizens and not by state legislatures. Thus the citizens must also approve any changes in state constitutions—except in Delaware, where the state legislature can amend the state constitution without voter approval. The current Texas Constitution emphasizes the idea of popular sovereignty in the preamble and bill of rights, prominently positioned at the beginning of the document.

Second, constitutions are contracts or compacts between the citizens and the government and cannot be violated. This principle is embodied in **social contract theory**, the notion that all individuals possess inalienable rights and willingly submit to government to protect these rights. In essence, the constitution binds the government and the people, providing the framework within which interaction occurs. The laws passed by legislatures must fit within the framework of the constitution.

Third, constitutions structure government, divide and assign power, and place limitations on government's power. Many assume that government can do anything not prohibited by the constitution, and thus it is necessary to expressly limit the power of government. The current Texas Constitution is very much an example of limitations on the power of state government.

The men (women could not vote until 1920) who assembled in a constitutional convention of 1875 had as their primary aim limiting the power of state government due to the perceived abuses of Radical Republican governor, Edmund J. Davis. The actions of the Radical Republicans in Congress and in Texas during Reconstruction may have intensified the desires of these men to weaken and limit government, but they were predisposed to this philosophy even before the Civil War. Although the Texas Constitution embraces all three principles, the idea of a limited government, in particular, is wholeheartedly embraced.

Characteristics Common to State Constitutions

Separation of Powers

Besides the ideals of popular sovereignty, compact or contract theory, and limited government, state constitutions share other common characteristics. First, all state constitutions embrace the idea of **separation of powers** provided in the U.S. Constitution. Power is divided among an elected executive, an elected legislature, and the judiciary. The separation of powers provides a check on the actions of government. Fear of concentration of power in a single person led the framers of the U.S. Constitution to separate powers and provide for a systems of **checks and balances**. Similarly, framers of the current Texas Constitution sought to distribute powers broadly among the branches of Texas government. Figure 2.1 is a diagram of the separation of powers between the three branches of the federal government, and Table 2.1 clearly articulates the powers of the legislature, the governor, and the judiciary in Texas.

All state constitutions embrace this idea. Fear of strong executive authority, experienced in Texas under Governor Edmund J. Davis and the Radical Republicans, led the framers of the 1876 Texas Constitution to fragment executive power. Today, voters elect the governor, the lieutenant governor, the comptroller, the

social contract theory
The idea that all individuals possess inalienable rights and willingly submit to government to protect these rights

separation of powers
Power divided between the legislative, executive, and judicial branches of government

checks and balances
Power granted by the Constitution to each branch of government giving it authority to restrain other branches

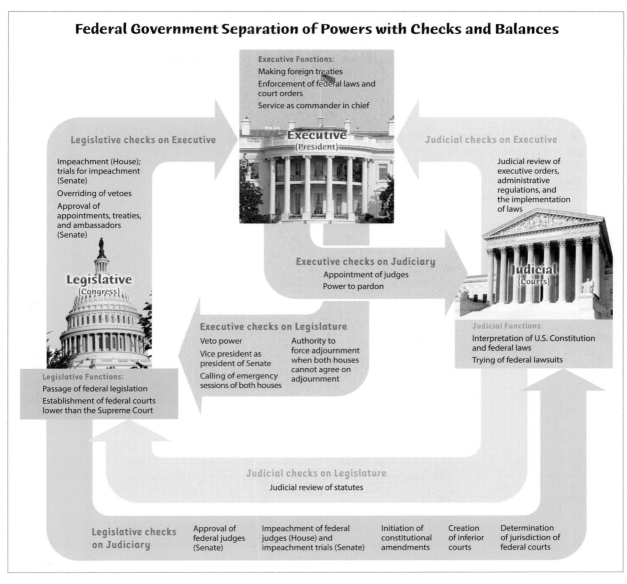

Federal Government Separation of Powers with Checks and Balances

Executive Functions:
Making foreign treaties
Enforcement of federal laws and court orders
Service as commander in chief

Executive
(President)

Legislative checks on Executive
Impeachment (House); trials for impeachment (Senate)
Overriding of vetoes
Approval of appointments, treaties, and ambassadors (Senate)

Judicial checks on Executive
Judicial review of executive orders, administrative regulations, and the implementation of laws

Executive checks on Judiciary
Appointment of judges
Power to pardon

Legislative
(Congress)

Judicial
(Courts)

Executive checks on Legislature
Veto power
Vice president as president of Senate
Calling of emergency sessions of both houses
Authority to force adjournment when both houses cannot agree on adjournment

Judicial Functions:
Interpretation of U.S. Constitution and federal laws
Trying of federal lawsuits

Legislative Functions:
Passage of federal legislation
Establishment of federal courts lower than the Supreme Court

Judicial checks on Legislature
Judicial review of statutes

| **Legislative checks on Judiciary** | Approval of federal judges (Senate) | Impeachment of federal judges (House) and impeachment trials (Senate) | Initiation of constitutional amendments | Creation of inferior courts | Determination of jurisdiction of federal courts |

FIGURE 2.1   Separation of Powers with Checks and Balances

CORE OBJECTIVE

Communicating Effectively...

Analyze the diagram in Figure 2.1 and the division of powers in Table 2.1 to describe the separation of powers and checks and balances in both theory and practice in Texas.

TABLE 2.1		
Separation of Powers in Texas Government		
The Legislature	**The Governor**	**The Judiciary**
Propose and pass laws	Limited appointment power of some executive officials and judges in cases of vacancies	Interpret the law
Power to propose constitutional amendments		Settle all disputes in matters of criminal and civil law
Power to tax and set the budget	Submits budget proposal to legislature	Popularly elected
Oversight power of state agencies and departments	Serves on boards; e.g., the Legislative Budget Board	
Impeachment power of judges and executive branch officials	Can call special sessions and dictate special session agenda	
	Veto and line-item veto power	

attorney general, the commissioner of the land office, the agricultural commissioner, the railroad commissioners, and the state board of education. The secretary of state is the only non-elected executive official; the position is appointed by the governor. This system is called a **plural executive system**, and it serves to limit the power of the governor by distributing executive power among the various independently elected officials.

plural executive system
System in which executive power is divided among several statewide elected officials

Bill of Rights

Like the U.S. Constitution, most state constitutions have very strong statements on civil liberties that secure basic freedoms. Most of the civil liberties protected in state constitutions duplicate those found in the U.S. document, but many state constitutions are more generous in securing liberties than is the U.S. Constitution. The Texas Constitution is no exception in this regard. The average citizen, upon reading the **bill of rights** section of the Texas Constitution, might well conclude that it is a very permissive document, granting equalities under the law to all citizens regardless of "sex, race, color, creed or national origin."[2]

bill of rights
A list of individual rights and freedoms granted to citizens within a constitution

Supreme Law of the State

Article 6 of the U.S. Constitution contains the **supremacy clause**. This makes the U.S. Constitution the supreme law of the land, and no federal or state **statute** may violate it. Because laws follow a hierarchy (owing to our federal system of government, discussed later in the chapter), federal law preempts state law, and state law preempts local law. Similarly, state law may not violate the state constitution, and state **statutes** are superior to local government **ordinances**.

A recent example of local ordinances potentially conflicting with a state statute involves the state issuing permits to citizens for carrying concealed handguns. Many local governments (cities, counties, and metropolitan transit authorities) passed regulations prohibiting the carrying of concealed handguns in some public places. Many of these gun laws have been struck down, though not all. Typically, local gun laws have been upheld only when they do not contradict state law, such as when local laws prohibit what the state prohibits, but more strictly. For example, in Cincinnati v. Baskin (2006), the defendant argued local law (prohibiting semi-automatic firearms with 10+ round capacity) was in violation of state law (prohibiting semi-automatic firearms with 31+ round capacity). While state law was found to be general law, the local law was determined to not be in conflict and was therefore applicable to the defendant.[3]

supremacy clause
A clause that makes constitutional provisions superior to other laws

statutes
Laws passed by state legislatures

ordinances
Laws passed by local governments

Evolution of the Texas Constitution: 1824–1876

We have identified several common features of constitutions. Throughout history, each transitional period for the region that became Texas, whether incorporating under Mexico, gaining independent nation status, becoming part of the United States, or moving through the troubled period before and after the Civil War, necessitated the creation of a new constitution. An examination of the various constitutions that have been drafted throughout Texas's history will show that not only are common features present throughout, but Texas's history and culture have also had a significant influence on the development of each constitution.

Constitutions under the Republic of Mexico

The first constitution to govern Anglos in Texas was the Republic of Mexico's Constitution of 1824. This constitution was federalist in concept, dividing governing authority between the nation and the states, breaking with the Spanish centralist tradition of a strong national government.[4] Under the provisions of the 1824 Constitution, the state of Coahuila y Tejas was formed. The new state was required to enact a state constitution that passed in 1827. It provided for a unicameral legislature, and Texas elected two representatives to the state legislature. This constitution, which lacked a bill of rights, provided a government structure with which the Anglos were mostly comfortable. Anglos simply disregarded sections of the constitution they found disagreeable. The sections Anglo settlers were most uncomfortable with were those designating Catholicism as the state religion and those that did not recognize slavery.

The suspension of the Mexican national constitution of 1824, and with it the state constitution of 1827, by Mexican president Santa Anna was a factor that led to the Texas revolution. One of the early Texas flags, supposedly flown at the Alamo, had the number 1824 superimposed on a red, green, and white emblem of the Mexican flag. This was a demand that the Constitution of 1824 be restored.[5]

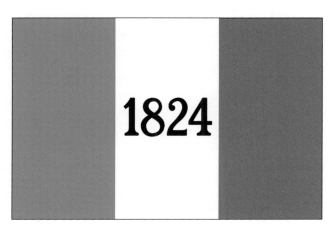

Early Texas flag depicting dissatisfaction with the suspension of the Republic of Mexico's 1824 Constitution

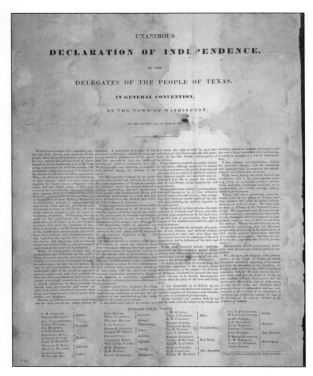

The Declaration of Independence 1836

The Republic of Texas Constitution of 1836

In 1836, when Texas declared itself a republic independent of Mexico (Map 2.1), a new constitution was adopted. This document was a composite of the U.S. Constitution and the constitutions of several southern states. It provided for a unitary, rather than federal, form of government. (See discussion on systems of government later in this chapter.) Signs of the distrust of government by the traditionalistic southerners who wrote the document are evident. They limited the term of the president to one three-year term with prohibitions against consecutive reelection. The president was also prohibited from raising an army without the consent of the congress. There were other

MAP 2.1   Republic of Texas From 1836 until 1845, Texas was an independent nation known as the Republic of Texas. In the treaty forced on Mexico by Texas, Mexico ceded land stretching to the headwaters of the Rio Grande. Although this land was never fully occupied by the government of the Republic, Texas claimed land in what is now part of the states of New Mexico, Oklahoma, Kansas, Colorado, and Wyoming.

features, such as freedom of religion and property rights protection, that had been absent in the 1824 and 1827 Mexican constitutions. Slavery, which had not been recognized by the Mexican government, was legalized.[6]

Statehood Constitution of 1845

The first Texas state constitution was adopted when Texas joined the Union in 1845. This document also reflected the traditionalistic southern culture, with a few notable exceptions that were adaptations of Spanish law. Women were granted property rights equal to those of men, especially in marriage—where women were given half the value of all property acquired during the marriage (communal property). In addition, a person's homestead was protected from forced sale to pay debts. These ideas were later adopted by many other states. The 1845 constitution also provided for limited executive authority, biennial sessions of the legislature, and two-year terms for most officials. Most of these features were included in later constitutions.

The Civil War and Reconstruction Constitutions of 1861, 1866, and 1869

In 1861, when Texas joined the Confederacy, another state constitution was adopted. It was essentially the same as the 1845 document, but with an added prohibition against the emancipation of slaves, a provision to secede from the Union, and a provision to join the Confederacy.

In 1866, a third state constitution was approved as a condition for rejoining the Union following the Civil War. This document abolished slavery, nullified the ordinances of secession, renounced the right of future secession, and repudiated the wartime debts of the state. This constitution was short-lived and overturned by Reconstruction acts of the U.S. Congress.

Texas adopted a new constitution in 1869. This fourth state constitution, which was approved under the supervision of the federal government's military rule, is called the Reconstruction constitution or the "carpetbagger's constitution." It represented a radical departure from past and future documents and reflected the centralization aspirations of the national Republicans. A four-year term was provided for the governor, who was also given the authority to appoint most state and many local officials. County courts were abolished, and much local authority and control was removed from the planter class. Public schools were centralized under state control and funded with a poll tax and the sale of public lands. African Americans were given the right to vote, and whites who had participated in the "rebellion" (Civil War) were disfranchised.[7]

The Constitution of 1876

The current Texas Constitution was written in 1875 at the end of Reconstruction and approved by the voters in 1876. None of the delegates present at the 1875 constitutional convention had participated in writing the 1869 constitution. These

Delegates to the 1875 Constitutional
Convention

men were landowners who had strongly objected to the centralist government under Reconstruction. As T. R. Fehrenbach put it, these men were

> mostly old Texans: John Henry Brown, Sterling C. Robertson, sons of empresarios, Rip Ford (Texas Ranger), John H. Reagan (Ex-Postmaster General of the Confederacy), and a bevy of generals who has [sic] worn the grey. Of the ninety members, more than twenty held high rank in the C.S.A. [Confederate States of America] This was a restoration convention . . . It was a landowners' group, including forty members of the Grange . . . This was an antigovernment instrument: too many Texans had seen what government could do, not for them but to them. It tore up previous frameworks, and its essential aim was to try and bind all state government within tight confines.[8]

The new constitution reflected the antigovernment sentiments of the traditionalistic/individualistic political culture of the state. It reimposed shorter terms of office, reestablished many statewide and local elected offices, and severely restricted the government's authority to act. The powers of both the legislature and the governor were restricted.[9]

CORE OBJECTIVE

Thinking Critically...

What is the impact of a constitutional convention dominated by one party? What were the consequences of the 1875 constitutional convention in the development of the Texas Constitution?

Culture Drives Institutions

The various Texas constitutions have all reflected the political climate of the state, demonstrating how political culture drives institutions. Consistent with the dominant views of the day, the 1845 constitution provided for limited government with little centralized power. The constitutions of 1861 and 1866 continued these principles of limited government. The present constitution not only reinstated but expanded the ideas of limited government. Only the Reconstruction constitution of 1869, which provided for a strong, centralized government, was a departure from these ideas. Its swift repeal at the end of Reconstruction indicates how southern whites utterly rejected these concepts. Many Texans today would not accept these concepts, either. In 1999, voters rejected two amendments that would have expanded the power of the governor to appoint and remove minor state officials. In addition, voters have rejected annual sessions of the legislature on several occasions, and there is a consistent voice for decentralization of decisions down to the local level. In short, the current Texas Constitution is very compatible with the political climate of the state. However, institutions also can independently impact political outcomes as well as shape political culture in the future. The Spanish constitutions contributed several key elements, including community property rights for women, which was a clear departure from English common law.

Important Sections of the Texas Constitution

There are 17 articles in the Texas Constitution in addition to a preamble and appendix. Because the Texas Constitution contains nearly 87,000 words, to discuss all sections in depth would be exhaustive. However, quite a few sections stand out as essential. A number of them are reflective of sections found in the U.S. Constitution; however, the Texas Constitution is significantly more detailed.

Article 1: Bill of Rights

The first article in the Texas Constitution is Article 1 Bill of Rights. Much like the U.S. Constitution, the Texas Constitution provides protection for freedom of speech and religion and protects the rights of the accused. Additional elements can be found in the Texas Constitution. For example, an equal rights amendment was inserted into the Texas Constitution in 1972, guaranteeing equality based on sex, race, color, creed, and national origin. The Texas Constitution ensures that the writ of habeas corpus will not be suspended and gives protection to crime victims. In 2009, the Texas Constitution was amended to give property owners additional rights, stating that private property cannot be taken by government for the purpose of "transfer to a private entity for the primary purpose of economic development or enhancement of tax revenues."[10] These rights add many of the elements of law found in the federal government and in other state constitutions. One of the amendments added to the Texas Constitution that conflicts with elements in some other state constitutions is Section 32, which defines marriage as a union between one man and one woman.

Article 2: The Powers of Government

Article 2 discusses separation of powers specifically. The Texas Constitution makes it clear that the system contains separate checks, as compared to the more implied structure noted in the U.S. Constitution, by stating "no person, or collection of persons, being of one of these departments, shall exercise any power properly attached to either of the others, except in the instances herein expressly permitted."[11]

Article 3: Legislative Department

Article 3 refers to the legislative branch. The Texas Constitution divides the Texas legislature into two branches: a senate and a house of representatives. The senate is to be composed of 31 members, and the house of representatives is to be 150 members. The constitution provides for the election system, terms of office of members, and required qualifications of both branches. Much like the U.S. Constitution, the qualifications for senators and representatives are minimal. The legislature is to meet every two years for 140 days. Unlike the U.S. Constitution, the Texas Constitution lays out in significant detail the rules of procedure that legislators must follow. Article 3, Section 24, provides the amount of compensation for legislators at $600 per month, with per diem expenses allowed. The Texas Ethics Commission, an agency whose membership is outlined in Article 3, sets the per diem amount and can choose to recommend a higher salary for legislators.

Article 4: Executive Department

Article 4 describes the executive branch, which consists of the governor, lieutenant governor, comptroller of public accounts, commissioner of general land office, and the attorney general, who are all elected. The secretary of state is appointed by the governor. Under Article 4, the Texas legislature sets the annual salary of the governor. The governor's term is set at four years and the constitution establishes no term limits. The governor is given the right to call a special session (which differs from an extraordinary session), during which members of the "Legislature may not consider any subject other than the appointment of electors at that special session."[12] The Texas Constitution purposefully provides for a fragmented executive branch and limits the powers of the governor. This is in keeping with much of the history and culture of the state, in which a general distrust of centralized power led to a preference for limited government.

Article 5: Judicial Department

Article 5 refers to the judicial branch. This is one of the branches whose structural elements are distinct from the design of the federal branches. The judicial department consists of multiple courts and, rather than having a single high court, the Texas Constitution provides for two high courts: the Supreme Court (eight justices and one chief justice) and the Court of Criminal Appeals (eight judges and one presiding judge). The Texas legislature has the right to create additional courts as it sees fit. Article 5 provides the requirements for judges. For example, a justice on the Texas Supreme Court must be "licensed to practice law in this state and [must be], at the time of election, a citizen of the United States and of this state, and [have] attained the age of thirty-five years, and [have] been a practicing lawyer, or a lawyer or judge of a court of record together at least ten years."[13] It should be noted, however, that not all judges need be lawyers. For example, county judges and justices of the peace are excluded from this requirement. In addition, the Texas Constitution provides for the election, rather than appointment, of judges. This has been a political concern wherein some citizens argue that the partisan election of judges may lead judges to base decisions on political reasons to ensure reelection. However, others argue that the election of judges provides for more direct involvement by the people in the democratic process.

Additional Articles

Article 6 concerns suffrage and provides the list of persons not allowed to vote in the state, including those who are under 18 years of age, deemed mentally incompetent by the court, and persons convicted of felonies. Article 7 focuses on education and provides for a system of free public schools as well as various systems of funding for primary and secondary schools. In addition, Article 7 provides for the establishment of state universities. Articles 9 and 16 define the creation and structure of counties in the state. These portions of the constitution are incredibly detailed, and the structure provided for counties leads to a fairly inflexible system that counties are required to abide by. Article 17 provides the means for amending the Texas Constitution.

Comparing the Structure of State Constitutions

Although they have some common characteristics, vast differences exist among state constitutions. According to legal experts and political theorists, there are some ideal characteristics that constitutions should possess. Ideally, a constitution should be brief and explicit, embody only the general principles of government, and provide the broad outlines of government subject to interpretation, especially through the court's power of judicial review. Constitutions should not be too detailed and specific, but should be broad and flexible. Furthermore, constitutions should provide broad grants of power to specific agencies and hold government officials accountable for their actions. Last, formal amendments to the constitution should be infrequent, deliberate, and significant.

Although it is worth identifying the qualities of an ideal constitution, it is important to understand that an "ideal" constitution does not necessarily equal good governance. The culture in which political institutions operate has a much more significant impact on governance. A good constitution serves to reinforce cultural expectations, but it is not sufficient in and of itself.

The U.S. Constitution meets these "ideal characteristics." There are only 4,543 words in the original document. It broadly outlines the basic principles of government and has been amended only 27 times. All but eight of these amendments involved issues of civil liberty, voting, and electoral questions. Very few of these amendments have altered the basic structure of the federal government. The document is flexible enough to allow for change without altering the basic document.

Few state constitutions can meet the ideal standards of brevity and few amendments. This is especially true of the Texas Constitution. Table 2.2 details information about all 50 state constitutions as of January 1, 2013. Several conclusions are obvious from examining this table. First, most states have had several constitutions. Only 19 states are still operating under their first constitution, and most of these are newer states in the West. Maine and Massachusetts are the only states of the "original 13" still operating under their first constitutions. Because of the Civil War and its aftermath, former Confederate states have had multiple constitutions.

Second, most state constitutions are very lengthy documents. Alabama's is the longest, with 376,006 words, including the amendments. The average state constitution is about 39,524 words. Some writers have pointed out that state constitutions have to be longer than the U.S. document because of the nature of state responsibility. Although this is true, it can also be argued that most state documents are of excessive length for other reasons, which is discussed later.

Third, most state constitutions have been amended more often than the U.S. Constitution; the average is about 142 times. Alabama is again the leader with 880 amendments. Fourth, state constitutions have a limited life span when compared with the U.S. Constitution. The average life span for a state constitution is ninety-five years.[14]

If we compare the Texas Constitution to the "average" state constitution, we find that it is longer than most, at 86,936 words, and has more amendments. It has been amended 474 times as of January 1, 2013.[15] Only six states have drafted more constitutions. One can easily conclude that most state constitutions, including Texas's, do not meet the criteria for an ideal constitution. Most are lengthy, detailed documents that require frequent alteration and might be more accurately described as statutory or legislative acts rather than constitutional law. This is especially true of the document that governs Texas.

Several other generalizations can be made about state constitutions. First, most create weak executives and strong legislatures. (This is discussed later in the text.) Second, all state constitutions contain articles on taxation and finance that limit how funds can be spent. Often taxes are **earmarked** for specific purposes (a common example is the gasoline tax for state highways). Third, all but a few constitutions prohibit deficit expenditures unless approved by voters in the form of a bond election. Finally, most state constitutions contain large amounts of detail. For example, the

earmarks
Money dedicated to a specific expenditure; for example, the excise tax on gasoline funds highway infrastructure

TABLE 2.2

Comparisons of State Constitutions, January 1, 2013

State or Other Jurisdiction	Number of State Constitutions	Dates of Adoption	Effective Date of Present Constitution	Estimated Length (Number of Words)	Number of Amendments	
					Submitted to Voters	Adopted
Alabama	6	1819, 1861, 1865, 1868, 1875, 1901	Nov. 28, 1901	376,006	1,209	880
Alaska	1	1956	Jan. 3, 1959	13,479	42	29
Arizona	1	1911	Feb. 14, 1912	47,306	274	151
Arkansas	5	1836, 1861, 1864, 1868, 1874	Oct. 30, 1874	59,120	198	99
California	2	1849, 1879	July 4, 1879	67,048	894	527
Colorado	1	1876	Aug. 1, 1876	66,140	339	158
Connecticut	2	1818, 1965	Dec. 30, 1965	16,401	31	30
Delaware	4	1776, 1792, 1831, 1897	June 10, 1897	25,445	0*	142
Florida	6	1839, 1861, 1865, 1868, 1886, 1968	Jan. 7, 1969	56,705	165	121
Georgia	10	1777, 1789, 1798, 1861, 1865, 1868, 1877, 1945, 1976, 1982	July 1, 1983	41,684	96	73
Hawaii	1	1950	Aug. 21, 1959	21,498	133	110
Idaho	1	1889	July 3, 1890	24,626	212	125
Illinois	4	1818, 1848, 1870, 1970	July 1, 1971	16,401	19	12
Indiana	2	1816, 1851	Nov. 1, 1851	11,476	79	47
Iowa	2	1846, 1857	Sept. 3, 1857	11,089	59	54
Kansas	1	1859	Jan. 29, 1861	14,097	126	96
Kentucky	4	1792, 1799, 1850, 1891	Sept. 28, 1891	27,234	76	42
Louisiana	11	1812, 1845, 1852, 1861, 1864, 1868, 1879, 1898, 1913, 1921, 1974	Jan. 1, 1975	69,876	248	176
Maine	1	1819	March 15, 1820	16,313	205	172
Maryland	4	1776, 1851, 1864, 1867	Oct. 5, 1867	43,198	264	228
Massachusetts	1	1780	Oct. 25, 1780	45,283	148	120
Michigan	4	1835, 1850, 1908, 1963	Jan. 1, 1964	31,164	73	30
Minnesota	1	1857	May 11, 1858	11,734	217	120
Mississippi	4	1817, 1832, 1869, 1890	Nov. 1, 1890	26,229	161	125
Missouri	4	1820, 1865, 1875, 1945	March 30, 1945	69,394	177	115
Montana	2	1889, 1972	July 1, 1973	12,790	56	31
Nebraska	2	1866, 1875	Oct. 12, 1875	34,934	354	230
Nevada	1	1864	Oct. 31, 1864	37,418	233	137

TABLE 2.2   *(Continued)*

Comparisons of State Constitutions, January 1, 2013

State or Other Jurisdiction	Number of State Constitutions	Dates of Adoption	Effective Date of Present Constitution	Estimated Length (Number of Words)	Number of Amendments Submitted to Voters	Adopted
New Hampshire	2	1776, 1784	June 2, 1784	13,060	289	145
New Jersey	3	1776, 1844, 1947	Jan. 1, 1948	26,360	81	46
New Mexico	1	1911	Jan. 6, 1912	33,198	298	165
New York	4	1777, 1822, 1846, 1894	Jan. 1, 1895	44,397	295	220
North Carolina	3	1776, 1868, 1970	July 1, 1971	17,177	38	31
North Dakota	1	1889	Nov. 2, 1889	18,746	271	154
Ohio	2	1802, 1851	Sept. 1, 1851	53,239	287	172
Oklahoma	1	1907	Nov. 16, 1907	81,666	360	193
Oregon	1	1857	Feb. 14, 1859	49,016	495	253
Pennsylvania	5	1776, 1790, 1838, 1873, 1968	1968	26,078	36	30
Rhode Island	2	1842, 1986	Dec. 4, 1986	11,407	14	12
South Carolina	7	1776, 1778, 1790, 1861, 1865, 1868, 1895	Jan. 1, 1896	27,421	687	498
South Dakota	1	1889	Nov. 2, 1889	27,774	233	217
Tennessee	3	1796, 1835, 1870	Feb. 23, 1870	13,960	62	39
Texas	5	1845, 1861, 1866, 1869, 1876	Feb. 15, 1876	86,936	652	474
Utah	1	1895	Jan. 4, 1896	17,849	169	117
Vermont	3	1777, 1786, 1793	July 9, 1793	8,565	212	54
Virginia	6	1776, 1830, 1851, 1869, 1902, 1970	July 1, 1971	21,899	56	48
Washington	1	1889	Nov. 11, 1889	32,578	180	106
West Virginia	2	1863, 1872	April 9, 1872	33,324	122	71
Wisconsin	1	1848	May 29, 1848	15,102	194	145
Wyoming	1	1889	July 10, 1890	26,349	128	100

*In Delaware, the state legislature amends the state constitution without voter approval.

Source: Book of the States 2013 (Council of State Governments, http://knowledgecenter.csg.org/kc/content/book-states-2013-chapter-1-state-constitutions).

original Texas Constitution contained a detailed list of items protected by the homestead protection provisions from forced sale for payment of debts. The list included the numbers of chickens, ducks, cows, pigs, dogs, and horses that were exempt.

Amending and Revising State Constitutions

All state constitutions provide procedures for amending and revising the document. Except in the state of Delaware, two steps are involved in changing constitutions: proposing amendments and citizen approval. In Texas, two-thirds of each house of the legislature must propose amendments, and a majority of the voters who vote on the amendment must approve.

Some states provide a variety of methods for proposing or recommending changes to the constitution. All state constitutions allow the legislature to propose changes. Most states require an extraordinary majority vote of both houses of the legislature to propose an amendment. Twenty-two states require only a majority; twenty two states require a two-thirds vote of the state legislature[16]; and eight require a three-fifths vote of the legislature.

A second method of proposing amendments to constitutions is by voter initiative. **Initiative** requires the collection of a prescribed number of signatures on a petition within a set time. Seventeen states allow initiative. Most states with initiative are western states that entered the Union in the late nineteenth or early twentieth century, when initiative was a popular idea. Only five states that allow for constitutional amendments by initiative are east of the Mississippi River. Texas does not have initiative. The Texas Republican party pushed the idea of initiative for many years, but in 1996 it was dropped from the party platform.

Most states, including Texas, allow the legislature to submit to the voters the question of calling a **constitutional convention** to propose amendments. This method is normally used for general revision and not for single amendments. Fourteen states have some provision for automatically submitting the question of a general convention to the voters periodically. If the voters approve, a convention is elected, it assembles, and it proposes amendments for voter approval.

Constitutional commissions are most often created by acts of the legislature, although there are other methods. These commissions usually submit a report to the legislature recommending changes. If the legislature approves, the proposed amendments are submitted to the voters. In Florida, the commission can bypass the legislature and go directly to the voters. Texas last used a commission in 1973 when the legislature created a 37-member commission to consider substantive and comprehensive revision to the Texas Constitution. After eight months of meetings and 19 public hearings, the Constitutional Revision Commission submitted recommendations to the 63rd Texas legislature.[17] Many issues, such as "right to work" provisions, were contentious and necessitated compromise. Other provisions, including bringing the multitude of local government clauses together in one article, represented vast improvements. Ultimately the committee's recommendations were rejected by the legislature on July 30, 1974, having failed to garner a two-thirds majority by 3 votes.

initiative

A process that allows citizens to propose changes to the state constitution through the use of petitions signed by registered voters; Texas does not allow constitutional revision through initiative

constitutional convention

An assembly of citizens who may propose changes to state constitutions through voter approval

Patterns of Constitutional Change

If we examine state constitutional amendment processes, several patterns emerge. The first involves the frequency of change. State constitutions are amended more frequently than the U.S. Constitution. One reason is that state constitutions deal with a wider range of functions. About 63 percent of state amendments deal with issues not covered in the U.S. Constitution. A good example of this is education. Even if we remove issues not covered in the U.S. Constitution, the rate of amendment is still 3.5 times the national rate.[18] Change is also related to length. Longer state constitutions are more likely to be amended.[19]

The second pattern involves the method used to amend. As indicated, most amendments (90 percent) are proposed by state legislatures. States that require large legislative majorities for initiation have fewer amendments proposed and approved. Most amendments proposed by legislatures also receive voter approval. About 63 percent of all amendments proposed since 1970 have been approved by the voters.[20]

In the 17 states that allow voters to initiate amendments, two patterns emerge: More amendments are proposed, and the voter approval success rate for initiative-generated amendments is about half the rate for those proposed by state legislatures (32 percent versus 64 percent).[21] This tells us that the initiative process does not screen out amendments that lack broad public support. Proposal by legislature does. Amendments that gain support from supermajorities (majorities at a specified level above a simple majority of 50 percent) are more likely to be politically acceptable. The legislature serves as a screening process to rule out unacceptable amendments.

Amending the Texas Constitution

All amendments to the Texas Constitution have been proposed by a two-thirds vote of each house of the legislature. From 1975 to 2013, the legislature has proposed 299 amendments for voter approval. The voters have approved 255 of the 299 amendments proposed and have rejected 44 (an 85 percent approval rate).[22]

Voter turnout for amendments tends to be quite low, for a variety of reasons. Most amendments appear on the ballot in November of odd-numbered years, when no statewide offices are up for election. Since 1960, the Texas legislature has proposed 379 amendments to the constitution. Of these, 298 were voted on in odd–numbered years, and 97 were approved in even-numbered years. Voter turnout for odd-year elections is lower than for even-year elections (see Table 2.3). In odd-year elections, less than 10 percent of the voting-age population participates.[23] This means that as few as 5 percent (plus one voter) could approve an amendment to the constitution. In

TABLE 2.3

Voter Turnout in Odd-Year Constitutional Amendment Elections

Year	Percent of Voting-Age Population Voting
2013	6.14
2011	3.77
2009	5.77
2007	6.31
2005	13.82 (Antigay marriage amendment)
2003	9.31
2001	5.57
1999	6.69
1997	5.32
1997	8.45 (Special election)
1995	5.55
1993	8.52
1991	16.60 (School tax reform)
1989	9.33
1987	18.60 (School tax reform)
1985	8.24
1983	6.91
1981	8.07

Source: Texas Secretary of State (http://www.sos.state.tx.us/elections/historical/70-92.shtml).

2005, there was a slight increase due to the antigay marriage amendment that was on the ballot. Texas submits more amendments in odd-numbered years than most states.

Second, statewide voter turnout rates are often skewed by election schedules in counties with large cities. For example, Harris County could have a greater impact on statewide elections if many city and school board elections are held in the same election cycle as constitutional amendments.. The Harris County vote could be significant if turnout statewide is very low. A strongly contested race for mayor of Houston could inflate the turnout rate in that city and affect statewide election results. The Harris County vote often constitutes about 30 percent of the total statewide votes cast on these amendments, despite the fact that registered voters in Harris County make up approximately 15 percent of the total number of registered voters in the entire state.

Third, **ballot wording** can also contribute to voter confusion and apathy about the political process. The state legislature dictates the ballot wording of all amendments. Sometimes this wording can be misleading or noninstructive unless the voter has studied the issue before the election. This example from the 1978 election is illustrative:

> For or against the constitutional amendment providing for tax relief for residential homesteads, elderly persons, disabled persons, and agricultural land; for personal property exceptions; truth in taxation procedures, including citizen involvement; for a redefinition [sic] of the tax base; for limitations on state spending; and for fair property tax administration.[24]

Most voters probably found this wording irresistible. Could any voter not favor tax exemptions for the elderly, the handicapped, homeowners, and farmers? Does any citizen oppose fair tax administration or citizen involvement? The amendment passed by an overwhelming majority. Another example of ballot-wording bias occurred in an amendment exempting personal property in Texas ports—the "freeport" amendment—which failed in 1987. The ballot read: "rendering to the exemption from ad valorem taxation, certain tangible personal property temporarily located within the states." But in 1989 the ballot read: "The constitutional amendment promoting economic growth, job creation and fair tax treatment for Texans who export goods." The amendment passed by a large majority. Ballot wording is apparently an important factor in the passage or rejection of amendments.

Fourth, the number of amendments and the subject matter of most amendments are not of interest to most voters, thus discouraging voter turnout. For example, in 1993, the voters were asked to approve 16 amendments to the constitution. The subjects of most of these amendments were financial: to authorize the issuance of bonds for economic development, pollution control, veterans' land, higher education, prisons, pensions, and agricultural development. In addition, one prohibited the establishment of an income tax without voter approval and one concerned delinquent taxes. Two separate amendments (Propositions 6 and 8) abolished the office of land surveyor in Jefferson and McLennan counties, and another amendment (number 15) allowed voters in any counties to abolish the office of land surveyor. One amendment cleared up Spanish land-grant titles in two counties. Another allowed the legislature to set qualifications for county sheriffs, and another allowed corporations additional means of raising capital. Except for one amendment dealing with an income tax prohibition, there was little in these amendments that was of interest to the average voter. This election is typical of most constitutional amendment elections. The seemingly trivial subject matter contributes to low voter interest and turnout. Only those people most affected by an amendment are likely to understand it and to vote. Most voters stay home because there is little else to bring them out to the polls on Election Day.

ballot wording

Description of a proposed amendment as it appears on the ballot; can be intentionally noninstructive and misleading to voters in order to affect voter outcome

Finally, voter ignorance of the issues is also a factor, although numerous sources provide ballot information. Issues are commonly reported in newspapers, on the nightly news, and on public radio broadcasting. Many county websites provide sample ballots beginning about a month in advance of an election. Unfortunately, many people remain uninformed regardless of the numerous avenues through which information can be accessed. This issue is discussed in more detail in Chapter 7.

Thus, odd-year elections, confusing or noninstructive ballot wording, issues that interest few voters, and voter ignorance all contribute to low voter turnout. A very small number of voters, stimulated by personal interests and supported by an active interest group, can amend the constitution without a majority of the voters becoming involved. Often, many voters are not even aware that an election is being held.

Several other observations can be made regarding the amendment processes in Texas. First, most amendments face little opposition. Texans have approved 474 amendments and rejected 178.[25] Most are supported by an organized interest group willing to spend money, gain support, and work hard for passage. Second, interest groups attempt to have their interests protected in the constitution. A vested interest, protected in the constitution, is more difficult to alter than one protected by state law alone, because state law can be changed easily in the next session of the legislature. The process of constitutional change requires a two-thirds vote of the legislature plus electoral approval.

A good example of such a protection in the constitution is the Permanent University Fund (PUF). The University of Texas and Texas A&M University are the only state schools that benefit from this fund, which has a value of approximately $11 billion. Other state universities have long felt that they deserved a share of this protected fund. Texas A&M and the University of Texas wanted to protect their funds and formed a coalition with non-PUF schools to support an amendment that created the Higher Education Assistance Fund (HEAF). This fund provides money to non-PUF universities. In the end, higher education funding for all state universities became protected in the state constitution.

Criticisms of the Texas Constitution

A number of criticisms can be levied against the Texas Constitution. These include length, wording, unclear organization, excessive detail, inflexibility, and constant change.

The Texas Constitution is the second longest state constitution in the nation, with much of its length coming in the form of amendments. For example, Article 1 Bill of Rights contains 33 Sections and Article 8 Taxation and Revenue contains 24 Sections. Including the index, the Texas Constitution is 228 pages.[26] Much of it is written in language that is unclear and that some consider outdated. For example, Article 4, Sec. 3 on election returns states:

> The returns of every election for said executive officers, until otherwise provided by law, shall be made out, sealed up, and transmitted by the returning officers prescribed by law, to the seat of Government, directed to the Secretary of State, who shall deliver the same to the Speaker of the House of Representatives, as soon as the Speaker shall be chosen, and the said Speaker shall, during the first week of the session of the legislature, open and publish then in the presence of both Houses of the Legislature . . .

In addition to the difficult language, the Texas Constitution is not organized in a manner that makes it easy to discover where items are located. Thus, there is the necessity of having both a table of contents and an index.

An ordinary system may not see excessive detail as problematic. However, the purpose of a constitution is to provide a broad foundation upon which a state government can rest. Although the Texas Constitution contains some broad foundational aspects, many of the components are so specific and detailed that they would be better placed in a legislative enactment. For example, Article 8, Taxation and Revenue, addresses topics such as homestead exemptions, assessment of lands designated for agricultural use, and ad valorem tax relief for items such as mobile drilling equipment and green coffee. Although these items may be important for government to address, their placement in the constitution, in contrast to being part of a statute or agency regulation, illustrates that many parts of the Texas Constitution are focused on specifics rather than on broad foundations.

The criticism that the Texas Constitution is both inflexible and at the same time constantly changing would seem contradictory. However, the inflexibility comes from the excessive detail referred to earlier. Broad statements allow for a wider use of discretion in interpreting and implementing constitutional provisions. The extreme detail found in a number of sections is one reason it is more difficult for government actors to use their discretion in interpreting and implementing it. For example, Article 9, Counties, lays out in detail such items as hospital districts, tax rates, and airport authorities. Counties become limited in what they can do under the Texas Constitution. Of course, for some people this is seen as an advantage rather than as a bug in the system. They believe that a constitution that frustrates the use of power by governmental authorities limits government and preserves their freedom.

The constant change comes from the stream of new amendments. These also contribute to excessive length. The constant changes tend to be incremental in nature, however, and as such, the Texas Constitution as a whole has not been drastically revised since the 1876 version upon which the current document is based. Although many reformers believe the constitution is therefore in need of a comprehensive revision, it is unlikely that such change can be achieved in the brief biennial legislative session in a state whose citizens tend to have a strong distrust of government.

Conclusion to the Texas Constitution

Many legal scholars have pointed out the need for a general revision of the current Texas Constitution. In the 1970s, a serious effort at total revision was unsuccessful. A commission of legal experts, acting as a constitutional commission, made recommendations to the state legislature for major changes. The state legislature, acting as a constitutional convention in 1974, deadlocked and adjourned without making any recommendations for change. The next regular session of the Texas legislature, in 1975, proposed eight separate amendments to the voters. In November 1975, the voters rejected all amendments by a two-to-one margin.

In 1999, two prominent members of the Texas legislature introduced a bill calling for general revision of the Texas Constitution. Then-Senator Bill Ratliff, Republican from East Texas, and Representative Robert Junell, Democrat from San Angelo, were the chairs of budget-writing committees in the senate and house in that session. Their bill called for some substantial changes in the current constitution. This proposal, which would have reduced the size of the current constitution to some 19,000 words in 150 sections, died in committee in both houses.

The 76th Legislature (1999) created the Select Committee on Constitutional Revision, and Speaker of the House James Laney appointed Representative Joe Driver as Chair. This committee has held hearings in various locations in the state and made suggestions for changes that could be characterized as elimination of deadwood and updating of wording. The committee did not see the need for general revision of the document nor the calling of a constitutional convention or commission.

The piecemeal process of amending the constitution every two years will likely continue for several reasons. Several reasons are generally cited for this. First is a lack of support for reform by significant political forces in the state. Strong political leadership from someone like the governor would be necessary. Neither Rick Perry nor his recent successor Governor Greg Abbott has indicated any interest in supporting reform efforts; supporting controversial issues such as revision of the constitution has little appeal or payoff. Currently, no statewide leader has been particularly vocal about supporting revision. In short, the political will to significantly change the constitution does not exist.

Second, the political culture of the state and the basic conservative nature of state politics do not support broad change. The current constitution supports the traditionalistic/individualistic political culture of the state. The document serves select groups of people and protects their interests and privileges, and these groups have the resources to maintain those protections. Senator Ratliff's and Representative Junell's 1999 proposal avoided many of the major controversies by leaving intact important interests that are well protected by the constitution; however, not all were protected.

Third, strong opposition from powerful lobby groups whose interests are currently protected by the document would make change difficult, if not impossible. In his opening address to the constitutional convention assembled in 1974, the vice chairman of the convention, Lt. Governor William Hobby, made the following observation:

> The special interests of today will be replaced by new and different special interests tomorrow, and any attempt to draft a constitution to serve such interests would be futile and also dishonorable.[27]

This convention adjourned without approving a new, rewritten constitution to be submitted to the voters. The special interests in the state had prevailed. The entire effort was, indeed, "futile and also dishonorable."

Fourth, one could cite a general lack of interest and support for change among the citizens of the state. Constitutional revision is not a subject that excites most citizens. The average Texan probably does not see the need for revision. Some proud Texans would take offense at the suggestion that the state document is flawed. The document drafted at the end of Reconstruction in the 1870s will probably continue to serve Texans for many years. The prospects for general revisions do not seem great. Evidence of this can be found in the 1999 election. In that year, the voters rejected three amendments that might be considered mildly progressive. Two of these amendments would have provided that the adjutant general of the national guard and the commissioner of health and human services were to serve at the pleasure of the governor. Another would have created a Judicial Compensation Commission providing procedures that are standard in most state constitutions today.

The American Federal System of Government

federal system of government

The division of powers between a national government and regional governments

unitary system of government

A system of government where all functions of government are controlled by the central/national government

confederal system of government

A system of government that divides power between a weak national government and strong, independently sovereign regional governments

Texas and the other 49 states operate within what is called a **federal system of government**. Broadly, this system provides for a sharing of powers between the national (federal) government and respective state governments. It provides for a balance of power and responsibilities between the national and state governments.

Although the United States is not unique among nations for having a federal system, most nations of the world have what is called a **unitary system of government**. Under a unitary government, power is centralized in a national government, and regional and local governments operate within powers granted by the national government. For example, in England the central government, through Parliament, governs the nation. Regional governments are subservient to the national government. In the United States, state governments have some powers reserved to them by the Constitution, and they can act independently of the national government within those areas.

Under a **confederal system of government**, most of the power rests with the regional and local governments, and the national government has only limited powers. Under the Confederate States of America, the national government found it impossible to compel state governments to contribute troops or supplies to the war effort. This lack of authority hampered the war effort during the American Civil War. Each state acted independently of the others and the national government.

In many respects, a federal system falls in between the unitary and confederal systems of government, illustrated in Figure 2.2. Power is divided between

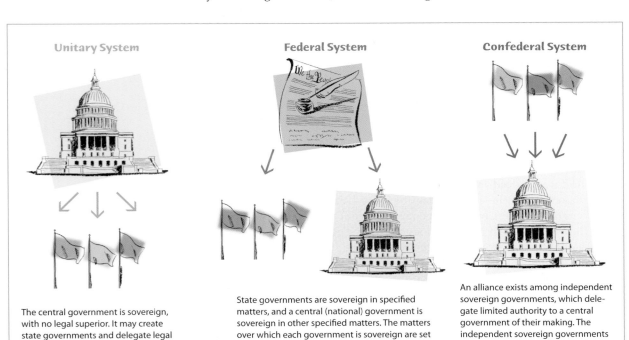

Unitary System

The central government is sovereign, with no legal superior. It may create state governments and delegate legal authority to them. It can also eliminate such governments.

Federal System

State governments are sovereign in specified matters, and a central (national) government is sovereign in other specified matters. The matters over which each government is sovereign are set forth in a constitution, which is the supreme law of the land. Dual sovereignty is the distinguishing characteristic of a federal system.

Confederal System

An alliance exists among independent sovereign governments, which delegate limited authority to a central government of their making. The independent sovereign governments retain sovereignty, with no legal superior, over all matters they do not delegate to the central government.

FIGURE 2.2   Systems of Government

the central government and between geographic units of government. In the U.S. system, these geographic units are called states. In other countries, such as Canada, these units of government are called provinces. The national government has powers and duties in assigned areas, and the regional governments have powers in assigned areas. In some cases, powers may overlap and in other areas both governments may possess similar powers. For example, both the federal and state governments have the power to tax and to spend money.

A federal system has a number of advantages. A key one, as Supreme Court Justice Louis Brandeis noted in 1932, is that states can be "laboratories" of democracy. In particular, he argued, "It is one of the happy incidents of the federal system that a single courageous state may, if its citizens choose, serve as a laboratory; and try novel social and economic experiments without risk to the rest of the country."[28] Another advantage, as the Supreme Court argued in Bond v. United States (2011), is that "By denying any one government complete jurisdiction over all the concerns of public life, federalism protects the liberty of the individual from arbitrary power."[29] Other advantages, as one law professor has pointed out, are that federalism can accommodate a diversity of preferences in a heterogeneous society, that the most appropriate level of government can be utilized for a particular purpose, and that the states can compete and their citizens can move to places that have an attractive particular mix of public policies.[30]

Constitutional Distribution of Powers

The U.S. Constitution distributes power between the national and state governments. The Constitution grants and denies powers. In some cases, powers are granted exclusively to the national government and in other cases exclusively to the states. In some cases, powers are granted to both the national and the state governments. The same can be said for denied powers. Some are denied to the national government, others are denied to the states, and some are denied to both.

Key Developments in American Federalism

Figures 2.3 and 2.4 present a clear summary of the division of powers between the national and state governments. Although the division of powers may seem straightforward, these figures belie the true complexity of our federal system of government. It is complicated, and the meaning of each power has been subject to interpretation by the federal courts. If we examine four areas of the Constitution and the courts' interpretations, we gain a much better understanding of American federalism. These four areas are the Necessary and Proper Clause versus the Tenth Amendment; the Interstate Commerce Clause; Equal Protection and Due Process Clause of the Fourteenth Amendment; and the power to tax and spend to promote the general welfare.

The "Necessary and Proper" Clause and the Tenth Amendment

Article 1, Section 8, paragraph 18 of the United States Constitution states that Congress shall have the power "To make all Laws which shall be necessary and proper for carrying into Execution the foregoing Powers, and all other Powers vested by this Constitution in the Government of the United States, or in any Department or Officer thereof." This seems to grant considerable power to the national government. However, the **Tenth Amendment** states: "The powers not delegated to the United States by the Constitution, nor prohibited by it to the States, are reserved to the States respectively, or to the people." This seems

Tenth Amendment
Amendment of the U.S. Constitution that delegates or reserves some powers to the state governments or to the people

NATIONAL POWERS

Punish offenses against the laws of the nation

Lay and collect taxes for the common defense and the general welfare

Coin and regulate money

Establish courts inferior to the U.S. Supreme Court

Raise and support armies

Administer the Capitol district and military bases

Declare war

Organize, arm, and discipline state militias when called to suppress insurrections and invasions

Provide for copyrights for authors and inventors

Regulate interstate and foreign commerce

Regulate the armed forces

Provide and maintain a navy

Establish standard weights and measures

Create naturalization laws

Punish the counterfeiting of money

Punish piracies and felonies on the seas

Develop roads and postal service

Define bankruptcy

FIGURE 2.3   Enumerated Powers of the National Government

to grant most powers not expressly granted to the federal government to the states, or that they would remain with the people. The meanings of these two sections of the Constitution were the cause of conflict early in the history of the Republic.

In 1790, Congress created a national bank under the advice of Secretary of the Treasury Alexander Hamilton. Although Article 8 of the Constitution does not grant Congress the right to create a national bank, it does grant it the power to borrow money, regulate commerce, and coin money. Hamilton thought that one could imply that Congress has the power to establish a bank into which money borrowed and coined could be deposited and commerce regulated. Thomas Jefferson objected to the creation of a national bank, fearing it could lead to centralization of power in the federal government. The argument basically came down to defining what exactly was "necessary and proper." Jefferson felt "necessary" meant "indispensable," whereas Hamilton felt "necessary" meant any manner that is deemed appropriate by Congress.

In 1819, the question of the meaning of the **Necessary and Proper Clause** reached the Supreme Court in the case of *McCulloch v. Maryland* (4 Wheaton 316 [1819]). The state of Maryland decided to tax a branch of the national bank located in Baltimore, Maryland. The Court accepted Hamilton's interpretation of the clause, and Justice Marshall, writing for the Court, stated, "Let the end be legitimate, let it be within the scope of the Constitution, and all means which are appropriate, which

Necessary and Proper Clause (Elastic Clause)

Statement in Article 1, Section 8, paragraph 18 of the U.S. Constitution that says Congress can pass any law necessary and proper to carry out other powers

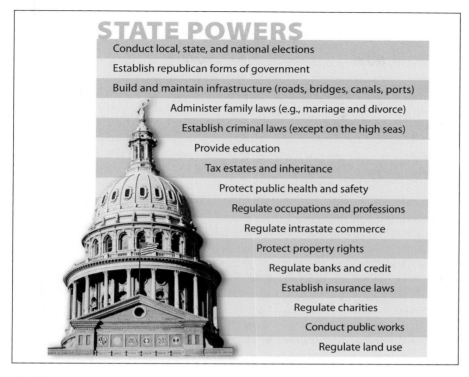

STATE POWERS

Conduct local, state, and national elections

Establish republican forms of government

Build and maintain infrastructure (roads, bridges, canals, ports)

Administer family laws (e.g., marriage and divorce)

Establish criminal laws (except on the high seas)

Provide education

Tax estates and inheritance

Protect public health and safety

Regulate occupations and professions

Regulate intrastate commerce

Protect property rights

Regulate banks and credit

Establish insurance laws

Regulate charities

Conduct public works

Regulate land use

FIGURE 2.4   Constitutionally Delegated and Reserved Powers of the State

are plainly adopted to that end, which are not prohibited but consistent with the letter and spirit of the Constitution are constitutional." This provides a very broad interpretation to the meaning of this clause, and it came to be called the "Elastic Clause" of the Constitution because it allowed Congress to decide the means to carry out ends, thus "stretching" its powers to meet its needs.

In addition, the McCulloch case also contributed to definitions of national supremacy. The Maryland law, taxing the bank, was found to be in conflict with the federal law establishing the bank. Article 6 of the Constitution says that federal law shall be the "supreme Law of the Land." State laws in conflict with national law are thus unconstitutional, and federal law would prevail over state laws. Without this interpretation, any state could choose to ignore national policy and go its own way. The supremacy clause provided for the creation of national policy with which states must comply.

Interstate Commerce Clause

Another troubling area was the question of interstate commerce. During the nineteenth century and most of the twentieth, the Supreme Court placed a very narrow interpretation on interstate commerce and applied it only to goods that were transported across state lines, leaving most regulation of commerce to the states. In the 1930s, during the Great Depression, the courts came under fire for their narrow view. Because of political pressure and changes in court membership, the meaning of interstate commerce came to be anything that had a substantial effect on national commerce. During the 1960s, the **Interstate Commerce Clause** was used to prohibit hotels and restaurants from being segregated by race. Georgia provides one example. In 1964, Lester Maddox, who would be governor from 1967 to 1971,

Interstate Commerce Clause

Article in U.S. Constitution that gives Congress the exclusive power to regulate commerce between the states; Congress and the courts determine what is interstate commerce refused to serve African Americans in a restaurant he owned. He felt he was not engaged in interstate commerce because he owned only one facility in one state. The court's interpretation was that, one, the food he served was shipped across state lines, and two, his establishment served people who potentially travelled across state lines. Therefore, he was engaged in interstate commerce.

Another question is when a state can prohibit the shipment of goods into that state. For example, in the past many states prohibited cattle from Texas to be shipped into their states because they were often infected with a tick fever. In another case, California prohibited citrus fruit from being imported because of infected crops in other states. Texas once prohibited California oranges from coming into Texas because of a fruit fly infection. All these cases address the issue of the legitimacy of trade barriers. If the prohibition on the importation of an item is truly to protect health, morals, and safety, and not a barrier imposed to restrict trade, it will be allowed. For example, if the reason for the barriers is to protect the health of cattle or oranges, then states may erect such barriers. Again, determination is up to the court. The courts will decide when barriers have been erected for legitimate purposes and when it is a restraint on interstate trade.

There are many areas of seeming contradiction when it comes to interstate commerce. From the narrow view to the expansion in interpretation during the Great Depression (enshrined in cases such as Wickard v. Filburn [1942] where the Court found that a farmer's growing of wheat for personal on-farm use was illegal as it exceeded a federally-mandated limit), the interpretation of the Interstate Commerce Clause has continued to evolve case by case. Similarly, some industries are regulated and others are not. The conclusion is that interstate commerce has become largely whatever the courts say it is. Critics of an expansive view of the commerce clause charge that it undermines the notion of the Constitution establishing a government of specific enumerated powers while strengthening the federal government at the expense of the states and individual liberty.

Equal Protection and Due Process Clause of the Fourteenth Amendment

The U.S. Bill of Rights provides for the protection of civil liberties and individual rights. Initially, the Bill of Rights applied only to actions of the national government that affected citizens. For example, the First Amendment states, "Congress shall make no laws respecting an establishment of religion. . . ." It says Congress—not Congress and the states.

In the aftermath of the Civil War, Congress passed and the states approved the Fourteenth Amendment, which for the first time ascribed rights to national as well as state citizenship, and extended some of the basic protections outlined in the Bill of Rights to African-American freed men that even state and local governments had to respect:

> "No State shall make or enforce any law which shall abridge the privileges or immunities of citizens of the United States; nor shall any State deprive any person of life, liberty or property, without due process of law, or deny to any person within its jurisdiction the equal protection of the law."

The **Equal Protection Clause** and the **Due Process Clause** mean that state and local governments must treat people equally and in accordance with established rules and procedures.

After World War I, the federal courts gradually began to apply the basic rights provided in the Constitution to the states. There were three primary areas where states were required to provide protection for citizens: civil liberties, criminal proceedings, and election laws.

Equal Protection Clause
Clause in the Fourteenth Amendment of the U.S. Constitution that requires states to treat all citizens equally

Due Process of Law Clause
Clause in the Fifth and Fourteenth Amendment of the U.S. Constitution that requires states to treat all citizens equally and that the state must follow certain rules and procedures

Civil liberties include such things as freedom of speech and religion. States may no longer require prayer in public schools or allow segregated schools. Criminal procedures include such things as protection against self-incrimination (so-called Miranda warnings) and the right to legal counsel in criminal procedures. Election laws overturned restrictive voter registration laws and white primaries. States were also forced to apportion legislative districts equally by population. (These issues are covered in more detail in later chapters.)

This gradual expansion of basic rights also expanded the role of the national government into areas that had traditionally been reserved to the states. Although state power may have been reduced, individual rights and liberties were expanded.

Power to Tax and Spend to Promote the General Welfare of Citizens

Article 1, Section 8, grants Congress the right to tax and spend to promote general welfare. The national government lacks the power to provide many basic services to citizens. Congress cannot, for example, operate schools and hospitals, build roads, or do many things state governments can. These powers are reserved to the states. The national government has only interstate police powers; however, the national government may provide money to state and local governments to provide these basic services.

In this area, the national government has had great impact on state and local authority. Congress can provide money to state and local governments and set standards for how the money can be spent. Congress supplies money to state governments to build and maintain roads and highways. When states accept this money, they must agree to some standard. Most college students might be aware of these standards as applied to highway funds: states must agree to set a drinking age of 21 if they accept federal money. At the time Congress passed this requirement, most states (30) already had 21 as the drinking age, 4 had the age of 20, 13 had the age of 19, and only 3 had the age of 18. However, many citizens felt that this was an unfair exercise of national authority and an intrusion into an area reserved to the states. Similar requirements applied to the 55-mile-per-hour speed limit in the 1970s, and some states initially refused to comply or enforce the rule.

The attitude of many state and local officials is that the national government should provide funds and then end its involvement in state affairs. They believe that the rules are often burdensome, inflexible, and unnecessary. There are probably cases where this is true; however, the positive side of these requirements is that they have led to improved uniformity in standards. For example, if you drive on an interstate highway anywhere in the United States (including Hawaii) there is a uniformity of highway signs and rules. Also, national requirements have led to improvements in accounting standards. State and local governments that accept federal money must comply with generally accepted accounting principles (GAAPs).

Some argue that the national government has eroded state power through the use of federal grants. In some cases the argument portrays the national government as an uncontrollable Leviathan preying upon the poor defenseless states. Nevertheless, Congress is not an independent force but consists of officials elected from states. When the federal government provides money to states for programs, those programs are passed by a majority vote of Congress, with the approval of the president.

In reaction to the criticism of federal encroachments into state powers, Congress has moved from **categorical grants** for specific purposes to grants that are much broader in scope, generally called **block grants**. This allows Congress to set general

categorical grants
Grants that may be used to fund specific purposes as defined by the federal government

block grants
Grants that may be used for broad purposes that allow local governments greater discretion in how funds are spent

CORE OBJECTIVE

Being Socially Responsible...

Considering the argument that the national government has eroded state power, to what extent should the government "promote general welfare"? What does promoting general welfare mean to you? In developing an understanding of state and local political systems and their relationship with the federal government, who do you think should play a greater role—the states or the federal government?

rules for how money can be spent and at the same time allows state and local officials to decide specific details. Over the past 50 years, states have been given much more control over how federal money is spent.

The Evolution of American Federalism

The real strength of the American federal system is flexibility. The relationship between the national government and state governments has altered and changed with time and political trends, and there is no reason to expect that this will not continue. Several models are used to describe this changing relationship over the past 230 years.

During most of the nineteenth and early twentieth centuries, a system called dual federalism operated. Under this model, there were rather specific areas of influence. The national government had primary delegated powers as defined in the Constitution, and the state governments provided most basic services to citizens. There was little financial assistance from the national government to states. Some have compared this to a layer cake with clearly defined areas of influence. Although this is called dual federalism, for much of the nineteenth century states were dominant. After the Civil War, the idea of states' rights over national power began to decline.

The second model used to describe federal–state relations is often called cooperative federalism. This relationship began in the 1930s with the Great Depression. The federal government began to supply more money to state and local governments to provide assistance to citizens. A cooperative relationship existed between the national and state governments to provide services to citizens.

During the 1960s, some saw a changed relationship with what came to be called creative federalism. President Johnson sought to create a Great Society through a massive expenditure of money to end poverty and lift all citizens in society. Under President Nixon, the system was referred to as new federalism. It involved giving state governments more discretion in program administration and so-called revenue sharing. President Reagan sought to give the states more power in spending grant money while reducing the amount of money available to state and local governments. Some viewed this as a return of both power and responsibilities to the states.

Under President Clinton, with emphasis from the Republicans in Congress, federal–state relations were called devolution of power. This basically means that states were given even greater authority on both program construction and administration.

When it comes to decisions about spending money, the evolution in the United States has been from one where the national government specified programs and provided money to support them to one where state and local governments are given greater power and authority to determine how federal programs are administrated in their states. Whereas federal grants to states declined as a percentage of federal expenditures during the Reagan administration, they grew under both Presidents Bush and Clinton. Federal grants are a form of financial assistance from a federal agency for a specific program or purpose. For example, the Texas Railroad Commission receives money annually from the Federal Recovery and Reinvestment Fund. About 24 percent of state expenditures are from the federal government. Of course, while states have greater power now than previously, they can still be coerced. Some grants, called categorical grants, have federal strings attached which specify to states where the money can and cannot be spent. This phenomenon is called coercive federalism. (We examine state financing more closely in Chapter 12.)

Relations between States in the Federal System

It is also important to understand the relations that exist between states, and between states and individuals. Article 4, Section 1, of the Constitution states, "Full Faith and Credit shall be given in each state to the public Acts, Records and Judicial Proceedings of every other state." For example, if your last will and testament is probated in a Texas court, other states must recognize that court action.

This seems like an obvious requirement, because it enables citizens to know that the rights they enjoy in their home state will be honored in another. However, this is not as simple as it seems. There are three good examples in the past 50 years where this clause in the Constitution was tested. The first is divorce. In the 1950s, it was difficult, in most states, to obtain a divorce. The state of Nevada was an exception. It granted divorces very easily. At first, some states refused to accept what were often called "quickie divorce mill" decisions. Eventually, all states had to recognize these divorces. Second, in the 1980s, some states refused to enforce child custody and support payments following divorce. There were cases where one parent in a divorce would move to another state and refuse to abide by the child custody or payment agreements. Eventually, federal courts forced all states to enforce these court decrees from other states.

The most recent example is the issue of gay marriage. The U.S. Congress passed, and President Clinton signed into law, the federal Defense of Marriage Act (DOMA) in 1996. When DOMA was signed into law, the argument that gay men and women should be allowed to marry was fringe opinion. Today (Oct. 2014), 19 states and the District of Columbia allow gay marriage. However, these marriages were not recognized by the federal government until recently, when Section 3 of DOMA was struck down by the Supreme Court. Section 3, as GLAAD notes, was the part of DOMA "that prevented the federal government from recognizing any marriages between gay or lesbian couples for the purpose of federal laws or programs, even if those couples are considered legally married by their home state." Thirty-one states have constitutional or statutory bans on gay marriage. Advocates of gay marriage argue that states are violating the full faith and credit clause by refusing to recognize gay marriages performed in other states. Congress, in Section 2

David Wegner, center left, and Molly Ryan Butterworth, center right, hold an enlarged copy of their recent marriage license during a rally at the Utah State Capitol in support of gay marriage in 2014

of DOMA, addressed this issue by stating that no state must accept another state's definition of marriage.

Several cases challenging DOMA and Proposition 8 in California, which banned gay marriage, were up for review in the 2012–13 term. In June 2013, the Supreme Court, in U.S. v. Windsor, struck down Section 3 of DOMA as unconstitutional. At the same time the Court dismissed Proposition 8 on procedural grounds instead of ruling on its constitutionality. This effectively left the previous lower district court ruling on the Proposition intact (originally *Perry v. Schwarzenegger* in 2010), a ruling which overturned the Proposition on constitutional grounds. Later in 2013, a U.S. district court dismissed Pennsylvania's argument that gay marriage is a state issue rather than a federal one, clearing the way for the Supreme Court to weigh in on the constitutionality of Pennsylvania's gay marriage ban. Similar cases are also underway in other states. The Court may finally end the gay marriage debate, although as of this writing, the Court has not taken up Section 2 of DOMA.

The U.S. Constitution, in Section 2 of Article 4, also secures what are known as the Privileges and Immunities of Citizenship. This clause means that the states cannot treat its citizens differently from citizens of other states, but this does not mean that states must treat residents and nonresidents the same in all cases. One particularly relevant example is out-of-state tuition at public universities. Differential rates can be charged for residents of Texas and residents of other states. The justification for different rates is that because state universities are publicly funded, residents of Texas rightfully should pay a lower tuition rate because they have been subsidizing higher education through taxes. This also applies to driver's licenses, hunting licenses, law licenses, and professional licenses.

Article 4, Section 1, says that in some areas a state must treat citizens of other states the same as they treat their own citizens; and Section 2 says that in other areas, residents and nonresidents can be treated differently.

CORE OBJECTIVE

Taking Personal Responsibility...

As a resident of Texas and a citizen of the United States, can you identify and discuss examples that reinforce the Full Faith and Credit Clause and the Privileges and Immunities Clause of the U.S. Constitution? Can you identify examples that, in your opinion, violate these principles?

Conclusion

As we have seen, one of the real strengths of the American federal system is its flexibility and ability to change with the times. This is obvious if you examine the national Constitution and observe how little the document has been altered in the past 200-plus years (see Table 2.4). A few of the structural amendments are often pointed to as examples. The Sixteenth Amendment gave the national government great financial resources and led to greater national influence over state spending decisions and policies. Many of the civil and voting rights amendments have had a greater impact on federal–state relations. The Fourteenth Amendment applied many of the first eight amendments to the states. Amendments were aimed at ending violations of civil and voting rights practiced by the states (for example, women's right to vote, poll tax).

Admittedly some changes were more profound than others. However, most were evolutional in nature and are not major structural changes. American federalism is a flexible system that will allow for change to meet future needs and challenges.

TABLE 2.4

Amendments to the Federal Constitution

Civil Liberties and Voting Rights		Structural Amendments	
Number	**Subject Matter**	**Number**	**Subject Matter**
1–8	Various civil liberties	10	Reserved powers
9	Other liberties that may exist	11	Sovereign immunity
13	End to slavery	12	Electoral College voting
14	Equal protection, due process of law	20	When the president takes office—lame duck amendment
15	Race and voting	22	Two terms for president
16	Income tax	25	Presidential disability
17	Direct election of senators	27	Congressional pay
19	Women's right to vote		
23	D.C. vote for president		
24	End poll tax as requirement for voting		
26	18-year-old right to vote		
18 & 21	Prohibition and repeal of prohibition on sale of alcohol		

Key Terms

ballot wording
bill of rights
block grants
categorical grants
checks and balances
confederal system of government
constitution
constitutional convention
Due Process of Law Clause

earmarks
Equal Protection Clause
federal system of government
initiative
Interstate Commerce Clause
Necessary and Proper Clause
    (Elastic Clause)
ordinances
plural executive system

popular sovereignty
separation of powers
social contract theory
statutes
supremacy clause
Tenth Amendment
unitary system of government

Notes

[1] Donald S. Lutz, "Toward a Theory of Constitutional Amendment," *American Political Science Review* 88 (June 1994): 355–370.

[2] *Texas Constitution,* art. 1, sec. 3a.

[3] "Local Authority to Regulate Firearms in Ohio," Law Center to Prevent Gun Violence, http://smartgunslaws.org/local-authority-to-regulate-firearms-in-ohio/.

[4] Fehrendbach, *Lone Star,* 146–147.

[5] Ibid., 206.

[6] Ibid., 222–23.

[7] Ibid., 411–14.

[8] Ibid., 434–35.

[9] Ibid., 436.

[10] *Texas Constitution,* art. 1, sec. 17.

[11] *Texas Constitution,* art. 2, sec. 1.

[12] *Texas Constitution,* art. 4, sec. 8(b).

[13] *Texas Constitution,* art. 5, sec. 2(b).

[14] Lutz, "Toward a Theory," 359.

[15] Book of the States 2012, http://knowledgecenter.csg.org/drupal/view-content-type/1502.

[16] Lutz, "Toward a Theory."

[17] Mary Lucia Barras and Houston Daniel, "Constitutional Convention of 1974," Texas State Historical Association, *Handbook of Texas Online,* http://www.tshaonline.org/handbook/online/articles/mjc07

[18] Ibid., 359.

[19] Ibid.

[20] Ibid., 360.

[21] Ibid.

[22] These figures are as of the general election in November 2013.

[23] Texas Secretary of State Voter Turnout, http://www.sos.
state.tx.us/elections/historical/70-92.shtml.

[24] Constitutional amendments ballot general election, 7
November 1978, tax relief amendment, H.J.R. 1.

[25] Book of the States 2013, http://knowledgecenter.csg.
org/kc/system/files/1.1_2013.pdf.

[26] *Texas Constitution* through 2011, http://www.tlc.state.
tx.us/pubslegref/TxConst.pdf.

[27] *Houston Chronicle,* 8 January 1974.

[28] New State Ice Co. v. Liebmann, 285 U.S. 262 (1932), in
http://caselaw.lp.findlaw.com/scripts/getcase.pl?na
vby=CASE&court=US&vol=285&&page=262.

[29] http://www.law.cornell.edu/supct/html/09-1227.
ZO.html.

[30] Alexander T. Tabarrok, "Arguments for Federalism,"
Hastings Law School, University of California, San
Francisco, September 20, 2001.

CHAPTER 3

The Texas Legislature

Upon completing this chapter,
you will be able to...

- **Demonstrate knowledge of the legislative branch of Texas government.**

Judge Gideon Tucker of New York wrote in an 1866 court decision, "No man's life, liberty, or property is safe while the legislature is in session." Although Tucker spoke these words within a narrow context, his statement has since been applied more broadly and can aptly describe generalized American distrust of government. This thought has been expressed by many others across the country, including some here in Texas. Its logic suggests the importance of the Texas legislature in state politics and the fear people have of government. The framers of the 1876 constitution distrusted government generally, but they were especially leery of executive authority and gave more power to the legislature than to the executive. (This sentiment harkens back to the drafters of the U.S. Constitution.) This does not mean that the office of governor is insignificant in state politics; governors play an important role. However, what power the governor of Texas possesses is derived primarily from informal sources. Courts and state agencies are also important, but the legislature is the most important institution in state government.

Legislative action is essential for many things. Money cannot be spent, taxes cannot be levied, state laws cannot be enacted or changed, and finally, in most states, the constitution cannot be amended without the approval of the legislature. Simply put, without actions by the legislature, most state governments would quickly come to a halt. In recent years, the federal government has shifted more responsibility to state governments, and state governments have taken the lead on some issues. This has resulted in state legislatures becoming even more important as policy-making bodies.

The Structure and Size of the Texas Legislature

The Texas legislature is **bicameral**, meaning it consists of two houses: the senate and the house of representatives. The Texas Senate has 31 members elected for four-year overlapping terms; half the membership is elected every two years. In the election that follows reapportionment

bicameral
Legislative body that consists of two houses

Texas State Capitol Building, Austin, TX

(essentially the second year of each decade), all seats in the senate are up for election. Lots are then drawn to determine who will stand for reelection in another two years (half of the senate) or in another four years (the other half). The most recent year in which the entire senate stood for election was 2012.

The Texas House of Representatives now consists of 150 members elected for two-year terms. The first house, elected following the adoption of the 1876 constitution, consisted of 93 members. After 1880, a new house seat was added for every 50,000 inhabitants until the membership reached 150 members.[1]

State legislatures vary in size. Alaska has the smallest senate, with 20 members, and Minnesota has the largest, with 67 senators. Lower house membership ranges from 40 in Alaska to 400 in New Hampshire. The New Hampshire House of Representatives is unusually large; the next largest house is Pennsylvania's, at 203.[2] The median size for state senates is 38; for the lower houses it is 100.

The Texas House and Senate are both quite small relative to the state's population. In 2010, there were about 811,147 constituents per state senate district and 167,637 constituents for each house district. Only California had more constituents per senator. In terms of the house, only California, New Jersey, and Arizona had more constituents per district. As of 2010, a Texas state senator represented more people than does a U.S. congressman![3] Population increases in Texas have only increased the number of people represented by each senator and house member.

The size of legislatures raises several issues. Large bodies might better promote the representation of local concerns and diverse interests within the state. However, statewide interests might go unrepresented. Another downside of large legislatures is that they can become inefficient at decision making or, in part because of the inefficiency, dominated by a few members (especially legislative leaders). This could certainly be said of Texas, where the relatively small senate is considered to be genteel and historically free of individual domination, and the relatively large house is less genteel and has historically been dominated by the speaker. Yet larger bodies would ensure that the senate and especially the house would be more democratic and closer to the people because state legislators would represent fewer constituents and smaller geographical areas. As one member of the United States' founding generation noted, smaller constituencies might also allow a wider array of people to participate in state politics rather than just the "rich" or "well born."[4] Debates about this subject at the state level are likely to follow many of the same arguments that the Federalists (such as James Madison) and the Anti-Federalists utilized in their classic battle over the size of the federal legislature.

Communicating Effectively...

In the preceding paragraph, an argument is made that smaller constituencies might allow a wider array of people to participate in state politics, rather than just the "rich" or "well born." How would you argue in favor of or against this statement?

General Characteristics of the Legislature

Sessions and Session Length

The Texas legislature meets in **biennial sessions** (every two years) for 140 days in odd-numbered years, beginning in January. Texas is one of only four states that still meet in biennial sessions. (Montana, Nevada, and North Dakota are the others.) At the end of World War II, only four states held annual sessions. Twenty states met annually by 1966 and 42 met annually by 1974. In recent decades, the trend toward annual sessions has continued, with Oregon convening its first annual session in 2011.[5]

Voters in Texas rejected a proposed change to annual sessions in 1969 and again in 1972. In keeping with the traditionalistic/individualistic political culture of the state (see Chapter 1), there is some concern that the more often the legislature meets, the more damage it can do. One political wag once joked that there was a typographical error in the original Texas Constitution, and that the founders had intended the legislature to meet for two days every 140 years.

At the end of the 140-day session, the Texas legislature must adjourn **(sine die)**. It cannot call special sessions or extend a session. In recent years, many state governments have placed limits on the number of days a legislature can stay in session; only 11 states do not limit the length of legislative sessions.[6] Another important factor is the ability of the legislature to call itself into special session (called **extraordinary session**). In Texas and 15 other states, the legislature cannot call itself into special session. The lack of ability to call special sessions makes the limit on the regular session even more meaningful. The legislature must finish its work in the prescribed time and then adjourn.

In Texas, only the governor may call **special sessions**. These sessions may not last more than 30 days each. However, there is no limit on the number of special sessions the governor may call. In Texas, the governor determines the subject matter of the session, thus limiting the range of topics the legislature can consider. This gives the governor tremendous power to set the legislature's agenda during special sessions, as well as a bargaining chip to persuade the legislature to do what the governor wants.

The Texas legislature's inability to call itself into special session also gives the governor stronger veto powers. If the governor vetoes a bill after the legislature has adjourned, the veto stands. This, in part, helps to explain why so few vetoes by the governor are overridden.

biennial session
Legislature meets every two years

sine die
Legislature must adjourn at end of regular session and cannot continue to meet

extraordinary session
Legislative session called by the legislature, rather than the governor; not used in Texas

special sessions
Sessions called by the governor to consider legislation proposed by the governor only

States like Texas that limit the number of regular session days are often forced to resort to special sessions. Budgetary problems, reapportionment issues, school finance, and prison funding have forced the Texas legislature into special sessions in past decades. The 83rd Legislature (2013) held three special sessions. They focused on abortion, redistricting, sentencing guideline reform for 17-year-olds convicted of capital murder, and transportation funding. The first special session was noteworthy for Senator Wendy Davis's long filibuster of a bill that would have put restrictions on abortions. This vaulted Davis into the public eye across the state and nation, although the limitations under consideration in the first special session were ultimately passed during the second special session. Many critics of Texas's biennial sessions point to the frequency of special sessions as evidence that the state needs to change to annual sessions. However, this would not come without trade-offs.

As we will see in Chapter 12, the tax structure in Texas is closely tied to economic conditions in the state. Predicting state revenues for two-year periods is extremely difficult. However, biennial sessions help the legislature to avoid reacting rashly in any particular situation because there is often time to reflect on a problem. Moreover, the nature of the perceived problem may change, especially in the economic realm. Therefore, biennial sessions may insulate politicians from being pressured to chase yesterday's economic news, given the lag before policy can be developed and have a meaningful impact. The advantages and disadvantages of annual and biennial sessions are presented in Table 3.1.

TABLE 3.1

Advantages and Disadvantages of Annual and Biennial Legislative Sessions

Arguments in Favor of Annual Sessions	Arguments in Favor of Biennial Sessions
The biennial format is unsuitable for dealing with the complex and continuing problems which confront today's legislatures. The responsibilities of a legislature have become so burdensome that they can no longer be discharged on an alternate-year basis.	There are enough laws. Biennial sessions constitute a safeguard against precipitate and unseemly legislative action.
More frequent meetings may serve to raise the status of the legislature, thereby helping to check the flow of power to the executive branch.	Yearly meetings of the legislature will contribute to legislative harassment of the administration and its agencies.
Continuing legislative oversight of the administration becomes more feasible with annual sessions, and that administrative accountability for the execution of legislative policies is more easily enforced.	The interval between sessions may be put to good advantage by individual legislators and interim study commissions, since there is never sufficient time during a session to study proposed legislation.
States may respond more rapidly to new federal laws which require state participation.	The biennial system affords legislators more time to renew relations with constituents, to mend political fences and to campaign for reelection.
The legislature cannot operate effectively in fits and starts. Annual sessions may help make the policy-making process more timely and orderly.	Annual sessions inevitably lead to a spiraling of legislative costs, for the legislators and other assembly personnel are brought together twice as often.
Annual sessions would serve to diminish the need for special sessions.	

Source: Table reproduced from National Conference of State Legislatures. See (http://www.ncsl.org/legislatures-elections/legislatures/annual-vs-biennial-legislative-sessions.aspx). Credit: William Keefe and Morris Ogul.

Salary

Some citizens believe that because the legislature meets for only 140 days every two years, it is part-time, and members should be paid accordingly. Legislative pay reflects this attitude. Texas pays the 181 members of the legislature $7,200 a year, plus an additional $150 per day while in session. In years when the legislature meets, the total compensation is $7,200 in salary plus $21,000 in per diem pay, for a total of $28,200. The Texas Ethics Commission sets the per diem rate.[7] Because most legislators must have a second residence in Austin while the session is going on, the per diem pay is not high. Housing and lodging costs in Austin are among the highest in the state. In years when the legislature is not in session, legislators receive their $7,200 in salary and may receive some additional per diem pay for off-session committee work.

The salary of the Texas legislature has not been increased since 1975.[8] As Table 3.2 indicates, of the 10 most populous states, Texas legislators are paid the least. Several attempts to change the state constitutional limit have been rejected by voters, and the low pay contributes to the small number of legislators who consider themselves full-time. Obviously, most legislators have other sources of income. Many are attorneys or successful businesspeople. Lack of high monetary compensation is very much in keeping with the traditionalistic political culture of the state, according to which only the elite should serve in the legislature. Other southern states (Florida, Georgia, and North Carolina) also have relatively low salaries.

Most citizens are effectively excluded from being legislators because they would not be able to devote the large amount of time required of legislative work and still earn a living. In reality, it is difficult to serve in the Texas legislature unless a person is independently wealthy, a "political consultant," or otherwise financially supported while in the legislature. In Texas, attorney-legislators with cases in court during the legislative session can have their cases delayed until the legislature adjourns. In fact, some attorney-legislators receive cases expressly because clients want to delay court action. Unlike many other states, Texas does not have a financial disclosure law that forces members to disclose their other sources of income. This leaves the sources of members' income an open question. Some might receive income as "consultants" to businesses with interests in current legislation. One could question the objectivity of members under these circumstances.

TABLE 3.2

Legislative Salaries in the 10 Most Populous States

State	Annual Salary, 2013
California	$90,526
Texas	$ 7,200
New York	$79,500
Florida	$29,697
Illinois	$67,836
Pennsylvania	$83,801
Ohio	$60,584
Georgia	$17,342
Michigan	$71,685
North Carolina	$13,951

Source: National Conference of State Legislators. See http://www.ncsl.org/research/about-state-legislatures/2013-ncsl-legislator-salary-and-per-diem.aspx.

Pay in other states varies greatly. The states with the lowest salaries are New Mexico, where there is no pay but a per diem expense based on federal policy ($154 per day), New Hampshire ($100 per year), and Alabama ($10 per day). At the high end is California at $90,526 per year; 16 other states pay salaries of more than $30,000 per year. Per diem expenses also vary greatly among the states. Texas, at $150 per diem, is higher than average.[9] Five states pay no expenses, and some provide a fixed amount for the year. Most states also provide additional expenses and income to people in leadership positions, such as committee chairs and presiding officers. Most states, including Texas, provide money to legislators for office and staff expenses, although there is great variation among the states.

Many states give members of the legislature retirement benefits. In Texas, legislators' retirement pay is linked to the salary of state district judges. Somewhat circularly, the salary of district judges is set by the Texas legislature. Therefore, legislators are able to increase their own retirement pay by voting to raise the pay of district judges.[10]

Texas appears to have generous retirement benefits. Legislators may retire at 60 years of age with 8 years of service and at 50 years of age with 12 years of service. According to the current formula, the pension provides $3,220 for every year in office; therefore, a retired lawmaker who served 8 years would receive $25,760 in benefits annually.[11] This high retirement may prompt some members to retire after achieving the minimum time requirement. They can count on cost-of-living pay raises as the legislature increases the salaries of district judges. Some increase can also come from cost-of-living adjustments given to all state retirees. In short, as an active member of the legislature, you are worth only $600 per month. Retire, and your pay increases substantially.

Staff and Facilities

The Texas legislature provides generous support for staff assistance. According to the most recent figures available, Texas trailed only three states in the total number of permanent and session-only staff.[12] Most members keep offices open on a full-time basis in their district, and many do so in the state capital as well. At the beginning of each session, senators and representatives establish their monthly allowance for salary and office expenses. During the 83rd Legislature (which met in 2013), the maximum amount each senator could spend on staff salaries and travel expenses was $38,000 per month.[13] The monthly allowance for representatives was set at $13,250 while in session and $11,925 while out of session.[14] In addition, standing committees have staff salary support during and between legislative sessions. The Texas Legislative Council has a large, professional staff to assist the legislature. It has produced one of the best Web pages of any of the states (http://www.tlc.state.tx.us/) and provides easy access for citizens during and between legislative sessions. The house also has the House Research Organization, which produces professional assistance to the legislature. The relatively recent renovations of the state capitol building have provided each senator and house member with excellent office and committee hearing space.

Qualifications for Legislators and Member Demographics

Setting aside for a moment the politics of state legislatures, let us examine the formal and informal qualifications for membership. Formal qualifications include age, citizenship, state residency, district residency, and qualified voter status.

Among the states, the lowest minimum age for house membership is 18 years and the upper minimum age is 25. Most states require U.S. citizenship, residency in the state from one to five years, and district residency for a year or less.

A Texas House member must be a U.S. citizen, a registered voter, at least 21 years of age, and must have lived in the state for at least two years and in the district they will represent for a minimum of 12 months. To be a Texas state senator, a person must be a U.S. citizen, a registered voter, at least 26 years of age, and must have been a Texas resident for at least five years and a district resident for at least 12 months.[15]

Formal requirements are minimal and do not constitute much of a barrier to holding office. More important are informal qualifications that limit many people's ability to serve. These include income, education, occupation, ethnicity, and gender. On these dimensions, state legislators tend not to represent the general population. Nationwide, legislators tend to be male, well educated, and professionals (often lawyers).

Other dimensions, sometimes called "birthright" characteristics, include characteristics such as race, ethnicity, religion, and national background. On these dimensions, representatives tend to mirror their district.[16] If the legislative district is predominantly Mexican American, the representative will likely be Mexican American; the same is true for predominantly African American districts. Even though legislators generally represent their constituents on these characteristics, legislators are usually better educated and from select occupational groups.

For example, in the 2001 session of the Texas House, 9 of the 14 African Americans were attorneys, and 16 of the 31 Mexican Americans were attorneys. All had a higher level of education than their constituents.[17] The same is also true for Anglo legislators. As of 2014, a total of 1,787 women, or 24.2 percent of all state legislators nationwide, were women; this represents a 7 percent increase in the number of female legislators since 2000. In 1971, only 344 women (4.5 percent of all legislators nationwide) served in state legislatures.[18] Although the first women to serve in a state legislature were elected to the Colorado House of Representatives in 1894, few women served until the early 1960s. The number of women rose steadily until the late 1990s, since which time gains have been more modest. Map 3.1 ranks the 50 states in terms of percentage of female legislators. In Texas, the number of women legislators has increased from one woman in each chamber in 1971 to 39 in 2014. This constitutes 21.5 percent of all seats in the state legislature. Seven of the women are senators and thirty-two are state representatives. Table 3.3 provides a demographic breakdown of the 83rd Legislature.

The numbers of Hispanics and African Americans have also increased in legislatures across the nation, in part because of reapportionment. Both ethnic groups are underrepresented in the Texas legislature when compared with their numbers in the population. In 2012, Hispanics made up 38.2 percent of the Texas population, yet they held only 21.1 percent of legislative seats in the 2013 session. In the same session, African Americans composed 12.3 percent of the Texas population and held 11.1 percent of seats in the legislature.[19]

Even with the changes in apportionment, minorities and women are still underrepresented in state legislatures. Most legislators are upwardly mobile white males. Most are from old, established, often wealthy families. The legislature is a good place to begin a political career. Having family and money helps launch that career. In addition, some professions, especially law, allow a person time to devote to legislative duties. A survey by the National Conference of State Legislatures shows that most legislators do not consider themselves full-time legislators, although the number who do has been increasing nationwide.

The percentage of attorneys in the Texas legislature is much higher than the national average. For example, in 2007 (the most recent year for which data are available), 15 percent of legislators nationwide were lawyers, whereas a third of

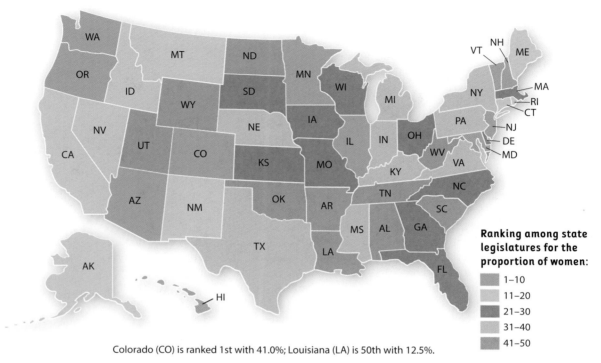

Ranking among state legislatures for the proportion of women:

- 1–10
- 11–20
- 21–30
- 31–40
- 41–50

Colorado (CO) is ranked 1st with 41.0%; Louisiana (LA) is 50th with 12.5%.

MAP 3.1   Percentage of Women Legislators by State

TABLE 3.3

Background of Members of the Texas Legislature, 2013

	House	Senate
Sex		
Male	119	24
Female	31	7
Age		
Under 30	2	0
30–39	25	0
40–49	43	5
50–59	46	14
60–69	30	12
70+	3	0
Incumbency		
Incumbents (and previously elected)	109	25
Freshmen	41	6
Party Affiliation		
Democrat	55	12
Republican	95	19

Source: Legislative Reference Library of Texas (http://www.lrl.state.tx.us/sessions/sessionSnapshot. cfm?legSession=83-0); Texas Tribune, Elected Officials Directory (http://www.texastribune.org/directory/)

Texas legislators were lawyers.[20] There is a higher-than-average percentage of businesspeople in the Texas legislature, and a lower-than-average percentage of schoolteachers. In some states, state employees can serve in the state legislature and keep their jobs as teachers. This is prohibited in Texas. A Texas state employee may not hold an elective and appointive office and receive pay for both.

Single-Member District Method of Election

Members of legislative bodies are most often elected from **single-member districts**. Under this system, each legislative district has one member in the legislative body. In Texas there are 31 senatorial districts and 150 house districts. The voters living in these districts elect one house and one senate member to represent the district. This system allows for geographical representation—all areas of the state choose representatives to the state legislature. Maps 3.2 and 3.3 show the senate and house districts for the entire state.

Some states use **multimember districts** for some legislative elections. Of all lower-house districts nationwide, 12 percent are multimember districts, but only 3 percent of senate seats are elected from multimember districts.[21] Although multimember election methods vary widely, the most common method is to elect two or three members per district. Voters cast one vote for each seat in the multimember

single-member districts
Districts represented by one elected member to the legislature

multimember districts
Districts represented by more than one member elected to the legislature

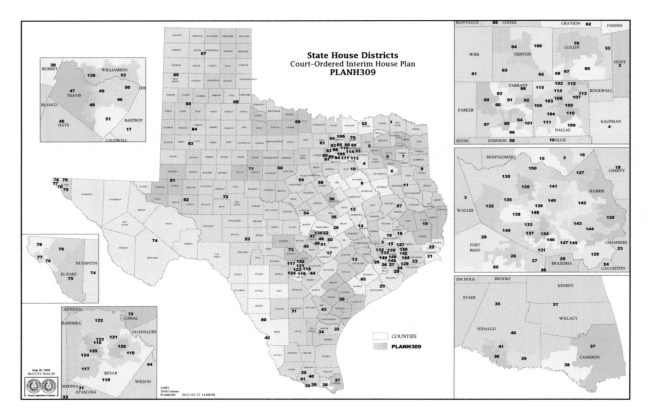

MAP 3.2   Texas State House Districts, 2012

district, and more than one state representative represents each voter. Table 3.4 shows the various multimember district systems used in other states.

Although Texas used multimember districts in the past, it most recently used them in the larger urban counties during the 1970s. The Legislative Redistricting

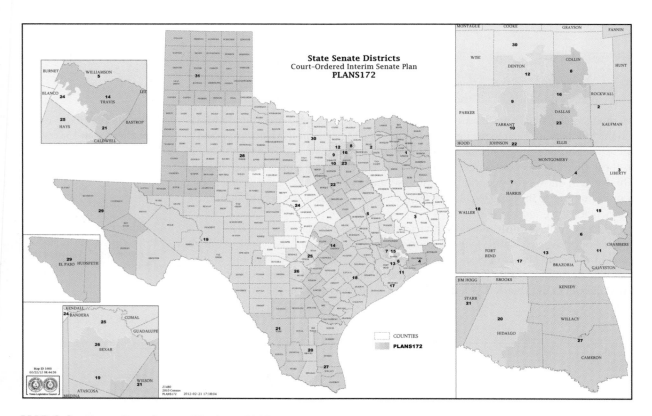

MAP 3.3 **Texas State Senate Districts, 2012**

TABLE 3.4

Multimember State Legislative Districts

State	Legislative Body	Number of Multimember Districts	Largest Number of Seats in a District
Arizona	House	30 of 30	2
Arkansas	House	3 of 96	2
Idaho	House	35 of 35	2
Maryland	House	44 of 63	3
Nevada	Senate	5 of 16	2
New Hampshire	House	99 of 193	11
New Jersey	House	40 of 40	2
North Carolina	Senate	8 of 42	2
North Dakota	House	49 of 49	2
South Dakota	House	35 of 35	2
Vermont	Senate	10 of 13	6

Source: National Conference of State Legislatures. See (www.ncsl.org).

Board, which is discussed later in this chapter, drew up this plan after the Texas legislature's plan was invalidated by federal court action. This board created 11 multimember districts with a total of 60 state representatives. The other 90 state representatives were elected from single-member districts. For example, Dallas County had 18 representatives elected by ballot place (Place 1 through Place 18). Candidates filed for a ballot place, and voters cast one vote in each of the 18 legislative races.

In 1971, the courts invalidated the Legislative Redistricting Board's multimember plan. Minority groups contested the plan, pointing out that the system allowed for a majority to elect all the representatives and for minorities to be frozen out. Some writers have called this the "Matthew effect," after the words of Matthew 13:12: "For whoever has to him more will be given, and he will have abundance; but whoever does not have, even what he has will be taken away from him."[22] In a single-member district system, a party or a candidate need win only a plurality of the vote in a district to win one seat. In countywide districts, a majority of the voters in the county can control all the seats. Under a single-member district system, districts can be drawn to the advantage of ethnic and political minorities within the county. Multimember districts promote majority representation or domination, and single-member districts can promote geographical representation. Depending upon how district lines are drawn, they can also promote racial and ethnic minority representation.

Reapportionment and Redistricting Issues

The U.S. Constitution requires that Congress reapportion the seats in the U.S. House of Representatives among the states following each federal census, every 10 years. The Texas Constitution likewise requires the state legislature to reapportion the seats following each federal census.[23] Two terms are usually used to describe this process: **reapportionment** and **redistricting**. The term *reapportionment* refers to the process of allocating representatives to districts; *redistricting* is the drawing of district lines. Table 3.5 presents the number of constituents per legislative district in the five most populous U.S. states. Each of the 150 house members in Texas represents about 167,637 people, and each of the 31 state senators represents approximately 811,147 people.

Apportioning seats in any legislative body is a highly political process. Each interest group within the state tries to gain as much as possible from the process. Existing powers, such as the majority party in the legislature, will try to protect their advantages. Incumbent legislators will try to ensure their reelection. The

reapportionment
Refers to the process of allocating representatives to districts

redistricting
The drawing of district boundaries

TABLE 3.5

Constituents per Legislative District

	2010 Population	Lower House	Upper House
California	37,253,956	465,674	931,349
Texas	**25,145,561**	**167,637**	**811,147**
New York	19,378,102	129,187	312,550
Florida	18,801,310	156,678	470,033
Illinois	12,830,632	108,734	217,468

gerrymandering
Drawing district boundary lines for political advantage

primary issues raised by reapportionment are equity of representation, minority representation, and **gerrymandering**, which is drawing district boundary lines for political advantage.

Equity of Representation

The issue of *equity of representation* is not new; it is perhaps as old as legislative bodies. Thomas Jefferson noted the problem in the Virginia legislature in the eighteenth century.[24] During most of the nineteenth century, legislative apportionment most often resulted in equity. In other words, each representative represented an equal number of citizens. Some states had provisions that limited the number of seats a single county could have. In the early twentieth century, population shifted from rural to urban areas, and gradually the rural areas were overrepresented in many state legislatures. In the 1960s, only two states (Wisconsin and Massachusetts) had rural/urban representation in the legislature that accurately reflected population distributions in the state.[25]

From 1876 until the 1920s, the Texas legislature made an effort to reapportion the seats after each census. This process was made easier by the addition of one seat for each increase of 50,000 in the population. From 1880 until 1920, a total of 57 seats could be added to the legislature to bring the total to 150 members. However, in 1930 and 1940, the legislature failed to reapportion legislative seats, and no new seats were added. Thus, in 1951 the Texas legislative seats had not changed since 1921, but major population shifts from rural to urban areas had occurred.[26] This was especially true during and immediately after World War II. These shifts in population created a serious disparity in representation between rural and urban areas of the state. Most urban counties were vastly underrepresented.

Legislative Redistricting Board (LRB)
State board composed of elected officials that can draw new legislative districts for the house and senate if the legislature fails to act

In an attempt to resolve the inequality of representation in the state, the Texas Constitution was amended in 1948 to create the **Legislative Redistricting Board (LRB)**. This board was given the authority to redistrict the seats in the Texas House and Senate if the legislature failed to act. The LRB is made up of the lieutenant governor, the speaker of the house, the attorney general, the comptroller of public accounts, and the commissioner of the general land office.[27]

The creation of the LRB and the threat of action forced the legislature to act in 1951. Representation shifted from rural to urban areas, but large urban counties were still underrepresented in 1952. This underrepresentation was due in part to a 1936 amendment to the Texas Constitution that limited the number of representatives any county could have to seven until the population reached 700,000, and then the county could have one additional representative for each 100,000 population.[28] For example, in 1952, had apportionment been based on population alone, each state representative would have represented about 50,000 people. This means that Dallas County would have increased from 7 to 12 representatives, Harris County from 8 to 16, and Bexar County (San Antonio) from 7 to 10. The constitution also prohibited any county from having more than one senator, no matter how large the county's population.

Baker v. Carr
Court case that required state legislative districts to contain about the same number of citizens

In 1962, in **Baker v. Carr**, the U.S. Supreme Court decided that these inequalities in the apportionment of legislative districts denied voters "equal protection of the law" and said that "as nearly as practicable, one man's vote would be equal to another's."[29] Two years later, in **Reynolds v. Sims**, the court ruled that both houses of state legislatures had to be apportioned based on population. The court rejected the analogy to the U.S. Senate, which is based on geographic units, and said, "Legislators represent people, not trees or acres. Legislators are elected by voters, not farms or cities or economic interests."[30]

Reynolds v. Sims
Court case that required state legislative districts for both houses to contain about the same number of citizens

These two cases forced all states to redistrict based on population and led to the "one person, one vote" rule. Over time, the general rule on reapportionment became that legislative districts could vary no more than 5 percent, plus or minus, from the mean population for districts. In Texas, the deviation from the mean for house and senate districts is between 2 and 3 percent.

In 1965, a federal district court ruled that the provisions in the Texas Constitution that limited a county to seven house seats and one senate seat were unconstitutional.[31] This forced the apportionment of both houses of the Texas legislature to be on the basis of population. The political consequences of these court decisions shifted power from rural to urban areas. (A discussion of the impact of these decisions on the makeup of today's Texas legislature follows later in this chapter.)

By the 1970s, the issue of equity of representation had not been settled, but this is no longer an issue. With advancements in computers, it is quite easy to draw districts with approximately the same number of people. Other issues, just as contentious, have replaced the equity issue.

Minority Representation

The second issue raised by redistricting is minority representation. According to current law, not only should legislative districts be approximately equal in population, they should also allow for minority representation. This issue was first raised in Texas in the 1970s when Texas used multimember districts in some large urban counties. Multimember districts were invalidated by court actions.[32]

The 1981 session of the legislature produced a redistricting plan that advanced minority representation in both houses. However, Bill Clements, the Republican governor, vetoed the senate plan, and the Texas Supreme Court invalidated the house plan. This forced the Legislative Redistricting Board to draw new districts. The new plan was challenged in federal courts and by the U.S. Justice Department, which ruled that the plan violated the federal Voting Rights Act because it did not achieve maximum minority representation. African Americans and Mexican Americans felt that the plan diluted their voting strength. A new plan, drawn up by federal courts, maximized minority representation by creating districts that contained a majority of ethnic minorities—"majority-minority" districts.

Similar battles took place in the 1990s. Minorities gained many seats, as did Republicans, who managed to take control of the Texas Senate for the first time in more than 100 years. In the 2001 session of the legislature, minorities did not gain significantly. In 2008, there were 16 African Americans in the Texas legislature (9 percent of the total seats). This was roughly average compared to the United States as a whole.[33] According to a 2009 study, there were 37 Hispanic legislators (20 percent of the total seats)—the second highest percentage of any state in the country. This number slipped slightly to 33 by 2013. The majority of these were Democrats, with only three Republicans.[34] In 2013, there were three Asian-American legislators, all in the House.[35]

Political and Racial Gerrymandering

Political gerrymandering is the drawing of legislative districts to achieve the political advantage of one political party over another. The term also has been applied to the practice of creating minority districts—**racial gerrymandering**. The practice dates to the early days of the Republic. In 1812, Governor Elbridge Gerry of Massachusetts drew a legislative district shaped somewhat like a

political gerrymandering
Drawing legislative districts to the advantage of a political party

racial gerrymandering
Legislative districts that are drawn to the advantage of a minority group

The original Gerrymander in Massachusetts, 1812

Hunt v. Cromartie
Court case that ruled while race can be a factor, it could not be the primary factor in determining the makeup of legislative districts

salamander. A political cartoonist for a Boston newspaper dressed up the outlines of the district with eyes, wings, and claws and dubbed it a "Gerrymander."

With the rise of the Republican Party, political gerrymandering in Texas has intensified. Until 2003, Republicans repeatedly charged that the Democrats reduced the number of potential Republican districts, especially in suburban areas. In the 1980s, the Republicans forged alliances with minority groups. Republicans supported the creation of racially gerrymandered majority-minority districts, and minority groups supported the Republican efforts. As we shall see subsequently, the creation of majority–minority districts has aided the Republicans as well as minorities.

A legal challenge to overturn the practice of creating majority–minority districts has been reviewed by the U.S. Supreme Court.[36] This challenge was aimed at U.S. congressional districts, rather than state house and senate districts, but it will eventually affect these. In ruling against three Texas U.S. congressional districts, the Court gave several reasons. Writing for the majority, Justice O'Connor stated that these districts were "formed in utter disregard for traditional redistricting criteria" (compactness) and that the shapes of the districts "are ultimately unexplainable on grounds other than the racial quotas established for these districts," resulting in "unconstitutional racial gerrymandering." Justice O'Connor also stated in her opinion that "districts can be oddly shaped but not bizarrely so."[37] While such a vague legal "standard" does not provide clear guidance, the Court is saying there is a limit to the use of race as a criterion for drawing legislative district lines.

In April 1999, the U.S. Supreme Court, in **Hunt v. Cromartie** (562 U.S. 541 [1999]), placed further limitation on the use of racial gerrymandering in drawing legislative districts. The Court said that although race can be a factor, it could not be the primary factor in determining the makeup of legislative districts. Partisan makeup can be a primary factor, but race cannot.

This is an obvious departure from the past practice of packing minorities into safe districts. It is clear that this new court ruling reduced the practice of racial gerrymandering. Although political party and race often coincide, it is now possible to pack minority Democrats into districts so long as race is not a primary factor. The fine art of gerrymandering has been with us since the development of political parties and will remain a part of the political landscape for years to come. Only the limits of political gerrymandering remain in question.

CORE OBJECTIVE

Being Socially Responsible...

To what extent should legislators use race when redistricting? Do you think redistricting is an appropriate tool to increase intercultural competency? Why or why not?

Redistricting in 2001 and 2003

In the 2001 session of the legislature, several issues relating to the redistricting process surfaced, and none were really new. Both parties hoped to gain seats through the redistricting process. Texas gained two additional U.S. congressional seats, for a total of 32, and the fight between Democrats and Republicans over these seats added to the controversy in the legislature.

With both parties almost evenly divided between the Texas House and Senate, even the shift of a few seats could change party control in either house. As the session wore on, the battle over redistricting intensified. Republican Party activists were more vocal in their criticism of the plans presented by the House and Senate Redistricting Committees than were the Democrats. The GOP chair, Susan Weddington, was especially critical of the house plan. She referred to the plan as a ". . . thinly veiled attempt to protect the careers of Speaker Pete Laney and incumbent politicians." Weddington said, "The Republican Party supports a fair redistricting plan that puts the interests of the people of Texas ahead of protecting incumbent politicians."[38] The chair of the House Redistricting Committee, Republican Delbert Jones of Lubbock, denied that this was the intention of the committee. Other house Republicans were pressured by their party and threatened with primary opponents if they did not support the GOP position on redistricting.

Some Republican attacks were also aimed at house committee chairs who were Republicans. The charge was that these committee chairs were supporting a plan that would keep current house speaker Pete Laney in power so they could keep their committee chairs in the next session should Laney be reelected. If a Republican replaced Laney in the next session, these Republican chairs would lose their positions. That is what happened.

At the same time, house minority members felt that they should gain more seats. The Mexican American Legal Defense and Education Fund and the League of United Latin American Citizens complained that the house committee recommendations did not take into account the growth in minority populations. Part of this dissatisfaction stemmed from the fact that the fastest growing areas of the state from 1990 to 2000 were in the predominantly white/Anglo suburbs of Houston, San Antonio, and Dallas. Although the inner cities of Houston and Dallas gained population, they did not increase as significantly as the surrounding suburban areas. In 1990, each house member represented about 109,000 people; by 2002, the number was approximately 139,000. For the senate, the numbers increased from 550,000 in 1990 to 673,000 in 2002. Harris County lost one of the 25 representatives it had in 1990. The 2000 population of Harris County was 3,400,578. Divide this by 25, and the result is 136,023, which is a deviation of 2.15 percent below the "ideal district" of 139,000. Although this is within the margin of acceptability, the Republican-controlled Legislative Redistricting Board gave the seat to the more Republican-leaning suburban area of Fort Bend County. Dallas and Fort Worth did not lose seats, but the suburban areas gained seats. The suburbs in the Austin (Travis County) area also gained seats.

There is one other important difference in reapportionment in the 2001 session of the legislature. In the 1980s and 1990s, the federal Voting Rights Act required state legislatures to consider racial makeup of districts. In April 1999, the U.S. Supreme Court in *Hunt v. Cromartie* ruled that race can be a factor, but not the predominant factor, in drawing legislative districts. In the same case, the Court again allowed the use of political party affiliation as a factor in drawing district lines (political gerrymandering). As indicated previously, minority groups tend to vote Democratic, and it may be possible to achieve the same results by using party rather than race in drawing district lines.

The Texas House and Senate adjourned the 2001 session without approving new redistricting plans. The senate rules require two-thirds (21 members) approval before a bill can be considered on the senate floor. The plan voted out of the committee did not receive enough support for floor consideration, so it died. The senate also failed to consider the house-approved plan.

As a result of this inaction by the senate, the Legislative Redistricting Board was then left to establish new districts for the Texas House and Senate. The LRB, consisting of the lieutenant governor, speaker of the house, comptroller, land commissioner, and attorney general, was dominated by Republicans. Only one member of this board was a Democrat—Speaker Laney, and he was effectively frozen out of the discussion. Lt. Governor Ratliff objected to the proceeding. The remaining three members, Attorney General Cornyn, Land Commissioner Dewhurst, and Comptroller Rylander, proceeded to draw districts that greatly favored Republicans. This board, however, cannot redistrict congressional districts, and Governor Perry refused to call a special session in 2001 to consider the issue. Instead, he stated that the matter was best left to the courts.

Therefore, the congressional district map used in the 2002 election cycle was drawn by a special three-judge federal court. While this may have favored Republicans in a majority of the districts, Democrats managed to win election in 17 of the 32 districts, leaving the Republicans with 15 districts. There were five districts that heavily favored Republicans but were won by Democrats. With these unexpected results, U.S. House Majority Leader Tom DeLay, a Republican from Sugarland, Texas, forwarded a plan to the Texas legislature in the 2003 session to redraw the 2001 court-ordered congressional district map.

Redistricting normally takes place every decade following the new federal census. In the 2003 session, Republicans controlled both houses of the Texas legislature for the first time in 130 years and used their new control to redistrict the state's 32 congressional districts. This mid-decade redistricting, or re-redistricting, was unprecedented. In part because of these redistricting efforts by the Legislative Redistricting Board, Republicans gained 16 house seats and 3 senate seats for the 2003 and 2005 sessions. The Republicans held 88 house and 19 senate seats. What follows describes how this happened and is an interesting case study of both the politics of redistricting and how the legislature works.

The Texas House, under the direction of newly elected Speaker Tom Craddick (R), took up the cause, and a new congressional district map was reported out of committee. The Texas Senate, under the direction of newly elected Lt. Governor David Dewhurst, did not debate the issue during the regular session because of the senate's two-thirds rule, which required 21 members of the senate to agree to allow a bill to be considered by the whole senate. Senate Democrats, with 12 members, refused to consider any bills.

The Texas House rules state that a quorum is two-thirds of the whole membership, or 100 members. A quorum must be present before the house can act. During the last week of the regular session in 2003, 52 Democrats left the state and took up residence in the Holiday Inn in Ardmore, Oklahoma. This boycott by the Democrats effectively prevented the house from acting, and the re-redistricting bill failed to pass. This boycott infuriated most of the state and national Republican leadership. Texas Rangers were sent to try to get the renegades back to Austin, but all efforts failed.

Despite much statewide opposition to continuing the re-redistricting battle, on June 19, 2003, Governor Rick Perry called a special session of the legislature, to begin June 30, to reconsider the re-redistricting proposal.

This move only heightened the degree of acrimony developing in the state at the time. For example, Clay Robison, an editorial writer for the *Houston Chronicle,* argued that the special session to examine redistricting was a "waste" of tax money. He also suggested that it showed Perry either had "a stubborn, partisan streak made meaner by his pique over the Democratic walkout" or that "he is a tail-wagging lap dog, eager to play 'go fetch' for the right wing of his party."[39]

Despite many misgivings, on July 8, 2003, the Texas House quickly passed a new congressional map by a highly partisan vote of 83 to 62. In this first special session, Lt. Governor Dewhurst left in place the two-thirds rule required to consider a bill on the senate floor.

While the Democrats held 12 seats, they could block the house-passed bill from being considered by the senate; however, several Democrats at first withheld their support for blocking the legislation. Some minority Democratic senators were offered passage of legislation favorable to their districts. Others were offered "safe" congressional seats in exchange for favoring re-redistricting. On July 15, 2003, Senator Bill Ratliff, a Republican from Mount Pleasant, joined 10 Democrats in blocking the re-redistricting bill.

Great pressure was applied to Lt. Governor Dewhurst to drop the two-thirds rule; however, many senators, both Democratic and Republican, opposed the change. Newspapers across the state urged Dewhurst to hold the line and not change the rules. Statewide polls showed Governor Perry losing support over the redistricting issue.

On July 28, 2003, 11 Texas senators fled to Albuquerque, New Mexico. Two things prompted this action. First, they anticipated that the governor was going to adjourn the first special session early and call a second special session immediately thereafter (which he did). The rumor was that the senate sergeant-at-arms had been ordered to lock the senators in the senate chamber as soon as the session was called to prevent them from busting a quorum. Second, Lt. Governor Dewhurst had stated he would suspend the two-thirds rule for future sessions.

While the Texas governor and Lt. governor were livid at the actions of these Democratic senators, the Democratic governor and Lt. governor of New Mexico were delighted and welcomed the 11 to the state. Republicans and Democrats held dueling press conferences, each accusing the other of wrongdoing. The governor at one point blamed the absent senators for preventing consideration of a bill to fund child health-care Medicaid benefits. Perry had earlier vetoed part of the state budget that would have allowed this funding.

A few hours after the second special session began and a quorum was present, the house passed the same redistricting bill passed in the first special session. The quick passage of the bill led some Democrats to question the fairness of the process because no debate or discussion was allowed.

The Republican senators in Austin attempted to force the return of the 11 Democrats by imposing fines. In the end, the fines amounted to $57,000 for each of the stray senators. The Republicans also took away the parking spaces of the boycotting senators. Some have questioned the legality of this action because a quorum was not present and, technically, the senate could not take action. The fines were later removed on the condition that there would be no more boycotts until the end of the term in January 2005.

The 11 Democratic senators stayed in New Mexico until the 30-day special session expired on August 26, 2003. They did not immediately return to the state because they were afraid that they would be arrested and taken to Austin for a third special session call. On September 3, 2003, the stalemate was broken when Senator John Whitmire, Democrat from Houston, broke the boycott and returned to the state.

On September 10, 2003, Governor Perry called a third special session of the legislature to consider redistricting. Some were surprised that a third session was called because a state poll by Montgomery and Associates, an independent research firm, found that most Texans were opposed to redistricting. In fact, only 47.9 percent of self-identified Republicans supported redistricting. The poll also showed the governor with a negative rating on job performance.

The house and senate quickly passed different redistricting bills, which went to a conference committee. These differences led to infighting among the Republicans, with the main issue being congressional districts in West Texas. House Speaker Tom Craddick wanted a district dominated by his hometown of Midland, but Senator Robert Duncan, Republican from Lubbock, wanted to keep Midland in a district with Lubbock.

The fight over the West Texas districts became so intense that Governor Perry and U.S. Congressman Tom DeLay became involved. Eventually Congressman DeLay was seen marching between house and senate chambers in the capitol. He claimed he was there as a diplomat, but most believed he was there as an enforcer. In the end, an entirely new map, unseen before DeLay's arrival, was produced by the conference committee and accepted by both houses in mid-October 2003.

Although many predicted that the DeLay redistricting map would be found in violation of the federal Voting Rights Act because it split minority voters rather than concentrating them into majority–minority districts, they were wrong. U.S. Attorney General Ashcroft issued a one-sentence letter saying that he did not object to the new map. At the time, Democratic Texas House members claimed that the professional staff of the U.S. Justice Department objected to the map, and they asked that the report be made public; however, it was not released. When it was later released, they were proved right.

A three-judge special court consisting of two Republicans and one Democrat approved the map, voting along party lines. The logic that prevailed, in essence, sets aside the Voting Rights Act by allowing minority voters to be divided into many congressional districts so long as the intention is to divide Democrats and not to divide minority voters. Partisan gerrymandering is considered legal. Because most minorities vote for Democrats, they can be split into many districts so long as the gerrymandering is partisan in intent. This established a new standard for redistricting. The U.S. Supreme Court later forced the change in four of these districts because they had diluted the voting strength of minorities.

Governor Perry, Congressman Tom DeLay, and the Republicans were successful in their redistricting efforts. In the 2004 election, the Republicans gained five Congressional seats and controlled the Texas delegation to Congress 21 to 11. Democrats entered the decade with a 17 to 15 majority. All targeted Democrats were either defeated or chose not to run. Only Congressman Chet Edwards won reelection in District 17.

In July of 2006, the U.S. Supreme Court heard an appeal to the DeLay redistricting. They ruled that nothing in the Constitution prohibited redistricting at mid-decade. However, they did order the redrawing of three Congressional districts because of concerns over minority representation.

It is interesting to note that on the national level, Republicans increased their control of the U.S. House of Representatives by six seats. Five of these came from the redistricting effort in Texas. Without this redistricting, the Republicans might not have retained control of the House of Representatives in the 109th Congress, which began in 2005.

Because of the continuing nationwide controversy over redistricting, some states have moved away from allowing the state legislature to develop the new redistricting maps and placed this in the hands of an independent commission. Although it is difficult to generalize on the various forms of these commissions, in 12 states, commissions are appointed and the members are not members of the state legislatures, state employees, or elected officials. These commissions draw district maps that must be accepted by the legislature. They are subject to review by the courts, but there is no information on this happening to date. Some other states have commissions, but the members are elected or appointed officials. For example, the Texas commission is made up entirely of elected officials. It is doubtful that Texas will move in the direction of a commission independent of the legislature.

Redistricting in 2011 and Beyond

The 2010 census showed that Texas increased in population by more than four million persons since the year 2000, for a total population of 25,145,561.[40] The necessary redistricting maps went into effect for the 2012 election cycle. Three maps needed to be redrawn in 2011: the Congressional districts of Texas (Texas gained four seats from the 2000 apportionment for a total of 36 seats in the United States Congress), the state of Texas House of Representative districts, and the state of Texas Senate districts. Redistricting can also have an impact on local election districts. However, because local districts often have their own specific rules, they are not within the scope of this discussion.

Debates in the Texas legislature over the 2011 redistricting were intense. The initial maps drawn by the Texas legislature favored Republicans by creating three additional Republican seats and one additional Democratic seat. The maps were submitted by Texas Attorney General Greg Abbott to a federal court in an attempt to gain preclearance for them as required under Section 5 of the 1965 Voting Rights Act. This is essential because Texas is one of a number of southern states required to submit redistricting maps for federal preclearance because of past discrimination in regard to voting and elections. Under this act, redistricting cannot discriminate in purpose or effect against minority populations. Concerns were raised about the maps because the majority of growth of population in Texas was in minority, most notably Hispanic, populations, and thus the maps were potentially discriminatory in nature by not showing concern for these demographic shifts. A series of legal battles ensued.

A federal court determined that the new maps were in violation of the Voting Rights Act and redrew the district maps in a way that would increase minority as well as Democratic power to some extent. These redrawn maps were then taken to the U.S. Supreme Court by the state of Texas, whereupon the court determined, in *Perry v. Perez* (2012), that in redrawing the maps the federal court must give additional deference to the desires of state policy and the state legislature.[41] Because they did not, the maps needed to be redrawn. So, another set of maps was drawn by the federal court that fell more in line with the Texas legislature's initial redrawn maps. These court-ordered interim maps are known as Plan S172 (Texas Senate), Plan H309 (Texas House), and C235 (Congressional).[42] The Texas legislature also engaged in creating a new set of maps and sought an order for declaratory judgment by the federal court to enact them.

In August 2012, the federal court determined that the maps drawn by the Texas legislature could not receive preclearance. The state is expected to appeal this decision to the U.S. Supreme Court. In the meantime, the court-ordered and court-drawn interim maps were used for the 2012 election cycle. In September 2012, the U.S. Supreme Court denied a request to stop the implementation of these interim maps by the League of United Latin American Citizens, which argued that the maps continue to violate Section 5 of the Voting Rights Act.

In addition to the impact that the redrawn maps have on partisan and minority voting, they have had a significant impact on a number of incumbent Texas House members whose districts, once considered safe, became highly contested. For example, in areas of East Texas, some longtime incumbents lost large amounts of district size. Chuck Hopson, from District 11, lost about 40 percent of his district, and Wayne Christian, from District 9, lost about 80 percent of his. Both incumbents lost in elections to newcomers—Hopson in a runoff election and Christian in a primary election. Some Texas lawmakers believe the legislative redistricting is largely at fault for this result.[43] Because of the numerous legal hurdles encountered during the redistricting process, it may be a number of years before the final decisions are made in regard to the Texas redistricting maps.

Getting Elected

Now that we know something about who is elected to state legislatures, we'll turn our attention to what it takes to win an election. As will be discussed in Chapter 8, running for office can be costly. Although most candidates for the state legislature face little or no opposition in either the primary or general election, there are exceptions. Even when candidates do not face opposition, they are likely to collect large amounts of money from various groups, especially from PACs.

In the 2010 election cycle, major candidates for the Texas House raised a total of $72 million. The senate candidates raised $11 million but only 16 seats were up for election in the senate, compared to 150 in the house.

Most money comes from contributors who live outside the senator's or representative's district. In the 2008 election cycle, only seven house members received 50 percent or more of their money from within the district. On average, only 19 percent of the money received by house members comes from within the district. In the senate, only three members in 2008 received 50 percent or more from residents living in their district; on average, 22 percent of a senator's money came from residents living in the district. Races in both the house and senate are financed by PACs and large contributors living outside their districts.

Competition for House and Senate Seats

As previously noted, in the one-party Democratic era in Texas (1870s to 1970s), most of the competition for all offices was in the Democratic Party primary. Today, competition is more likely to be in the general election, but many seats are in relatively safe districts. In the 2010 election, a total of 89 of 150 house seats had at least two candidates running. In the 2004 election, only 25 seats were competitive. In the past eight years, the level of competition in the Republican Party primary elections increased. Some of this competition was related to former house speaker Craddick, who was known to seek opponents for those members who opposed his agenda and threatened his continuation as speaker. Even with this increase in competition, most incumbents still survive election challenges.

Party voting is a measure of the strength of a political party in the legislative district based on voter support for the party's candidates in previous elections. This is also a measure of party competition. Studies of party competition for seats in the U.S. House and Senate define **noncompetitive districts** as any district in which either party receives 55 percent or more of the votes. A district in which party vote is between 44 and 54 percent is considered competitive.[44] The measure used here to gauge party competitiveness is the combined vote received by either party for all offices/candidates in the district in the 2000 general election. This is the composite party vote. Thus, a house or senate district in which the Republican Party candidates for statewide office collectively received 55 percent or more of the votes is considered a safe Republican district. Table 3.6 shows the number of competitive and noncompetitive seats in the Texas House and Senate from the 2014 General Election.

The second variable is racial composition of the district, which is the percentages of minority and nonminority populations of the district. If we compare these two characteristics (party competition and minority population in the district) using some simple statistics, we can see that most Texas House and Senate seats fall into two categories: noncompetitive Republican Anglo districts and noncompetitive Democratic minority districts. The creation of minority-majority districts results in the creation of safe Republican districts. Because minority support for Democratic candidates is always very high, concentrating minorities in districts also concentrates Democratic Party support in these districts. Many remaining districts are noncompetitive Republican districts. Other studies have found the same is true for U.S. congressional districts.[45]

One reason for the low competition in Texas legislative races is racial and political gerrymandering. Competition in such districts is most likely to occur at the primary level and when there is no incumbent. Competition in the general elections is less likely. Safe Democratic districts exist primarily in two places: South Texas, where there are concentrations of Mexican Americans, and East Texas, the traditional stronghold of Democrats. Republicans are strong in the Panhandle and the German Hill Country. Metropolitan areas of the state also contain both safe Democratic and safe Republican districts—Democrats in the inner city and Republicans in the suburbs.

noncompetitive districts
Districts in which a candidate from either party wins 55 percent or more of the vote

TABLE 3.6
Competitive and Noncompetitive Seats in the Texas House and Senate, 2014 Election

	Safe Democratic	Safe Republican	Competitive	Unopposed*
House	51 (34%)	94 (63%)	5 (3%)	103 (69%)
Senate	3 (20%)	11 (73%)	1 (7%)	7 (47%)

Source: Data compiled from Texas Secretary of State 2014 November General Election Candidates (http://www.sos.state.tx.us/elections/candidates/general/2014-gen-sbs.shtml) and the Texas Tribune (http://www.texastribune.org/2014/elections/scoreboard/).

*"Unopposed" means a candidate ran without opposition from the other major party but may or may not have been opposed by a third-party candidate; unopposed candidates were also included in the "safe" count for their respective party.

CORE OBJECTIVE

Thinking Critically...

As we have discussed, both the demographics and the voting patterns have changed in Texas, and some districts have become more competitive, especially for Democrats in South Texas and in inner-city districts. Referring to the previous discussion and Table 3.6, discuss what these shifts mean for future elections and the composition of the Texas House and Senate.

Each election year, only about one-third of the House members face opposition in the general election. Most members who seek reelection are reelected. Even fewer face opposition in the primary elections. Unless legislators are in a competitive district, they can generally stay as long as they like. Most voluntarily retire after a few years of service.

Term Limits

term limits
Limitations on the number of times a person can be elected to the same office in state legislatures

Although turnover in state legislatures nationwide is quite high, many states adopted formal **term limits** for state legislators to legally limit long tenures in any particular seat. From 1990 to 1996, 21 states approved term limits for both house and senate seats. Of these states, 14 have imposed these limits with constitutional amendments and 7 by statutes.[46] These limits were approved despite the fact that self-limiting of terms was working for many years. For example, "nationally, 72 percent of the house members and 75 percent of the senators who served in 1979 had left their respective chamber by 1989."[47] The Texas legislature is not term limited, but it has individually self-imposed "term limits" that have allowed for regular turnover.

Turnover in State Legislatures

turnover
The number of new members of the legislature each session

One could conclude from the lack of competition for Texas legislative seats that there would be low turnover of the membership. This is not the case. **Turnover** refers to the number of new members of the legislature each session. Turnover is high in all state legislatures, and normally it is higher for the lower house than for the upper chamber.[48]

In the 1980s and 1990s, some states had very high turnover due to the implication of term limits. Excluding those years, the average turnover in state legislatures around the country is around 25 percent for the lower house and about 15 percent for the upper house.[49] Table 3.7 lists the number of years of service for members of the Texas legislature. In 2011, there were 34 freshmen members in the house and 1 new member of the senate. In 2013, there were 41 freshmen house members (the largest contingent of new members in several decades) and 6 new senators.[50]

Over time, turnover rates in Texas are very high. Turnover is not due mainly to electoral defeat; most members voluntarily retire from service. Retirement around the country is prompted by relatively low pay, the lack of professional staff assistance, redistricting, the requirements of the job, the demands upon one's family, fundraising demands, and the rigors of seeking reelection.[51] Some use the office as a stepping-stone to higher office and leave to become members of Congress or take statewide

---

TABLE 3.7

Years of Service of Members of the 83rd Legislature

	House		Senate	
	Number	Percent	Number	Percent
20+	12	8%	6	19%
14–19	17	11%	4	13%
8–13	28	19%	6	19%
<1 – 7	53	35%	9	29%
1st	41	27%	6	19%

Source: House of Representatives. See: (http://www.house.state.tx.us/_media/pdf/members/senior.pdf) and Texas Senate See: (http://www.capitol.state.tx.us/Members/Members.aspx?Chamber=S)

office. In Texas, the retirement benefits are excellent for those serving a relatively low number of years in the legislature, so leaving office can actually be financially wise.

Why is turnover significant in state legislatures? It can be argued that high turnover contributes to the amateurish nature of state legislatures (which could be good or bad, depending on your view). In recent years, this has been especially significant in those states with term limits. If 20 to 25 percent of the members are new each session, these new members are learning the rules and finding their way. This allows a few "old timers" to control the legislative process.

Leadership Positions in the Texas Legislature

In any legislative body, those holding formal leadership positions possess considerable power to decide the outcome of legislation. In the Texas legislature, power is very much concentrated in the hands of two individuals: the speaker of the house and the lieutenant governor. These two individuals control the output of legislation.

Speaker of the House

The members of the house elect the Speaker of the Texas House of Representatives by majority vote. The election of the **speaker of the house** is the first formal act of the members in each legislative session. The secretary of state presides over the election. Only occasionally is the outcome of this election in doubt. Who the speaker will be is generally known far in advance of the beginning of the session, and this individual spends considerable time lining up supporters before the session begins. In all but a few cases, the person elected is a long-time member of the house and has support from current members. When one-third of the members are new, the person elected speaker may also have to gain support from some of these new members. It is illegal for candidates for speaker to formally promise members something in exchange for their vote, but key players in the election of the speaker often receive choice committee assignments.

It should be noted that for many years the Texas House of Representatives operated on a bipartisan basis. In the 2001 session of the legislature, Democrats controlled the house, and Democrat Pete Laney was speaker. Bipartisanship was much more apparent in committee assignments and the overall tone of the session. In the 2003 through 2007 sessions, much of this bipartisanship disappeared when the Republicans held a majority of the seats in the house and Representative Tom Craddick became speaker. In the 2003 session, partisanship was the order of the day, the tone set by Speaker Craddick. Representative Dawnna Dukes (Democrat from Houston) stated that the Republicans did not feel the need to compromise on issues since they controlled a majority of the seats. However, this sentiment may have reflected partisanship itself and the historic nature of the shift in house leadership as much as anything.

Former Speaker Laney served in the Texas House from 1969 to 2004 and chaired several important committees. Incumbent speakers are almost always reelected. A new speaker is chosen only after the death, retirement, or resignation of a sitting speaker. Traditionally, speakers served for two terms and retired or moved to higher offices. From 1951 to 1975, no speaker served more than two terms. In 1975, Billy Clayton broke with this tradition and served for four terms. Gib Lewis, who succeeded Clayton, served for five terms, as did Laney.[52]

speaker of the house
Member of the Texas house, elected by the house members, who serves as presiding officer and generally controls the passage of legislation

Speaker Joe Straus bangs the gavel
to start the 83rd Legislative Session

Tom Craddick was first elected speaker for the 2003 session. He was the first Republican speaker since Reconstruction. After serving three terms as speaker, Craddick was not reelected in 2009. In the 2008 election, the Republicans barely held onto a majority (76/74). Before the 2009 session even began, a long-standing "Anybody but Craddick" movement gained momentum and ultimately led to the election of San Antonio-area legislator Joe Straus as the speaker for the 81st Legislature. The move to oust Speaker Craddick began in earnest in early January 2009 when what journalist Ross Ramsey called the "Polo Road Gang" of 11 moderate Republican legislators met at the Austin home of Rep. Byron Cook to discuss a challenge to the speaker and to select an alternative candidate. Straus, a moderate Republican first elected to the House in 2005, was chosen on the fifth ballot as a compromise selection. This Polo Road Gang of Republicans was then joined by a few more Republicans and 65 Democrats to push Craddick out.[53] It did not ultimately require much of a push, because Craddick quickly decided not to seek reelection once the writing was on the wall.[54] Straus has been speaker since that time. However, he has earned the ire of conservative and Tea Party Republicans who would like to see a speaker who they think is more in line with their views.[55]

Speaker Straus was a departure from past speakers in that he had served only two terms before being elected. He had a shaky start but finished the session with some minor success. In the 2010 elections, the Republicans increased their control from 78 members to 101, and Straus was reelected to a second term.

Many believe that speaker of the house is the most powerful position in Texas government. There is no doubt that the speaker is extremely powerful. Generally, speakers have the power to direct and decide what legislation passes the house. The speaker gains power from the formal rules adopted by the house at the beginning of each session. These rules allow the speaker to do the following:

1. Appoint the chairs of all committees.
2. Appoint most of the members of each standing committee. About half of these committee seats are assigned based on a limited seniority system. In reality, the backers of the speaker often use their seniority to choose a committee assignment, thus freeing up an appointment for the speaker.
3. Appoint members of the calendar and procedural committees, conference committees, and other special and interim committees.
4. Serve as presiding officer over all sessions. This power allows the speaker to recognize members on the floor who want to speak, generally interpret house rules, decide when a vote will be taken, and decide the outcome of voice votes.
5. Refer all bills to committees. As a rule, bills go to subject matter committees. However, the speaker has discretion in deciding what committee will receive a bill. Some speakers used the State Affairs Committee as their "dead bill committee." Bills assigned to this committee usually had little chance of passing. Also, the speaker can assign a bill to a favorable committee to enhance its chances of passing.

These rules give the speaker control over the house agenda. The speaker decides the chairs of standing committees, selects a majority of the members of all committees, and refers bills to committees. The selected chairs are members of the "speaker's team." Few bills pass the house without the speaker's approval. For example, in the 2005 session of the legislature, House Bill 1348, which would have limited campaign contributions from corporations and labor unions, was being co-sponsored by two-thirds of the members of the house, both Democrats and Republicans. The bill was not given a hearing by the Elections Committee because of the influence of the speaker.

Lieutenant Governor

Unlike the speaker of the house, the voters in a statewide general election elect the **lieutenant governor** for a four-year term. The lieutenant governor does not owe his or her election to the legislative body, is not formally a senator, and cannot vote except in cases of a tie. One might assume that the office was not a powerful legislative office. In most states this is true; however, the lieutenant governor in Texas possesses powers very similar to those of the speaker. Lieutenant governors can do the following:

1. Appoint the chairs of all senate committees.
2. Select all members of all senate committees. No formal seniority rule applies in the senate.
3. Appoint members of the conference committees.
4. Serve as presiding officer and interpret rules.
5. Refer all bills to committees.

On the surface, it appears that the lieutenant governor is more powerful than the speaker. Lieutenant governors do not owe their election to the senate, and they have all powers possessed by the speaker. The reality is different. The powers of the lieutenant governor are assigned by the formal rules of the senate, which are adopted at the beginning of each session. What the senate gives, it can take away. Lieutenant governors must play a delicate balancing role of working with powerful members of the senate, often compromising in the assignment of chairs of committees and committee membership. The same is true for all other powers. Thus, the lieutenant governor must forge an alliance with key senators to effectively utilize these powers.

From 1876 to 1999, the Democrats controlled the lieutenant governor's office. They controlled the senate from 1876 to 1997. Until recently, party control was not a factor. It is often suggested that if the lieutenant governor and the senate are ever of opposite parties, the powers of the lieutenant governor could be diminished. Such concerns have been voiced in the past few years, and given the pattern in other states, this seems quite likely. Having such a powerful lieutenant governor is unusual among the states. In only five other states (Alabama, Georgia, Mississippi, South Carolina, and Vermont), the lieutenant governor can appoint committee members and assign bills to committees. In Arkansas, the lieutenant governor can assign bills to committees but does not appoint committees.[56]

In most states, the lieutenant governor is not a powerful leader. Eight states do not have lieutenant governors (Arizona, Maine, New Hampshire, New Jersey, Oregon, Tennessee, West Virginia, and Wyoming).[57] In the 26 states where their only legislative duty is to serve as the presiding officer, most lieutenant governors attend a senate session only when their vote is needed to break a tie.[58] Most lieutenant governors are figureheads who stand in when the governor is out of state.

lieutenant governor
Presiding officer of the Texas Senate; elected by the voters of the state

Former Lt. Governor David Dewhurst

In states where the lieutenant governor is a figurehead, or when there is no lieutenant governor, the senate elects one of its members to be the presiding officer, called the pro tempore, president of the senate, or speaker of the senate.[59]

Thus, the office of lieutenant governor in Texas is quite different from the office in most other states. This has not always been true in Texas. J. William Davis in his book, *There Shall Also Be a Lieutenant Governor,* traces the concentration of power in this office to the actions of Allan Shivers and Ben Ramsey during the 1940s and 1950s. Over a period of several years the office gained power in the senate.[60]

The 1999 session was the first since Reconstruction where Republicans held the majority of the senate seats and the lieutenant governor's office. Then-Lt. Governor Rick Perry retained the powers usually given to lieutenant governors. Retaining those powers depends upon a lieutenant governor's ability to compromise and get along with the 31 members of the senate. Acting Lt. Governor Ratliff, who filled the position in 2000 when Perry assumed the governorship after George W. Bush moved to the White House, retained these powers. This was not surprising because he was a member of the senate and was elected by that body to be lieutenant governor. Republican senators ensured that former Lt. Governor David Dewhurst kept these powers when he won the office in 2002. It is not in the interests of the Republicans, with their current 20 seats in the senate, to break with the lieutenant governor, because it takes 21 votes to bring a bill up for debate on the floor of the senate.

The speaker and the lieutenant governor also have other **extra legislative powers**. They appoint members of other state boards, or they serve as members of such boards. For example, they appoint the members of the Legislative Budget Board, which writes the state budget, and they serve as the chair and vice chair of this board. These are important powers because these boards make policy. The state budget, for instance, is a policy statement in monetary terms. The budget decides what agencies and programs will be funded and in what amounts.

The speaker and the lieutenant governor also serve as members of the Legislative Redistricting Board. This board meets if the legislature fails to redraw house or senate districts. The decision of this board is subject to change only by court action.

extra legislative powers
Legislative leaders serve on boards outside of the legislature

Committees in the House and Senate

standing committees
Committees of the house and senate that consider legislation during sessions

Most of the work of the legislature is done in **standing committees** established by house and senate rules. Besides the standing committees, there are also subcommittees of the standing committees, **conference committees** to work out differences in bills passed by the two houses, temporary committees to study special problems, and **interim committees** to study issues between sessions of the state legislature.

conference committees
Joint committees of the house and senate that work out differences in bills passed in each chamber

Of these, the standing committees are the most important. In most sessions, there are 14 standing committees in the senate and 41 in the house. In the recent 83rd Legislature, there were 18 in the senate and 38 in the house. These are listed in Table 3.8. The chairs of these standing committees have powers similar to those of the speaker and lieutenant governor at the committee level. They decide the times

interim committees
Temporary committees of the legislature that study issues between regular sessions and make recommendations on legislation

and agendas for meetings of the committee. In doing so, they decide the amount of time devoted to bills and which bills get the attention of the committee. A chair that strongly dislikes a bill can often prevent the bill from passing. Even if the bill is given a hearing, the chair can decide to give that bill to a subcommittee that might kill the bill. As in most legislative bodies, power in Texas is heavily concentrated

TABLE 3.8

Standing Committees of the Texas House and Senate, 83rd Legislature

Senate Committees	House Committees
Administration	Agriculture & Livestock
Agriculture, Rural Affairs, and Homeland Security	Appropriations
Business & Commerce	Business & Industry
Criminal Justice	Calendars
Economic Development	Corrections
Education	County Affairs
Finance	Criminal Jurisprudence
Government Organization	Culture, Recreation & Tourism
Health & Human Services	Defense & Veterans' Affairs
Higher Education	Economic and Small Business Development
Intergovernmental Relations	Elections
Jurisprudence	Energy Resources
Natural Resources	Environmental Regulation
Nominations	General Investigating & Ethics
Open Government	Government Efficiency & Reform
State Affairs	Higher Education
Transportation	Homeland Security & Public Safety
Veteran Affairs & Military Installations	House Administration
	Human Services
	Insurance
	International Trade & Intergovernmental Affairs
	Investments & Financial Services
	Judiciary & Civil Jurisprudence
	Land & Resource Management
	Licensing & Administrative Procedures
	Local & Consent Calendars
	Natural Resources
	Pensions
	Public Education
	Public Health
	Redistricting
	Rules & Resolutions
	Special Purpose Districts
	State Affairs
	Technology
	Transportation
	Urban Affairs
	Ways and Means

Source: Texas Senate. See: (http://www.senate.state.tx.us/75r/senate/Commit.htm) and House of Representatives. See: (http://www.house.state.tx.us/committees/)

in the individuals who make up the house and senate leadership, and who control the agendas and actions of the legislature. Few bills can pass the legislature without the support of these individuals.

CORE OBJECTIVE

Taking Personal Responsibility...

It has been stated that the success of legislation depends largely on a relative few individuals who make up the leadership in the Texas House and Senate. Do you think the speaker of the house and the lieutenant governor have too much control over the passage of bills? How can you influence legislation? What can individuals do to affect legislation?

Functions

Lawmaking

The Texas legislature has, as one of its main functions, the responsibility to create, alter, and enact laws for the state. Laws are submitted, created, and enacted by the two branches of the Texas legislature. This is the main duty and function of legislative bodies in general.

Budget and Taxation

One of the most essential laws enacted by the Texas legislature is the biennial budget. The Legislative Budget Board submits a recommended budget to the legislature. The governor's office also submits an executive budget. The legislature uses these two documents to help create and enact the budget that will be in place for the state until the next legislative session. The Senate Finance Committee and House Appropriations Committee begin the process of creating the budget bill for the legislature. The budget bill follows a similar process as other bills in the legislature, but it passes to the state comptroller prior to being sent to the governor.

The Texas legislature establishes the state sales tax, which is the main source of revenue for the state. Additional taxes can be established, such as franchise taxes on businesses or "sin" taxes on activities the legislature may want to discourage, such as the purchase of alcohol and tobacco. The Texas legislature has not chosen to establish a state income tax.

Oversight

Another key responsibility of the legislature is to keep track of what state agencies are doing, assess their performance, and determine whether they provide necessary functions. The legislature has a number of mechanisms by which it examines these state agencies in order to fulfill this "oversight" duty. One form of oversight is through the use of committees, whereby a committee may call representatives of agencies to testify at a hearing. Whereas this is a common tactic used in the federal government, it is less effective for the Texas legislature because of the limited legislative session. Another means of oversight is through financial mechanisms—for example, the actions taken by the Legislative Budget Board and by the Legislative Audit Committee. A final means of oversight is the Sunset Advisory Commission.

The Texas legislature established this commission in 1977 as a major means of oversight of state agencies. The commission reviews about 130 state agencies on a rotating basis to determine whether there is a continued need for the agency under review. This works out to each agency being reviewed, on average, about every 12 years. The commission then makes a recommendation to the legislature regarding whether agencies should be continued or abolished. See Figure 3.1 on how this process works.[61]

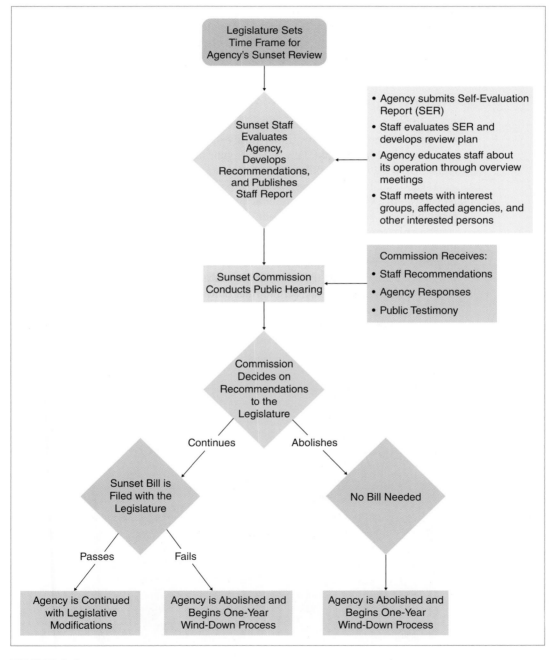

FIGURE 3.1   **Sunset Advisory Commission Review Process**

Procedures

All legislatures have formal rules of procedure that govern their operations. These rules prescribe how bills are passed into law and make the process of passing laws more orderly and fair. These rules also make it difficult to pass laws. A bill must clear many hurdles before it becomes a law. Rules that make it difficult to pass bills have two results: they prevent bills from becoming law without careful review, and they preserve the status quo. In the traditionalistic/individualistic political culture of Texas, these rules protect the ruling elite and enable them to control the legislative process. Thus, it is more important to understand the impact of rules on legislation than to have a detailed understanding of the actual rules. This will be the basic approach used here to explain how laws are made in Texas.

Formal Rules: How a Bill Becomes a Law

Figure 3.2 lists the formal procedures in the Texas House and Senate for passing a bill. Each bill, to become law, must clear each step. The vast majority of bills that are introduced fail to pass. Few bills of major importance are passed in any given legislative session. Most bills make only minor changes to existing law.

At each stage in the process, the bill can receive favorable or unfavorable actions. At each step, a bill can die by either action or inaction. There are many ways to kill a bill, but only one way to pass a bill. To pass, a bill must clear all hurdles.

The rules of the Texas Senate have a conserving force on legislation. Before the sixtieth day of the legislative session, a bill can clear the senate with a simple majority vote. Few bills pass before the sixtieth day. After the sixtieth day, before a bill can be considered on the floor of the senate, a two-thirds vote is required. Technically, after the sixtieth day, senate rules state that bills must be considered in the order they are reported out of committees. If bills are not considered in the order reported out of committees, a two-thirds vote is required. By design, bills are never considered in the order reported out of committee. If two-thirds of the senators

Texas House of Representatives

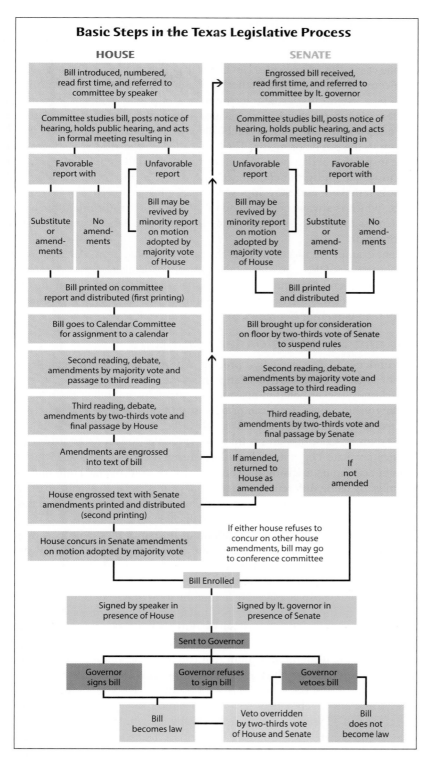

FIGURE 3.2   Basic Steps in the Texas Legislative Process This diagram displays the sequential flow of a bill from the time it is introduced in the Texas House of Representatives to final passage and transmittal to the governor. A bill introduced in the senate follows the same procedure, flowing from senate to house.

agree to consider the bill, it can pass by a simple majority. Because of this rule, few bills that are not supported by more than a simple majority of the senators clear the senate. This rule makes the senate a conserving force in the legislative process.

In some cases, the formal rules can be used to hide actions of the legislature. It is not uncommon in legislative bodies to attach **riders** to appropriations bills. A rider can be a subject matter item (creation of a new state regulatory board) or a money item (money for a park in a legislator's district). In the Texas legislature, the practice adds a new twist. Riders can be attached to appropriations, and they are not known to the public or media. They are called **closed riders**. They are closed to public inspection and appear only after the appropriation bills have passed the house and senate and go to conference committee. In the conference committee the cloak is removed, and they appear for public inspection for the first time. At this stage, which is always near the end of the session, the likelihood of change is remote. Unless there is a governor's veto, these closed riders become law without public comment.

A recent example of this dealt with the Bush School at Texas A&M University. In the 1999 session of the legislature, the Bush School (College) was separated from the College of Liberal Arts and made a separate school (college) within the university, and its budget was increased by several million dollars. This was done at the request of then-Governor George W. Bush.

Major and Minor Calendars and Bills

To fully understand the legislative process, we must distinguish between major and minor bills, because state legislators treat them very differently. As political scientist Harvey Tucker noted in his study of calendars and bills, "the major criterion distinguishing major from minor bills is political: the level of conflict the bill is expected to generate within the Legislature."[62] Two organizations, the former Federal Advisory Commission on Intergovernmental Relations and the Citizens Conference on State Legislators, have both recommended that state legislatures use different calendars to distinguish between major, controversial bills and minor, or local bills. By using different calendars, legislatures can better manage their limited time and devote attention to important matters. Texas is one of 36 states that use both a local and a consent calendar in both chambers.

The Texas House has two different **calendars** for minor bills—the local calendar and the consent calendar. To be assigned to these calendars, a bill must meet tests established by house rules. Local bills must not have an effect upon more than one of the 254 counties in the state. Bills for the consent calendar must be minor, noncontroversial bills. To be placed on either the local or the consent calendar, bills must meet two further criteria. First, they must receive unanimous support in the substantive house committee handling the bill. Second, the **Local and Consent Calendars Committee** must approve them. If this committee does not approve the bill, it is sent to the **Calendars Committee** (regular calendars) for assignment to another calendar. A bill may be removed from the local or consent calendar if five members object during floor debate. Also, if debate exceeds 10 minutes, the bill is withdrawn and effectively killed.[63] These procedures safeguard against important bills being approved without adequate review by the whole house.

Table 3.9 demonstrates the fate of bills in the Texas legislature. As the table shows, only about 25 percent of all bills introduced in the house and senate make it into law. Most bills die at the committee level, and some are dead on arrival. Some bills are introduced to satisfy a constituency, and the member has no intention of working to pass the bill.

---

rider
Provision attached to a bill that may not be of the same subject matter as the main bill

closed rider
Provisions attached to appropriations bills that are not made public until the conference committee meets

calendars
Procedures in the house used to consider different kinds of bills; major bills and minor bills are considered under different procedures

Local and Consent Calendars Committee
Committee handling minor and noncontroversial bills that normally apply to only one county

Calendars Committee
Standing committee of the house that decides which bills will be considered for floor debate and to which committee they will be assigned

TABLE 3.9

Bill Survival Rate in the Texas Legislature

	77th (2001)	78th (2003)	79th (2005)	80th (2007)	81st (2009)	82nd (2011)
Total Bills	100%	100%	100%	100%	100%	100%
Deliberated by committee in originating chamber	70%	64%	68%	70%	70%	70%
Passed by committee in originating chamber	50%	46%	47%	48%	47%	46%
Floor consideration in originating chamber	41%	37%	35%	40%	34%	36%
Pass originating chamber	40%	35%	33%	37%	33%	34%
Deliberated in second chamber	35%	30%	27%	31%	26%	28%
Passed by committee in second chamber	33%	29%	27%	31%	26%	28%
Floor consideration in second chamber	29%	25%	25%	26%	20%	24%
Pass second chamber	29%	25%	24%	25%	19%	24%
Pass both chambers	29%	25%	24%	25%	19%	24%
Passed into law	27%	24%	24%	24%	19%	23%
Vetoed	1%	1%	<1%	1%	1%	<1%

Source: Adapted from Harvey J. Tucker, "Legislation Deliberation in the Texas House and Senate." Paper presented at Annual Meeting of Midwest Political Science Association, Chicago, Illinois, April 15–18, 2004. Data in this table updated by Harvey Tucker.

There are three calendars for major bills: the emergency calendar, the major state calendar, and the general state calendar. The Calendars Committee has the authority to assign bills to these calendars. This power is rarely challenged. The distinction among the major calendars is not important until the final days of the legislative session, when time is limited.

A few similarities and differences exist between major and minor bills. The bills are identical in three ways:

1. They originate in either chamber.
2. They are equally as likely to be vetoed.
3. They receive final action toward the end of the legislative session.

Major and minor bills are treated differently in six ways:

1. Major bills are introduced earlier in the session than minor bills.
2. Companion bills are introduced in the other chamber more frequently for major bills than for minor bills.
3. Major bills are more evenly distributed across committees; minor bills are more concentrated in a few committees.
4. Major bills are amended more frequently than minor bills.
5. Major bills are more likely to be killed; minor bills are more likely to be passed by the legislature.
6. Final actions to kill major bills occur later in the session than final actions to kill minor bills.[64]

Legislative Workload and Logjams

According to much of the literature on state legislatures, most bills pass the legislature in the final days of the session. This scenario suggests that the legislature "goofs off" for most of the session and then frantically passes bills just before adjournment, producing laws that are given only "hasty consideration, of poor quality and are confused and inferior."[65]

In Texas, it is true that most legislation is passed in the final two weeks of the session. About 80 percent of all bills passed in this time period. The question remains: Does this result in poor quality and inferior legislation? The answer is, probably not. One must understand the process of setting the agenda in the Texas legislature.

First, bills may be introduced at any time prior to the session and up until the sixtieth day of the 140-day session. After the sixtieth day, only local bills, emergency appropriations, emergency matters submitted by the governor, and bills with a four-fifths vote of the house may be introduced. Thus, for the first 60 days, the agendas for both houses are being set. After the sixtieth day, the legislature begins to clear these agendas. As indicated, most bills die in committees and are never assigned to a calendar. Killing a bill in committee is an action by the legislature, and it occurs at a regular rate during the session.[66] The bill is dead if it does not make it out of committee. This leaves only about a third of all bills for further consideration late in the session. As Harvey Tucker observes:

> Once the agenda has been set it is cleared at a fairly even rate. Final action on most bills passed occurs at the end of the session by design. Conflicting and complementary bills are reconciled. Bills tied directly or indirectly to the state budget are delayed until the final days of necessity. The legislature is not able to appropriate funds until the Comptroller of Public Accounts certifies the amount of revenues that will be available. The "certification estimate" is not made until the very end of the legislative session, because, among other reasons, the estimate must be informed by any actions the legislature takes that would affect state revenues.[67]

Thus, the image of the legislature as goofing off for 120 days is not accurate. The nature of the legislative process requires the passage of major legislation near the end of the session. Also, about half the bills that pass toward the end of the session are minor bills, and they are cleared late for different reasons than are major bills.

Thus, the formal rules of the house and senate are very important factors in determining how and what kind of legislation gets passed. These rules have the effect of preserving the status quo. It is very difficult to pass legislation and very easy to kill a bill. Although the Texas legislature is not remarkably different from most other legislatures in this respect, in Texas these rules protect the status quo of the traditionalistic/individualistic political culture of the state.

Informal Rules

informal rules

Set of norms or values that govern legislative bodies

In addition to the formal rules, there are also **informal rules**, or legislative norms, that all state legislators must learn if they are to be successful. Political scientists Lee Bernick and Charles Wiggins identified eleven norms that were generally accepted in their study of a sample of state legislatures. These included the following: Legislators should *not*

Conceal the real purpose of a bill or purposely overlook part of it to assure passage.
Deal in personalities during floor debate.
Give first priority to your reelection in all of your lawmaking activities.
Introduce as many bills and amendments as possible.
Be a thorn in the side of the majority by refusing unanimous consent.
Become known as a spokesperson for a special interest group.
Speak on issues you know little about.
Become known as a "loner."

Seek as much publicity as possible to look good to the people back home.

Talk to the press or others about decisions reached in private.

Avoid taking a position on legislation before the final vote or roll call.[68]

Of course, each legislature will have a different set of norms and place different values on them. In fact, only the first norm on the list was accepted in all states examined in the study. However, the next three norms in the list were accepted in at least 10 of the 11 states. Texas, however, was the only state where those three prescriptions did not meet the criteria for a legislative norm. In particular, dealing in personalities during floor debate was viewed as acceptable behavior by a significant number of members in Texas, whereas in the other states only a few members viewed this as appropriate.[69] It is also worth noting that Texas legislators were a lot less concerned with "blabbing" to the press about private deals than those in other states.

Legislators must learn the norms of their legislature and adhere to them, or they might find themselves ineffective or even isolated. The informal rules can be nearly important as the formal rules governing the legislature.

Legislative Roles

Members of the legislature are expected to play many roles during the legislative sessions. We have already discussed formal leadership roles. Each speaker will approach the job in different ways. Historically, most speakers have exerted very tight control over the house and dominated the legislative process. This was true of Billy Clayton, speaker from 1975 to 1983. However, Gib Lewis, who followed Clayton, exerted much less control. He allowed the members of his team—namely, committee chairs—to control the process, and he himself took a much more "laid back" attitude. Pete Laney was more like Billy Clayton in that he controlled the house. Tom Craddick of Midland followed a role similar to that of Speakers Laney and Clayton.

Great differences can also exist in lieutenant governors' leadership styles. For instance, Bill Hobby, the son of a former governor, served as lieutenant governor for 18 years (1972–90). Hobby, a very quiet, low-key person, seldom forced his will on the members of the senate. He preferred to work behind the scenes and forge compromises.

Hobby chose not to run for reelection in 1990, and Bob Bullock succeeded him. Bullock had served for 16 years as the state comptroller and had developed a reputation for strong, effective leadership, but he often went out of his way to make enemies. Bullock's leadership style as lieutenant governor was almost the opposite of Hobby's. Stories have circulated of shouting matches and angry behavior, sometimes even in open sessions of the senate. The senate seemed to adjust to Bullock's style of leadership, and he managed to get much of his agenda passed. Hobby and Bullock illustrate very different ways to be effective leaders of the senate.

Rick Perry, while serving as the Texas agricultural commissioner from 1995–1999, did not have the reputation of a compromiser; however, judging from all reports, he performed quite effectively as lieutenant governor in the 1999 session. Lt. Governor Dewhurst was something of a political unknown, having served only four years as land commissioner prior to his election. Dewhurst's performance received mixed reviews. He was an effective leader in the regular sessions and was viewed by some as more partisan in the three special sessions.

Powerful Republican leaders ensured that he kept the broad powers normally given to lieutenant governors.

Leadership in legislative bodies can take many forms. In addition to formal leadership roles, some members develop reputations as experts in particular areas of legislation and are looked to by other members as leaders in those areas. Being recognized by other members as the expert in some area of legislation obviously increases one's influence. For instance, a person who is a recognized expert on taxation issues can use this reputation to forge coalitions and pass tax legislation.

Representational Roles

delegate
Representational role of member that states that he or she represents the wishes of the voters

trustee
Representational role of a member that states that the member will make decisions on his or her own judgment about what is best for voters

Constituencies have expectations about the roles of their legislators. For centuries, members of legislatures have argued about the representational role of a legislator. Who do legislators represent? Are they **delegates**, sent by the voters to represent the voters' interests, or are they **trustees**, entrusted by the voters to make decisions based on their best judgment? The delegate role is perceived as being more democratic—as doing what the people want. The trustee role can be characterized as elitist—as doing what one thinks is best.

In reality, members may play both the delegate and the trustee roles, depending upon the issue before them. For example, in 1981 the Texas legislature passed a bill prohibiting commercial fisherman from catching redfish in some waters in the Gulf of Mexico. The bill was written and advanced by sport fishermen. Representatives from coastal communities in Texas voted as delegates—with the commercial fishermen and against the bill. Representatives from the Panhandle, however, were free to vote as trustees. In matters affecting the livelihood of Panhandle ranchers but not coastal fisheries, these representatives would reverse their voting roles. Which role representatives play is largely dependent on how the issues affect their district. The problem with this is that local interests can take the forefront, leading legislators to neglect long-term statewide or larger public interests.

Partisan Roles

Party has traditionally not been a strong factor in the Texas legislature. Members of both parties are given committee assignments. Texas contrasts with states with a tradition of strong partisanship, where party leadership roles are important, formal leadership positions are assigned on the basis of party, and party leaders try to ensure that party members support party positions on issues.

In the past, coalitions in the Texas legislature have organized more around ideology than around party. The 1970s saw the formation of the "Dirty Thirty" coalition of liberal Democratic and conservative Republican house members to fight the conservative Democrats. This uneasy alliance of those excluded from leadership positions was short lived.

In more recent years, conservative Republicans and Democrats organized the Texas Conservative Coalition to fight what they view as liberal ideas. Other caucuses represent Hispanics and African Americans. In 1993, the Republicans formed a caucus to promote the election of Pete Laney as speaker. As a reward, they were assigned several committee chairs. However, partisan factors have played a much larger role in the Texas legislature in recent years.

In 2003 session, this partisanship was evident in the redistricting battles. With the Republicans in control of both the house and the senate in the 2003 session, there was promise of bipartisan cooperation. For example, the new speaker, Tom Craddick, promised to continue bipartisanship and appointed 14 (29.2 percent)

Democrats to chair committees. However, there was little evidence of bipartisanship beyond that.

The sessions from 2003 to 2007 were instead marked by deep partisanship by Speaker Craddick. In fact, some members started calling him Speaker Auto-Craddick. He subsequently lost his speakership to Republican Joe Straus from San Antonio in the 2009 session. As discussed earlier, Speaker Straus came to power through a small coalition of Republicans who joined Democrats to wrest the position from Craddick. Key Democrats who helped engineer Straus's victory were given decent committee assignments by the new Republican speaker.[70] Some Democratic members, though, felt the party should have received more committee chairs and thus gave Straus mixed reviews at the start of his term. However, conservative Republicans have never been happy with Straus and have maintained their criticism of him throughout his tenure in the speakership. This led one commentator to describe Straus as "a political piñata for his party's conservatives."[71]

Legislative Professionalism versus Citizen Legislatures: Where Does Texas Stand?

In the preceding discussion, we have often made comparisons between the Texas legislature and the legislatures of other states. For example, we noted that few states have as many constituents per house and senate district as Texas, and that Texas is one of only four states to have biennial sessions. Political scientists have also compared state legislatures in terms of their level of **legislative professionalism**. According to Peverill Squire, legislative professionalism can be measured using data on "pay, session length, and staff resources."[72] States with higher legislative pay, longer sessions (such as no limits on the length of regular sessions), and more staff support are deemed more professional. One could say that states with part-time legislators who get lower pay, shorter or biennial sessions, and fewer staff resources are less professional or, more positively, **"citizen legislatures."**[73] Compared to all other states, Texas ranks the fifteenth most professional in the latest Squire Legislative Professionalism Index. New Hampshire has the least professional legislature (or the strongest citizen legislature), and California has the most professional.

legislative professionalism
Legislatures with higher pay, longer sessions, high levels of staff support are considered more professional

citizen legislatures
Legislatures characterized by low pay, short sessions, and fewer staff resources

Conclusion

Thomas R. Dye comes to three conclusions on state legislatures, all of which could be said to apply to the Texas legislature.[74] First, Dye observes that

> State legislatures reflect socioeconomic conditions of their states. These conditions help to explain many of the differences one encounters in state legislative politics: the level of legislative activity, the degree of inter-party competition, the extent of party cohesion, the professionalism of the legislature . . . [and] the level of interest group activity.[75]

This means that the legislature is greatly influenced by the social and economic conditions in the state, and

that policies passed by the legislature reflect those conditions. This certainly applies to Texas.

Second, legislatures function as "arbiters of public policy rather than initiators" of policy change.[76] State legislatures wait for others—state agencies, local governments, interest groups, and citizens—to bring issues to them for resolution. Someone other than members of the legislature write most bills introduced. The rules make it much easier to delay legislation than to pass it. Leadership most often comes from others outside the legislature, often the governor. With a few exceptions this applies to Texas.

Third, legislatures "function to inject into public decision making a parochial influence."[77] By this Dye means that state legislatures tend to represent local legislative interests and not statewide interests. Legislators are recruited, elected, and reelected locally. Local interests will always be dominant in determining how legislators vote on proposed legislation. Frequently, no one represents statewide interests. This conclusion certainly applies to Texas. Statewide interests often get lost in the shuffle to protect and promote local interests.

Key Terms

Baker v. Carr
bicameral
biennial session
calendars
Calendars Committee
citizen legislatures
closed rider
conference committees
delegate
extra legislative powers
extraordinary session
gerrymandering
Hunt v. Cromartie

informal rules
interim committees
legislative professionalism
Legislative Redistricting Board
   (LRB)
lieutenant governor
Local and Consent Calendars
   Committee
multimember districts
noncompetitive districts
political gerrymandering
racial gerrymandering
reapportionment

redistricting
Reynolds v. Sims
rider
sine die
single-member districts
speaker of the house
special sessions
standing committees
term limits
trustee
turnover

Notes

[1] *Texas Constitution*, 1876, art. 3, sec. 2.

[2] Council of State Governments, *Book of the States, 2012* (Lexington, Ky.: Council of State Governments, 2012), 118, Table 3.3.

[3] National Conference of State Legislatures, 2010 Constituents Per State Legislative District Table. http://www.ncsl.org/legislatures-elections/legislatures/2010-constituents-per-state-legislative-district.aspx.

[4] On this and other points related to the size of the legislature, see Anti-Federalist writings such as Brutus's "III" from the *New York Journal*, November 15, 1787 or Cato's "Letter V" from the *New York Journal*, November 22, 1787. These quotations come from Brutus.

[5] Rich Jones, "State Legislatures," *Book of the States*, 1944–95, 99; National Conference of State Legislatures, Annual Versus Biennial Legislative Sessions. http://www.ncsl.org/research/about-state-legislatures/annual-versus-biennial-legislative-sessions.aspx.

[6] National Conference of State Legislatures, Annual Versus Biennial Legislative Sessions. http://www.ncsl.org/research/about-state-legislatures/annual-versus-biennial-legislative-sessions.aspx.

[7] Legislative Reference Library of Texas, Answers to frequently asked questions about the Texas Legislature. http://www.lrl.state.tx.us/genInfo/FAQ.cfm#legPay.

[8] Texas State Historical Association, Texas Legislature. http://www.tshaonline.org/handbook/online/articles/mkt02.

[9] National Conference of State Legislatures, 2013 NCSL Legislator Compensation Data. http://www.ncsl.org/research/about-state-legislatures/2013-ncsl-legislator-salary-and-per-diem.aspx.

[10] Robert T. Garrett, "Texas lawmakers move to indirectly boost their own pensions," Dallas Morning News, May 13, 2013. http://www.dallasnews.com/news/politics/state-politics/20130513-texas-lawmakers-move-to-indirectly-boost-their-own-pensions.ece.)

[11] Ross Ramsey, "Legislators With Benefits, Even When They Stray," Texas Tribune, April 12, 2012, http://www.nytimes.com/2012/04/13/us/texas-legislators-with-benefits-even-when-they-stray.html.)

[12] National Conference of State Legislatures. Size of State Legislative Staff. http://www.ncsl.org/research/about-state-legislatures/staff-change-chart-1979-1988-1996-2003-2009.aspx.

[13] Senate Journal, Eighty-Third Legislature - Regular Session, First Day. http://www.journals.senate.state.tx.us/sjrnl/83R/pdf/83RSJ01-08-F.pdf.

[14] House Journal, Eighty-Third Legislature, Regular Session. http://www.journals.house.state.tx.us/hjrnl/83R/pdf/83RDAY02FINAL.pdf

[15] Texas Secretary of State, Qualifications for Office. http://www.sos.state.tx.us/elections/candidates/guide/qualifications.shtml; University of Texas at Austin, Texas Politics, The Legislative Branch. http://texaspolitics.laits.utexas.edu/2_3_0.html.

[16] Thomas R. Dye, *Politics in States and Communities*, 7th ed. (Englewood Cliffs, N.J.: Prentice Hall, 1991), 157.

[17] Harvey Tucker and Gary Halter, *Texas Legislative Almanac 2001* (College Station: Texas A&M University Press, 2001).

[18] Center for American Women and Politics, Women in State Legislatures 2014. http://www.cawp.rutgers.edu/fast_facts/levels_of_office/documents/stleg.pdf.

[19] University of Texas at Austin, Texas Politics, Race and Ethnicity in the Texas Legislature. http://www.laits.utexas.edu/txp_media/html/leg/features/0304_02/race.html.

[20] National Conference of State Legislatures. Legislators' Occupations in All States, 1976, 1986, 1993, 1995, 2007 (Percentages). http://www.ncsl.org/research/about-state-legislatures/legislator-occupations-national-data.aspx.

[21] Malcolm E. Jewell and Samuel C. Patterson, *The Legislative Process in the United States* (New York: Random House, 1985), 21.

[22] Samuel C. Patterson, "Legislators and Legislatures in the American States," in *Politics in the American States: A Comparative Analysis,* 6th ed., eds. Virginia Gray, Herbert Jacob, and Kenneth N. Vine (Boston: Little, Brown, 1996), 164.

[23] *Texas Constitution,* art. 3, sec. 26.

[24] Leroy Hardy, Alan Heslop, and Stuart Anderson, *Reapportionment Politics* (Beverly Hills, Calif.: Sage, 1981), 18.

[25] Gordon E. Baker, *The Reapportionment Revolution: Representation, Political Power and the Supreme Court* (New York: Random House, 1966).

[26] Wilbourn E. Benton, *Texas: Its Government and Politics,* 2nd ed. (Englewood Cliffs, N.J.: Prentice Hall, 1966), 141.

[27] *Texas Constitution,* art. 3, sec. 28.

[28] Ibid., sec. 26a.

[29] *Baker v. Carr,* 369 U.S. 186 (1962).

[30] *Reynolds v. Sims,* 377 U.S. 533 (1964).

[31] *Kilgarlin v. Martin,* 1965.

[32] *Graves v. Barnes,* 343 F. Supp. 704 (W.D. Tex. 1972); *White v. Register,* 412 U.S. 755 (1973).

[33] National Conference of State Legislatures, African-American Legislators 2009. http://www.ncsl.org/research/about-state-legislatures/african-american-legislators-in-2009.aspx.) (Need new FN here: National Conference of State Legislatures, 2009 Latino Legislators.

[34] National Conference of State Legislatures, 2009 Latino Legislators. http://www.ncsl.org/research/about-state-legislatures/latino-legislators-overview.aspx; National Hispanic Caucus of State Legislators, Hispanic State Legislator Information. http://www.nhcsl.org/hispanic-state-legislator-information.php.

[35] Corrie MacLaggan, "Texas House Race Draws Focus to Vietnamese Voters," *Texas Tribune,* January 10, 2014.

[36] *Bush v. Vera,* 517 U.S. 952 (1996).

[37] Ibid.

[38] R. C. Ratcliffe, "Re-mapping of the Districts Draws Fire: 18 Incumbents Would Square Off," *Houston Chronicle,* 24 April 2001, p. 1.

[39] Clay Robison, "Bush, DeLay in the Lobbying Game," *Houston Chronicle,* June 22, 2003, http://www.chron.

com/CDA/archives/archive.mpl/2003_3665599/bush-delay-in-the-lobbying-game.html.

[40] Texas Legislative Council. http://www.tlc.state.tx.us/redist/redist.htm.

[41] *Perry v. Perez,* 565 U.S. (2012).

[42] Texas Legislative Council. http://www.tlc.state.tx.us/redist/redist.htm.

[43] Longview News Journal. http://www.news-journal.com/news/local/did-new-voting-lines-doom-incumbent-east-texas-legislators/article_16361306-5135-55f5-befa-506fdf5887a6.html.

[44] Gary C. Jacobson, *The Politics of Congressional Elections,* 3rd ed. (New York: HarperCollins, 1992).

[45] Kevin A. Hill, "Does the Creation of Majority Black Districts Aid Republicans? An Analysis of the 1992 Congressional Election in Eight Southern States," *Journal of Politics* 57 (May 1995): 348–401.

[46] *Book of the States, 1994–95,* 29, table A. Also see the website of the National Conference of State Legislatures (www.ncsl.org).

[47] *Book of the States, 1994–95,* 27.

[48] Samuel C. Patterson, "Legislative Politics in the States," in *Politics in the American States,* 6th ed., eds. Virginia Gray and Herbert Jacob (Washington, D.C.: Congressional Quarterly Press, 1996), 179–186.

[49] *Book of the States, 2004.*

[50] Ross Ramsey, "Texas Lawmakers Put Down Their Swords," *New York Times,* May 26, 2013, http://www.nytimes.com/2013/05/26/us/texas-83rd-legislative-session-characterized-by-agreement.html?pagewanted=all); Jonathan Tilove, "Texas House returns with largest contingent of new members in 40 years," *Austin American-Statesman,* January 5, 2013, http://www.statesman.com/news/news/state-regional-govt-politics/texas-house-returns-with-largest-contingent-of-new/nTnpq/

[51] Lawrence W. Miller, *Legislative Turnover and Political Careers: A Study of Texas Legislators, 1969–75,* Ph.D. dissertation, Texas Tech University, 1977, 43–45.

[52] *Presiding Officers of the Texas Legislature, 1846–2002* (Austin: Texas Legislative Council, 2002).

[53] Ross Ramsey, "Texas Lawmakers Put Down Their Swords," *New York Times,* May 26, 2013, http://www.nytimes.com/2013/05/26/us/texas-83rd-legislative-session-characterized-by-agreement.html?pagewanted=all); Jonathan Tilove, "Texas House Returns with Largest Contingent of New Members in 40 Years," *Austin American-Statesman,* January 5, 2013, http://www.statesman.com/news/news/state-regional-govt-politics/texas-house-returns-with-largest-contingent-of-new/nTnpq/.

[54] Gary Scharrer, "Craddick: 'I'm Not Running for Speaker,'" *Houston Chronicle,* January 14, 2009. http://blog.chron.com/texaspolitics/2009/01/craddick-im-not-running-for-speaker/.)

[55] http://www.breitbart.com/Breitbart-Texas/2014/02/16/Shining-Light-On-House-Speaker-Joe-Straus.

[56] *Book of the States, 1998–99,* 48, table 2.13.

[57] Ibid., 33, table 2.9.

[58] Ibid., 48, table 2.13.

[59] In Tennessee, the speaker of the senate also holds the title of lieutenant governor.

[60] J. William Davis, *There Shall Also Be a Lieutenant Governor* (Austin: University of Texas, Institute of Public Affairs, 1967).

[61] Sunset Advisory Commission, Sunset in Texas 2013-2015. https://www.sunset.texas.gov/public/uploads/files/reports/Sunset%20in%20Texas%202013-2015.pdf

[62] Harvey Tucker, "Legislative Calendars and Workload Management in Texas," *Journal of Politics* 51 (August 1989).

[63] Harvey Tucker, "Legislative Calendars and Workload Management in Texas," *Journal of Politics* 51 (August 1989): 633.

[64] Harvey J. Tucker, "Legislative Workload Congestion in Texas," *Journal of Politics* 49 (1987): 557.

[65] Ibid.

[66] Ibid., 569.

[67] Ibid., 575.

[68] E. Lee Bernick and Charles W. Wiggins, "Legislative Norms in Eleven States," *Legislative Studies Quarterly* 8.2 (May 1983): 194–195.

[69] Ibid., 194.

[70] Ross Ramsey, "Now It Starts," *Texas Tribune,* February 16, 2009. http://www.texastribune.org/2009/02/16/now-it-starts/.

[71] Ross Ramsey, "Speaker's Original Band of 11 Shrinks to Four," *Texas Tribune,* September 9, 2013. http://www.texastribune.org/2013/09/09/speakers-original-band-11-shrinks-four/.

[72] Peverill Squire. "Measuring State Legislative Professionalism: The Squire Index Revisited." *State Politics & Policy Quarterly* 7:2 (Summer, 2007): 211–227.

[73] William Ruger and Jason Sorens. "The Citizen Legislature." Goldwater Institute Policy Brief. June 22, 2011.

[74] Dye, *Politics in States and Communities,* 192–193.

[75] Ibid., 192.

[76] Ibid., 193.

[77] Ibid.

CHAPTER 4

The Executive Department and the Office of the Governor of Texas

*Upon completing this chapter,
you will be able to...*

- **Demonstrate knowledge of the executive branch
of Texas government.**

The governor is the most salient political actor in state government. Whether the true power center of the state is embodied in the occupant of the office or elsewhere, the office is the focal point of state government and politics. The expectation is that governors will be leaders in their state.

Qualifications

Formal Qualifications

In most states the formal qualifications to be governor are minimal. All but six states set a minimum age requirement, and most require a candidate to be a resident of the state for 5 to 10 years preceding election. Also, most states require governors to be U.S. citizens and qualified voters.

In Texas the formal qualifications are simple: One must be at least 30 years of age, a citizen of the United States, and a resident of the state for five years preceding election. There is no requirement to be a registered voter. In fact, in the 1930s W. Lee O'Daniel ran for governor, stressing that he was not a "professional politician." To prove his point, he made an issue of not being a registered voter.

Informal Qualifications

Experience

Informal qualifications are more important. Nationwide, most governors have held elected office before becoming governor. An examination of the 933 people who have served as governor in the United States between 1900 and 1997 reveals that the most common career path to that office is to begin in the legislature, move to statewide office, and then move to the governor's office. Others who have been elected governor have served as U.S. senator or representative, and a few have served in local elected

informal qualifications
Additional qualifications beyond the formal qualifications required for men and women to be elected governor; holding statewide elected office is an example.

97

offices (such as mayor). Some governors gain experience as appointed administrators or as party officials. Between 1970 and 1999, only 10 percent of all people elected governor had no prior political office experience.[1] Having held elected office is an important informal qualification for becoming governor.

The national statistics generally apply to most Texas governors. Table 4.1 lists the men and women who have served since 1949 and their prior office experience. Only two had not held elected office. The recently retired governor, Rick Perry, followed a rather typical pattern. He served in the state legislature, as agricultural commissioner, and as lieutenant governor prior to becoming governor when George Bush resigned to assume the office of President of the United States. Perry was elected governor in his own right in 2002, 2006, and 2010. He did not run for a fourth term. Incoming governor Greg Abbott [R] served under Perry as Attorney General. He previously served on the Texas Supreme Court, as appointed by George W. Bush.

Ethnicity

Besides electoral experience, there are many other informal qualifications. Nationwide, most people who have served as governors have been white, wealthy, well-educated, Protestant males. Only two African Americans, Douglas Wilder of Virginia and Deval Patrick of Massachusetts, have been elected as governor. Several Hispanics have served as governor, including Tony Anaya, Jerry Abodaca, Bill Richardson, and Susan Martinez in New Mexico; Bob Martinez in Florida; Paul Castro in Arizona; and Brian Sandoval in Nevada.

Women

More women have served as governor in recent years. In 1924, Wyoming elected the first woman governor, Nellie T. Ross, who served one term. She succeeded her husband, who died in office. Also in 1924, Texans elected Miriam A. Ferguson governor. "Ma" Ferguson was a "stand-in" for her husband, Jim Ferguson, who had been impeached, removed from office, and barred from seeking reelection.

TABLE 4.1		
Previous Public Office Experience of Texas Governors, 1949–2014		
Governor	**Term of Office**	**Previous Offices**
Allan Shivers	1949–57	State senate, lieutenant governor
Price Daniel	1957–63	U.S. Senate
John Connally	1963–69	U.S. Secretary of the Navy[*]
Preston Smith	1969–73	Texas House and Senate, lieutenant governor
Dolph Briscoe	1973–79	Texas House
Bill Clements	1979–83 1987–91	Assistant Secretary of Defense[*]
Mark White	1983–87	Attorney General
Ann Richards	1991–1994	County office, state treasurer
George W. Bush	1995–2001	None
Rick Perry	2001–2014	State legislature, agricultural commission, and lieutenant governor
Greg Abbott	2015–	Attorney General, Texas Supreme Court Jurist

[*]Appointed offices. No electoral experience before becoming governor.

Source: James Anderson, Richard W. Murray, and Edward L. Farley, *Texas Politics: An Introduction*, 6th ed. (New York: HarperCollins, 1992), 166–188.

Mrs. Ferguson was reelected in 1932. Similarly, in 1968, Lurleen Wallace was elected governor of Alabama as a stand-in governor for her husband, George Wallace, who could not be reelected because of term limits. Although Ferguson and Wallace were stand-in governors for husbands ineligible for reelection, several women have been elected in their own right. Aside from Ferguson, Texas has had one other female governor: Ann Richards. She was elected in 1990 and served from 1991 to 1995.

As of 2014, 27 states have elected a total of 36 women as governor (see Map 4.1).[2] Arizona is the first state where three women have held the office in succession. The number of women serving as governor will undoubtedly increase. As of this writing, 5 women are serving as governors, 11 women are serving as lieutenant governors, and 56 women are serving in other statewide elected offices.[3] For women as well as men, service in statewide office is a good stepping-stone to the governor's office.

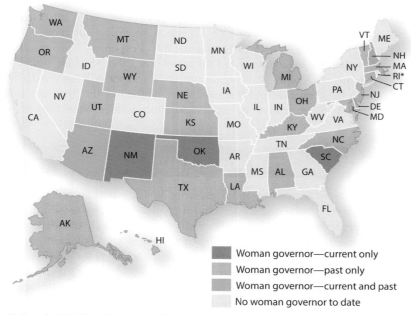

Woman governor—current only
Woman governor—past only
Woman governor—current and past
No woman governor to date

* In November 2014, Rhode Island elected its first female Governer, Gina Raimando [D].

MAP 4.1   Women Governors

CORE OBJECTIVE

Communicating Effectively...
Analyze Map 4.1. What inferences can be drawn from the data?

Wealth

Historically, the men who have served as governor of Texas have generally had one thing in common—wealth. A few, such as Dolph Briscoe and Bill Clements, were very wealthy. If not wealthy, most have been successful in law, business, or politics before becoming governor. Ann Richards was something of an exception to these informal qualifications. She was not wealthy nor from a wealthy family, and she had no business or law experience. Governor Bush is an example of past governors in terms of background, with a famous family name and family wealth. Governor Perry, while claiming the status of a sharecropper's son, came from a family with a moderate, middle-class background.

Salary

Nationwide, governors receive much higher pay than state legislators. As of 2010, salaries ranged from a low of $70,000 in Maine to a high of $179,000 in New York. The Texas salary of $150,000 per year is above the mean salary of $90,000 in 2010.[4] In addition, Texas also provides the governor with a home in Austin, an automobile with a driver, an airplane, and reimbursement for actual travel expenses. Texas governors also receive a budget for entertaining and for maintaining the governor's mansion. Compared with members of the state legislature, the governor in Texas is extremely well paid. Given the demands and responsibilities of the job, the governor is not overpaid compared with executives of large corporations who earn much more.

Succession to Office and Acting Governor

Most states provide for a successor if the governor dies or leaves office. In 43 states, lieutenant governors advance to the office if it is vacant for any reason. In the 7 states without lieutenant governors, another officeholder, usually the leader of the state senate, succeeds to the governor's office. In 19 states, the lieutenant governor and the governor are separately elected. In 24 states, the governor and lieutenant governor are jointly elected. They run as a "team," much as candidates for president and vice president do. In these cases, the candidate for governor picks the lieutenant governor. In Texas, the lieutenant governor becomes governor if the office is vacated. Following the lieutenant governor, the order of succession is as follows: president pro tempore of the Texas Senate, the speaker of the house, and the attorney general. In the unlikely event that the attorney general is no longer able to discharge the duties of governor, the Texas Constitution stipulates that succession follows the chief justices of the Court of Appeals in ascending order.

acting governor
When a governor leaves a state, the position is held by the lieutenant governor, who performs the functions of the office

When governors leave their states, lieutenant governors become **acting governors**. Sometimes problems arise with this arrangement. For instance, in 1995, Arkansas Governor Jim Guy Tucker had problems with Senate President Pro Tem Jerry Jewell, who was acting as governor in the absence of the lieutenant governor. Jewell "granted two pardons and executive clemency to two prison inmates."[5] Also, the Arkansas lieutenant governor, Republican Mike Huckabee, "signed a proclamation for a Christian Heritage Week after Tucker declined to do so earlier."[6]

In Texas, Governor Rick Perry may hold the record as serving the most time as acting governor when Governor George W. Bush was campaigning for president outside the state. When serving as acting governor, the lieutenant governor in

Texas receives the same pay as the governor. Lieutenant Governor David Dewherst also served as acting governor for a great deal of time while Governor Perry was out of state running for the Republican presidential nomination in 2012.

Postgubernatorial Office

For some governors, the office is a stepping-stone to other offices. Some go on to the U.S. Senate, and several have been elected President of the United States. In Texas, former governor W. Lee O'Daniel served as U.S. senator from 1941 to 1949, and George W. Bush became president in 2001. Postgubernatorial administrative service in the federal government is also common. Presidents often call upon former governors to head departments. President George H. W. Bush chose former New Hampshire governor John Sununu as his chief of staff. Bill Clinton chose Bruce Babbitt, former governor of Arizona, as secretary of the interior and he also appointed former Governor Richard Riley of South Carolina as secretary of education. Former Texas governor John Connally served as secretary of the treasury under President Richard Nixon. President George W. Bush selected several governors to be in his cabinet, as did President Barack Obama. However, for most governors (64 percent nationwide), the office is the peak of their political careers and they retire to private life.[7] This statistic is true for most Texas governors. George W. Bush was the first Texas governor since 1941 to go on to higher elected office.

James E. Ferguson [D] was the 26th Governor of Texas for three years until his impeachment in 1917. He tried to regain the governorship in 1918 but lost in the Democratic primary to William P. Hobby.

Removal from Office

All states except Oregon have a procedure for removing governors by a process generally called impeachment. Technically, the lower house of the legislature adopts articles of impeachment, and then a trial on these articles of impeachment is held in the senate. If the senate finds the governor guilty by a two-thirds vote, he or she is removed from office. Together the two steps—the adoption of articles of **impeachment** and **conviction** by the senate—are commonly called impeachment. Sixteen U.S. governors have had impeachment trials, and eight have been removed from office.[8] Technically, impeachment is a judicial process, but it is also a very political process. Impeached governors have generally been guilty of some wrongdoing, but they are often removed for political reasons.

Four impeachments illustrate the highly political nature of the process. Governor Jim Ferguson of Texas (1915–1917) is one example. Ferguson was indicted by the Texas House, technically for misuse of state funds, and was convicted and removed from office by the senate. In reality he was impeached because of his fight with the University of Texas board of regents. When Ferguson could not force the board of regents to terminate several professors who had been critical of him or force the resignation of board members, he used his line-item veto authority to veto the entire appropriations bill for the University of Texas.[9] This veto led to his impeachment. Ferguson tried to prevent his impeachment by calling the legislature into special session. Because only the governor may decide the agenda of a special session, Governor Ferguson told the legislature it could consider any item it wanted, except impeachment. This ploy did not work, and he was removed from office. Courts later upheld Ferguson's impeachment.

A few years after the Ferguson affair in Texas, Oklahoma impeached two consecutively elected governors. These two impeachments were as political as the one

impeachment

The process by which some elected officials, including governors, may be impeached (accused of an impeachable offense) by the lower house adopting articles of impeachment

conviction

Following adoption of articles of impeachment by the lower legislative house, the senate tries the official under those articles; if convicted, the official is removed from office in Texas. In 1921, many African Americans were killed in several race riots. The most noted of these occurred in the Greenwood area of Tulsa, Oklahoma. Thirty-five square blocks of this segregated African American community were burned and destroyed and more than 40 people were killed. The next year, John C. Walton was elected governor as a member of the Farmer-Laborite party. Walton tried to break up the Ku Klux Klan in the state, and this led to his impeachment. The lieutenant governor, Martin Trapp, served out the remainder of Walton's term but was unable to run for reelection because Oklahoma had a one-term limit at that time. Henry S. Johnson was elected governor in 1926 as a pro-KKK candidate and refused to use his office to quell Klan activity in the state. Johnson used the National Guard to try to prevent the legislature from meeting to consider his impeachment. The legislature was kept out of the state capitol building and had to meet in a hotel in Oklahoma City. Johnson was convicted and removed from office. He had been indicted on 18 counts and found not guilty on all charges but one—"general incompetence"—for which he was impeached.[10]

The impeachment of Evan Mecham in Arizona in 1988 was equally political. Mecham made a number of racist remarks and had become a source of embarrassment in the state. Technically, he was impeached for misuse of state funds during his inaugural celebration. All these governors had technically committed some malfeasance of office, but they were impeached for political reasons.

recall
The removal of the governor or an elected official by a petition signed by the required number of registered voters and by an election in which a majority votes to remove the person from office

Fifteen states also allow **recall** of the governor; Texas does not. Many Texas home-rule cities do allow recall of city councils and mayors. Recall involves having petitions signed by a specific number of voters, followed by an election where, if a majority approves, the governor can be recalled or removed from office. Two governors have been recalled. Lynn J. Frazier of North Dakota was recalled in 1921, the same time when governors were being impeached in Texas and Oklahoma. In 1988, Governor Mecham of Arizona was spared a recall election when impeached by the legislature.[11] In 2003, Gray Davis of California was recalled. With so few examples of recall, it is impossible to make any generalizations on the politics of recall. In 2011, the voters of Wisconsin voted against recalling Governor Scott Walker. More than 60 percent of voters did not like the idea of using a recall to remove a governor.

Formal Powers of the Governor

Most governors do not have extensive formal powers. The formal powers of the office of governor can be measured using six variables: election of other statewide executives, tenure of office, appointment powers, budgetary powers, veto powers, and control over party. By examining each of these variables, we can compare the formal powers of governors and, more specifically, assess the powers of the Texas governor.

Election of Other Statewide Executives

plural executive system
System in which executive power is divided among several statewide elected officials

The ability of the Texas governor to control administrative functions through formal appointive and removal powers is exceptionally weak. The voters elect many important state administrators. Texas is, therefore, a good example of the **plural executive system** structure. Map 4.2 provides a comparison of the number of elected executive officials in all states. Texas voters elect the lieutenant governor (discussed in Chapter 3), attorney general, comptroller of public accounts, state land commissioner, agricultural commissioner, the railroad commission, and the state board of education.

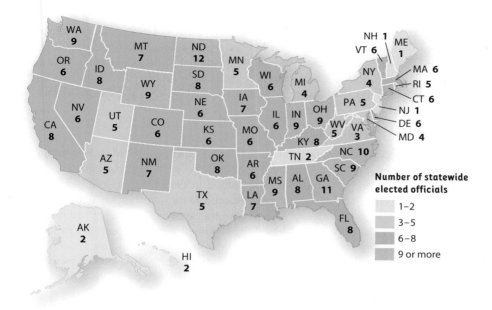

MAP 4.2　**Total Number of Statewide Elected Officials for Each State, Executive Branch**

The election of people to head administrative units of government is a concept dating to the 1820s with the election of Andrew Jackson. Known as Jacksonian statehouse government, the belief is that the ballot box is the best way to select administrators and make them accountable to the public. In the aftermath of Reconstruction in the 1870s, the current constitution reintroduced the idea of electing almost all officeholders and limiting the governor's ability to appoint them.

Office of the Attorney General

This office was created under the 1876 Texas constitution. The **attorney general** serves as the legal counsel to the governor, the legislature, and most of the other agencies, boards, and commissions in state government. Most of the work of the attorney general involves civil law rather than criminal law. The attorney general's office, with some 3,700 state employees, is responsible for representing the state in litigation, enforcing state and federal child support laws, providing legal counsel to state officials, and enforcing state laws. Criminal functions of the office are primarily limited to those cases appealed to federal courts. The most common examples of these criminal cases are death penalty appeals. Occasionally, the attorney general's office may assist local criminal prosecutors when invited to do so. Although the functions of the attorney general are usually civil and not criminal in nature, this does not prevent most candidates who run for the office from emphasizing their commitment to law enforcement and being tough on criminals.

Most of the resources of this office are devoted to collection of child support payments, collection of delinquent state taxes, administration of the Crime Victims' Compensation program, and investigation of Medicare fraud. Despite this rather mundane list of functions, the office has important political functions. The most important of these is to issue so-called AG (attorney general) opinions on legal questions. Often when the legislature is in session, the AG will be asked for an opinion on a pending piece of legislation. These AG opinions can have an impact on the course of legislation. Often, a negative AG opinion will kill a bill's chances of passing.

attorney general

Chief counsel to the governor and state agencies; limited criminal jurisdiction

The office of attorney general is also an important stepping-stone to the governor's office. In recent years, several candidates for governor have been former attorneys general (John Hill, Mark White, Jim Mattox and most recently Greg Abbott). Dan Morales was the first Mexican American to be elected to the office. He did not seek reelection in 1998, and in 2002 he ran and lost a bid to become the Democratic Party nominee for governor. John Cornyn, the AG from 1998 to 2002, was elected to the U.S. Senate in 2002.

Comptroller of Public Accounts

comptroller of public accounts
Chief tax collector and investor of state funds; does not perform financial audits

Another constitutional office created in 1876, the **comptroller of public accounts** has been assigned many additional duties over the years and currently functions as the chief fiscal and revenue forecasting office. In 1966, the office of treasurer was abolished, and the comptroller became responsible for investing state funds.

In many states and in the private sector, the term is "controller," rather than "comptroller" as used in Texas. Generally, in government the controller has a pre-audit responsibility for ensuring that funds can be spent for specific functions. In Texas, the comptroller not only has the preaudit responsibility but also serves as the chief tax collector (a function normally associated with the office of treasurer), revenue forecaster, and investor of state funds.

The comptroller is responsible for collecting 31 taxes for the state and collects the sales tax for some 1,169 local governments (1,018 cities, 117 counties, and 34 special districts).[12] The property tax division also conducts annual audits of property appraisal districts in the state to ensure uniformity in appraisals. This uniformity is important to improve the equity of state aid to local school districts. (See Chapter 6 on local government.)

Former governor Bob Bullock served as comptroller for many years. During his tenure, the office expanded the information and management functions and developed a fiscal forecasting model essential to projecting revenues in a two-year budget cycle. John Sharp, who succeeded Bullock as comptroller, continued and expanded the information management programs of the office. Also under Sharp, the office developed the Texas Performance Review teams to evaluate the effectiveness of government operations and ensure the most efficient use of state funds. These reviews were estimated to have saved the state more than $1.3 billion in the 1998–1999 biennium fiscal years. Similar management information and efficiency audits are available to assist local governments. Most of these programs were kept in place by Sharp's successor, Carole Keeton Strayhorn (1999–2007), and Susan Combs (2007–2015).

The office also provides assistance to the private sector through the provision of information. The State of Texas Econometric Model is used to forecast state economic growth, keep track of business cycles, and generally provide information on the health of the economy of the state. Finally, the office is responsible for investing state funds. This involves investing and securing fund balances that average $8.6 billion during the year.[13]

CORE OBJECTIVE

Being Socially Responsible...

How does the comptroller promote effective involvement in regional, national, and global communities?

Commissioner of the General Land Office

Texas is one of only four states to have a **land commissioner**.[14] In Texas, the office was created under the 1836 constitution to administer state-owned land. When Texas entered the Union in 1845, the agreement between the former republic and the U.S. government was that Texas kept its public debt and its public land. When Texas became a state, most of the land was state owned. Today the state of Texas owns and manages 20.3 million acres, including open beaches and submerged land 10.3 miles into the Gulf of Mexico.

The land commissioner's office is responsible for leasing state lands and generating funds from oil and gas production. The office is also responsible for overseeing the Veterans' Land Board and Veterans' Land Fund. This fund loans money to Texas veterans to purchase rural land. Finally, the land office is responsible for maintaining the environmental quality of the state's open beaches along the Gulf Coast.

land commissioner
Elected official responsible for administration and oversight of state-owned lands and coastal lands extending 10.3 miles into the Gulf of Mexico

Commissioner of Agriculture

The Texas Department of Agriculture (TDA) was created by statute in 1907. A commissioner of agriculture, elected in a statewide election, heads the department. The TDA has the dual, and sometimes contradictory, roles of promoting agricultural products and production and regulating agricultural practices, while also protecting the public health from unsafe agricultural practices. For example, the TDA must both promote cotton production and sales in the state and regulate the use of pesticides.

The TDA has six major functions: marketing of Texas agricultural products, development and promotion of agricultural products, pesticide regulation, pest management, product certification and safety inspection, and inspection and certification of measuring devices (including gasoline pumps, electronic scanners, and scales).

Although the agriculture commissioner is not as publicly visible as the other statewide elected officials, it is an important office to a large section of the state's economy—those engaged in agriculture. Texas's economy has become more diversified in recent years, but agriculture is still a significant player. Major agribusinesses and others in agriculture in the state pay close attention to who serves as the agriculture commissioner.

The Texas Railroad Commission

The **Texas Railroad Commission** (RRC) was created in 1891 under the administration of Governor James S. Hogg to regulate the railroad monopolies that had developed in the state. The commission was also given regulatory authority over terminals, wharves, and express companies. The commission consists of three members who are elected in statewide elections for six-year staggered terms, with one member elected every two years. The member up for election, by convention, always serves as chair of the commission.

In the 1920s, when oil and natural gas production developed in the state, the task of regulating the exploration, drilling, and production of oil and natural gas was assigned to the RRC in part because it was the only state regulatory agency at the time. When motor truck transport developed in the state, regulation of the trucking industry was also assigned to the RRC. In part because of federal rules and regulations, the original role of regulating railroads and the later role of regulating trucking have diminished to minor roles, reduced primarily to concern with safety issues. The regulation of the oil and gas industry is the RRC's primary function today.

Texas Railroad Commission
State agency with regulation over some aspects of transportation and the oil and gas industry of the state

Many have been critical of the RRC over the years because of close ties between the elected commissioners and the oil and gas industry they regulate. (See Chapter 10 on interest groups.) Large campaign contributions from oil and gas PACs have raised questions about the commission being co-opted by the industry it regulates. Also, like the agriculture commissioner, the RRC has the dual role of promoting oil and gas production in the state and regulating the safety and environmental aspects of the industry (for example, promoting the development of pipelines to carry petroleum products as well as overseeing the safety of such pipelines). A similar conflict may exist between the RRC's task of regulating and promoting the mining of minerals (especially lignite coal) in the state.

The role of the RRC that most directly affects citizens in the state is that of setting the rates charged by local natural gas companies. Natural gas companies must have the rates they charge residential and commercial customers approved by the RRC. The RRC also regulates the safety of natural gas systems.

It has been suggested that the name of this agency be changed to better reflect its function. As discussed in the previous session of the legislature, the present name is confusing to voters and does not reflect its functions. Some say that this voter confusion is useful to the oil industry in controlling the commission.

The State Board of Education

Unlike the other offices discussed in this section, the governing body for public elementary and secondary education in the state has varied greatly in form and structure over the years. Originally, in 1884, an elected school superintendent governed Texas schools. In 1929 an appointed state board was created. In 1949 the Gilmer-Aikin Act created the Texas Education Agency (TEA) with an appointed superintendent of education. An elected state board was added in the 1960s. In 1984 the elected board was reduced from 21 members who were elected from congressional districts in the state to 15 members appointed by the governor. In 1986 the board was again changed, and members were elected from 15 districts. The current board, called the State Board of Education, nominates a person to the governor to be commissioner of education.

In recent years, the authority of the state board has been greatly reduced by actions of the state legislature. The political battle over the power of the state board revolved around social conservatives' (Christian right) success in electing members to the board and the actions taken in setting curriculum standards and textbook selection issues. Public infighting among members of the board diminished its effectiveness. The legislature has removed several functions, most significantly the selection of textbooks, from the state board, in part because of the infighting and control by this faction. One of the main issues has been the teaching of evolution in biology classes. Some members of the board want the curriculum to reflect a creationist approach to human existence.

CORE OBJECTIVE

Taking Personal Responsibility...

What can you do to become more actively engaged in the civic discourse about the role of the State Board of Education?

Tenure of Office

Tenure of office is both the legal ability of governors to succeed themselves in office and the term length. Historically, the tenure of governors has been less than that for most other statewide elected state officials, in part because of term limits.[15] Term limits for governors have been a fixture since the beginning of the Republic. In the original 13 states, 10 of the governors had one-year terms. States first moved to two-year terms, then four-year terms. In the 1960s, states borrowed from the federal Constitution the idea of limiting governors to two four-year terms.[16] Southern states were the last to move to longer terms. Many southern states once prohibited the governor from serving consecutive terms in office. Today, only Virginia retains this provision. Map 4.3 provides a comparison of gubernatorial term limits.

Tenure is an important determinant of power. If governors can be continually reelected, they retain the potential to influence government until they decide to leave office. Only 14 states do not limit how long a person can serve as governor. When prevented from being reelected by term limits, governors suffer as "lame ducks" toward the end of their terms. Long tenure also enables governors to carry out their programs. Short terms (two years) force governors to continually seek reelection and make political compromises. Only two states retain the two-year term—Vermont and New Hampshire.

Longer tenure is also an important factor in the governor's role as intergovernmental coordinator. Building up associations with officials in other states and in Washington is important and takes time. Short tenure makes it difficult for governors to gain leadership roles in this area and has the effect of shortchanging the state that imposes them.[17]

The Texas governor has the strongest tenure—four-year terms with no limit on the number of terms. Dolph Briscoe was elected to a two-year term in 1972. In that same election, Texas changed to a four-year term, which became effective in 1975. Briscoe was reelected to serve one four-year term (1975–79). After Briscoe, governors Clements, White, and Richards were limited by voters to one term, although Clements did later regain the governorship. He served from 1970 to 1983, lost to Mark

tenure of office
The ability of governors to be reelected to office

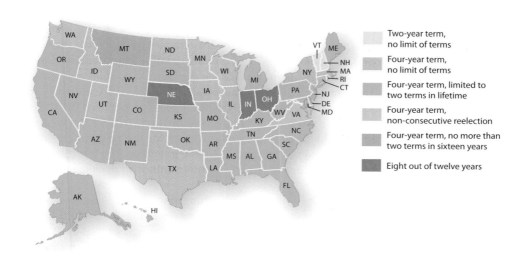

Two-year term, no limit of terms

Four-year term, no limit of terms

Four-year term, limited to two terms in lifetime

Four-year term, non-consecutive reelection

Four-year term, no more than two terms in sixteen years

Eight out of twelve years

MAP 4.3   Term Limits for Governors

White for one term, and then retook the governorship from 1987 to 1991. George W. Bush was the first governor to be elected to two consecutive four-year terms. However, Bush served only six years because he was elected president in 2000.

Few Texas governors have served more than four years in office. Since 1874, 19 Texas governors have served for four years; most of these (15) were for consecutive two-year terms. Seven served for two years, four served six years, and only one (Allan Shivers, 1949–57) served for eight consecutive years—four 2-year terms.[18] Bill Clements served for eight nonconsecutive years. Thus, the history of Texas governors is not one of long tenure. Serving two 2-year terms was the norm for most of the state's history. From 1874 until 1953, no person served more than four years as governor in Texas.[19]

Had Governor Bush not been elected president in 2000, he would have been the first governor to serve two consecutive four-year terms. Former Governor Perry was the first governor to be elected to three consecutive four-year terms. Upon finishing his final term in January 2015, he served a total of 14 years. As a result of Governor Perry's long tenure, many Texans are calling for gubernatorial term limits. Perry's record has been under much scrutiny, with some journalists accusing him of "crony capitalism."

Governor's Appointment Powers

If the governor can appoint and remove the heads of most state agencies, he or she can better control the administration of programs. Historically, governors have not had strong appointive powers. For most of the nineteenth century, the traditional method of selecting the heads of state agencies was by election. This is called Jacksonian statehouse democracy. President Andrew Jackson expressed ultimate faith in the ballot box for selecting administrators. Toward the end of the nineteenth century, there was a proliferation of agencies headed by appointed or elected boards and commissions. The governor was just one of many elected state officials and had little formal control over state administration.[20] Governors often share power with many other elected individuals. Such arrangements are known as plural executive structures. Figure 4.1 is a diagram of the administrative structure of the Texas state government and is divided into three categories: statewide elected offices, single-head agencies appointed by the governor, and boards and commissions appointed by the governor.

Equally important to the appointive power is the power to remove administrators, which is discussed in a later section of this chapter. Without the power of removal, the appointive powers of the governor are greatly diminished. Beginning in the early twentieth century, the powers of the governor to appoint and remove officials were increased in some states. This expansion of executive authority has increased in the past three decades in many states.[21] This has not been the pattern for much of the South or for the office of governor in Texas. In 2001 the voters in Texas even rejected an amendment that would have made the adjutant general of the Texas National Guard subject to removal by the governor. The traditionalistic culture does not support the idea of strong executive authority, even for relatively minor offices.

Of the 172 agencies in the Texas, the governor appoints a few agency heads; the most significant is the secretary of state, who serves as the chief record keeper and election official for the state. The governor also appoints the executive directors of the departments of Commerce, Health and Human Services, Housing and Community Affairs, and Insurance, the Office of State-Federal Relations, and the Fire Fighters' Pension Commission. The governor appoints the head of the Texas

VOTERS IN STATE ELECT	GOVERNOR APPOINTS		
	Agency Heads	Boards and Commissions	
Lieutenant Governor	Secretary of State	General Government	Licensing and Professional Examining Boards
Attorney General	Adjutant General of the National Guard	Health and Human Services	Public Safety and Criminal Justice
Comptroller of Public Accounts	Director of Housing and Community Affairs	Higher Education Boards of Regents	Natural Resources
Commissioner of the General Land Office	Director of Office of State-Federal Relations	Other Education	Employee Retirement Boards
Commissioner of Agriculture	Executive Director of Texas Education Agency	Business Regulation	Interstate Compact Commissions
Railroad Commission (three members)	Commissioner for Health and Human Services	Business and Economic Development	Water and River Authorities
State Board of Education (fifteen members)	Eight other minor agencies	Regional Economic Development	Judicial

FIGURE 4.1   **The Administrative Structure of State Government in Texas**

National Guard and appoints the executive director of the Texas Education Agency from recommendations made by the elected Texas State Board of Education. The governor also appoints the chief counsels for the Public Utility Commission, the Insurance Commission, and the State Office of Administrative Hearings.

Thus, significant portions of state government are beyond the direct control of the governor because several agency heads are elected. In terms of numbers, most agencies are controlled by independent boards and commissions over which the governor has minimal direct control. These independent state agencies are usually governed by three-, six-, or nine-member boards or commissions appointed by the governor for six-year, overlapping, staggered terms. Usually, one-third of the membership is appointed every two years. In total, the number of governing and policy-making positions filled by gubernatorial appointment is about 2,800.[22] If the governor stays in office for two terms (eight years), she or he will have appointed all members of these agencies and boards and can have indirect influence over them (see Table 4.2). The governing board chooses the heads of these agencies. A good example of this is the president of a state university, who is selected by the board of regents, whose members are appointed by the governor. The governor often exercises influence with his or her appointees on the board of regents. In 2002, it was rumored that Governor Perry strongly supported the selection of retiring Senator Phil Gramm for president of Texas A&M University. All of Governor Perry's appointees supported Gramm. (Although Phil Gramm was not appointed president of Texas A&M, his wife Wendy, an accomplished academic in her own right, was appointed to the A&M Board of Regents, and she served from 2001 to 2005.[23])

The governor also appoints a number of persons to non-policy-making and governing boards that make recommendations to the governor or other state officials. These boards are not discussed in detail in this chapter. However, many of these non-policy-making boards recommend changes in policy and programs. Others are simply window dressing and allow the governor to reward supporters. Most often, these non-policy-making boards do not require senate approval.

TABLE 4.2

Texas Governor Appointments to Policy-Making and Governing Boards, Commissions, and Agencies

Type of Agency	Number of Agencies	Number of Appointees
General Government	31	244
Health and Human Services	31	366
Higher Education Boards and Regents	12	117
Other Education	16	149
Business Regulation	9	37
Business and Economic Development	24	176
Regional Economic Development	32	276
Licensing and Professional Examining Boards	39	461
Public Safety and Criminal Justice	22	158
Natural Resources	16	156
Employee Retirement Boards	8	53
Interstate Compact Commissions	8	24
Water and River Authorities	18	210
Judicial	18	151
Others	18	251
Totals	302	2,838

Source: Data supplied by the Texas State Governor's Appointment Secretary, Freedom of Information Request, August 2000. Categories for state agencies are by the author. List can be obtained from Governor's Appointment Secretary, State Capitol, Austin, TX (updates to 2010).

senatorial courtesy

The courtesy of the governor clearing his or her appointments with state senator from the appointee's home district

Some gubernatorial appointments are subject to approval by a two-thirds vote of the senate. In these cases, the governor must clear his or her appointments with the state senator from the appointee's home district. This limits the discretion of the governor. This process is known as **senatorial courtesy**. If the senator from an appointee's home district disapproves of the appointment, the senate might not confirm the appointee. Senatorial courtesy does not apply to all gubernatorial appointments, especially the non-policy-making boards.

The discretion of the governor is also limited by other factors. For example, some boards require geographic representation. Members of river authority boards must live in the area covered by the river authority. Good examples of this are the Trinity River Authority and the Lower Colorado River Authority. Other boards require specified professional backgrounds. Membership on the Texas Municipal Retirement Board, for instance, is limited to certain types of city employees—such as firefighters, police, and city managers.[24]

However, political limits are placed on the governor's ability to appoint people. Interest groups pay close attention to the governor's appointments to these boards and commissions and try to influence the governor's choices. The governor may have to bend to demands from such groups. Chapter 10 discusses this subject in more detail.

In Texas, the appointive power of the governor, even with these formal limitations, allows the governor to indirectly influence policy by appointing people with similar policy views to serve on these boards and commissions. It is unlikely that a governor will select men and women with whom he or she differs on major policy issues. This broad appointive power allows the governor to influence policy even after leaving office, because some of the appointees remain on these boards and commissions after the governor's term ends. Ann Richards used her appointive powers to increase the number of women and minorities serving on these boards and commissions. Richards's successor, George W. Bush, appointed some women and minorities, but tended mainly to appoint white businessmen to these positions. Governor Perry, for the most part, appoints white business leaders as well.

In some states, a single person, appointed and serving at the pleasure of the governor, heads most agencies. The structure is much like that of the federal government, where the president appoints members of his own cabinet and they serve at his pleasure. Only a handful of state agencies in Texas meet this model.

Secretary of State

The **secretary of state** (SOS) is a constitutional office, appointed by the governor with approval of the state senate. The constitution and state statutes assign many duties to this office, which can be lumped into three broad categories: elections, record keeping/information management, and international protocol. As the chief election official, the SOS is responsible for overseeing voter registration, preparation of election information, and supervision of elections. The SOS issues rules, directives, and opinions on the conduct of elections and voter registration. These duties allow the secretary some latitude in the interpretation and application of the state election code. For example, the SOS has some latitude in how vigorously he or she encourages citizens to register and vote.

A second duty of the SOS is to serve as the official keeper of state records. This includes records on business corporations and some other commercial activities. The office also publishes the *Texas Register*, which is the source of official notices or rules, meetings, executive orders, and opinions of the attorney general that are required to be filed by state agencies. Through the protocol functions of the office, the SOS provides support services to state officials who interact with representatives of foreign countries.

In a few cases, the office of secretary of state has been an important stepping-stone to higher office. It is a highly visible office, and the secretary is often in the public eye, especially with the duties as chief election official. It is without doubt the most important single-head agency appointment that the governor makes. The most noted example is Mark White, who became attorney general and later governor. Former Governor Bush picked his secretary of state to become White House counsel in his administration.

Commissioner for Health and Human Services

This office was created in 1991 to coordinate a number of health-related programs and agencies. The governor appoints the commissioner for a two-year term with the approval of the state senate. The commissioner has oversight responsibility over 11 separate health and welfare programs, which are directed by boards, councils, or commissions. The commissioner is not directly responsible for the administration of these programs but has oversight and review functions. Those programs include aging; alcohol and drug abuse; the blind, deaf, and hard-of-hearing; early childhood intervention; juvenile probation; mental health and retardation; rehabilitation; and departments of Health, Human Services, and Protective and Regulatory Services. Although this office has little direct administrative control, it can and often does have impact on policy. The commissioner serves as a spokesperson for the governor in health and welfare matters.

secretary of state
Chief election official and keeper of state records; appointed by the governor

Office of State-Federal Relations

The governor appoints the executive director of the Office of State-Federal Relations. As the name suggests, this office coordinates relations between state and federal officials. The office has existed since 1971 and is the primary liaison between the governor's office and federal officials. To some degree this office becomes an advocate for the state in dealing with the Texas congressional delegation and federal agencies.

Adjutant General of the National Guard

This office was created by the Texas Constitution and is responsible for directing the state military force under the direction of the governor. The governor serves as commander-in-chief of the guard. The **military powers** of the governor are quite limited and come into play only in times of natural disaster or civil unrest. The governor appoints the adjutant general of the National Guard and can direct the guard to protect the lives and property of Texas citizens. The most common use of this power is during natural disasters, when the guard is employed to help evacuate people, protect property, and supply food and water to victims. The size of the National Guard (nationwide and in Texas) is determined and funded by Congress as a reserve force to the regular army.

In the 1999 November election, Texas voters rejected a constitutional amendment that would have allowed the governor to appoint and remove the head of the National Guard. As with other appointees, the governor may appoint the head of the National Guard, but not remove him or her except on approval of the state senate.

military powers
Powers giving the governor the right to use the National Guard in times of natural disaster or civil unrest

Other Single-Head Agencies

The remaining state agencies to which the governor makes a single appointment are not of great significance in terms of policy or politics. This is not to say that they are insignificant, but simply of less importance. These agencies often receive little or no attention from the average citizen or the press. They include the Department of Housing and Community Affairs; Department of Commerce; State Office of Administrative Hearings; Executive Director of Health Care Information Council; Insurance Commissioner; Public Utility Commission Council; and the Fire Fighters' (volunteers) Pension Commission Executive Director. In addition, five interstate compact commissions govern the rivers in Texas. The governor appoints the executive director of each of these commissions.

Boards and Commissions

In addition to these elected and appointed officials, the governor also appoints about 2,838 members to 302 state **boards and commissions**. These administrative units carry out most of the work of state government. The board or commission usually appoints the head of the agency (e.g., chancellor of a university or executive director of a state agency) and in varying degrees is responsible for policy and administration of the agency. Most operate quite independently from other agencies of state government, except the legislature.

Given the lack of central control and the decentralized nature of state government in Texas, it is striking that things work as well as they do. For example, some 18 separate agencies provide health and welfare services. In addition to the Department of Agriculture, the General Land Office, and the Railroad Commission—all having some control over environmental and natural resources—at least seven other agencies with independent boards or commissions have some authority in

boards and commissions
Governing body for many state agencies; members appointed by the governor for fixed term

this area. These include the Texas Commission of Environmental Quality, the Texas Parks and Wildlife Department, the Soil and Water Conservation Board, and the Water Development Board.

In this conservative state with a strong belief in the free market there are, nonetheless, no fewer than 38 separate professional licensing and examining boards. Every profession likely has a state agency that licenses and regulates it. Just a few examples are accountants, architects, barbers, chiropractors, cosmetologists, dentists, exterminators, funeral directors, land surveyors, medical doctors, two kinds of nurses, pharmacists, physical therapists, podiatrists, and veterinarians. Most often a professional group asks for regulation by the state. When such a group advocates government regulation and licensing, it claims its primary interest to be protecting the public from incompetent or dishonest practitioners. This may be partially true; however, regulation also has the added benefit of the development of rules favorable to the group and limiting entry into the profession. Two good examples are the water-well drillers and landscape architects. (See Chapter 10 on interest groups.) Also, professionals always make the argument that the people appointed to the boards by the governor should be knowledgeable about the profession they are governing. Knowledge is one factor, but the danger is that these boards and commissions, dominated by members of the profession, will be more interested in making rules and regulations favorable to the group than to protect the public. Because of this fear, in recent years, the appointment of at least some members of the board from outside the profession has become the norm—for example, nonphysicians are on the State Board of Medical Examiners.

Twelve college governing boards oversee the institutions of higher education in the state. These boards are required to coordinate their activities and gain approval for some activities and programs from the State Higher Education Coordinating Board. Within these broad guidelines, each university governing board is relatively free to set policy, approve budgets, and govern their universities. Again, governance is decentralized, with only minimum control from the state and almost none from the governor.

Appointment and Campaign Contributions

Governors have also been known to appoint their campaign supporters to governing boards and commissions. People who were loyal supporters, especially those giving big campaign contributions, are often rewarded with appointment to prestigious state boards and commissions. University governing boards are especially desired positions. Listed in Table 4.3 are the contributions Governor Perry received from individuals who were appointed to state boards and commissions.

Removal Powers

The other side of the power to appoint is the power to remove persons from office. U.S. presidents may remove many of their appointees, but state governors are often very restricted by the state constitution, statutes creating the agency, or term limits set for appointees. Some states allow the governor to remove a person only for cause. This requires the governor to make a case for wrongdoing by the individual. Of course, the governor can force the resignation of a person without formal hearings, but the political cost of such forced resignations can be quite high and beyond what the governor is willing to pay.

In Texas, the removal power of the governor is very weak. Before 1981, Texas state law was silent on the issue of removal. In 1981 the constitution was amended

TABLE 4.3

Governor Rick Perry Campaign Contributions and Appointments to Boards and Commissions

Appointed Office Category (% of All Appointments)	Average Appointee Contribution	No. of Appointments	Percent Involving Donations	Total Appointee Donations
Education (12%)	$10,616	135	35%	$1,433,093
Humanities (4%)	8,316	45	44%	374,220
Natural Resources (12%)	6,410	133	42%	852,556
Insurance (1%)	6,167	15	20%	92,500
Finance (4%)	3,940	41	32%	161,527
Corrections/Security (9%)	2,673	100	22%	267,278
Other (7%)	2,171	79	27%	171,535
Housing (2%)	1,982	17	29%	7,000
Infrastructure/Transportation (3%)	1,938	39	46%	77,296
Law (7%)	1,501	78	36%	117,080
Health/Human Services (14%)	958	153	16%	146,507
Economy (6%)	840	62	26%	52,070
Licensing (18%)	559	198	25%	110,712
Retirement	248	28	29%	6,950
Total	$ 3,446	1,123	32%	$3,870,324

Source: TPJ.org "Well-appointed boards." See: (http://info.tpj.org/page_view.jsp?pageid=979)

to allow governors, with a two-thirds vote of the senate, to remove any person they personally appointed. Governors may not remove any of their predecessors' appointees. To date, no person has been formally removed from office using this procedure, but it does provide the governor with some leverage to force an appointee to resign. It might also be used to force a policy change favored by the governor. It does not, however, allow the governor to control the day-to-day administration of state government.

In 2010 Governor Perry became openly involved in the removal of some members of these appointed boards when he demanded the resignation of a member of the Texas Tech Board of Regents who was supporting his rival, Senator Kay Bailey Hutchison, in the Republican primary.

Other evidence that the governor may try to control the decisions of an appointed board occurred when Governor Perry tried to influence the appointment of the chancellor of the University of Texas system. Regents say that Perry called and suggested they support John Munford, a former state senator, over Francisco Cigarroa, a well-qualified academic.[25] Perry has also tried to influence appointments of positions at the Texas A&M system where his former chief of staff, Mike McKinney, was chancellor. These include a former president and the vice president of student affairs, General Joe Weber, a roommate of the governor while they were students at Texas A&M University.

Budgetary Powers

budgetary powers

The ability of a governor to formulate a budget, present it to the legislature, and execute or control the budget

Along with tenure of office and appointive/executive authority, **budgetary powers** are an important determinant of executive authority. Control over how money is spent is at the very heart of the policy-making process. Some writers define a budget as a statement of policy in monetary terms. If the governor can control budget formation and development (the preparation of the budget for submission to the legislature) and budget execution (deciding how money is spent), the governor can have a significant influence on state policy. Four kinds of constraints can undercut the governor's budgetary authority:

- The extent to which the governor must share budget formation with the legislature or with other state agencies
- The extent to which funds are earmarked for specific expenditures and the choice on how to spend money is limited by previous actions
- The extent to which the governor shares budget execution authority with others in state government
- The limits on the governor's use of a line-item veto for the budget

In 40 U.S. states, the governor is given "full" authority over budget formation and development.[26] In those states where the governor is given authority for budget formation, agencies must present their requests for expenditures to the governor's office, which combines them and presents a unified budget to the legislature. In some states, the governor is limited regarding how much he or she can reduce the budget requests of some state agencies. If the governor can change the requests of agencies, this gives him or her tremendous control over the final form of the budget submitted to the legislature. A common practice of state governments is to earmark revenue for specific purposes. For example, funds received through the gasoline tax are commonly earmarked for state highways. This also limits the discretion of the governor.

Budget execution authority is more complex. Governors and others control budget execution in a variety of ways. If the governor controls the appointment of the major department heads of state government, he or she will have some discretion in how money is spent. The governor may decide not to spend all the money appropriated for a state park, for example. Administrative discretion over how money is spent is a time-honored way to expand executive authority over the budget.

Another area where governors can often exercise control over budgets is veto authority. All but seven U.S. governors have a **line-item veto** that allows them to exercise great influence over the budgetary process.[27]

In Texas the governor's budgetary powers are exceptionally weak, except in the area of the line-item veto. The governor is not constitutionally mandated to submit a budget. This power is given to the **Legislative Budget Board** (LBB), an agency governed by the speaker of the house and the lieutenant governor. State agencies must present budget requests to the LBB, and the LBB produces a budget that is submitted to the legislature. Historically, governors have submitted budget messages to the legislature, often in the form of reactions to the LBB proposed budget.

In Texas many funds are earmarked by the previous actions of the legislature. One estimate from the LBB is that more than 80 percent of all funds are earmarked for specific expenditures, such as highways, teachers' retirement, parks, and schools. This will be discussed in Chapter 12.

The Texas governor has very limited authority over budget execution. Outside the governor's immediate office, control over the budget rests with other state agencies over which the governor has little or no control. Only in cases of fiscal crisis can the governor exercise any influence. A constitutional amendment approved in 1985 created the Budget Execution Committee, composed of the governor, the lieutenant governor, the comptroller, the speaker of the house, and chairs of the finance and appropriations committees in the senate and house. The Budget

line-item veto
The ability of a governor to veto part of an appropriations bill without vetoing the whole bill

Legislative Budget Board
State agency that is controlled by the leadership in the state legislature and that writes the state budget

Execution Committee can exercise restraints over the budget if there is a fiscal crisis, such as a shortfall in projected revenue.

The one area where the Texas governor does have influence over budget decisions is the line-item veto. The governor can veto part of the appropriations bill without vetoing the entire bill. The legislature determines what a line item is. It can be a department within an agency, or the entire agency. For example, Governor Clements once vetoed the line items appropriating money to operate the systems administration offices of the University of Texas and Texas A&M University. He did not veto all money appropriated to these schools, just the funds for the operation of the systems offices. The governor might line-item veto money for a state park without having to veto the money for all state parks.

The legislature can override this veto by a two-thirds vote of each house. However, as we saw in Chapter 3, appropriations bills generally pass in the last days of the session, so the legislature has adjourned by the time the governor vetoes items. Because the legislature cannot call itself back into session ("extraordinary" sessions), overriding a line-item veto is impossible. The governor may call special sessions, but he or she controls the agenda. If the governor thought there was a chance of a veto override, this would not be included in the agenda of the special session.

Thus, the line-item veto is a very important power possessed by the Texas governor, but more important than the actual veto is the threat of a veto. Historically, governors have used this threat to discipline the legislature. It is not uncommon for the governor to threaten to veto a local line item, such as an item creating a new state park in a legislator's district. This threat to veto local appropriations can be used to gain legislative support for items important to the governor but unrelated to the park. It should be noted that typically governors do not veto many bills. Although exceptions occasionally occur, as a general rule, threats are more important than the actual veto.

Nationally, the U.S. Congress granted the president of the United States a limited line-item veto. The U.S. Supreme Court declared this act unconstitutional. Although many have advocated that the president needs the line-item veto to control congressional spending, a constitutional amendment will be required to grant this power. If this happens, presidents might use the threat of veto to control members of Congress and gain their support for other programs.

Legislative Powers

legislative power
The formal power, especially the veto authority, of the governor to force the legislature to enact his or her legislation

The line-item veto can be viewed as a budgetary power, but it is also a **legislative power**. There are also other types of vetoes. All governors possess some form of veto authority, but this varies among the states. (See Table 4.4.) Forty-three states have formalized **partial vetoes**, where the legislature can recall a bill from the governor so that objections raised by the governor can be changed and a veto avoided.[28] Texas does not have a formal partial veto process; however, the governor can still state objections to a bill before it is passed and thus seek to effect changes in legislation. Formalizing the process would shift some power to the office of governor and give the governor more say in the legislative process.

partial veto
The ability of some governors to veto part of a nonappropriations bill without vetoing the entire bill; a Texas governor does not have this power except on appropriations bills.

Requirements for overriding a governor's veto also vary widely among the states. Most states require a two-thirds vote to override, although a few allow a simple majority.[29] In Texas, the governor has very strong veto authority. The office possesses a general veto and line-item veto, with a two-thirds vote of each house required for override. Very few vetoes have been overturned. From 1876 to 1968, only 25 of 936 vetoes were overridden in the legislature. Most of these

TABLE 4.4	
Veto Authority of State Governors with Override Provisions	
Type of Veto	**No. of Governors**
General veto and item veto: two-thirds legislative majority needed to override	37
General veto and item veto: simple legislative majority needed to override	6
General veto, no item veto: special legislative majority to override[*]	6
General veto, no item veto: simple legislative majority to override	1

[*]Most common is three-fifths vote. Not all occurred by three-fifths vote, so depending on the precise method, the data changes slightly.

Source: Thad L. Beyle, "Governors: The Middlemen and Women in Our Political System," in *Politics in the American States,* 8th ed., eds. Virginia Gray and Russell L. Hanson. Washington D.C.: Congressional Quarterly Press, 2004.

vetoes occurred before 1940. This low number of veto overrides is primarily due to late passage of bills and adjournment of the legislature. Only one veto has been overturned in recent years, and it was not a significant bill. In 1979, during his first term, Bill Clements vetoed 52 bills. The legislature, in an attempt to catch the governor's attention, overrode the veto on a bill that limited the ability of county governments to prohibit hunters from killing female deer.[30] Since 1979, no vetoes have been overridden by the legislature.

In 15 other states besides Texas, the legislature may not call a "special" session. These are usually called *extraordinary sessions* to distinguish them from *special sessions,* which are called by the governor. States where the legislature cannot call extraordinary sessions add to the power of the governor to veto bills. In the 2001 session of the Texas legislature, Governor Perry set a new record by vetoing 82 bills. If the Texas legislature could have called an extraordinary session, there is little doubt that it would have happened and that some vetoes would have been overridden.

Thus, the veto authority of the Texas governor is significant. Accomplishing a two-thirds override (in both house and senate) is very difficult. If the legislature has adjourned, it is impossible. For these reasons, there have been few overrides.

Some governors have a pocket veto, meaning that they can veto a bill by not signing it. The governor just "puts the bill in a pocket" and forgets about it. The Texas governor does not have a pocket veto. If the legislature is in session, the governor has 10 days to sign a bill or it becomes law without his or her signature. If the legislature has adjourned, the governor has 20 days to sign a bill or it becomes law without a signature. Sometimes governors do not like a bill but do not want to veto it. Letting the bill become law without a signature can be a way of expressing displeasure short of an actual veto.

In recent years, some U.S. governors have used the line-item veto to eliminate more than a line item in the appropriations bill. In Arizona, the Republican-controlled legislature twice sued Democratic governor Janet Napolitano, claiming that she misused her line-item veto authority. The most recent case involved Napolitano's veto of a bill involving a state employee pay plan. The governor vetoed a section of the bill that exempted employees making more than $47,758 from the state merit pay plan. The Republicans contend that this is a misuse of her constitutional authority.

Governor's Control over Party

Governors are expected to be leaders of their political party and in most states are recognized as such. In the one-party era in Texas, the Democratic candidate for governor picked the state party chair and controlled the state party organization. Often such control was based on a personal following rather than a well-organized party structure. Governor Bill Clements, a Republican, made use of his election to build the party in the state, especially during his second term. He managed enough control over the Republican Party and its elected house members to thwart Democratic control of the legislature on some issues.

Today, governors might influence the choice of party leadership, but they do not control the party. George W. Bush found himself in the uncomfortable position of having to work with a state party chair chosen by the social conservatives. Governor Bush would probably have made a different choice for party chair. He did not attend the meeting of the Republican Party convention in 2000. He claimed to be very busy campaigning for president. This may have been the first time a sitting governor did not attend his or her state's party convention. It indicated the level of disagreement between the governor and the party leaders. As the two-party system matures in Texas, party leadership by the governor will have to become more of a fixture in state politics. Except when he was in a primary election with a tough opponent, Governor Perry did not embraced the social conservatives' program or the party platform, in part because of personal beliefs and in part because it is a popular idea in the state.

Administrative Agencies of State Government

In addition to the office of governor, a number of state agencies make up what might be called the state bureaucracy. The term *bureaucracy* often implies a hierarchy of offices with levels of power leading to a centralized controlling authority. This term does not describe the overall structure of state government in Texas, because there is no overall central governing, controlling authority. Government authority in Texas is very decentralized and resides within many independent state agencies. In addition, many independent boards, commissions, and agencies operate independently of the governor. Power is decentralized among many officials. This decentralized structure of power is in keeping with the traditionalistic and individualistic political culture of the state.

State Employees

Most of the funds appropriated by the state legislature go to pay for personnel. This is the largest single expenditure for all state governments. Figure 4.2 shows a breakdown of the four largest state agencies by total number of employees. Texas has no general civil service system or central personnel agency. Each agency creates its own set of rules and regulations regarding personnel practices and procedures. Most states, however, have a central personnel system and some form of civil service system that formulates personnel policies and procedures. In keeping with the decentralized nature of state government, the personnel system in Texas is also decentralized. Approximately 76 percent of Texas state employees work in the five major functional areas of state government: corrections, highways, public welfare, hospitals, and higher education.

The number of state employees has declined slightly in recent years due in part to the performance review audits conducted by Comptroller John Sharp. Among the 15 most populous states, Texas ranks tenth in the number of state

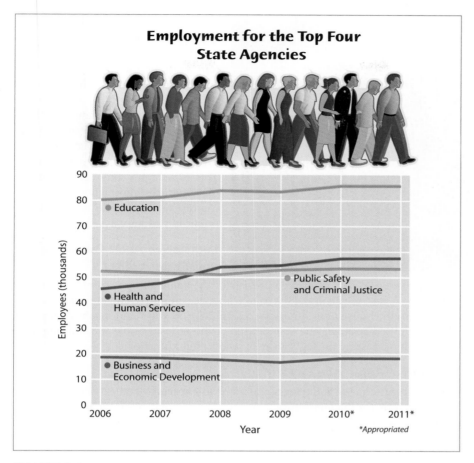

FIGURE 4.2   Employment for the Top Four State Agencies Largest State Agencies. Among the 15 most populous states, Texas ranks tenth in the number of state employees per 10,000 population. Still, the state of Texas is the largest single employer in Texas.

employees per 10,000 population. Still, the state of Texas is the largest single employer in Texas.

Legislative Agencies

In addition to the executive agencies, there are also several legislative agencies. These are units controlled by the leadership in the Texas House and Senate. Their purpose is to provide legislative oversight of the executive agencies and to assist the legislature in its lawmaking functions.

Legislative Budget Board

The Legislative Budget Board (LBB) is primarily responsible for preparing the state budget. It is composed of the lieutenant governor, the speaker of the house, four senators, and four representatives. All agencies that receive state funds from the state budget must submit their requests for appropriations to the LBB. The LBB reviews these requests and proposes a budget to the state legislature. Unlike most other states, in Texas the governor plays a very limited role in budgeting.

The Texas Legislative Reference Library was originally created in 1909 as the Legislative Reference Division of the Texas State Library. In 1969, the Reference Division was separated out into its own library directly under the authority of the Texas Legislature. The Library houses an extensive collection of print and online media, including documents going back to the1850s.

Texas Legislative Council

The speaker of the house, the lieutenant governor, four senators, and four state representatives control this agency and appoint the executive director. The agency was created in 1949 to assist the legislature in drafting bills, conducting research on legislation, producing publications, and providing technical support services. This is a highly professional agency that produces information for the legislature, which is made available to the public in various ways.

Legislative Audit Committee and State Auditor's Office

The Legislative Audit Committee consists of the lieutenant governor, the speaker of the house, and the chairs of the senate finance committee and state affairs committee, and the house appropriations committee and ways and means committee. This committee appoints the state auditor, who is responsible for auditing state agencies and assisting the legislature in its oversight functions.

Legislative Reference Library

This organization assists the legislature in doing research and serves as a depository of records for the legislature. Located in the state capitol, the library is open to other state agencies and members of the public also engaged in legislative research.

Judicial Agencies

Several agencies, which can be called judicial agencies, are under the supervision of the state supreme court (civil matters). Except for budgeting of money by the legislature, these agencies are relatively free of legislative oversight. The state bar, which licenses attorneys, receives no state appropriations. The remaining agencies are responsible for court administration (Office of Court Administration), operations of the state law library, and certification of legal licenses and specializations.

Judicial Powers

judicial powers
The ability of a governor to issue pardons, executive clemency, and parole of citizens convicted of a crime

Governors are also given limited **judicial powers** to grant pardons, executive clemency, and parole. Historically, governors have misused this power. This has led to the creation of some checks on governors' ability to exercise this authority. In Texas, James "Pa" Ferguson was accused of misusing this power, especially during the second term of his wife, "Ma" Ferguson (1933–35). It was charged that Jim Ferguson sold pardons and paroles to convicted felons.[31] These charges led to the creation of the state pardons and paroles board. Today this eighteen-member board, appointed by the governor, recommends the action the governor can take in such matters and serves as a check on the process. Independent of board action, the governor may grant only one 30-day stay of execution for any condemned prisoner. This board must recommend all other actions by the governor.

In the Fergusons' defense, many of the pardons were given to people who were in prison because they had violated the Prohibition laws. Former Lt. Governor Hobby put it this way: "Prohibition's laws filled the prisons and ruined lives . . . The Fergusons may have rightly concluded that the state was better served by these men . . . supporting their families." [32]

In 2010, Governor Haley Barber of Mississippi attracted national attention by pardoning some 200 individuals as he was leaving office. This has led to much discussion about limiting a governor's power to pardon.

Ex Officio Boards and Commissions

A number of state agencies are headed by boards whose membership is completely or partially made up of designated state officials who are members because of the position they hold. Examples of these officials are the statewide elected officials—governor, lieutenant governor, speaker of the house, attorney general, and land commissioner. Examples of these agencies are the Bond Review Board, the Legislative Redistricting Board, and the Budget Execution Committee.

Multi-Appointment Boards

Finally, some state agencies have governing boards whose members are appointed by more than one elected official. This is to prevent any one individual from dominating the selection process and the outcome of decisions. An example of such an agency is the Texas Ethics Commission, which has four members appointed by the governor, two by the lieutenant governor, and two by the speaker of the house, and which oversees campaign contributions and lobbying activities.

Democratic Control and Bureaucratic Responsiveness

The concept of democratic control requires that state agencies be responsible to the people—that is, that state agencies respond to demands placed on them by citizens. With Texas state administrative agencies operating quite independently of each other, and overall administrative control being absent from state government, agencies are often able to respond only to clientele groups they serve and not the public generally. (See Chapter 10 on interest groups for a more complete discussion of agency capture.)

In other states, accountability in a more general sense is ensured by giving the governor broader power to appoint agency heads (rather than independent boards and commissions) who serve at the pleasure of the governor. Also, some states have given the governor broad budgetary control over state agencies. Agencies are required to submit budget requests to the governor, who produces a state budget that is submitted to the state legislature. As discussed previously, in Texas the governor plays almost no role in the budgetary process; the Legislative Budget Board performs this function.

State government in Texas is so fragmented and responsibility so divided that holding anyone responsible for state government is impossible. Although citizens may blame the governor when things go wrong, and governors may claim credit when things go right, in truth the governor is responsible for very little and deserves credit for much less than most claim. An example of this is a governor who claims to have created hundreds of jobs in the state when, in fact, a governor has very little to do with the economy or job creation.

Sunset Review

Sunset Advisory Commission

Agency responsible for making recommendations to the legislature for change in the structure and organization of most state agencies

Given the lack of overall, central control in state government and the limited and weak authority of the governor, in 1977 the Texas legislature created the 10-member **Sunset Advisory Commission** to review most state agencies every 12 years and recommend changes. This commission consists of five state senators, five representatives, and two public members.

The sunset process is the "idea that legislative oversight of government operations can be enhanced by a systematic evaluation of state agencies."[33] The process works by establishing a date on which an agency of state government is abolished if the legislature does not pass a law providing for its continuance. The act does not apply to agencies created by the Texas Constitution, and some state agencies are exempt, such as state universities. Sunset asks the basic question: "Do the policies carried out by an agency need to be continued?"[34]

In the years of sunset review in Texas, 37 state agencies have been abolished. Most were minor state agencies with few functions. Most notable were the Boll Weevil Commission, the Battleship Texas Commission, and the Stonewall Jackson Memorial Board. More important than abolition is the review process. By forcing a review of an agency every 12 years, the legislature is given the opportunity to recommend changes to improve the efficiency and effectiveness of state government. In many cases, functions of state agencies are transferred to other agencies, and agencies are combined or merged. Sunset review has also forced many agencies that operate much out of the public's attention into the limelight. This is especially true of those agencies that license professions. Sunset review resulted in the appointment of non-professionals to these agencies in an effort to promote the broader interests of the public over the narrower interests of the agency and its clientele. Table 4.5 lists the activities of the Texas Sunset Advisory Commission over the past 30 years.

TABLE 4.5

Overview of Sunset Activities in Texas, 1979–2014

Year	Session	Reviews	Agencies Continued	Agencies Abolished	Functions Transferred
1979	66	26	13	7	6
1981	67	28	23	3	2
1983	68	32	29	3	0
1985	69	31	23	6	1
1987	70	20	17	1	1
1989	71	30	22	3	2
1991	72	30	20	3	5
1993	73	31	22	1	5
1995	74	18	14	0	2
1997	75	21	18	0	2
1999	76	25	22	1	1
2001	77	25	19	1	1
2003	78	29	23	1	2
2005	79	29	21	2	4
2007	80	20	14	1	1
2009	81	27	20	2	2
2011	82	29	19	2	4
2013	83	24	19	0	1
	Total	475	358	37	42
			83%	8%	9%

Source: Texas Sunset Advisory Commission, Past Review Cycles, April 2014. See: (http://www.sunset.texas.gov/review-cycles)

Powers of the Texas Governor in Comparative Context

If we take the six indicators of power—election of other statewide executives, tenure of office, governor's appointment powers, budgetary powers, veto powers, and governor's control over party—and compare the Texas governor with the other 49 U.S. governors, the Texas office is comparatively weak in formal powers because of the limitations placed on administrative and budgetary powers, although the office is strong on tenure and veto authority (see Table 4.6.) The formal weakness in the office of governor is very much in keeping with the traditionalistic/individualistic political culture of the state. As was discussed earlier, the present constitution was written in a time when limited government was very much on the minds of the framers of the constitution. Having experienced strong executive authority during Reconstruction, these framers wanted to limit the governor's ability to act, especially in budgetary and administrative matters. They succeeded. In recent years the powers of the Texas governor have been increased somewhat, but the office is still very weak on the budgetary and administrative dimensions. Given this formal weakness, Texas governors must use all their informal powers of persuasion and their political skills if they are to be successful. Also, in recent years the voters have rejected constitutional amendments that would have expanded the governor's ability to appoint and remove agency heads.

TABLE 4.6

Summary of Institutional Powers of Governors by State

Alabama	2.8	Montana	3.5
Alaska	4.1	Nebraska	3.8
Arizona	3.4	Nevada	3.0
Arkansas	3.6	New Hampshire	3.2
California	3.2	New Jersey	4.1
Colorado	3.9	New Mexico	3.7
Connecticut	3.6	New York	4.1
Delaware	3.5	North Carolina	2.9
Florida	3.6	North Dakota	3.9
Georgia	3.2	Ohio	3.6
Hawaii	3.4	Oklahoma	2.8
Idaho	3.3	Oregon	3.5
Illinois	3.8	Pennsylvania	3.8
Indiana	2.9	Rhode Island	2.6
Iowa	3.8	South Carolina	3.0
Kansas	3.3	South Dakota	3.0
Kentucky	3.3	Tennessee	3.8
Louisiana	3.4	**Texas**	**3.2**
Maine	3.6	Utah	4.0
Maryland	4.1	Vermont	2.5
Massachusetts	4.3	Virginia	3.2
Michigan	3.6	Washington	3.6
Minnesota	3.6	West Virginia	4.1
Mississippi	2.9	Wisconsin	3.5
Missouri	3.6	Wyoming	3.1
		50 average	**3.5**

Source: Thad L. Beyle, "Governors," in *Politics in the American States*, 9th ed., eds. Virginia Gray and Russell L. Hanson. Washington D.C.: Congressional Quarterly Press, 2008.

CORE OBJECTIVE

Thinking Critically...

We discussed six factors that influence the strength of the power of the governor. Those six factors are the number of elected statewide executives; tenure of office; the governor's appointive powers; the governor's budgetary powers; the governor's veto powers; and the extent to which the governor controls his or her political party. What can you conclude about the powers of the governor?

Informal Powers

Although the office of Texas governor is formally very weak, the office can be strong politically. The governor's primary political resource is the ability to exert influence. The governor is the most visible officeholder in the state and can command the attention of the news media, holding press conferences and announcing new decisions on policy issues. Such news conferences usually are well covered and reported by the press and other media. This enables the governor to have an impact on the direction of state government. The governor can also stage events that are newsworthy to emphasize things she or he is interested in changing.

The popularity of the governor in public opinion polls is also an important aspect of informal leadership. Governors who consistently rank high in popularity polls can use this fact to overcome opposition to their policies and reduce the likelihood of opposition, both to policies and electoral challenges. A governor who is weak in public opinion polls becomes an easy target for political opponents.

In very general ways, governors are judged on their leadership abilities. Some governors develop reputations as being indecisive, whereas others become known as effective, decisive leaders. The characterization attached to the governor will affect his or her ability to be effective. The media will begin to repeat the reputational description of the governor, and if this happens often enough, the reputation will become "fact." Therefore, developing a good image is very important.

The power and respect accorded to governors have varied greatly over time. During the colonial period, there was very little; some have argued that the American Revolution was a war against colonial governors. The experiences of southern states following Reconstruction led to a return of weak governors in the South. An old Texas saying states, "The governor should have only enough power to sign for his paycheck." In recent times, the power and prestige of the office have increased, as evidenced by recent presidential politics. In both Democratic and Republican parties, many presidential candidates have been former governors. In the past 40 years, only President George H. W. Bush and President Barack Obama have not served as governors prior to becoming president. Today the office of governor has assumed new significance because of a change in attitude toward the role of the federal government. In the past 50 years, every congress promised to return power and responsibility to state governments and to allow states more flexibility in administering programs funded by the federal government. Even without the renewed significance of the office, and even though many governors have little formal power, governors are important players in state politics.

Roles

Citizens expect governors to play many roles. First, the governor is expected to be the **chief legislator**, formulating long-term policy goals and objectives. In this capacity the governor recommends policy initiatives to state legislators and coordinates with state agencies that administer programs and implement policies. Although governors do not formally introduce bills, passing legislation requires the support of legislative leaders to carry their program forward. Often governors spend considerable time and energy developing these relationships. If the governor is of one party, and the other party dominates the legislature, it is more difficult to pass legislation.

The governor must act as **party chief**. As the most important party official in the state, the governor leads the party and aids its development and growth. This role is important in promoting the party's position on political issues and shaping its policy initiatives. The governor is the most visible member of the party, helping legislators and other elected officials in their reelection efforts, raising money for the party, and creating a favorable image of the party in the state.

In addition, the governor serves as the ceremonial leader of the state. The **ceremonial duties** can be demanding. The governor receives many invitations to speak, make presentations, and cut ribbons. Some governors become trapped in the safe, friendly environment of ceremonial duties and neglect or avoid the other duties of their office. For governors with an agenda for action, getting caught in a "ceremonial trap" is a diversion from more important and difficult objectives. Governors can, however, use ceremonial duties as communication opportunities to promote their programs. They must carefully choose which invitations to accept and which to delegate to others or decline. Ceremonial appearances, such as a commencement speaker, provide an opportunity to generate favorable press coverage and support for one's programs. Former Governor Bush used these opportunities to promote his state programs and his race for the presidency.

In recent years, a new role for the governor has been added to that list—**crisis manager**. Governors are expected to react to crises, such as natural or man-made disasters. How well the governor reacts to these situations may very well have an impact on reelection chances. For example, during Hurricane Katrina in Louisiana, Governor Blanco was not viewed as a strong leader, thus influencing her decision not to seek reelection in 2007.

Finally, the governor is expected to be the chief **intergovernmental coordinator**, working with federal officials and officials in other states. The governor must also work with the state congressional delegation of U.S. senators and representatives, the president, and cabinet officials to promote the interests of the state.

In Texas, like many other states, the formal powers of the governor are very weak. Without explicit authority, the governor must develop and use the power and prestige of the office to persuade others to accept his or her legislative agenda. This informal leadership trait, the power to persuade others, is perhaps the most important and necessary "power" the governor must develop. Governor Perry used his considerable charm and tenure to persuade the legislature to go along with his programs; over time, his influence and power in the office increased.

chief legislator
The expectation that a governor has an active agenda of legislation to recommend to the legislature and works to pass that agenda

party chief
The expectation that the governor will be the head of his or her party

ceremonial duties
The expectation that a governor attends many functions and represents the state; some governors become so active at this role that they get caught in a "ceremonial trap" and neglect other duties.

crisis manager
The expectation that the governor will provide strong leadership in times of a natural or man-made disaster

intergovernmental coordinator
The expectation that a governor coordinates activities with other state governments

The Governor's Staff

In Texas, the trend in recent years has been to expand the staff of the governor's office. In 1963, when he became governor, John Connally made the first use of a professional staff of advisors. Previous governors often appointed only a handful of individuals who were loyal to them politically, but not necessarily highly professional. Other governors since Connally have added to the governor's staff. Today an organizational chart is necessary to maintain lines of authority and responsibility. Currently, the governor has a staff of about 200.

Each governor is going to make different use of her or his staff. In recent years most have used their staff to keep track of state agencies over which the governors themselves have little or no direct control. The staff also gathers information and makes recommendations on changes in policy that impact most areas of state government. A message from a member of the governor's staff to a state agency is taken seriously. A report issued by the governor's office automatically attracts the attention of significant state leaders and the news media. Often the governor must use the information gathered to wage a public relations war with the legislature or state agencies. In Texas, the increases in the size, professionalism, and complexity of the governor's staff have become necessary to offset the limited formal control the governor has over state government.

Conclusion

Even though governors in most states do not have much formal power, the office has great importance in state politics. In recent years, the importance of the office has increased. Of the last five U.S. presidents, four have been state governors before their move to the White House. The office has become increasingly visible in both state and national politics. The need for strong leadership in this office will continue to increase.

Texas is now the second-largest state in population and one of the leading states in industrial growth. The governor's lack of formal power makes the task of governing this large, diverse, and economically important state challenging. Some reform of the powers of the governor is still needed, but it is doubtful that such changes will occur. The political culture of the state does not support that change. Leadership will have to come from force of will and personality, not from formal changes in structure. Interest groups are not supportive of transferring power from state agencies they can dominate to agencies under the control of a single individual appointed by the governor. Although the Sunset Advisory Commission has had a positive impact on some agencies, general reorganization of state government is not likely anytime soon.

Key Terms

acting governor
attorney general
boards and commissions
budgetary powers
ceremonial duties
chief legislator
comptroller of public accounts
conviction
crisis manager

impeachment
informal qualifications
intergovernmental coordinator
judicial powers
land commissioner
Legislative Budget Board
legislative power
line-item veto
military powers

partial veto
party chief
plural executive system
recall
secretary of state
senatorial courtesy
Sunset Advisory Commission
tenure of office
Texas Railroad Commission

Notes

[1] Thad L. Beyle, "Governors: The Middlemen and Women in Our Political System," in *Politics in the American States,* 6th ed., eds. Virginia Gray and Herbert Jacob (Washington, D.C.: Congressional Quarterly Press, 2004), 197.

[2] Center for American Women and Politics. (2014). *Statewide Elective Executive Women 2014* [Fact Sheet]. Retrieved from http://www.cawp.rutgers.edu/fast_facts/ levels_of_office/documents/stwide.pdf

[3] Ibid.

[4] *Book of the States,* 2010, table 4.3, 199.

[5] *Book of the States,* 1994–95, 66.

[6] Ibid.

[7] Thad L. Beyle, "Governors," in *Politics in the American States,* 4th ed., eds. Virginia Gray, Herbert Jacob, and Kenneth N. Vine (Boston: Little Brown, 1983), 217.

[8] Ann Bowman and Richard C. Kearney, *State and Local Government* (Boston: Wadsworth Cengage Learning, 2011), 206.

[9] Benton, *Texas,* 222–224.

[10] Victor E. Harlow, *Harlow's History of Oklahoma,* 5th ed. (Norman, Okla.: Harlow, 1967), 294–315.

[11] Daniel R. Grant and Lloyd B. Omdahl, *State and Local Government in America* (Madison, Wis.: Brown & Benchmark, 1987), 260.

[12] Legislative Budget Board, *Fiscal Size-Up,* 1998–99. Biennium: Texas State Services, 4–6, Austin.

[13] Ibid., 4–7.

[14] *Book of the States,* 1996–97, 33–34.

[15] S. M. Morehouse, *State Politics, Parties and Policy.* (New York: Holt, Rinehart & Winston, 1981), 206.

[16] Beyle, "Governors: The Middlemen and Women in Our Political System," 230.

[17] Ibid., 231.

[18] Allan Shivers was elected lieutenant governor in 1946. Governor Beauford H. Jester died in July 1949. Shivers then became governor, and he was reelected in 1950, 1952, and 1954.

[19] *Texas Almanac* 1994–95, 519.

[20] Beyle, "Governors: The Middlemen and Women in Our Political System," 221.

[21] Ibid., 231.

[22] *Guide to Texas State Agencies* (Austin: University of Texas, Lyndon B. Johnson School of Public Affairs, 1994).

[23] Governor Perry's Patronage, Texas for Public Justice, September 2010. www.tpj.org.

[24] Ibid.

[25] http://www.allbusiness.com/government/ government-bodies-offices-heads-state/12890062-1 .html.

[26] Ibid.

[27] Beyle, "Governor: The Middlemen and Women in Our Political System," 234.

[28] Ibid., 235.

[29] *Book of the States,* 1998–99, table 2.3, 20.

[30] Anderson, Murray, and Farley, Texas Politics, 122.

[31] Deborah K. Wheeler, *Two Men, Two Governors, Two Pardons: A Study of Pardon Policy of Governor Miriam Ferguson.* Unpublished copyrighted paper, presented at State Historical Society Meeting, March 1998, Austin.

[32] Bill Hobby, "Speaking of Pardons, Texas Has Had Its Share," *Houston Chronicle,* 18 February 2001, 4c.

[33] *Fiscal Size-Up* 2002–03, 242.

[34] Texas Sunset Advisory Commission, *Guide to the Texas Sunset Process,* 1997, Austin, 1991, 1.

CHAPTER 5

The Court System in Texas

Upon completing this chapter,
you will be able to...

- **Demonstrate knowledge of the judicial branch**
  of Texas government.

Texans share with citizens in the rest of the United States a conflicting view of how courts should function in a democratic society. In part, this conflicted understanding arises from the two primary sources of law: legislatures and courts.

When we say "law" in the context of a legislature, we mean a present, binding requirement imposed on all citizens in a given category, such as all minors under the age of 21, or all divorced parents, or all people who drive vehicles, or all people who work. The law in this sense applies to all people in a category of citizens, without exceptions. It embodies majority rule, or *majoritarianism.*

Courts also create law, but they do so by evaluating individuals on a case-by-case basis. Under our common law system, each opinion that a court hands down enjoys equal status with a statute as "law." But the courts ask a different question than the legislature does: Given that a statute has created a general requirement, are there

Solicitor General Ted Cruz presents the state's position in the Texas Supreme Court on Wednesday, July 6, 2005, in Austin, Texas. Supreme Court justices, at left, heard oral arguments from both sides in the ongoing court battle over how Texas pays for public education.

special circumstances that should lead the court to deal with a particular individual differently? For example, a party could argue that if a general law was applied to them, it would violate their constitutional rights. Courts, therefore, write decisions that will later apply to everyone who is in the same category of citizens as the party in court, but they analyze the law in a way that accounts for individual circumstances. Legal scholars sometimes refer to this approach to the law as *countermajoritarianism:* where special circumstances exist that make the application of the general law to a specific individual illegal. In these situations, courts carve out an exception despite the will of the majority expressed in the statute.

These two conflicting roles of the law translate into contradictory views of how law should function, both in Texas and in the country. First, citizens think the court system should be above politics. Courts are expected to act in nonpolitical ways, interpreting our nation's Constitution as individual challenges arise: That is, regardless of generally applicable legislation that theoretically embodies the majority will, the courts should evaluate each case without preexisting assumptions about who should prevail in a specific case. This is the countermajoritarian role of the courts. Justice is often portrayed as a blindfolded woman holding the scales of justice in her hand. Most Americans firmly believe that courts should be blind to political bias: Fairness, it would seem, requires neutrality.[1]

Second, Americans also want state courts to be responsive to the electorate, "especially if they play prominent roles in molding and implementing public policy."[2] But how can courts be simultaneously above politics and responsive to the electorate?

Surprisingly, most citizens do not see a conflict between these two ideas. They think that courts should both dispense pure justice and do so according to the wishes of the electorate. Courts are placed in this position because they make decisions on matters ranging from domestic and family law to criminal law, and they serve as the final arbitrator of highly political decisions. In playing the dual roles of decision maker and policy maker, courts function very differently from other institutions.

Court Decision Making

The courts' approach to decision making is quite different from that of the executive and legislative branches.[3] Unlike the legislature or governor, who can initiate policy changes, courts evaluate individual disputes that arise in cases that parties file with them. Cases that Texas courts decide may have an important impact on different sectors of the state's population: All school children, all property taxpayers, and all landowners, for example, may be affected by a single decision involving school-specific children, taxpayers, or landowners. Most cases do not involve policy questions, however, but deal only with controversies between individuals. Another way of expressing the role of the courts is that they resolve individual conflicts by interpreting and enforcing existing rules and laws. But in doing so they may create law that plays an important role in the lives of far more people than the individuals who actually participated in the case.

Parties who want a court to resolve their dispute must satisfy *strict rules of access.*[4] Although any citizen may approach the legislature or the governor, courts have rules that limit access to them. Individuals must have "standing." This means that the case must involve real controversies between two or more parties, and someone must have suffered real damage. Courts do not deal in hypothetical or imaginary controversies. In short, they do not play "what if" ("What if I hit this person? What will the court do?").

Courts are governed by *strict procedural rules* that determine when and how facts and arguments can be presented.[5] These rules prevent the introduction of some evidence in a criminal case. For example, evidence gathered by the police in an illegal search may not be allowed.

Generally, a court's decisions affect only the cases being considered by the court and not other cases before other courts.[6] However, a court's decision serves as precedent for parties in the future with a similar dispute. For example, if a trial court rules that a city ordinance in one city is invalid, this does not invalidate all similar ordinances in other cities. Another year later, however, someone in another city may challenge a similar ordinance on similar legal grounds, in which case the earlier decision will serve as legal precedent for invalidating the ordinance in the second case. The court must evaluate each case separately and then decide whether earlier decisions apply to the present case.

The rulings of appellate and supreme courts serve as especially important precedents for future legal decisions. Under the principle of **stare decisis**—"to stand by that which was decided before"—courts must follow principles announced in former cases and diverge from these only when they can show good cause for doing so. In this way, appellate courts affect how trial courts make decisions; however, each case in a lower court might be affected slightly differently.

Courts also differ from other branches of government in that, to the extent possible, they seek to evaluate cases with **objectivity**.[7] Unlike governors and legislators, courts may not appear to be political in their decision making, even though judges' decisions might be affected by political considerations. Judges must base their decisions on the federal and state constitutions, statutes, and earlier court decisions. A court's decision may have unintended or even deliberate political consequences, but the law binds a court's decision-making process to a greater extent than in the executive and legislative branches.

Thus, courts differ from governors and legislators in the way they make decisions. They must maintain a passive role, enforce rules that restrict access to the courts, uphold strict rules of procedure, confine their decisions to the specifics of the cases before them, and maintain the appearance of objectivity. By doing this, courts help to reinforce the legitimacy of their decisions and their place as the final arbitrators of conflict. This in turn reinforces the concept that the rule of law, and not the rule of arbitrary actions by individuals, governs.

stare decisis
Court decisions depending on previous rulings of other courts

objectivity
The appearance that courts make objective decisions and not political ones

Judicial Federalism

Article III of the United States Constitution established the Supreme Court and gave Congress the authority to create other lower federal courts. Article VI of the U.S. Constitution makes federal law the *supreme law of the land*. Any direct conflicts between federal and state law must be resolved in favor of federal authority.

States create their own courts. As a result, 50 separate jurisdictions have complete court systems that exist side by side with the federal courts. Federal courts hear cases involving federal laws, and state courts hear cases involving state laws. Although some cases might be held in either state or federal court, most cases go to state courts rather than federal courts. There are two high-profile examples, however, of cases that were tried in federal rather than in state courts. One is the 1995 bombing of the Alfred P. Murrah Federal Building in Oklahoma City. Although murder is a crime in Oklahoma, a bombing of a federal facility that results in the death of a federal government employee is a federal crime. Another example is the case of the "Unabomber," in which persons were injured or murdered by a series of bombs, most of which were sent through the U.S. mail, from the late 1970s to the mid-1990s. Both of these cases were tried in federal court. Initially, state prosecutors indicated that they might also file state murder charges against the Unabomber suspect. This did not happen.

Few other countries have dual court systems. Ours developed because of the United States' federal system of government. State courts existed during the colonial period and continued after the adoption of the U.S. Constitution in 1789. State courts act primarily in areas where the federal government lacks authority to act.

Trial and Appellate Courts

There are two kinds of state courts: trial courts and appellate courts. They differ in several important ways. First, **trial courts** are localized. Jurisdiction is limited to a geographic area, such as a county.[8] Second, only one judge presides over a trial court, and each court is considered a separate court. Third, citizens participate in trial court activity. They serve as members of juries and as witnesses during trials. Fourth, trial courts are primarily concerned with establishing the facts of a case (such as a determination that a person is guilty). Fifth, trial courts announce decisions immediately after the trial is finished.[9]

Appellate courts, on the other hand, are centralized, often at the state level. More than one judge presides, citizen participation is virtually absent, and, of most importance, appellate courts decide points of law, not points of fact. An appeal of a murder conviction from a trial court to a higher court is not based on points of fact (Is the person guilty?) but on points of law (Were legal procedures followed?). Trial courts establish guilt; appellate courts decide whether proper procedures have been followed. For example, in Texas, all death penalty cases are automatically appealed to the Texas Court of Criminal Appeals. The issue is not the guilt or innocence of the person but whether all procedures were properly followed in the trial court and whether the defense adequately defended the person charged.

The Structure of State Courts

Most states provide for three levels of courts: trial courts, appellate courts, and a supreme court. The structure of courts in Texas is more complicated, as shown in Figure 5.1. Texas has several levels of trial courts and appellate courts. Trial courts include the justices of the peace, municipal courts, county courts, district courts, and special purpose courts, such as probate, juvenile, and domestic relations courts. Texas has 14 intermediate appellate courts and 2 "supreme" appellate courts: one for civil cases (Supreme Court) and one for criminal cases (the Court of Criminal Appeals).

Magistrate or Minor Courts

All states provide for some type of minor or magistrate court, usually called the justice of the peace. These courts hear cases involving misdemeanors, most often traffic violations and minor civil cases. In Texas there are two courts at this level:

---

trial courts

Local courts that hear cases; juries determine the outcome of the cases heard in the court.

appellate courts

Higher-level courts that decide on points of law and not questions of guilt or innocence

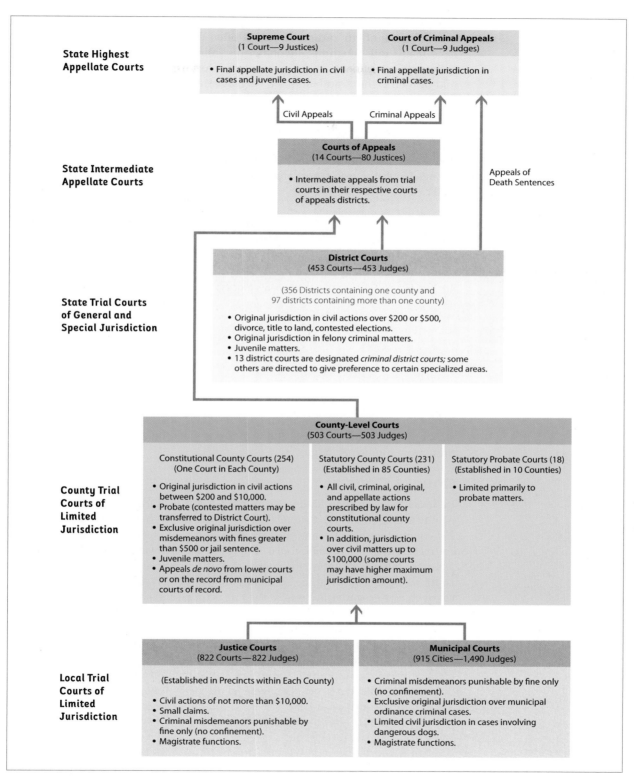

FIGURE 5.1   Court Structure of Texas

SOURCE: Texas Courts Online. (http://www.courts.state.tx.us/)

magistrate functions
Preliminary hearings for persons charged with a serious criminal offense

justices of the peace (JPs) and municipal courts. Municipal courts hear cases involving violations of city ordinances, most often traffic violations. These courts also have **magistrate functions**, involving preliminary hearings for persons charged with a serious offense. These persons are informed of the charges against them, told of their rights, and bail is set. As magistrates, municipal judges and JPs can also issue search-and-arrest warrants. JP courts also perform these magistrate functions and hear minor criminal cases, most of which involve traffic tickets issued by the Texas Highway Patrol or county deputy sheriffs. JP courts also serve as small claims courts in Texas. Municipal courts do not.[10] Jurisdiction in small claims is limited to a maximum of $15,000. Of the cases in the JP courts, 90 percent are criminal misdemeanor cases: most are traffic cases (66 percent) and only 10 percent are civil cases.

CORE OBJECTIVE

Communicating Effectively...

Analyze Figure 5.1. Describe the appeals process for a civil case filed in county court.

Another interesting difference between JP and municipal courts is that JPs can perform marriages, whereas municipal court judges cannot. Although municipal judges have tried to have this changed, they have not been successful. The reason is that JPs charge a fee for performing marriages, and they have challenged competition from municipal judges.

County Courts

In Texas there are two kinds of county courts: constitutional county courts and county courts at law. The state constitution creates a county court in each of the 254 counties in the state, and the state legislature has created 505 statutory county courts at law and 18 probate courts. County courts at law are created in large urban counties. In those counties, the constitutional county court ceases to function as a court, and the "county judge" becomes almost exclusively an administrative officer or county executive but retains the title of judge and some limited judicial functions. The state constitution determines the jurisdiction of constitutional county courts. The jurisdiction of county courts at law is set by the act passed by the legislature creating the court and varies from court to court. The general levels of jurisdiction are shown in Figure 5.1.

County courts primarily hear intermediate criminal and civil cases. Most criminal cases are misdemeanors. On average, more than one million cases are pled in Texas county courts each year. The most common type of cases are driving while intoxicated (DWI), worthless checks, violation of drug laws, and traffic appeals cases from city and justice courts.

County courts also serve as appellate courts for cases heard by JP and municipal courts. All JP and most municipal courts in Texas are trial de novo courts and not courts of record. In **trial de novo courts**, no record of the proceeding is kept, and cases may be appealed for any reason. It is a common practice in Texas to appeal

trial de novo courts
Courts that do not keep a written record of their proceedings; cases on appeal begin as new cases in the appellate courts

traffic tickets to the county court, where, due to heavy caseloads, they are buried. If a person has the resources to hire a lawyer, there is a good chance the ticket will be "forgotten" in case overload.

District Courts

In most states, major trial courts are called district or superior courts. These courts hear major criminal and civil cases. Examples of major criminal cases (felonies) are murder, armed robbery, and car theft. Whether a civil case is major is generally established by the dollar amount of damages claimed in the case.

In Texas in 2014, there were 457 district courts. These courts are created by the state legislature. Large urban counties generally have several district courts. In rural areas, district courts may serve several counties. The jurisdiction of these courts often overlaps with county courts, and cases may be led in either court. Other cases must begin in district courts.

Appellate Courts

Ten states do not have courts of appeal, and 23 states have only one court of appeal. The other states, primarily large urban states, have several courts of appeal.[11] Texas has 14 courts of appeal with 80 judges elected by districts in the state. Only California has more judges and courts at this level. These courts hear all civil appeals cases and all criminal appeals except those involving the death penalty, which go directly to the Court of Criminal Appeals.

Supreme Courts

All states have a supreme court, or court of last resort. Oklahoma, like Texas, has two supreme courts.[12] Oklahoma copied the idea from Texas when it entered the Union in 1907. The highest court in Texas for civil matters is the Texas Supreme Court, and the highest court in Texas for criminal cases is the Court of Criminal Appeals. Each court consists of nine judges who are elected statewide for six-year overlapping terms.

Judicial Selection

Under the U.S. Constitution, all federal judges are appointed by the president and serve for life. A lifetime appointment means that a judge continues to serve during good behavior and can be removed only for cause. Among the states, a variety of methods are used to select judges. Seven of the original 13 states allow some judges to be appointed by the governor and serve for life. Four states, also among the original 13, allow the legislature to elect judges.[13] Some states use partisan elections to select certain judges. Candidates must run in a primary and in a general election. Still other states elect particular state judges in nonpartisan general elections. And finally, some states use the **merit system, or Missouri system**, to select specific judges. Under this plan, the governor appoints judges from a list submitted by a screening committee of legal officials. After appointment, a judge serves for a set term and is then subjected to a retention election in which the voters decide whether the judge retains the office.

The method of selection also varies between courts within some states. For example, in some states, appellate court judges are chosen by a merit system and the voters elect trial court judges. Table 5.1 and Figure 5.2 show the number of

merit system, or Missouri system
A system of electing judges that involves appointment by the governor and periodic retention election

states using each selection method for appellate and trial courts. Most states have moved away from partisan election of judges and use either a nonpartisan election or a merit system.

TABLE 5.1

Methods of Selecting Judges

Method of Selecting Judges	Number of States Using Method[*]
Appellate Court Judges	
Legislative election	2
Appointment by governor	3
Partisan election	7
Nonpartisan election	14
Merit plan	24
Trial Court Judges	
Legislative election	2
Appointment by governor	2
Partisan election	11
Nonpartisan election	16
Merit plan	19

[*] Does not add to 50 because some states use more than one method to select judges. For example, district judges are elected, whereas appellate judges are appointed.

Source: Council of State Governments, *The Book of the States, 2013* (Lexington, Ky.: Council of State Governments, 2013), Tables 5.6 and 5.7.

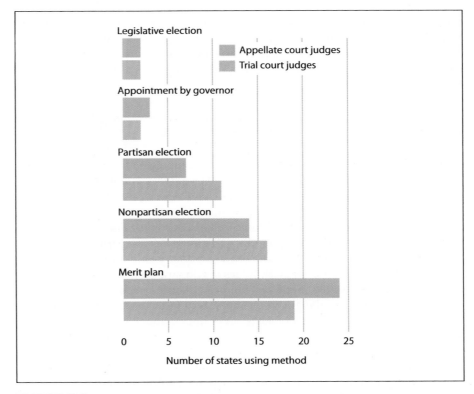

FIGURE 5.2   Method of Selecting Judges

TABLE 5.2

Judicial Selection of State Supreme Court Judges

Partisan Election	Nonpartisan Election	Missouri Plan	Appointment
Alabama	Arkansas	Alaska	Connecticut
Illinois	Georgia	Arizona	Delaware
Louisiana	Idaho	California	Hawaii
New Mexico	Kentucky	Colorado	Maine
Pennsylvania	Michigan	Florida	Massachusetts
Texas	Minnesota	Indiana	New Hampshire
West Virginia	Mississippi	Iowa	New Jersey
	Montana	Kansas	New York
	Nevada	Maryland	Rhode Island
	North Carolina	Missouri	South Carolina
	North Dakota	Nebraska	Vermont
	Ohio	Oklahoma	Virginia
	Oregon	South Dakota	
	Washington	Tennessee	
	Wisconsin	Utah	
		Wyoming	

Table shows how judges are normally selected. Some judges in partisan and nonpartisan systems may get their initial seat by appointment of the governor.

Source: Methods of Judicial Selection. 2014. American Judicature Society. 11 June 2014 (http://www.judicialselection.us/judicial_selection/methods/selection_of_judges.cfm?state=).

Table 5.2 shows how states initially select judges to the supreme court in that state. As was indicated earlier, some states use different methods to select appellate court judges.

Judicial Selection in Texas

In Texas, trial court judges are elected in **partisan elections** for four-year terms, and all appellate court judges are elected in partisan elections for six-year terms. The only exceptions to this are municipal court judges. Most municipal judges are appointed by the mayor or the city council (1,527 are appointed and only 16 are elected). The question of judicial selection has been an issue in Texas for almost two decades. In 1995 the Texas Supreme Court established the Commission on Judicial Efficiency to make recommendations on the method of judicial selection, and other issues, to the 1997 session of the Texas legislature, but the legislature took no action on the recommendations. In the 1999 session of the legislature, several bills were introduced to change judicial selections, but none passed. In 2001, seven bills were introduced that called for the appointment or **nonpartisan election** of some judges in Texas. None passed. And in 2003, six such bills were introduced, and none passed. In 2005, 2007, 2009, and 2011, session bills were led to move to nonpartisan elections or the merit system; none passed.

Although the election of judges can be problematic, most Texans do not like the idea of giving up their right to elect judges. Other issues in Texas judicial selection include voting by familiar name rather than qualifications, voting by straight ticket, judicial campaign contributions, and lack of minority representation in judicial elections.

partisan election
Method used to select all judges (except municipal court judges) in Texas by using a ballot in which party identification is shown

nonpartisan election
Election in which party identification is not formally declared

CORE OBJECTIVE

Being Socially Responsible...

What impact, if any, do you think partisan election of judges has on judicial outcomes?

Familiar Names Can Skew Judicial Elections

Several events have brought the issue of judicial selection to the forefront in Texas today. The first of these is electoral problems. Although elections are at the very heart of any democracy, they are imperfect instruments for deciding the qualifications of the persons seeking office. This is especially true for judicial offices, for which qualifications are extremely important. The average voter in Texas will be asked to vote for judges for the Texas Supreme Court and the Court of Criminal Appeals and, in large urban counties, several district judges, county judges, and JPs. Most voters go to the election booth with scant knowledge about the qualifications of judicial candidates, and they often end up voting by **name familiarity**.

There are two good examples of this happening in Texas. In 1976 voters elected Don Yarbrough to the Texas Supreme Court. Yarbrough was an unknown attorney from Houston who won nomination as the Democratic candidate and claimed after the election that God had told him to run. Many voters had thought he was Don Yarborough, who had run unsuccessfully for governor. Still others thought he was Ralph Yarbrough, who had served in the U.S. Senate for two terms. Judge Yarbrough was forced to resign after about six months because criminal charges were filed against him. He was later convicted of perjury and sentenced to five years in jail, but he jumped bond.

In 1990 there was a similar case of voting based on name familiarity. Gene Kelly won the Democratic Party primary for a seat on the Texas Supreme Court. Some citizens thought he was the famous dancer and film star from the 1950s and 1960s. However, this Gene Kelly was a retired Air Force judge with little nonmilitary experience. Kelly lost to Republican John Cornyn after extensive television commercials questioned his competency.

name familiarity
Practice in Texas of voting for judges with familiar or popular names

Straight Ticket Voting

Another electoral problem that has surfaced in recent years is straight ticket voting. Texas is one of 14 states allowing straight ticket voting. The **straight ticket voting system** allows a voter to vote for all candidates in a party by making a single mark. In 1984 many incumbent Democratic judges lost their seats in large urban counties to unknown Republican challengers because of Republican straight ticket voting. Other examples have occurred since 1984. In Harris County in 1994, only one incumbent Democrat was reelected, and Republicans defeated 16 Democrats because of straight ticket voting. In 2008, voters reversed this and returned Democrats to most judicial offices in Harris County. Many of the Republicans elected lacked judicial experience, and some had no courtroom experience. Also in 1994, Steve Mansfield, an individual who had very limited legal experience and

straight ticket voting system
System that allows voters to vote for all candidates of a single political party by making a single mark and that has resulted in an increase in the number of Republican judges

no experience in criminal law, was elected to the Texas Court of Criminal Appeals, the highest court for criminal matters in Texas. After the elections, questions were raised about Mansfield's qualifications. In his state bar application, he had failed to acknowledge that he was behind in his child support payments. This raised the possibility that he could be disbarred and therefore ineligible to serve. Some state-wide officials called for his resignation.

A similar case occurred in the 2002 election. Steven W. Smith, the chief litigant behind the Hopwood case that limited the use of racial quotas in selecting law school students at the University of Texas, won election to the Texas Supreme Court. Despite being a Republican, he had little support from statewide party officials and few endorsements from state bar associations; he still managed to win election because of straight ticket voting. He received about the same percentage of votes as other Republican candidates for statewide judicial office. A study by Richard Murray at the University of Houston demonstrated that about 54 percent of the votes cast in Harris County in both 1998 and 2002 were straight ticket votes. A Republican running for countywide office had a 14,000 vote head start.[14]

These incidents, along with more recent cases of straight ticket voting, have caused some to call for nonpartisan election of state judges. In every session since 1995, bills have been introduced that called for the nonpartisan election of district judges and a merit system for appellate judges. Yet another suggestion is to prohibit straight ticket voting in judicial races, which has been considered in past sessions. This would force voters to mark the ballot for each judicial race. Given the recent success of Republicans in gaining control of the legislature and the judiciary, this idea might lack strong support in the legislature.

Campaign Contributions

Another issue is campaign contributions. Under the Texas partisan election system, judges must win nomination in the party primary and in the general election. Two elections, stretching over 10 months (January to November), can be a costly process. In 1984, Chief Justice John L. Hill spent more than $1 million to win the chief justice race. The cost of this race and other experiences caused Hill and two other Democratic justices to resign from the supreme court in 1988. They called for a merit system to replace partisan elections. These resignations, along with other openings on the court, resulted in six of the nine seats on the supreme court being up for election. The total cost of these six races exceeded $10 million. One candidate spent more than $2 million.[15]

Races for district judgeships can also be very costly. Money often comes from law firms that have business before the judges who receive the money. Other money comes from interest groups, such as the Texas Medical Association, which has an interest in limiting malpractice tort claims in cases before the courts. The Public Broadcasting System's *Frontline* television series ran a program titled "Justice for Sale," about the Texas courts and money. This report detailed how eight justices on the supreme court in 1994 received more than $9 million, primarily from corporations and law firms. In the 2002 election cycle, five of nine seats on the court were up for election, including the chief justice. Close to $5 million had been raised by November of 2002. Many of these contributions came from large law firms that had cases before the court. This practice continues to this date.

Does money influence the judiciary?

According to Texans for Public Justice, the three Republican incumbent justices on the November 2008 ballot raised a total of almost $1.6 million for their reelection campaigns through the end of June 2008. The justices took 65 percent of this money from courtroom contributors who had recent business before the same justices. The justices' dependence on courtroom contributions ranged from a low of 60 percent for Chief Justice Wallace Jefferson to a high of 71 percent for Justice Dale Wainwright. The Democrats challenged these justices (see the next section) and raised a total of $722,167, taking 69 percent of it from lawyers and litigants who had recent business before the Texas Supreme Court.[16]

The basic question raised by these contributions is their impact on judicial impartiality. Do these contributions influence judges' decisions? A 1999 poll conducted by the Texas Supreme Court found that 83 percent of Texans think money influences judges.[17] In 2006, a Texans for Public Justice study found that the supreme court is more likely to hear cases filed by large contributors. Because of the volume of cases, the high court accepted only about 11 percent of all petitions filed, but they were seven and a half times more likely to hear cases filed by contributors of $100,000 and ten times more likely from contributors of $250,000.[18] Respect for the law declines when people lose confidence in the courts. This should be of concern to all citizens.

Gender and Minority Representation in the Texas Judiciary

When asking how the gender, race, or ethnicity of Texas judges compares with these same traits in the state's general population, it is important to remember why the question is relevant. Many studies have asked whether such differences between judges and citizens appearing in their courts result in biased decisions.[19] We will never know the extent to which such bias exists or what forms it takes.

However, the racial, ethnic, and gender composition of Texas judges matters to our more general sense of fair treatment under the Constitution. We know that many provisions in the Bill of Rights seek to provide citizens with the elements of a fair criminal or civil trial: The state must fairly obtain evidence used in a criminal trial,[20] cannot force defendants to confess,[21] must provide procedures for a fair and speedy trial,[22] and must ensure the selection of fair and impartial juries in civil trials.[23] Further, we know that the Fourteenth Amendment guarantees citizens in each state due process and equal protection of the laws regardless of race, ethnicity, or gender.[24] This means that the Bill of Rights provisions for fair trials apply to the states and prohibit racial, ethnic, or gender bias in conducting trials.

With respect to at least one aspect of a fair trial—a fair and impartial jury—we know that the Fourteenth Amendment forbids eliminating jurors solely on the basis of their race,[25] ethnicity,[26] or gender.[27] When we consider the racial, ethnic, and gender composition of Texas judges, we have a general sense that our Constitutional right to a fair trial prohibits courts from biasing their results based on characteristics that should not influence how a court decides. In a general sense, Texans have, in fact, indicated in recent years that the gender, race, or ethnicity of judges can affect the fairness of state courts.[28] We don't know when or if these forms of bias creep into the process, but our general

Texas Supreme Court Justice Eva A. Guzman, sworn into office at the Texas Capitol on Jan. 11, 2010, is a well respected law judge who grew up in an impoverished Houston home.

sense of fairness suggests that electing judges from a diverse array of backgrounds will lessen whatever bias does exist.

If fair courts require judges that roughly reflect the ethnic, racial, and gender diversity of the Texas population, statistics indicate that the state still falls short. Approximately 49.6 percent of the state's general population is male.[29] However, 67 percent of Texas judges are male.[30]

Despite this disparity, the number of female judges in the state is significant and growing. Even as early as 1995, some major metropolitan areas in Texas saw a significant increase in the number of female judges. At that time, for example, almost half of the 59 sitting district court judges in Harris County were female.[31] As of 2013, 42 percent of justices serving on Texas Courts of Appeals were female,[32] and women have filled two or three of the nine seats on the Texas Supreme Court at different times in recent history.[33] Two women serve on the Texas Supreme Court and 4 of the 9 justices on the Texas Court of Criminal Appeals are women as of the Nov. 2014 election. Approximately 32.8 percent of all Texas judges are female.[34]

Statistics regarding ethnicity or national origin are especially significant in Texas given the fast-growing Hispanic population in the state. Of all Texas judges, in 2013 78 percent identify as "Caucasian" (or white) of non-Hispanic origin.[35] In the general population, by contrast, 44.5 percent of Texans identified themselves as white and non-Hispanic.[36] Sixteen percent of all judges are identified as Hispanic.[37] By contrast, 38.2 percent of the Texas population identified itself as Hispanic or Latino.[38]

Perhaps the most striking disparity between the composition of Texas judges and the state's general population can be seen among African Americans, who constitute 12.3 percent of the Texas population.[39] However, only 4.1 percent of all Texas judges are black.[40] Additionally, Figure 5.3 shows the disproportionate numbers of racial minorities incarcerated in Texas. Though African Americans only make

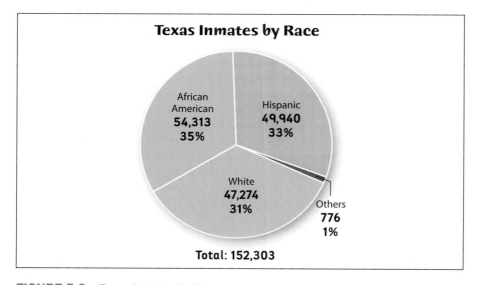

FIGURE 5.3   Texas Inmates by Race

SOURCE: Texas Department of Criminal Justice, Fiscal Year 2012 Statistical Report, Demographic Highlights (http://www.tdcj.state.tx.us/documents/Statistical_Report_FY2012.pdf).

up about 12 percent of the population in Texas, 35 percent of those incarcerated in Texas prisons are African American. One important commentator on the racial, ethnic, and gender composition of the Texas judiciary has observed with regard to African Americans:

> The low representation of African Americans is especially noteworthy since African Americans have disproportionately high rates of arrest and conviction in criminal cases. Worse, they represent an extremely high proportion of death row inmates. Though recent appointments to the Supreme Court have increased the visibility of African American judges, the racial make-up of the defendants and judges in the criminal court system continues to draw criticism.[41]

CORE OBJECTIVE

Thinking Critically...

As you learned from the discussion on minority representation in the Texas judicial system, African Americans represent 12.3 percent of the population of Texas, but only 4.1 percent of all judges in Texas are black. Compare these facts with Figure 5.3. What do you think accounts for the disproportionate number of African Americans incarcerated in Texas?

The "Appointive-Elective" System in Texas

Reformers, some of whom were elected through the current partisan system, have called for change to Texas's judicial selection process. Both nonpartisan and merit systems have been suggested. Some have pointed out that the state already has an **appointive-elective system**. The Texas governor can fill any seat for district or appellate court that becomes vacant because of death or resignation, or any new district court position created by the legislature. Vacancies in the county courts and justice of the peace courts are filled by the county governing body, the County Commissioners Court. Persons appointed to fill vacancies serve until the next regular election for that office, when they must stand for regular election.

appointive-elective system
In Texas, the system of many judges gaining the initial seat on the court by being appointed and later standing for election

Historically, many judges in Texas initially receive their seats on the courts by appointment. The data are not complete for all time periods, but enough is available to show that this is a common practice. Between 1940 and 1962, about 66 percent of the district and appellate judges were appointed by the governor to their first term on the court. In 1976, 150 sitting district court judges were appointed.[42] Table 5.3 shows data on appointments of sitting judges in 2013.

Judicial Selection: Is There a Best System?

The debate in Texas over judicial selection will continue in future sessions of the legislature. Judicial selection revolves around three basic issues. Citizens expect judges to be (1) competent, (2) independent and not subject to political pressures, and (3) responsive, or subject to democratic control. Each method used by the

TABLE 5.3

Texas Judges Serving in 2013 Who Were Appointed to Their Initial Seat on the Court

	Appointed		Elected	
	Number	Percent	Number	Percent
Supreme Court	6	67%	3	33%
Court of Criminal Appeals	2	22%	7	78%
Court of Appeals	42	53%	37	47%
District Courts	159	36%	285	64%
Criminal District Courts	2	15%	11	85%
County Courts at Law	59	25%	177	75%
Probate Courts	5	28%	13	72%
Constitutional County Courts	44	17%	210	83%
Justice of the Peace Courts	218	27%	597	73%
Municipal Courts	1,541	99%	20	1%

Source: Office of Court Administration, *Annual Statistical Reports, Fiscal Year 2013.* See Profile of Appellate and Trial Judges, (http://www.courts.state.tx.us/oca/judinfo.asp).

TABLE 5.4

Strengths and Weaknesses of Judicial Selection Methods

Method of Selection	Issue		
	Competence	Independence	Responsiveness
Appointment by governor	Strong	Strong	Weak
Election by legislature	Mixed	Strong	Weak
Merit/Missouri Method	Moderate	Moderate	Weak
Partisan election	Weak	Weak	Strong
Nonpartisan election	Mixed/Weak	Mixed/Weak	Strong

Source: Ann O. Bowman and Richard C. Kearney, *State and Local Government* (Boston: Houghton Mifflin, 1990), 286–297.

states to select judges has strengths and weaknesses regarding each of these issues (see Table 5.4).

When judicial selection is by appointment by the governor, there is great potential for selection of judges who are competent. However, it does not ensure competence. Governors can use judicial appointments to reward friends and repay political debts. All U.S. presidents, some more than others, have used their judicial appointive powers to select federal judges with political philosophies similar to their own. Governors do the same thing. In such cases, questions of judicial competence are sometimes raised.

Governors are not likely to select unqualified people for judicial appointments; however, governors might not be able to convince the best candidates to agree to serve. The appointive system probably rules out the completely incompetent, but it does not necessarily result in the appointment of the most competent people to serve as judges. Once appointed, judges are not responsive to voters and can exercise great independence in their decisions.

Election by the legislature is a system left over from colonial America when much power rested with the state legislature. It is used only in South Carolina and

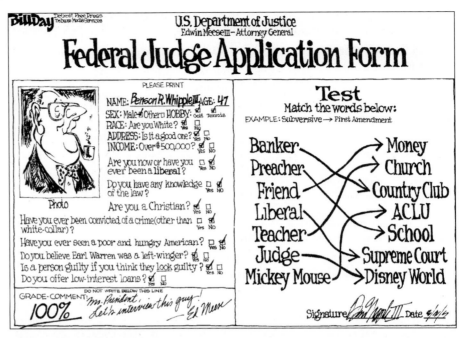

Some methods of selecting judges do not always result in the selection of qualified individuals. Bill Day. Reprinted by permission of United Features Syndicate, Inc.

Virginia. This system tends to select former legislators as judges. In South Carolina, the number of judges who formerly were legislators is very close to 100 percent. Appointment is viewed as a capstone to a successful legislative career.[43]

Nonpartisan election is one system being given serious consideration in Texas. This system would reduce the cost of campaigns and eliminate the problem of straight ticket voting. Voters would have to base their decisions on something other than party label. It would not necessarily result in the selection of more competent judges, but it would prevent the kind of large-scale changes in judgeships that happened in Harris County in 1994 and Dallas County in 2008. As indicated before, it has also been suggested that Texas prohibit straight ticket voting for judicial candidates, requiring voters to mark the ballot for each judicial race.

The merit, or Missouri, plan is also being given consideration as a method of selecting judges. Under this system, the governor would appoint judges from a list of acceptable (and, it is to be hoped, competent) candidates supplied by a judicial panel and perhaps ranked by the state bar association. Once appointed, the judge would serve for a set term and stand for retention in an election. In this retention election, voters could vote to either retain or remove the judge from office. The system is used by many states; 21 states use it for appellate judges, and 15 for trial judges.

It would seem that the merit plan would be strong on the issues of competency and responsiveness; however, there is little evidence that it results in the selection of more competent judges.[44] There is also evidence that it is weak on responsiveness. In retention elections, the judge does not have an opponent.[45] Voters vote to retain or remove. Several writers have pointed out that it is difficult to defeat someone with no one.[46] In the states that use this system, most judges are retained; fewer than 1 percent are ever removed.[47] One study showed that between 1964, when the system was first used, and 1984, only 22 of 1,864 trial judges were defeated.[48] When judges are removed, it is usually because of either an organized political effort to remove them from office or gross incompetence.

Some states have variations on these plans. In Illinois, judges are elected using a partisan ballot, but they must win 60 percent of the vote in a retention election to remain in office. In Arizona, judges in rural counties are elected in nonpartisan elections, but judges in the most populous counties are appointed. These variations might also be considered in Texas.

In short, no perfect system exists for selecting judges. All methods have problems. Also, there is no evidence that any one of these judicial selection methods results in the selection of judges with "substantially different credentials."[49] The only exception is that in the states where the legislature elects judges, more former legislators serve as judges.

Removing and Disciplining Judges

Most states provide some system to remove judges for misconduct. Impeachment, a little-used and very political process, is provided for in 43 states, including Texas. Five states allow for recall of judges by the voters.[50] One state, New Hampshire, allows the governor to remove a judge after a hearing. In five states, the legislature can remove judges by a supermajority vote (a two-thirds vote is most common). In recent years, the trend in the states has been to create a commission on judicial conduct to review cases of misconduct by judges and remove them from office. To date, 49 states have established judicial conduct commissions. Also, the method of removal of judges can depend on the level of the judgeship—for instance, trial judges versus appellate judges.

In Texas, the state supreme court may remove any judge from office. District judges may remove county judges and justices of the peace. The State Commission on Judicial Conduct may recommend the removal of judges at all levels. This 12-member commission conducts hearings and decides whether "the judge in question is guilty of willful or persistent conduct that is inconsistent with the proper performance of a judge's duties."[51] The commission can privately reprimand, publicly censure, or recommend that the state supreme court remove the judge.

The use of review commissions to reprimand, discipline, and remove judges is a good check on the actions of judges. If Texas adopts the merit, or Missouri, plan, this commission would probably increase in importance as a check on judges.

The Legal System

The American legal system can be broadly divided into civil and criminal branches. Civil cases are those between individual citizens and involve the idea of responsibilities, not guilt. Criminal cases are those cases brought against individuals for violations of law—crimes against society. Figures 5.4 and 5.5 present a breakdown of caseloads by type for both district and county courts in Texas.[52]

Under civil law, all individuals who believe they have cause or have been injured by others may file a civil lawsuit. Courts decide whether the case has validity and should be heard in the court.

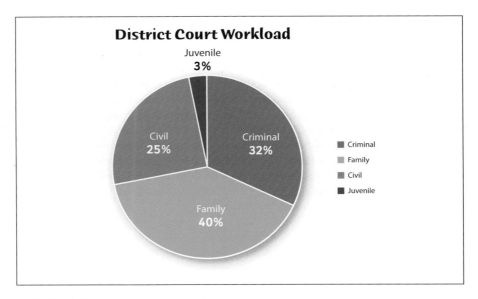

FIGURE 5.4   District Court Workload, 2013

SOURCE: Office of Court Administration, *Annual Statistical Reports, Fiscal Year 2013*. See: Activity Details for District Courts (http://www.courts.state.tx.us).

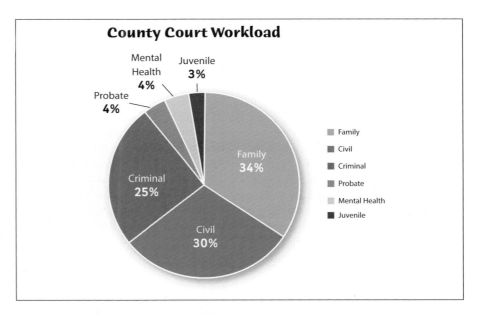

FIGURE 5.5   County Court Workload, 2013

SOURCE: Office of Court Administration, *Annual Statistical Reports, Fiscal Year 2013*. See: Activity Details for Statutory County Courts and Activity Details for Constitutional County Courts, (http://www.courts.state.tx.us).

Grand Jury

grand juries
Juries of citizens that determine if a person will be charged with a crime

Although any citizen may file a civil suit in court, a screening body must review criminal cases. The U.S. Constitution requires the use of **grand juries** to serve as a screening mechanism to prevent arbitrary actions by federal prosecutors. Some states use the grand jury system for some criminal cases, although in recent years the use of a formal hearing before a judge, which is called an **information or an administrative hearing**, has become more common. The judge reviews the facts and decides whether enough evidence exists to try the case.

Texas uses both grand juries and administrative hearings. A citizen may waive his or her right to review by a grand jury and ask that a judge review the charges. In Texas, grand juries consist of 12 citizens chosen by district judges in one of two ways. The district judge may appoint a grand jury commission that consists of three to five people.[53] Each grand jury commissioner supplies the judge with three to five names of citizens qualified to serve on a grand jury. From these names, the judge selects 12 citizens to serve as a grand jury. In the other method, the district judge can have 20 to 75 prospective grand jurors summoned in the same manner used for petit juries (described in the next section). From this group, the district judge selects 12 citizens who are called grand jurors.[54]

Most grand juries serve for six months. They often screen major criminal cases to decide whether enough evidence exists to go to trial. Grand juries are supposed to serve as filters to prevent arbitrary actions by prosecuting attorneys, but they do not always serve this function. The district attorney often dominates grand juries. Most grand jury members are laypeople who have never served before, and they frequently follow the advice of the prosecuting attorney. Although grand juries may conduct investigations on their own, few do. Those that do conduct investigations are sometimes termed "runaway grand juries" by the media.

A study by the *Houston Chronicle* presented evidence that some judges in Harris County had been given names of citizens for the grand jury by prosecutors from the district attorney's office. The study also demonstrated that many of the same citizens serve on grand juries year after year. Judges justified the repeated use of the same people for grand juries based on the difficulty of finding people to serve. Often, older, retired citizens volunteer to serve.[55]

Thus, a grand jury might not always serve the function of protecting citizens from arbitrary action by prosecutors. For this reason, a person may ask for an administrative hearing before a judge. During grand jury proceedings, the accused may not have an attorney present during the hearing; during an administrative hearing, however, the attorney is present and can protect the accused.

In Texas the prosecuting attorney leads minor criminal cases in county courts. The county court judge, who determines whether the case should proceed to trial, holds an "administration" hearing. Criminal cases in the county court are generally less serious than those led in district courts. They consist of DWI/DUI, minor theft, drug, assault, and traffic cases.

Petit Jury

Both criminal and civil cases can be decided by a petit (pronounced *petty*) jury. For **petit juries**, the Texas Government Code allows jurisdictions to draw upon two sources for jury selection. A jury pool may be selected randomly from voter registration lists or from a list of licensed drivers.[58] In criminal and civil cases, the defendant has the right to a trial by jury but may waive this right and let the judge decide the case.

Most people charged with a crime plead guilty, often in exchange for a lighter sentence. On average in Texas, over a million cases are filed in county courts each year, and fewer than 5,000 result in jury trials. Less than one-third of cases in the district courts are criminal cases. Most cases end in a plea bargain and never go to trial. The person charged agrees to plead guilty in exchange for a lesser sentence. The judge hearing the case can accept or reject the agreement.

information or administrative hearing
A hearing before a judge who decides if a person must stand trial; used in place of a grand jury

petit juries
Juries of citizens that determine the guilt or innocence of a person during a trial; pronounced *petty* juries

If all criminal cases were subject to jury trials, the court system would have to be greatly expanded. Many additional judges, prosecuting attorneys, and public defenders would be needed. In addition, many more citizens would have to serve on juries. The cost of this expanded process would be excessive, and even though citizens support "getting tough on criminals," they would balk at paying the bill.

Crime and Punishment in Texas

Today we hear a lot about crime and the rising crime rate. Political candidates often use the crime issue as a campaign strategy to prove to voters they will be "tough on criminals." It is a safe issue that offends few voters.

But how much crime is there nationally and in Texas? What factors seem to contribute to higher crime rates? Who commits most of the crimes? What impact does punishment have on crime rates? What is the cost of crime and punishment?

Crime has decreased in the United States over the past several decades, although less in Texas than in the United States as a whole (see Figure 5.6). Texas still ranks fifth among the 15 most populous states in total crime per 100,000 population.

Many factors contribute to the crime rate. Most crimes are committed in larger cities. If we compare the 50 states, we find a strong correlation between the percentage of the population living in urban (metropolitan) areas and crime rates. This in part explains the crime rate in Texas, because about 80 percent of the population of Texas lives in metropolitan areas.

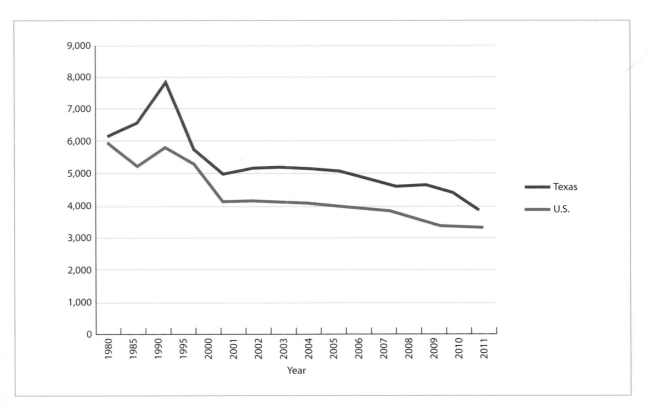

FIGURE 5.6   Crime Rates per 100,000, 1980–2011

TABLE 5.5

Persons Arrested for Crime by Sex, Race, and Age

	Percentage of Arrests
Sex	
Male	75.0%
Female	25.0%
Race	
White*	69%
Black	28%
Others	3%
Age	
Under 18 years of age	14%
Over 18 years of age	86%

*Includes Hispanics

Source: U.S. Census Bureau, *The 2012 Statistical Abstract,* Tables 324 and 325, (http://www.census.gov/compendia/statab/cats/law_enforcement_courts_prisons/arrests.html).

A strong relationship also exists between age, sex, and crime. People below 18 years of age commit almost 14 percent of the crimes, and males commit about 75 percent of all crimes. It has been suggested that if society could lock up all men between 18 and 25 years of age, crime would decline tremendously. Race is also a factor in crime. African Americans constitute about 13 percent of the U.S. population, yet, as shown in Table 5.5, they constitute almost 30 percent of persons arrested for crimes.

Juvenile Justice

As of 2013, 26.6 percent of the Texas population was under 18 years of age.[57] Both state and federal law in the United States treat juveniles differently under the law than adults. A citizen is a juvenile until he or she reaches the so-called age of majority, which in Texas is age 17 for civil and criminal responsibility before the law.[58] "Juvenile justice" includes not only those minors charged with civil or criminal wrongdoing, but also those who, through no fault of their own, find themselves wards of the state.

Texas state and local governments are charged with at least three general legal duties in cases involving minors. The first is *in loco parentis,*[59] which means that the state must act in the place of the parent to protect the interests of the child, even without a formal legal relationship. The second is *parens patriae,* which refers to the inherent power of the state to protect persons legally incapable of protecting themselves before the law.[60] The third is the "police powers doctrine": the duty of the state to protect the health, safety, and welfare of its citizens.[61] The state acts as a caretaker for the minor, a defender of his or her legal interests, and at the same time the guardian of public safety.

Because these duties are complex and difficult to carry out, Texas "juvenile justice" encompasses a large network of state and local authorities charged with meting out justice while also providing for the interests of minors. This network includes judges who must determine whether a minor faces full criminal responsibility as an adult; state agencies that must provide needed detention and living facilities; and caseworkers, lawyers, and other experts assigned to work on cases who must exercise discretion to act in the best interests of minors but also parents and crime victims.

Under certain circumstances, juveniles may be tried as adults.

From a legal perspective, Texas looks at juvenile justice as part of family law. As a result, the Juvenile Justice Code is actually Title III of the Texas Family Code, Chapters 51 through 61. The Juvenile Justice Code addresses a vast array of issues that arise when a minor is accused of wrongdoing: the jurisdiction of juvenile courts; appointment of counsel; minors suffering from mental problems or drug addiction; the rights of parents on the one hand and victims on the other. Texas faces restrictions on prosecuting or convicting a minor for crimes unless the juvenile court judge allows the minor to be tried as an adult in a nonjuvenile court. The juvenile court judge can consider whether the crime was against a person, whether the minor had a prior record, whether the minor's mental state at the time of the crime indicated criminal intent, whether the minor committed several crimes in the same transaction, and similar issues.[62]

Studies have shown that the legal system designates minors as adults for trial in a random way, and that reform of this decision-making process is needed.[63] Even if tried as an adult, a minor cannot be sentenced to life imprisonment without parole or to death if he or she committed the crime before the age of 18.[64] Nevertheless, minors tried as adults are not really the worst offenders in the juvenile system, but compared to other juvenile offenders, they face more serious consequences later in life from long sentences and criminal records that are more difficult to keep confidential.[65]

Courts that have jurisdiction to consider matters pertaining to juveniles range from the lowest level, such as justices of the peace, to constitutional county courts, statutory family law courts, county courts at law, and district courts. The 14 courts of appeals as well as the Texas Supreme Court and Court of Criminal Appeals review juvenile cases at times.[66] Some counties have dedicated either district courts or county courts at law to deal exclusively with juvenile cases. Harris County has three such "juvenile district courts"; Dallas County has two.[67]

Courts evaluate cases against juveniles, but local and state agencies carry the vast majority of responsibility for this population. At present, at least 168 local probation departments, in conjunction with district attorneys, complete most phases of a juvenile justice case. This includes a minor's intake, predisposition investigation, prosecution, as well as possible probation.[68]

Until 2011, two state agencies bore responsibilities for administering the juvenile justice system: the Texas Youth Commission and the Texas Juvenile Probation Commission. The Youth Commission managed 15 detention centers and nine halfway houses throughout the state to house juveniles before they were formally charged with offenses, before a court had disposed of their cases, and before they were released, for example.[69] The Juvenile Justice Probation Commission oversaw the entire juvenile justice system at the local level and coordinated state-local communication.[70] Because of controversies, however, the Texas legislature abolished both agencies in 2011 and created one agency—the Texas Juvenile Justice Department[71]—to carry out all duties each agency had originally handled. As a result, a great deal of uncertainty remains as to what shape Texas juvenile justice will take in the future.

Despite the uncertainties that now exist, statistics indicate that juvenile crimes are decreasing in Texas. Despite the legislature's 2007 decision to release minors in detention facilities who had been convicted of misdemeanors (minor offenses), the crime rate committed by juveniles has decreased in Texas from 2008 until 2009.[72]

As reflected by the number of juveniles referred to local probation authorities across the state as well as the number of minors processed by the Juvenile Justice Probation Commission, the rate of juvenile crime also decreased in 2010.[73] These trends suggest a hopeful future for the new state agency, the Texas Juvenile Justice Department, charged with carrying out wide-ranging and difficult responsibilities.

CORE OBJECTIVE

Taking Personal Responsibility...

Currently, at what age does the State of Texas consider a person an adult in criminal and civil proceedings? At what age do you think the state should require individuals to take personal responsibility?

The Effect of Punishment on Crime Rates

The attitude among most Texans is, "If you do the crime, you should do the time." Juries in Texas give longer sentences than the average nationwide (see Table 5.6).

However, the average time served in Texas is less than the national average, and the percentage of sentence served by violent offenders in Texas is also lower than the national average because of the longer sentences imposed by juries. The length of time served has increased in recent years because of an increase in available prison space. It will probably continue to increase, and the cost of keeping people in jail for longer periods of time will have to be weighed against the cost of other programs that might reduce crime.

Texas has one of the highest rates of incarceration. The incarceration rate in Texas as of 2013 was 601 per 100,000. Texas had tied with Alabama in the early 2010's for fourth-highest incarceration rate until 2013 when Texas sank to become fifth overall. Table 5.7 lists the 10 states with the highest incarceration rates. In raw numbers, there were 166,372 prisoners in Texas in 2012. This represents a 3.4 percent decrease from 2011 and a 4 percent increase from 2000.[74]

TABLE 5.6

Average Time Served by Texas Prisoners and Prisoners Nationwide

Type of Offense	Length of Average Sentence (years)		Average Time Served (years)		Percentage of Sentence Served	
	Nation	Texas	Nation	Texas	Nation	Texas
All violent offenses	6.8	9.9	4.2	7.6	62%	77%
Property	4.3	5.2	1.7	3.0	39%	57%
Drug	4.8	5.8	1.7	2.8	34%	49%

Source: Texas Data: Texas Department of Criminal Justice, *Statistical Report Fiscal Year 2011* (http://www.tdcj.state.tx.us/documents/Statistical_Report_2011.pdf); National Data: Bureau of Justice Statistics, *Table 9: Fiscal Releases from State Prison, 2009:* National Corrections Reporting Program: Sentence length of state prisoners, by offense, admission type, sex, and race. (http://bjs.ojp.usdoj.gov/index.cfm?ty=pbdetail&iid=2056).

TABLE 5.7	
Top 10 Incarceration Rate per 100,000 Residents by State	
State	Rate
Louisiana	893
Mississippi	717
Alabama	650
Oklahoma	648
Texas	**601**
Arizona	583
Georgia	542
Florida	524
Missouri	518
Idaho	499

Source: U.S. Department of Justice, *Bureau of Justice Statistics, Prisoners in 2013 - Advance Count,* July 2013 (http://www.bjs.gov/content/pub/pdf/p12ac.pdf.) Appendix Table 8.

Rehabilitation of Offenders

In Texas, as elsewhere, the criminal justice system should serve three broad purposes: to deter future criminal action, to punish criminal activity, and to rehabilitate the offender so that he or she does not break the law again upon returning to society.

To comprehend how critical it is to rehabilitate convicted criminals in Texas, we should consider a few basic statistics. First, crime rates in Texas have remained stagnant or dropped since the turn of the twenty-first century.[75] 2010 was no exception: The vast majority of crimes tracked as either crime reports or arrests dropped an average of 6 percent from 2009 to 2010 among juveniles and adults alike.[76] Further, the crime rates did not change significantly from 2001 until 2009.[77] Nevertheless, 740,905 Texans are under some form of criminal supervision, and more than 150,000 are imprisoned.[78] Both in terms of raw numbers and the rate at which it imprisons its citizens, Texas ranks among the top two or three in the nation.[79] Further, Texas built at least 94 prisons from 1980 until 2004, increased its spending on prisons by 1,600 percent between 1980 and 2004, and saw a 566 percent increase in its incarcerated population during the same time period.[80]

In other words, the crime rate is stagnating or declining, but the number of prisons, inmates, and public resources devoted to the criminal justice system has continued at high levels. Under these circumstances it becomes paramount to decrease **recidivism**, or the rate at which criminal offenders commit crime after they leave the state's custody. The statistics on repeat offenders as of 2004 were not encouraging: one estimate indicates that, from 1980 until 2004, approximately 65,169 inmates left Texas prisons and returned to their communities, and an estimated 23,070 returned to the prison system within three years.[81] Other studies confirm that, for juveniles and adults alike, the most likely repeat offenses will occur within three years of release from some form of criminal supervision.[82] Disturbingly, a high percentage of repeat offenders will commit a different category of crime than the one for which they were convicted.[83] Moreover, more than half of repeat offenses involve technical violations of the terms of probation rather than actual crimes against third parties.[84]

Clearly, Texas needs to find ways to improve its criminal justice system in general, and this includes the manner in which the state rehabilitates past offenders. The Rehabilitation Programs Division of the Texas Department of Criminal Justice administers and manages rehabilitation programs alongside other state and local

recidivism

The rate at which criminal offenders commit crime after they leave the state's custody departments in the criminal justice system that deal with issues such as parole, pardons, and health issues, as well as faith- and community-based organizations.[85] The stated goal of the Rehabilitation Programs Division is to develop a unified approach that deals with the criminal offender throughout the incarceration and post-release supervision period.[86]

There are signs that some of these efforts are working. In 2004, for example, 31.9 percent of released inmates returned to prison within three years. In 2007, that percentage had dropped to 24.3.[87] In 2011, the Texas Department of Criminal Justice released an evaluation of released offenders who had completed rehabilitation programs the legislature expanded in 2007.[88] For offenders released in 2007, the report found that recidivism rates were significantly lower for those who participated in the programs, which included the faith-based InnerChange Freedom Initiative (IFI), the Substance Abuse Felony Punishment (SAFP) Program, and the Violent Offender Reentry Initiative (SVORI).[89] Most of these programs decreased the three-year recidivism rate, and one—the SAFP Program—reduced recidivism by almost 14 percent.[90] In 2008, Texas also reported that its incarceration rate had dropped by 31 prisoners per 100,000 residents.[91] Texas needs to continue improving its rehabilitation programs to decrease the rates of incarceration and repeat offenses.

Death Penalty

It has often been suggested that the death penalty can reduce crime. The death penalty was outlawed in the United States in 1972 (*Furman v. Georgia*) because it was unfairly applied to many crimes and because of the lack of safeguards in place in many states. In 1976, the U.S. Supreme Court established guidelines under which a state could reinstate the death penalty (*Gregg v. Georgia*).

Texas is the leading state in both sentencing people to death and the number of prisoners executed. Since the death penalty was reinstated in the state in 1976, and executions began in 1982, Texas has executed 481 of the 1,289 people executed nationwide. Texas, with about 7 percent of the total population in the United States, has had 35 percent of the executions. Also, there is no shortage of people in Texas waiting to be executed. In October of 2013, there were 287 people on death row awaiting execution in Texas. At the rate of one execution per week, it would take more than five years to execute those persons. In 1995, Texas executed 19 of the 51 people executed nationwide. In 2000, Texas executed 40 of the 84 people executed nationwide.

Most executions (82 percent) have been in southern states. The death penalty fits well within the dominant traditionalistic culture of the South. In Texas and many other southern states, juries can set the sentence for all crimes, and juries might be more inclined than judges to impose the death penalty. As Table 5.8 shows, some states sentence many prisoners to death but carry out few executions.

The Harris County Factor

Although Texas leads the nation in both the number of persons sentenced to death and the number of executions, Harris County contributes a disproportionate share. In fact, Harris County (Houston) has contributed more death row inmates than the other large urban counties combined. Only five states (including Texas) have condemned more people to death (California, Florida, Pennsylvania, and North Carolina). Most counties in Texas contribute very few death row inmates. From 2007 to 2010, 43 death sentences were imposed in 21 counties, which represents only 8 percent of all counties in Texas. Of those 43 sentences, 13 were from Dallas and Harris County.[92]

TABLE 5.8

Death Row Inmates by State

Total Number of Death Row Inmates as of October 1, 2013: 3,088

State	Number Waiting to Be Executed	State	Number Waiting to Be Executed
California	741	Oklahoma	54
Florida	412	South Carolina	50
Texas	287	Missouri	49
Alabama	197	Mississippi	48
Pennsylvania	193	Arkansas	38
North Carolina	159	Oregon	36
Ohio	143	Kentucky	34
Arizona	125	Delaware	18
Georgia	94	Indiana	13
Louisiana	88	Idaho	12
Tennessee	81	Nebraska	11
Nevada	80	Connecticut	11
U.S. Government	59		

Source: Death Penalty Information Center. See (http://www.deathpenaltyinfo.org/documents/FactSheet.pdf).

What factors contribute to the large number of death sentences in Texas, and in Harris County in particular? First, the statutes in Texas for assigning a death sentence are among the least complicated. A jury must first answer two questions: (1) Did the defendant act intentionally, and (2) Is the defendant a future threat to society? If a person commits murder while committing another crime (rape, robbery) or kills two people, or kills a police officer, a firefighter, or child, or is a murderer for hire and did it intentionally and is a threat, the person can receive the death sentence. These standards make it easy for juries to answer yes, and approve a death sentence.

Second, the Texas Court of Criminal Appeals almost never reverses a death sentence. Until recently, only 11 of 300 capital cases have been reversed or sent back to lower courts. In 2011, the Court of Criminal Appeals upheld all cases brought before it. Recently, this court failed to reverse a death sentence when the defense attorney slept during part of the trial. The chief justice of the court, Judge Sharon Keller, in her campaign for election, stated that failure to execute condemned murderers was a violation of human rights.[93] Likewise, the U.S. Fifth Circuit is reluctant to overturn appeals. This court upheld the conviction in the case of the sleeping defense attorney. Thus, the likelihood of winning a case on appeal in Texas is small. The purpose of appellate courts is to check on procedures and processes in lower courts and make sure no mistakes are made. Judging by the number of reversals, few mistakes are made in Texas district criminal courts. Those that are found are ruled as not important in most cases. Finally, the Texas Board of Pardons and Paroles, often the final recourse for those with failed appeals, is even less apt to make changes. In the 5-year period from 2007 to 2011, the Board of Pardons and Paroles reviewed 139 clemency cases. Out of those, only four cases were recommended for commutation of sentence (see Table 5.9).[94] As Table 5.9 shows, even if the board makes a recommendation, the governor is unlikely to approve. In the 13 years Governor Perry was in office, he commuted only 31 capital sentences, and 28 of those cases were solely due to a U.S. Supreme Court decision banning capital punishment of minors.[95]

TABLE 5.9

Clemency Actions by the Board of Pardons and Paroles, 2007–2011

Clemency Type	Cases Considered by the Board	Cases Recommended by the Board	Cases Approved by the Governor
Commutation of Sentence	78	4	2
Reprieves of Execution	57	0	0
Conditional Pardons	4	0	0
Total Death Penalty Actions	139	4	2

TABLE 5.10

Public Opinion on the Death Penalty in Texas

Which of the following characterizes your opinion on the death penalty for those convicted of violent crimes?

Strongly support	42%
Somewhat support	31%
Somewhat oppose	11%
Strongly oppose	10%
Don't know	5%

Generally speaking, do you believe the death penalty is applied fairly or unfairly in Texas today?

Fairly	51%
Unfairly	28%
Don't know	21%

If you could choose between the following two approaches, which do you think is the better penalty for murder?

The death penalty	53%
Life imprisonment with absolutely no possibility for parole	37%
Don't know	10%

Source: University of Texas/*Texas Tribune* May 2012 Poll, *Texas Politics* (http://texaspolitics.laits.utexas.edu/11_9_14.html).

Money is also a factor in determining whether the prosecuting attorney will ask for a death sentence. Smaller, rural counties often lack the money to prosecute a death sentence case. Even large urban counties often find that death sentence cases will strain their budgets. Harris County is an exception to this, which partly explains the reason for so many death sentence convictions. The budget for the Harris County District Attorney's office is $30 million, and it has a staff of 230 assistant district attorneys. Dallas County, by contrast, has a budget of about $20 million. Some of the difference is due to a lower caseload in Dallas. Harris County also has a total of 22 felony courts (compared to 8 in Dallas County). Of the 22 Harris County courts, all but two judges are former prosecutors in the Harris County District Attorney's Office.[96]

One can question the high rate of death sentences in Texas and the procedures for appeal. Despite these shortcomings, the public heavily favors the death penalty: 73 percent of Texans support the death penalty versus 61 percent of those polled nationally.[97] Table 5.10 provides public opinion data of Texans polled about the death penalty. Texas favors the death penalty more strongly than the nation as a whole and thinks the death penalty is a deterrent to crime. Also, Texans feel safer because of the death penalty.

Little evidence suggests that the death penalty is a deterrent to crime. Endless delays and appeals and the long time span between the sentence and the execution reduce the effectiveness of the death penalty. In Texas the average time from sentence to execution is 10.6 years.[98] David Lee Powell spent the longest amount of time on death row—31 years.[99] Powell was finally executed in June of 2010, making him the 460th person executed by the state of Texas. No public officials are advocating a return to public executions, but it has been suggested that this might increase the power of the death sentence as a deterrent to crime. However, most crimes are not capital crimes, so the death penalty would do little, even under "ideal circumstances," to reduce the crime rate.

Additionally, inmates on death row are invariably poor and disproportionately African American or Hispanic. Few middle- and upper-class Anglos are sentenced to death in capital cases. This disparity in sentencing raises questions about equity under the law. Of the 515 people executed in Texas between December 1982 and August 2014, 231 (45 percent) were white, 190 (37 percent) were black, and 92 (18 percent) were Hispanic. Only 5 were female.[100]

Impact of Income and Poverty on Legal Services

To understand the profound impact of economic status on the ability to obtain legal representation or participate effectively in the legal system, some basic statistics describing the population of Texas are necessary. In 2013, the United States census estimated that 26,448,193 people lived in Texas.[101] Of these, approximately 17.4 percent lived below federally defined poverty thresholds for the size family they lived in and with the income of wage earners in that family.[102] As of 2013, the federal poverty threshold for an individual under the age of 65 was $12,119.00; for two people, this figure increased to $15,679.00.[103]

When we discuss legal services for the poor, we should focus on the entire population below the poverty line and not just those who might themselves become a party to some kind of civil or criminal lawsuit. This is because anyone, from an infant to an elderly person, may require some form of legal services: legal issues arising from the quality of care given to an infant and health issues related to an elderly person may both require legal representation, for example. Moreover, we cannot assume that Texans below the poverty line are the only ones who cannot afford the help of an attorney. Legal aid services for the poor often use twice the federal poverty threshold as their guideline for free legal services, for example.[104] The result: roughly speaking, over 4 million Texans[105] live below federal poverty thresholds and have no prospect whatsoever of paying for legal services; probably twice this figure or more have no realistic prospect of obtaining legal help.

Texas addresses these citizens' need for legal representation with a patchwork of public and private resources at the state and local levels. Attorneys may pay a percentage of their income into the Texas Interest on Lawyers' Accounts program, which distributes money contributed to nonprofit legal services for the poor.[106] Free or reduced-fee legal representation is referred to as *pro bono,* short for *pro bono publico,* or "for the public good." Private law firms sometimes require their attorneys to devote a percentage of their time to *pro bono* work, often coordinated through the Texas Bar Association's Lawyers Giving Back program.[107] University legal clinics[108] and nonprofit organizations[109] provide representation to a small number of indigent clients on a wide range of civil and criminal matters, such as immigration, environmental protection, family and domestic abuse matters, criminal defense, and death penalty defense. The Texas Bar Association[110] and local bar associations[111] offer referral services to attorneys who may work for reduced rates if a client is poor. Courts can appoint defense counsel in criminal cases. The Texas Access to Justice Commission is a state agency that funds indigent legal services for thousands of clients—primarily with problems related to marriage, child custody, and domestic abuse, and other issues—but the future of legal help funded by this agency is in jeopardy because the state legislature has not assured them of future funding.[112] Whether in civil or criminal matters, the result is that Texas provides little assistance to indigent citizens for their legal needs. For example, Texas ranks last in the 50 states for indigent criminal defense spending.[113] The ultimate result: tens of thousands of low-income Texans likely represent themselves *pro se*—without an attorney—in legal matters that will have an impact on the rest of their lives.[114]

Conclusion

In the twenty-first century, the court system in Texas faces many challenges. Methods of selecting judges will continue to be controversial. Some change in these methods will probably occur. Texans may want to think about their approach to dealing with the high crime rates in the state. Although voters seem anxious to approve bonds for the construction of more prisons, they are reluctant to consider other approaches to crime control. The long-term cost of having the highest prison population and the highest execution rate in the world should be weighed against the cost of alternative programs that might more effectively reduce crime.

Key Terms

appellate courts
appointive-elective system
grand juries
information or administrative
    hearing
magistrate functions

merit system, or Missouri system
name familiarity
nonpartisan election
objectivity
partisan election
petit juries

recidivism
stare decisis
straight ticket voting system
trial courts
trial de novo courts

Notes

[1] Herbert Jacob, "Courts: The Least Visible Branch," in *Politics in the American States,* 6th ed., eds. Virginia Gray and Herbert Jacob (Washington, D.C.: Congressional Quarterly Press, 1996), 254.

[2] Ibid.

[3] Dye, *Politics in States and Communities,* 8th ed., 227.

[4] Ibid.

[5] Ibid.

[6] Ibid.

[7] Ibid., 228.

[8] Jacob, "Courts," 253.

[9] Ibid., 256–258.

[10] Office of Court Administration, Texas Judicial Council, *Texas Judicial System Annual Report* (Austin: Office of Court Administration, 1994), 31–33.

[11] *Book of the States,* 1998–99, 131–32, table 4.2.

[12] Ibid., 186–189.

[13] Delaware, Maine, Massachusetts, New Hampshire, New Jersey, New York, and Vermont have some judges who are appointed by the governor and can be removed only for cause. Connecticut, Rhode Island, South Carolina, and Virginia have legislative elections; judges serve for life with good behavior. See Jacob, "Courts," 268, Table 7.2. Also see *Book of the States,* 1994–95, 190–193, Table 4.4. There are some slight variations between the Jacob table and the table in *Book of the States.* This is probably due to interpretations by the writers. Because of minor variations among states, classification differences are possible.

[14] *Houston Chronicle,* "A Closer Look at Harris County's Vote," 14 November 2002, 32A.

[15] Anthony Champagne, "Campaign Contributions in Texas Supreme Court Races," *Crime, Law, and Social Change* 17 (1992): 91–106.

[16] Texans for Public Justice, *Courtroom Contributions,* February 2012.

[17] Texans for Public Justice, *Courtroom Contributions Stain Supreme Court Campaigns,* http://info.tpj.org/reports/courtroomcontributions/courtroomcontributions.pdf.

[18] Texans for Public Justice, "Billable Ours: Texas Endures Another Attorney Financed Supreme Court Race." http://info.tpj.org/reports/supremes06/supremes06.pdf.

[19] See, for example, Sherrilyn A. Ifill, "Judging the Judges: Racial Diversity and Representation on State Trial Courts," 39 Boston College Law Review 95 (1998). http://lawdigitalcommons.bc.edu/bclr/vol.39/iss1/3.

[20] See Fourth Amendment to the United States Constitution.

[21] See Fifth Amendment to the United States Constitution.

[22] See Sixth Amendment to the United States Constitution.

[23] See Sixth Amendment to the United States Constitution.

[24] See Fourteenth Amendment to the United States Constitution.

[25] *Batson v. Kentucky,* 476 U.S. 79 (1986).

[26] *United States v. Martinez-Salazar,* 528 U.S. 304 (2000).

[27] *J.E.B. v. Alabama,* 511 U.S. 127 (1994).

[28] In a 1998 study, with respect to gender, only 50 percent of respondents agreed that men and women are treated alike in Texas courts, and 62 percent believed that there are too few female judges in Texas. Texans expressed even greater concern about fairness with regard to race. Only 41 percent reported that "the courts treat all people alike regardless of race," and 55 percent believe that there are too few minority judges. Supreme Court of Tex., Tex. Office of Court Admin. & State Bar of Tex., PUBLIC TRUST & CONFIDENCE IN THE COURTS AND THE LEGAL PROFESSION IN TEXAS: SUMMARY REPORT (1998), http://www.courts.state.tx.us/pubs/publictrust/index.htm. (Study cited in Anthony Champagne and Kyle Chet, "The Cycle of Judicial Elections: Texas as a Case Study," 29 Fordham L.J. 29(3) article 7 (2001), http://ir.lawnet.fordham.edu/ulj).

[29] Quickfacts, "States," http://quickfacts.census.gov/qfd/states/48000.html.

[30] Texas Politics: 2 Oct 2012: "Profiling Texas Judges." Liberal Arts Instructional Technology Services, University of Texas at Austin, 3rd Edition—Revision 6, http://www.laits.utexas.edu/txp_media/html/just/features/ 0403_01/judges.html.

[31] Sherrilyn A. Ifill, "Judging the Judges: Racial Diversity and Representation on State Trial Courts," 39 Boston College Law Review 95 at p. 96, note 7 (1998), http://lawdigitalcommons.bc.edu/bclr/vol.39/iss1/3.

[32] http://www.houston-opinions.com/Tex-App-Female-Justices-and-Male-Justices-on-the-Texas-Courts-of-Appeals-gender-ratio-html.

[33] Texas Office of Court Administration, "Texas Supreme Court," http://www.supreme.courts.state.tx.us/court/justices.asp(three female justices 2001–2005).

[34] Texas Office of Court Administration, *Annual Statistical Reports, Fiscal Year 2013.* Profile of Appellate and Trial Judges, http://www.courts.state.tx.us/pubs/AR2012/jud_branch/3-judge-profile.pdf.

[35] Ibid.

[36] Quickfacts, "States," http://quickfacts.census.gov/qfd/states/48000.html.

[37] Texas Office of Court Administration, *Annual Statistical Reports, Fiscal Year 2013.*

[38] Quickfacts, "States," http://quickfacts.census.gov/qfd/states/48000.html.

[39] Texas Office of Court Administration, *Annual Statistical Reports, Fiscal Year 2013.*

[40] Quickfacts, "States," http://quickfacts.census.gov/qfd/states/48000.html.

[41] Texas Office of Court Administration, "Profile of Appellate and Trial Judges" (as of December 30, 2003), http://www.courts.state.tx.us/publicinfo/AR2003/jb/judge_profile.pdf.

[42] Kramer and Newell, *Texas Politics,* 3rd ed. (New York: West, 1987), 281.

[43] Herbert Jacob, "The Effect of Institutional Differences in the Recruitment Process: The Case of State Judges," *Journal of Public Law* 33, no. 113 (1964): 104–119.

[44] Bradley Canon, "The Impact of Formal Selection Processes on Characteristics of Judges—Reconsidered," *Law and Society Review* 13 (May 1972): 570–593.

[45] Richard Watson and Rondal G. Downing, *Politics of the Bench and Bar: Judicial Selection under the Missouri Nonpartisan Court Plan* (New York: John Wiley, 1969).

[46] Dye, *Politics in States and Communities,* 8th ed., 236.

[47] William Jenkins, "Retention Elections: Who Wins When No One Loses," *Judicature* 61 (1977): 78–86.

[48] William K. Hall and Larry T. Aspen, "What Twenty Years of Judicial Retention and Elections Have Told Us," *Judicature* 70 (1987): 340–347.

[49] Craig F. Emmert and Henry R. Glick, "The Selection of Supreme Court Judges," *American Politics Quarterly* 19 (October 1988): 444–465.

[50] *Book of the States,* 1998–99, 138–148, Table 4.5.

[51] Commission on Judicial Conduct, *Annual Report,* 1994 (Austin: Commission on Judicial Conduct, State of Texas, 1994).

[52] Office of Court Administration, *Annual Report for the Judiciary, Fiscal Year 2013,* http://www.courts.state.tx.us/pubs/AR2011/toc.htm.

[53] Interview with District Court Judge John Delaney, Brazos County Courthouse, November 1995.

[54] *Texas Code of Criminal Procedure,* arts. 19.01—20.22.

[55] *Houston Chronicle,* "Murder Case Testing Grand Jury Selection," 2 March 2002, 1A and 16A.

[56] *Texas Government Code,* sec. 62.001.

[57] People Quick Facts, http://quickfacts.census.gov/qfd/states/48000.html.

[58] Texas Family Code section 51.041(a).

[59] See, for example, definition of "in loco parentis" in the Free Legal Dictionary, http://legal-dictionary.thefreelegaldictionary.com/in+loco+parentis.com.

[60] See, for example, definition of "parens patriae" in the Free Legal Dictionary, http://legal-dictionary.thefreelegaldictionary.com/prens+patriae.com.

[61] See, for example, definition of the police power doctrine in the Free Legal Dictionary, http://legal-dictionary.thefreelegaldictionary.com/Police+powers.com.

[62] Texas Family Code section 54.02.

[63] Michele Deitch, *Juveniles in the Adult Criminal Justice System in Texas,* LBJ School of Public Affairs, University of Texas at Austin, Special Project Report, March 2011: http://www.utexas.edu/lbj/sites/default/files/file/news/juvenilestexas--final.pdf.

[64] Death penalty: see Tarlton Law Library, Jamail Center for Legal Research, Texas Death Penalty Law: Resources and Information about the Death Penalty Law in Texas, http://www.tarltonguides.law.utexas.edu/texas-death-penalty. See also Texas Penal Code section 8.07(c). Life sentence: see *Miller v. Alabama*, United States Supreme Court, June 2012.

[65] Ibid. See also provisions relating to expunging or keeping confidential the criminal records of minors: Texas Government Code section 411.081 (orders of non-disclosure), Texas Family Code section 58.003 (sealing juvenile records); Texas Family Code section 58.203 (automatic restriction of access to juvenile records except by law enforcement officers).

[66] http://www.txcourts.gov/oca/pdf/Court_Structure_Chart.pdf.

[67] http://www.justex.net/courts/Juvenile/JuvenileCourts.aspx.

[68] http://www.tjjd.texas.gov/about.aspx.

[69] http://www.tyc.state.tx.us/about/history.html.

[70] http://www.tyc.tx.us/about_us/juv_justice_overview.html. See also Texas Human Resource Code Chapter 141.

[71] Pursuant to Senate Bill 653 passed by the 82nd Texas Legislature and signed by the governor, the Texas Juvenile Justice Department (TJJD) was created on December 1, 2011, and the existing Texas Juvenile Probation Commission (TJPC) and Texas Youth Commission (TYC) were abolished. On December 1, 2011, operations of both TJPC and TYC were transferred to the new TJJD and all references to TJPC and TYC were changed to the new name. http://www.tjjd.texas.gov.

[72] Efforts to revoke probation for a new offense or rule violation dropped from 2008 to 2009; statewide referrals to juvenile probation dropped 4.3 percent from 2007 to 2008; juvenile referrals in Bexar and Dallas Counties dropped significantly in 2007–2008. See " Right on Crime: Reform in Action," http://www.rightoncrime/reform-in-action/state-initiatives/texas/; citing the following: "Total of Reported Juvenile Activity," Office of Court Administration, Fiscal Year 2008, 21 Dec. 2009, http://www.courts.state.tx.us/pubs/AR2008/juvenile/2-juvenile-activity-by-co-fy08.pdf.; "Total of Reported Juvenile Activity," Office of Court Administration, Fiscal Year 2009, 21 Dec. 2009, http://www.courts.state.tx.us/pubs/AR2009/juvenile/2-juvenile-activity-by-co-fy09.pdf; "Texas Youth Commission and Texas Juvenile Probation Commission Coordinated Strategic Plan Fiscal Year 2010," 8 Dec. 2009, 12 Jan. 2010, http://www.tyc.state.tx.us/about/TJPC_TYC_Coordinated_Strategic_Plan_FY2010.pdf; "Bexar County Juvenile Probation Monthly Trend Report," 15 July 2009, 10 Jan. 2010, http://www.co.bexar.tx.us/bcjpd/JVD_uploads/Monthly_Trend_Report_2009_06.pdf; Dallas County 3rd Quarter FY 2009 Performance Measures, 21 Oct. 2009, 10 Jan. 2010, http://www.dallascounty.org/department/budget/documents/3rdQuarter09PerfMeasure.pdf.

[73] Texas Juvenile Justice Department, The State of Juvenile Probation Activity in Texas 2009–2010 (November 11, 2011), citing Texas Juvenile Justice System Statistical Report Calendar Years 2009–2010, http://www.tjjd.texas.gov/statistics/staisticsdetail.aspx.

[74] U.S. Department of Justice, Bureau of Justice Statistics, Prisoners in 2013, June 2013, (http://www.bjs.gov/content/pub/pdf/p12ac.pdf.)

[75] Texas Department of Public Safety: Annual Report of Data Collection for 2009 (released 2010), http://www.txdps.state.tx.us/director_staff/public_information/2010CIT.pdf.

[76] Ibid.

[77] Ibid.

[78] Robert Perkinson, "Fast Facts" from Texas Tough: the Rise of America's Prison Empire (2011). http://texastough .com/resources/facts/.

[79] Ibid.

[80] Ibid.

[81] Ibid.

[82] Texas Legislative Budget Board, *Statewide Criminal Justice Recidivism and Revocation Rates* (2005), http://www.lbb.state.tx.us/PubSafety_CrimJustice/3_Reports/Recidivism_Report_2005.pdf.

[83] Ibid.

[84] Ibid.

[85] Texas Department of Criminal Justice: Rehabilitation Programs Division. http://www.tdcj.state.tx.us/divisions/rpd/index.html.

[86] Website for Texas Department of Criminal Justice: Rehabilitation Programs Division. http://www.tdcj.state.tx.us/divisions/rpd/index.html.

[87] Allan Turner, "Study Praises Texas for Prison Reforms But Comes with a Warning," *Houston Chronicle*, April 12, 2011. http://www.chron.com/news/houston-texas/article/Study-praises-Texas-for-prison-reforms-but-comes-1689770.php.

[88] Joseph A. Adams, "Texas Rehabilitation Programs Reduce Recidivism Rates," Right on Crime, May 16, 2011. http://www.rightoncrime.com/2011/05/texas-rehabilitation- programs-reduce-recidivism-rates/.

[89] Ibid.

[90] Ibid.

[91] United States Bureau of Justice Statistics (2009), "Prisoners in 2008," http://bjs.ojp.usdoj.gov/content/pub/pdf/p08.pdf.

[92] Texas Coalition to Abolish the Death Penalty, Texas Death Penalty Developments in 2010: The Year in Review, www.http://tcadp.org/TexasDeathPenaltyDevelopments 2010.pdf.

[93] *Houston Chronicle*, 9 February 2001, 6.

[94] Texas Board of Pardons and Paroles, Publications, Annual Reports 2007–2011, http://www.tdcj.state.tx.us/bpp/publications/publications.html.

[95] *The Texas Tribune*, "Under Perry, Executions Raise Questions," (September 2012), http://www.texastribune.org/texas-people/rick-perry/under-perry-executions-raise-questions/.

[96] *Houston Chronicle*, 4 February 2001, 1A, 24A–27A.

[97] Gallup Poll, Support for the Death Penalty, October 2012, http://www.gallup.com/poll/1606/death-penalty.aspx.

[98] Texas Department of Criminal Justice, Death Row Information, Executions December 7, 1982 through April 17, 2014, http://www.tdcj.state.tx.us/death_row/dr_executions_by_year.html. Death Row Information, Executed Offenders, 17 April 2014, http://www.tdcj.state.tx.us/death_row/dr_executed_offenders.html.

[99] Ibid.

[100] Ibid.

[101] Quick Facts, http://quickfacts.census.gov/qfd/states/48000.html.

[102] Ibid.

[103] See (http://www.census.gov/hhes/www/poverty/index.html)

[104] The law clinics at Tulane University in New Orleans, Louisiana, use twice the poverty threshold as their guideline for representation, for example. See (http://www.tulane.edu/~telc/more.html.)

[105] Based on the 2013 United States census estimates for population and the percentage of Texans below federal poverty thresholds, approximately 4,601,985 citizens.

[106] http://www.tealjf.org/attorneys/whatisiolta.aspx.

[107] www.texasbar.com/AM/Template.cfm?Section=Lawyers_Giving_Back.

[108] For example, the legal clinics at the University of Texas and Saint Mary's University: see www.stmarytx.edu/law/index.php?site=centerforlawandsocialjustice and www.utexas.edu/law/clinic.

[109] The Texas Civil Rights Project, for example. See http://www.texascivilrightsproject.org.

[110] See discussion of state bar referral program at www.texasbar.com.

[111] The Lawyer Referral Service of Central Texas, for example, makes approximately 10,000 referrals per year. See http://www.austinlrs.com.

[112] Bobby Cervantes, "Legal Aid to Low-Income Texans at Risk, Groups Say," Texas Politics, *San Antonio Express News* and *Houston Chronicle,* February 16, 2011. http://blog.mysanantonio.com/texas-politics/2011/02/legal-aid-to-low-income-texans-at-risk-groups-say/.

[113] Robert Perkinson, "Fast Facts" from Texas Tough: The Rise of America's Prison Empire (2011). http://texastough.com/resources/facts/.

[114] Bobby Cervantes, " Legal Aid to Low-Income Texans at Risk, Groups Say," Texas Politics, *San Antonio Express News* and *Houston Chronicle,* February 16, 2011. http://blog.mysanantonio.com/texas-politics/2011/02/legal-aid-to-low-income-texans-at-risk-groups-say/.

CHAPTER 6

Local Governments in Texas

Upon completing this chapter,
you will be able to...

- **Describe local political systems in Texas.**

Local governments in Texas and throughout the United States are hiding in plain sight. Evidence of local government is all around us: paved streets, sidewalks, clean water, fire stations, police cars, parks, and schools. Yet many citizens are either unaware or uninterested in the operations and procedures of local governments and local government elections. Most citizens show as little interest in the former as the latter. Voter turnout in local government elections is consistently the lowest year in and year out when compared to federal and state elections.

At least 80 percent of Texans live in urban areas and rely on local governments for a host of services, and they have been increasing their demands for a greater range of services. Local governments, in short, provide some of the services that make our modern lives possible. Even the 20 percent of Texans who live in rural areas rely on services from county governments and special districts. It is important for us, as Texans, to understand how local governments work and affect our lives.

Austin City Hall

Federalism Revisited

The United States is characterized by its highly decentralized system of government. This lack of centralization has its roots in the historic fear of a strong national government and the principles of federalism enshrined in the U.S. Constitution. Federalism is the political principle that assigns different functions to different levels of government. In Chapter 2 we focused on the relationship between the central government and the various state governments in our federalist structure. Local governments add another layer. Decentralization and the lack of intergovernmental coordination are trends in Texas government and throughout the United States. Nationwide, there are approximately 89,000 local government units, and Texas has almost 5,000 of them. Counts for 2012 on the number of local governments by category are presented in Table 6.1 (revised as of Sept 2013).

Creatures of the State

In a federal system in which multiple governments share authority over the same territory, states possess police powers—the authority to regulate the health, safety, and morals of their citizens. These powers, granted under the 10th Amendment, are exercised through the enactment and enforcement of statutes. Enforcement here includes not just what we more commonly think of as 'police' power (actual police forces; the people in uniform) but also legal sanctions and other methods of nonphysical coercion. States are allowed to form local governments to aid the states in the performance of their police powers. Constitutionally, municipalities and other local governments are legal **creatures of the states**. This means municipal and other local governments are constrained by the same legal limits as are states and lack any legal existence independent of state action. On the other hand, unitary governments, while also able to form creatures of the state, strictly dictate what those governments can and cannot do. Unlike in a federal system where states are granted all those powers not expressly given to the national government, unitary systems are much more centralized. State-level governments receive only those powers expressly granted by the central governing authority. The same principle goes for municipalities and other local governments.

The states, in our federal system, have substantial discretion in the authority they grant their local governments, and local governments within each state have different types of authority. We can categorize local governments by the amount

creatures of the state
Local governments are created by state government, and all powers are derived from the state government; there are no inherent rights for local governments independent of what the state grants to them

TABLE 6.1

Number of Local Governments in the United States and Texas, 2012

	United States	Texas
Counties	3,031	254
Cities	19,522	1,214
Townships	16,364	—*
School districts	12,884	1,079
Special districts	37,203	2,600
Totals	89,004	5,147

*Texas does not have townships.

Source: U.S. Census Bureau, *2012 Census of Governments: The Many Layers of American Government*. See (http://www2.census.gov/govs/cog/2012/2012_cog_map.pdf).

of authority granted to them by the states; there are general-purpose and limited-purpose local governments. General-purpose governments are granted broad discretionary authority to act on a range of issues and to control their own spending, revenue, and personnel, and to establish and modify their own governmental structures. Conversely, limited-purpose governments are granted rather narrow authority to act and have little leeway over revenue, spending, and personnel; the structure of their governments is set by the state.[1]

Examples of limited-purpose government in Texas include school districts and counties. A school district has but one function—education. Its taxing authority is limited to the property tax, and many personnel issues are controlled by a state agency. Texas counties are also limited-purpose governments. State law severely restricts county authority and revenue sources, and all 254 Texas counties share the same government structure.

Municipalities are the most visible example of general-purpose governments in Texas. Home rule Texas cities (see the following section) are granted the authority to pass any ordinance not expressly forbidden by the state constitution or state laws, and they have multiple sources of revenue. Texas home rule cities have greater discretion in deciding their government structure, and the state has limited authority over cities' personnel decisions. Consequently, not all local governments are created equal, although all are legal creatures of their states. Cities, counties, special districts, and school districts all have their unique aspects.

General Law Cities and Home Rule

City governments are municipal corporations, granted a corporate charter by their state. The term *municipality* derives from the Roman *municipium,* which means a "free city capable of governing its local affairs, even though subordinate to the sovereignty of Rome."[2] A city's charter is its constitution; it provides the basic organization and structure of the city government and outlines the general powers and authority of its government and officials. Cities in Texas are chartered as either a **general law city** or a **home rule city**. The charters for general law cities are spelled out in state statutes, and those cities must choose from the seven charters provided in these statutes.[3] There are approximately 938 general law cities in Texas.[4]

After the approval of a state constitutional amendment in 1912, Texas cities with populations of at least 5,000 may be chartered as home rule cities.[5] Most cities with such populations choose to be home rule cities. Home rule allows local citizens a greater range of governmental structure and organization and allows such cities the authority to pass ordinances not prohibited by state law. Although there is no specific grant of power to cities in the state constitution, cities can pass any ordinance that does not conflict with state law or violate the state constitution. For example, no state law establishes the number of city council members, but the state constitution does establish a ceiling of four years for terms of office.

Prohibitions on local government action can be implicit or explicit. For example, there is no explicit prohibition against cities passing an ordinance banning open alcohol containers in vehicles. Several Texas cities passed such ordinances in the 1980s before there was a state law against open containers. However, state courts ruled that the regulation of alcohol was a state function and, by *implication,* Texas cities could not pass ordinances banning open alcohol containers in vehicles.

The home rule provisions of the Texas Constitution allow great latitude in governing local affairs. Once adopted, home rule charters may be amended solely with the

general law city
Cities governed by city charters created by state statutes

home rule city
Cities governed by city charters created by the actions of local citizens

approval of the city voters. Usually a charter review commission or the city council proposes amendments. Approximately 243 home rule charters allow voters to initiate charter amendments,[6] yet at times state law allows home rule councils to amend their charters, without the vote of their citizens, on specific issues. For example, the Texas legislature periodically passes a law permitting city councils a calendar window to change their municipal election date to November. In the fall of 2004, the San Marcos city council, in response to such a state law, changed the city election month from May to November despite the City of San Marcos Charter provision that explicitly granted that authority to its citizens voting on the proposed charter amendment.

Incorporation: The Process of Creating a City

incorporation
Process of creating a city government

The process of establishing a city is known as **incorporation** because, legally, cities are municipal corporations. Local citizens need to petition the state and ask to be incorporated as a city. Second, an election is held, and a simple majority of the voters need to approve the establishment of a city with explicitly drawn territorial boundaries. Then the state issues a municipal corporate charter.

In Texas, for incorporation to proceed, first, a minimum population of 201 citizens must be living within a two-square-mile area. Second, 10 percent of the registered voters and 50 percent of the property owners in the area to be incorporated must sign petitions asking that an election be held. If the petition is deemed valid, the county judge calls an election. If a simple majority of the voters approve incorporation, the city is granted a general law charter, and a second election is held to elect city officials.[7]

extraterritorial jurisdiction
City powers that extend beyond the city limits to an area adjacent to the city limits

There are some limits regarding where cities can be established. By Texas law, all cities have **extraterritorial jurisdiction** (ETJ), and it extends beyond the city limits.[8] General law cities have only one-half mile of ETJ. The ETJ distance increases as the cities' populations increase, and may extend for five miles for cities with populations above 250,000. ETJ is important because it provides a city some measure of regulatory control over the growth (zoning, construction, etc.) of surrounding areas. It is illegal for a city to be incorporated within the ETJ of an existing city unless the existing city approves. This provision was intended to prevent smaller towns from impeding the growth of existing cities within their own ETJs. Cities may expand by annexing land within their ETJ.

Annexation

Cities may annex land within their ETJ. Annexation is the process by which cities legally add adjoining unincorporated territory to the total land area of the city. Texas cities have broad annexation powers. The city council, by majority vote, can unilaterally annex land, and the residents living in the area being annexed have no voice or vote in the process. This provision in state law, coupled with the ETJ provisions, provides Texas cities with room to expand. In every session of the Texas legislature, many bills are introduced to restrict Texas cities' ability to annex land. Though some restrictions have been placed on home rule cities in the past, Texas cities still have broad annexation authority when compared to many other states.

Annexation has become an increasingly contentious issue in Texas and elsewhere. Cities annex for a number of reasons. First, cities annex so that they will not be surrounded by other incorporated cities. Annexation of one city by another requires the consent of the annexed city, which happens rarely, so encirclement means the end of growth. Second, and connected to the first, cities annex to protect and enhance their tax base. New land means new property taxes, new sales taxes, and larger population. Finally, cities annex to become more important politically.

Larger populations mean greater political clout, more federal grant money, and more representatives elected to the state legislature and the U.S. Congress.

The rapid growth in Texas cities created counterpressures from people who had been enjoying the benefit of a nearby city without paying for those benefits before their property was annexed. A new annexation law was passed by the Texas legislature in 1999. It requires cities to give a three-year notice before annexation formally begins, to create a service plan and deliver those services within two and a half years, and to arbitrate with the residents of the proposed annexed area. However, in 2009, the attorney general issued an opinion stating that the three-year requirement does not pertain to "sparsely populated areas."[9] Even in the face of these limitations, it is inevitable that cities will be even more important to Texas in the future.

Types of City Government

Cities in the United States and Texas use two basic forms of city government: mayor-council and council-manager. Additionally, the mayor-council system has two variations: the strong mayor system and the weak mayor system. A third form of local government, the commission, is used by only a few cities nationwide; it is not used by any city in Texas, but the commission form is discussed later in this chapter because it once played an important role in the development of local government in Texas.

Council-Manager Government

The **council-manager form** of government is the most popular form of government in Texas today. It arose during the Progressive Era (1901–1920) out of concern about the corruption and inefficiency of large cities dominated by political machines. Figure 6.1 outlines the structure of the council-manager form. Amarillo was the first city to adopt it in 1913, and Dallas and San Antonio are the largest adopter

council-manager form
Form of government where voters elect a mayor and city council; the mayor and city council appoint a professional administrator to manage the city

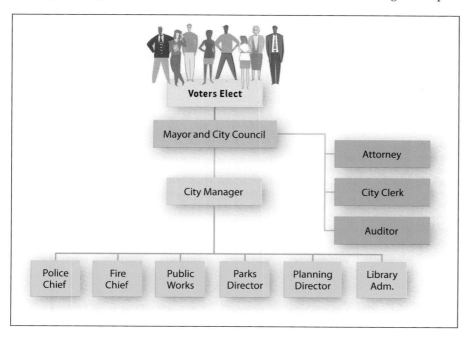

FIGURE 6.1   Council-Manager Form of City Government

cities today. Except for Houston, all major cities in Texas use the council-manager form of government. Under this system, the voters elect a small city council (usually seven members), including a mayor. The council hires a city manager, who has administrative control over city government. The city manager appoints and removes the major heads of departments of government and is responsible for budget preparation and execution.

The mayor and city council are responsible for establishing the mission, policy, and direction of city government. More specifically, the mayor and council generate policy while all administrative authority rests with the city manager. The mayor and council roles in administration and management are greatly reduced. Figure 6.2 shows the roles of the council and mayor on the four dimensions of city government: mission, policy, administration, and management. In Figure 6.2, the curved line illustrates the division between the council's and the manager's spheres of activity (the council's tasks to the left of the line, the manager's to the right). This division roughly approximates a "proper" degree of separation and sharing; shifts to the left or right would indicate improper incursions. The council and mayor dominate the areas of mission and policy, and the city manager dominates the areas of administration and management.

Role of the Mayor

The role of the mayor in city governments is often misunderstood because of the variations in the roles of the office. The mayor is the presiding officer of the council

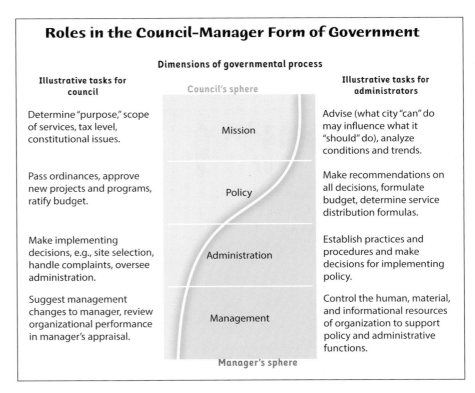

Roles in the Council-Manager Form of Government

Dimensions of governmental process

Illustrative tasks for council	Council's sphere	Illustrative tasks for administrators
Determine "purpose," scope of services, tax level, constitutional issues.	Mission	Advise (what city "can" do may influence what it "should" do), analyze conditions and trends.
Pass ordinances, approve new projects and programs, ratify budget.	Policy	Make recommendations on all decisions, formulate budget, determine service distribution formulas.
Make implementing decisions, e.g., site selection, handle complaints, oversee administration.	Administration	Establish practices and procedures and make decisions for implementing policy.
Suggest management changes to manager, review organizational performance in manager's appraisal.	Management	Control the human, material, and informational resources of organization to support policy and administrative functions.

Manager's sphere

FIGURE 6.2   Roles in the Council-Manager Form of Government The curved line suggests the division between the council's and the manager's spheres of activity (the council's tasks to the left of the line, the manager's to the right). This division roughly approximates a "proper" degree of separation and sharing; shifts to the left or right would indicate improper incursions.

and most often has a vote on all issues. (A small number of cities have the mayor vote only in case of a tie vote.) The mayor usually lacks any type of veto, though a few cities such as El Paso do extend veto power to the office. Laws are passed by a majority vote of the total council membership, not just a majority of those present. The mayor in this form is the "head of state," the symbolic leader and the embodiment of his or her city, but is not the head of government.

The council, including the mayor, selects only four city government officials: the manager, the attorney, the clerk (sometimes called secretary), and the municipal judge. (Some cities elect the municipal judge.) The city council passes ordinances (also called laws), sets policies for the government, and provides guidelines to the city staff on such issues as the budget, taxes, and fees and spending. The council is considered part-time, so members are paid only a nominal salary or none at all.

Role of the City Manager

Because so many cities in Texas use the council-manager form of government, some understanding of the role of the **city manager** is essential. Texas has always been a leader in the use of this form of government. O. M. Carr, the first city manager in Amarillo, strongly influenced the formation of the International City Managers (Management) Association.[10]

city manager
Person hired by the city council to manage the city; serves as the chief administrative officer of the city

Under the council-manager form of government, the voters elect a city council and mayor. Generally, these are the only elected officials in city government, although a few cities elect a city judge. The council, in turn, appoints the city manager and may remove the manager for any reason at any time; managers serve at the pleasure of the city council. In smaller general law cities in Texas, the position might be called a city administrator rather than a manager, but the duties are essentially the same.

Most managers are trained professionals. Today many managers have a master's degree in public administration and have served as an assistant city manager for several years before becoming city manager. All but a few city managers are members of the International City Management Association (ICMA) and, in Texas, are also members of the Texas City Management Association (TCMA). These organizations have codes of ethics and help to promote the ideas of professionalism in the local government management. This expertise and professionalism sets city governments apart from county governments in Texas, where the voters elect most all officeholders, and professionalism is often absent. Because city managers appoint and can remove all major department heads and are in charge of the day-to-day management of city government, they can instill a high level of professionalism in the city staff.

Although the manager's primary role is to administer city government, managers can and do have an impact on the councils' policy decisions. Managers provide information and advice to the council on the impact of policy changes in city government. Professional managers attempt to provide information that is impartial so the council can make an informed decision. Councils sometimes delegate this policy-making process to city managers, either openly or indirectly, by failure to act. When this happens, councils are neglecting their duty of office and are not serving the citizens who elected them. Over the past 100 years, the council-manager form of government has functioned well in Texas. Texas cities have a national reputation of being well managed and highly professional in their operations.

Weaknesses of the Council-Manager Form

The council-manager form has some weaknesses. The council members are part-time and usually serve for a short amount of time. Second, because the city manager is not directly answerable to the voters, citizens may believe they lack influence. Third, owing to political coalitions on a council, a city manager may be able to ignore large parts of the community when it comes to provision of simple city services such as sidewalks and serviceable streets. Finally, a powerful city manager can skew and hide information from the council so as to control council policy decisions before they are even made.

Mayor-Council Government

Mayor-council government is the more traditional form that developed in the nineteenth century. There are two variations of mayor-council government—weak executive and strong executive (see Figures 6.3 and 6.4.). Under the **weak mayor form of government** (also known as the weak executive form), the formal powers of the mayor are limited in much the same way that the Texas governor's formal powers are limited. First, the mayor shares power with other elected officials and with the city council. Second, the mayor has only limited control over budget formation and execution. Third, the number of terms the mayor can serve is limited. Fourth, the mayor has little or no veto authority.[11]

weak mayor form
Form of government where the mayor shares power with the council and other elected officials

CORE OBJECTIVE

Communicating Effectively...

Compare Figures 6.1, 6.3, and 6.4 with Table 6.2. Discuss the fundamental differences between weak mayor, strong mayor, and council-manager forms of government. Which do you prefer and why?

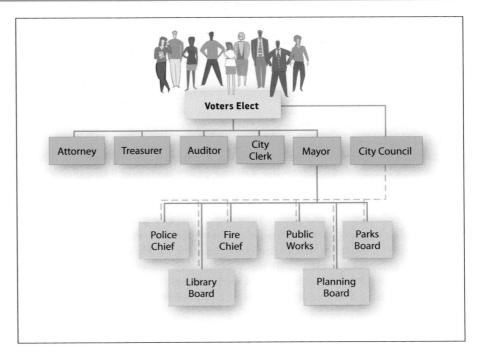

FIGURE 6.3   Weak Mayor-Council Form of City Government

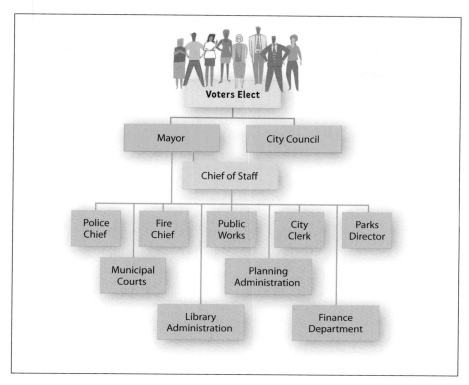

FIGURE 6.4   Strong Mayor-Council Form of City Government

Under a strong executive or **strong mayor form of government**, the mayor can appoint and remove the major heads of departments, has control over budget formation and execution, is not limited by short terms or term limits, and can veto actions of the city council.

Houston and nearby Pasadena are the two largest home rule cities using the mayor-council form.[12] Only Houston has a strong mayor. The Houston mayor can appoint and remove department heads and is responsible for budget formation and execution. However, the office has no veto authority, has a short term (two years), and is limited to three terms. Many more mayor-council forms exist in the general law cities in Texas than in the home rule cities. Formally, however, all have very weak mayors. Their powers are provided in the state statutes, and no form provided in the state laws can be classified as a strong executive. A comparison of the council-manager, weak-mayor, and strong-mayor forms of government is provided in Table 6.2.

strong mayor form
Form of local government where most power rests with the mayor

TABLE 6.2

Comparison of Council-Manager, Weak-Mayor, and Strong-Mayor Forms of Government

Council-Manager Form	Weak-Mayor Form	Strong-Mayor Form
A city manager hired by city council is responsible for administration. City manager appoints and removes department heads. City manager is responsible for budget preparation and execution.	Power of the mayor is limited and divided among city council and other elected officials. Mayor has limited control over budget. Mayor has term limits. Mayor has no veto authority.	Mayor can appoint and remove major department heads. Mayor controls budget. Mayor is not restricted by term limits. Mayor has veto power.

Commission Form of Government

commission form

A form of local government where voters elect department heads who also serve as members of the city council

The **commission form** of government is not used by any home rule city in Texas, but it deserves mention because of its impact on local Texas governments. The city of Galveston popularized this form of government in the early part of the twentieth century. In 1901, a major hurricane destroyed most of Galveston and killed an estimated 5,000 people. At the time, Galveston was the only major port on the Texas Gulf Coast and was a kingpin in the cotton economy of the state. It was in the interests of all Texans to have the city and port rebuilt. A delegation of Galveston citizens approached the Texas legislature for funds to help in the rebuilding effort. Then-Governor Joseph D. Sayers was opposed to state funding without some state control. The governor proposed that he be allowed to appoint five commissioners to oversee the rebuilding of the city, and he threatened to line-item veto any appropriations without this control. The legislature balked at the idea of locally appointed officials because of the experiences during Reconstruction under the administration of Edmund J. Davis. John Nance Garner, who served as vice president for two terms under Franklin Delano Roosevelt, was speaker of the Texas House at that time and said that without the threat of a line-item veto, it would be impossible to find five men in Galveston who supported the commission form of government. The governor and legislature compromised; initially, the governor appointed three commissioners, and the voters elected two. Later, all were elected.[13]

The new commission in Galveston worked in a very expeditious manner and quickly rebuilt the port city. This efficiency attracted nationwide attention. Many other cities adopted this new form of government, assuming that its form had caused the efficiency. It was a very simple form (see Figure 6.5) when compared to the older weak mayor system and the attendant long ballot of elected officials. In most commission forms, the voters elected five commissioners. Each commissioner was elected citywide by the voters as the head of a department of city government and

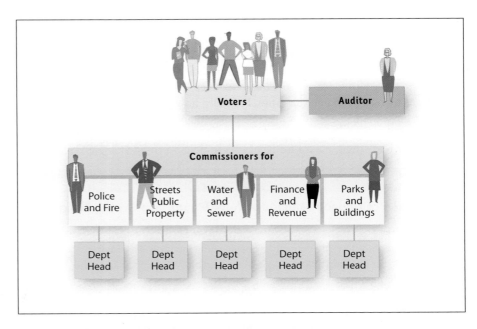

FIGURE 6.5 **Commission Form of City Government**

was also a member of the city commission (the legislative body). Thus, the system combined both executive and legislative functions into a single body of government.

This combination seemed to allow for quick action, but it also created many problems. Between 1901 and 1920, many cities adopted the commission form of government, but after 1920, very few cities adopted it, and many began to abandon the form. By the end of World War II, few commission governments remained. Even Galveston abandoned the form in the 1950s.[14] These abandonments were caused by several fundamental weaknesses in the form.

Weaknesses of the Commission Form of Government

The first weakness was that voters did not always elect competent administrators. Citizens voted for candidates based on apparent qualifications. For example, a failed banker might run for finance commissioner and stress his banking experience.[15] Voters might have no way of knowing that his banking experience had been a failure and would, instead, vote on apparent qualifications. The failed banker's bank might be happy to see him depart and not challenge his qualifications.

Second, the combination of legislative and executive functions, although efficient, eliminated the separation of powers and its checks and balances. Commissioners were reluctant to scrutinize the budget and actions of other commissioners for fear of retaliation. Logrolling (exchanging political favors) set in: You look the other way on my budget and programs, and I will on yours.

Third, initially the commission had no leader. The commissioners rotated the position of mayor among themselves. This "mayor" presided over meetings and served as the official representative of the city but was not in a leadership position. This lack of a single, strong leader was a major shortcoming in the commission government. One writer describes it as a ship with five captains.[16] Later variations called for a separately elected mayor with budget and veto authority. Tulsa, Oklahoma, one of the last, larger cities to use the form, gave the mayor these powers.[17]

Impact on the Evolution of Local Government

The major contribution of the commission form of government was that it served as a transition between the old weak mayor form, with many elected officials and a large city council, and the council-manager form, with no elected executives and a small city council. Many cities altered their charters, stripping the administrative power from the commissioners and assigning it to a city manager. Many Texas cities retained the term *commission* as a name for the city council. Lubbock retained the five-member commission until the 1980s, when it was forced to increase the size of the council and use single-member district elections.

Municipal Election Types

The two most common municipal election types are at-large election systems and single-member district systems. Two additional systems used in Texas are cumulative voting and preferential voting.

At-Large Election Systems

In the beginning of the twentieth century, many cities, led by early commissions, chose to move away from the single-member district system and began to elect council members at large, by all voters in the city. There are several variations of the **at-large election system**, which are summarized in Figure 6.6.

at-large election system
System where all voters in the city elect the mayor and city council members

At-large by place

This is the most common such system used in Texas. In this system, candidates file for at-large ballot positions, which are usually given a number designation—Place 1, Place 2, and so on. Voters cast one vote for each at-large ballot position, and the candidate with a majority is elected to that place on the city council.

At-large by place with residence wards required

In this system, candidates file for a specific place as in an at-large by place system; however, these candidates must live in a section, area, or ward of the city to file for a specific place. Mayors can live anywhere in the city. All voters in the city elect them at large.

At-large no place

This is the least common system used in Texas. In this system, all candidates seeking election to the council have their names placed on the ballot. If there are ten candidates seeking election and five open seats, each voter is instructed to cast one vote each for five candidates. The top five vote getters are elected. With this method, it is not uncommon for a candidate to win with only a plurality (less than a majority) of the vote.

FIGURE 6.6   Variations of At-Large Voting Systems

At-large by place is the most common form of at-large voting in Texas. In this system, candidates file for at-large ballot positions, which are usually given a number designation—Place 1, Place 2, and so on. Voters cast one vote for each at-large ballot position, and the candidate with a majority is elected to that place on the city council.

At-large by place with residence wards required is a system by which candidates file for a specific place, just as in at-large by place. However, each place on the ballot is assigned to a specific geographic area, and a candidate must live within that section, area, or ward of the city to file for a specific place. Abilene, Texas, uses this form. The city is divided into two wards with three council seats in each ward. The mayor can live anywhere in the city, and the mayor and council are elected at-large by all city residents.

At-large no place is the least common system in Texas. Under this system, all candidates seeking election to the council have their names placed on the ballot. If 10 candidates are seeking election for five open seats, each voter is instructed to cast one vote each for five candidates. The top five candidates with the most votes win. With this method, it is not uncommon for a candidate to win with only a plurality (less than a majority).[18]

Last, some cities use a combination of at-large and single-member district systems. Houston is a prime example. Voters elect 11 council members from single-member districts, and five council members and the mayor are elected at large by all voters in the city.[19]

Single-Member District Election Systems

In **single-member district** elections, each city council seat is assigned to a specific district. The city is divided into election districts of approximately equal populations, and the voters in these districts elect a council member. In a true single-member district system, only the mayor is selected at large. Usually, candidates for a particular council seat must reside within the district for which they are running. Though some municipalities use multimember district systems, all district elections in Texas are single-member district systems.

Prior to 1975, almost no Texas cities used the single-member district (SMD) system. When the 1965 Voting Rights Act took effect, the language surrounding racial discrimination in polls was targeted at specific districts in specific states with known problems. Section 4, for example, targeted those election sites with disenfranchising tactics (such as literacy tests) and required federal intervention.[20] Section 5, the centerpiece of the legislation, subjected those targeted states and counties to preauthorization requirements for any election-related legislation and to federal monitors during election time.[21] But going into the 1970s, with southern states attempting to circumvent the law with at-large voting (to limit the concentration and effect of black votes), Congress began to make changes. One of the outcomes: the growth of single-member districts across the United States. At the federal level, it was believed that in a single-member district a minority group could be the majority, thereby electing their desired candidate.[22] Since the Voting Rights Act was amended in 1975 and applied to Texas, many cities have changed from an at-large system to single-member districts. Most of the major cities have been forced to change to SMD for at least some of the city council seats.

In cities that have changed from at-large to SMD systems, the number of minority candidates elected to the city council has increased substantially. There is some evidence that SMD council members approach their role differently than at-large council members do. A study of council members in Houston, Dallas, San Antonio, and Fort Worth found that council members from SMDs showed greater concern for neighborhood issues, engaged in vote trading, increased their contacts with constituents in their districts regarding service requests, and became more involved in administrative affairs of the city.[23]

Although SMD council members might view their job as representing their districts first and the city as a whole second, no evidence shows that the distribution of services changes dramatically. District representation may be primarily symbolic.

single-member district
A system where the city is divided into election districts, and only the voters living in that district elect the council member from that district

CORE OBJECTIVE

Being Socially Responsible...

Compare at-large election systems and single-member district systems. An argument in favor of single-member district systems is that they increase minority representation in local government. In your opinion, does increased minority representation increase intercultural competency? Why?

Symbolism is not insignificant, though, because support for local governments can be increased as minority groups believe they are represented on city councils and feel comfortable contacting their council member.

Cumulative and Preferential Voting Systems

cumulative voting

A system where voters can concentrate (accumulate) all their votes on one candidate rather than casting one vote for each office up for election

In a **cumulative voting system**, each voter has votes equal to the number of seats open in the election. If five seats are open, each voter has five votes and may cast all five votes for one candidate (cumulating their votes), one vote each for five candidates, or any combination or variation. Several cities and school districts have adopted this system as an alternative to single-member districts. This system is preferred by voting rights activists as a means of increasing minority representation. In May 2005, the Amarillo Independent School District became the largest government body using the system in Texas.[24]

preferential voting

A system that allows voters to rank order candidates for the city council

The **preferential voting system** is also referred to as the instant-runoff system. It allows voters to rank their candidates for city council. All candidates' names are listed on the ballot, and the voter indicates the order of his or her preferences (first, second, third, and so on). Using a complicated ballot-counting system, the most-preferred candidates are elected. Although no city in Texas uses this form today, Gorman and Sweetwater used it in the past.

Advocates of the cumulative voting system and the preferential voting system argue that they allow minority interests to vote for candidates without having to draw single-member districts and possibly risk the accompanying gerrymandering (see Chapter 3). Some evidence shows, as in the case of the Amarillo Independent School District, that these alternative systems result in more minority candidates being elected.[25]

Regardless of the system used to elect city council members, some city charters allow for a person to be elected with a plurality of the vote—less than a majority. In Texas, if the city council term of office is longer than two years, a majority vote is required. This may necessitate a runoff election if no one has a majority.

Nonpartisan Elections

nonpartisan elections

Election in which party identification is not formally declared

Another facet of municipal elections in Texas is that they are all technically nonpartisan. In **nonpartisan elections**, candidates run and appear on the ballot without any party designation. The Texas Election Code allows home rule cities to conduct partisan elections, but no city in Texas does so.[26]

Nonpartisan elections were a feature of the reform movement in the early part of the past century and were aimed at undercutting the power of partisan big-city political machines. Reformers said that there is no Democratic or Republican way to collect garbage, pave streets, or provide police and fire protection, so partisanship should not be a factor in city decisions.

Texas cities adopted the nonpartisan system largely because the state was a one-party Democratic state for over 100 years, and partisanship, even in state elections, was not a factor as long as candidates ran as Democrats. However, it should be noted that the use of a nonpartisan ballot does not eliminate partisanship from local politics. Partisanship simply takes new forms and new labels are applied.

For decades in several Texas cities, "nonpartisan organizations" successfully ran slates of candidates and dominated city politics. Most noted among these organizations were the Citizens Charter Association in Dallas, the Good

Government League in San Antonio, and the Business and Professional Association in Wichita Falls and Abilene.[27] The influence of these groups has declined, but slate making is not unknown today in Texas politics. Partisanship has been a factor in city elections recently in San Antonio, Houston, and Dallas, especially in mayoral races. Without a doubt, partisanship will be a factor in city politics in the years ahead. Although the Tea Party is not a political party, its social conservative views most closely align with the Republican Party. In 2010, many candidates in local elections ran as "Tea Party approved." Although local elections are explicitly nonpartisan, it is quite easy, especially in large cities such as Dallas, Houston, and San Antonio, for voters to glean a candidate's political leanings.

Voter Turnout in Local Elections

Voter turnout in Texas municipal elections is varied but tends to be low for several reasons. One reason is that some cities conduct local elections in off years. This means that some city elections are held when no state or federal legislative or executive elections are being held (off-off-year elections—e.g., 2009, 2011, 2013), some are held when state elections and U.S. House of Representative elections are being held (off-year elections—e.g., 2010), and only one out of four municipal elections are held the same year as presidential elections (e.g., 2012). Second, many Texas cities hold their elections in May, rather than in November when most people expect elections to be held. Voter turnout rates in the City of Austin municipal elections, which are held in May, usually hover around 10 percent.[28] In comparison, voter turnout rates in the City of Dallas, which holds local elections in November, was about 62 percent in 2008 and 38 percent in 2010.[29] Third, many times the candidates' races are not contested. This has happened so often that a state law went into effect in 1991 allowing cities and school boards to cancel elections if no seat was contested. A fourth reason is the lack of media coverage in city elections. Most election news coverage of city races concentrates on mayors' races, and both electronic and print media of major cities ignore suburban city elections. Even local small-town or suburban newspapers virtually ignore city elections in their home communities, arguing that readers are not interested in local issues and races.

The lack of interest in municipal elections is disturbing because city government has such authority over so many aspects of people's daily lives, including streets and sidewalks, police and fire departments, building codes, speed limits, noise ordinances, and zoning and land use designations.

CORE OBJECTIVE

Taking Personal Responsibility...

Local government directly impacts people in their daily lives. What can you do to improve local governance?

County Governments

county government
Local unit of government that is primarily the administrative arm of a state government. In most states, it does not provide urban-type services.

The oldest type of local government in the United States is **county government**, an adaptation of the British county unit of government that was implemented in this country. County governments exist in all states except Connecticut, which abolished them in 1963, and Rhode Island (which never needed them). Louisiana calls counties "parishes," from the French influence, and Alaska calls them "boroughs." The number of counties varies greatly among the states. Alaska, Delaware, and Hawaii each have three county governments, whereas Texas has 254.[30]

County governments were originally intended to be a subdivision, or an "arm," of state government to perform state functions at the local level. For example, voter registration, which is a state function, is handled at the county level. Most commonly, the county tax office handles voter registration, although in some large counties a separate elections department may handle this function. Similarly, county governments issue marriage licenses, birth certificates, and automobile registrations, and operate state courts. County governments act as an arm of the state in all these activities.

Besides performing state functions, county governments also provide local services. The level of services provided varies from state to state; counties in some states provide many local services. In Texas, however, counties provide only very limited local services. Generally, Texas counties provide road construction and repair and police protection through the sheriff's department. Some urban county governments operate hospitals or health units, libraries, and parks.

In some states, urban counties are major providers of urban services. In Texas, city governments usually provide these services. Urban services include water supply, sewage disposal, planning and zoning, airports, building codes and enforcement, mass transit systems, and fire protection. With few exceptions, Texas counties cannot perform these functions. Texas counties most closely resemble the traditional rural county governments that perform functions for the state: recording vital statistics, operating state courts and jails, administering elections, and maintaining roads and bridges. Texas counties can also assist in the creation of rural fire protection districts. In Harris County, the government may assist in the creation of master water and sewer districts to combine many smaller ones.

The distinguishing feature of county government is population. Of the 3,007 counties in the United States, most are rural with small populations. About 700 counties have populations of less than 10,000, and fewer than 200 have populations of more than 250,000. In Texas, 58 percent of the population lives in the 10 largest urban counties (see Table 6.3). Texas also has the distinction of having the smallest county by population in the United States. Loving County had a population of 82 in 2010, an increase from 18 in 1980, which was attributable to the oil boom.[31]

Urban Texans tend to identify with city governments rather than with county government. People think of themselves as residents of Houston, not Harris County. Some city residents might not be able to name the county where they reside. This stems in part from their identification with a service being provided, such as police protection. Residents of rural areas are more likely to identify with the county rather than the city, for many of the same reasons.

The Structure of County Government

All Texas county governments have the same basic structure, regardless of the county's size. This structure mirrors the fragmented structure of state government.

It can most accurately be described as weak or plural executive. Voters elect the heads of major departments of county government (see Figure 6.7). These provisions appeared in the constitution of 1876. The writers of this document distrusted appointive authority and trusted the electorate to choose administrators.[32]

TABLE 6.3	
The 10 Largest Counties in Texas, 2010	
County and (Major City)	**2010 Population**
Harris (Houston)	4,092,459
Dallas (Dallas)	2,368,139
Tarrant (Fort Worth)	1,809,034
Bexar (San Antonio)	1,714,773
Travis (Austin)	1,024,266
El Paso (El Paso)	800,647
Collin (Plano)	782,341
Hidalgo (McAllen)	774,769
Denton (Denton)	662,614
Fort Bend (Sugar Land)	585,375
Total	14,614,417
Percentage of total population of Texas in the 10 largest counties	58%

Source: U.S. Census Bureau, *2010 Census.*

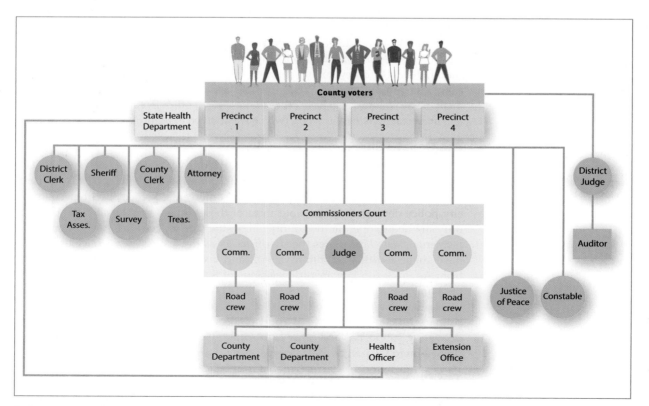

FIGURE 6.7   Structure of County Government in Texas

The County Commissioner's Court

commissioner's court
Legislative body that governs a
Texas county

In Texas, the governing body of county government is the county **commissioner's court**, composed of the constitutional county judge and four county commissioners. The county judge is elected at large, and each commissioner is elected from a single-member district called a commissioner precinct. Like most other state officeholders, these officials are elected for four-year terms in partisan elections. Even though this body is termed the commissioner's court, it is not a court but a legislative body. Its duties include passing local ordinances, approving budgets and new programs, and oversight of county government.

The county judge presides as the chair of the commissioner's court, participates as a full member in deliberations, and has a vote on all matters. The constitution assigns judicial duties to this office, but the occupant does not have to be a licensed attorney; the constitution states that the constitutional county judge must be "well informed in the law." In 72 urban counties, where the state legislature has created county courts of law, the constitutional county judge performs only very limited judicial functions. The judicial functions of constitutional county courts (described in Chapter 5) are transferred to the county courts of law, and the constitutional county judge acts as the primary administrative officer of the county.

Like other legislative districts, commissioner precincts eventually became malapportioned. In 1968, the U.S. Supreme Court ruled that the one-person-one-vote rule applied to these election districts. The Commissioner's Court in Midland County claimed it was a court and not a legislative body, and therefore the one person, one vote rule did not apply. The U.S. Supreme Court disagreed and ruled that it was a legislative body and not a court, and that election districts had to be equally apportioned.[33] This means that each district should comprise roughly the same number of residents, or potential voters.

There are seven constitutionally prescribed county officers elected by the voters: sheriff, district attorney, county attorney, tax assessor/collector, district clerk, county clerk, and county treasurer. These officials act as heads of departments of government. Some counties also have other minor elected officials, such as county surveyor and inspector of hides and wools (which was created to reduce cattle and sheep theft).

The County Sheriff

county sheriff
Elected head of law enforcement
in a Texas county

The **county sheriff** is elected countywide for a four-year term and serves as the law enforcement officer for the county. Sheriffs can appoint deputy sheriffs. In rural counties, the sheriff may be the primary law enforcement officer. In urban counties, city police departments carry out most of these duties, and the sheriff's primary duty may be to operate the county jail. In the smaller counties (fewer than 1,800 residents), state law allows the sheriff to act as the tax assessor/collector.[34] Some have suggested that combining sheriff and tax collector is a frightening leftover from Anglo-Saxon law, inspiring visions of Sherwood Forest, the Sheriff of Nottingham, and Robin Hood.

The voters also elect constables, who serve as law enforcement officers. Their primary function is to serve as court officers for the justice of the peace courts—delivering subpoenas and other court orders. Constables may also provide police protection in the precinct they serve.

The County and District Attorneys

The county and district attorneys are the chief prosecuting attorneys for criminal cases in the county, the county attorney at the county court level and the district attorney at the district court level. Each county has a county court and usually several district courts that reside in the constituent districts that make up a given county. Not all counties have county attorneys. In counties with a county attorney, this office usually prosecutes the less-serious criminal offenses before county courts, and the district attorney prosecutes major crimes before the district courts.

The County Tax Assessor/Collector

The tax assessor/collector is responsible for collecting revenue for the state and county. Before 1978, this office also assessed the value of all property in the county for property tax collection purposes. In 1978, these functions were transferred to a county-wide assessment district. There are 254 of these tax appraisal districts in the state, and they are governed by a board elected by the governing bodies of all governments in the jurisdiction—counties, cities, school districts, and special districts. Although this office still has the title assessor, few occupants serve in this capacity today. Most still collect county property taxes, sell state vehicle licenses and permits, and serve as voter registrars. The voter registration function is a carryover from the days of the poll tax.[35]

The County and District Clerk

The county clerk is the chief record keeper for the county; the clerk keeps track of all property records and issues marriage licenses, birth certificates, and other county records. Although normally the function of voter registration rests with the tax assessor/collector, in some counties this function has been transferred to the county clerk, who in all counties is responsible for conducting elections.

The district clerk is primarily a court official who maintains court records for county and district courts. The clerk schedules cases in these courts and maintains all records, acts, and proceedings of the court, along with keeping a record of all judgments. The district clerk also administers child support payments and maintains accounts of all funds derived from fines and fees collected by the office.[36]

The County Treasurer

The county treasurer is responsible for receiving, maintaining, and disbursing all county funds, including general revenue and special revenue funds. The county treasurer is the chief liaison between the commissioner's court and the depository banks, and the treasurer is responsible for maintaining a record of all deposits, withdrawals, and reconciling all bank statements. The county treasurer may also at times be designated as the chief investment officer for the county.[37]

The County Auditor

The district judge or judges in the county appoint the county auditor. The county auditor's responsibility is to oversee the collection and disbursement of county funds. The auditor reports to the district judge or judges. Not all counties have auditors. Counties with populations of less than 10,000 are not required to have auditors. In larger counties (with populations greater than 250,000), the auditor acts as a budget officer unless the commissioner's court appoints its own budget officer.[38]

Weaknesses of County Government in Texas

The weaknesses in county government in Texas can be broadly divided into two kinds: (1) inherent weaknesses in the plural executive form of government, and (2) the inability of county governments to confront many problems in urban areas.

West Texas volunteer firefighters clean a fire unit at their headquarters on Friday April 19, 2013. Only two days prior, the West Fire Dept. responded to a fertilizer company explosion which caused several fatalities and extensive damage to the community.

As we have already seen, the plural executive structure of county government in Texas is a product of the nineteenth century and the general distrust of centralized executive authority. The plural executive structure lacks centralized authority, and the elected officials can, and often do, act quite independently of each other. Although the county commissioner's court does exercise some control over these department heads, it is primarily limited to budgetary matters. After a budget is approved, elected officials can make many independent decisions.

Elected officials also hire their own staffs. After each election, personnel at the county courthouse can change dramatically. For example, new sheriffs hire their own deputy sheriffs. The patronage ("spoils") system in some courthouses results in a less-professional staff.

As indicated in our discussion of the judiciary in Chapter 5 and in the discussion of the commission form of city government in this chapter, elections are imperfect instruments for determining the qualifications of candidates, and voters do not always select the most competent person to administer departments. The appointment of department heads is more likely to result in the selection of competent persons. A lack of professionalism and competence is a frequently noted problem with officials in some counties.

In most (201 of 254) Texas counties, each county commissioner is responsible for road repair within the boundaries of the precinct in which the commissioner is elected.[39] As a result, there are four separate road crews, each under the direction of a commissioner. Although there is some sharing of equipment, duplications and inefficiencies are common. Commissioners have also been known to use their road crews to reward supporters with more favorable attention to road repairs that affect them directly.

County government was designed to meet the needs of and provide services to a rural population. In rural areas of the state, it still functions adequately. However, in large urban counties, this form of government has many weaknesses.

Inability to Provide Urban Services

The first of these weaknesses is the inability to provide urban-type services. Dense urban populations demand and need services that are unnecessary in rural areas. Usually, county governments are powerless under state law to provide even the most basic services common to city governments, such as water and sewer services. In the 1999 session of the legislature, Harris County was given limited authority to assist in the formation of "master" water and sewer districts by consolidating many small suburban districts.

Citizens living on the fringe of cities are forced to provide these services themselves or to form other governments, such as a water district, to provide these services. In recent years, garbage (solid waste) collection and disposal have become a problem in the urban fringe areas. Many citizens must contract with private collectors for this service. Some counties help residents by providing collection centers, often operated by private contractors. In the area of fire protection, counties often help rural residents to establish volunteer fire departments. However, counties are not permitted to operate fire departments. Each rural fire department goes its own way, and there is often a lack of coordination between departments. Training and equipment are generally below the standards of full-time city fire departments. Counties sometimes contract with city governments to provide fire protection for the county, although this practice has declined in recent years because the state has made it easier to form and finance rural fire districts.

Lack of Ordinance Authority

County governments also lack general ordinance authority. City governments in Texas may pass any ordinance not prohibited by state law, but county governments must seek legislative approval to pass specific ordinances. For example, county governments may not pass ordinances on land use (zoning) or building codes that regulate construction standards. A citizen buying a home in a rural area is largely dependent upon the integrity of the builder.

Even where counties have been given the authority to regulate activities, they often fall short. For example, counties were given the authority to pass ordinances regulating the construction of septic systems. Some counties failed to pass such ordinances, and many failed to adequately inspect the installation of septic systems. In some counties, this function was transferred to the state health department in 1992.

Inequity of Financial Resources

Finally, a related problem with county governments is the inequity of financial resources and expenditures. A few counties have a sales tax, but most rely almost exclusively on the property tax. Most of this tax is paid by citizens living inside cities and not in the unincorporated, rural areas of the county. For example, in the tax year 2010 in Brazos County, the total taxable property was $13.7 billion. Most of this value ($10.8 billion) was located within the cities of Bryan and College Station, leaving only $1.2 billion in rural Brazos County.[40] Thus, most (79 percent) of the cost of county government was paid for with property tax money from the two cities. Although county residents pay little of the cost to operate county governments, they receive many services from them (such as road construction and repair and police protection) that are not provided to city residents by the county. City residents receive these services from their city and pay city taxes. City residents are paying twice for services they receive only once. This financial inequity goes unnoticed by most citizens.

Possible Reform of County Government

Since the 1930s, there have been suggestions to reform county government in Texas. The rhetoric often called for county government to be "brought into the twentieth century." In Texas, apparently all such reforms skipped the twentieth century and have to wait for sometime in the twenty-first century. Whereas other states have modernized county governments, Texas has steadfastly refused all efforts for change. One suggestion that has been a frequent agenda item over the past 70 years is to allow for county home rule, which would allow the voters in each county to adopt a local option charter.[41] Voters could then approve any form of government not prohibited by state law; no county would be forced to change its form of government. This might result in the adoption of a strong executive form of government similar to the strong-mayor or council-manager forms popular with Texas cities. Even though this suggestion seems quite reasonable, it has been strongly opposed by the many county elected officials in Texas who see this as a threat to their jobs.

The Texas Association of Counties (TAC) is an umbrella organization that represents elected county officials—sheriffs, tax collectors, treasurers, judges, commissioners, and so on. The TAC has opposed granting county governments home rule. This group is politically powerful and has many supporters throughout the state. One group within the TAC, the Conference of Urban Counties (CUC), has shown mild support for home rule. The CUC represents 36 metropolitan county governments in Texas where home rule would have the greatest impact. The CUC is not pushing home rule issues and is more concerned with representing the unique interests of urban counties.

County officials often have very provincial attitudes about the role of county government. The idea of expanding county services is foreign to many county officials. They seem content with the status quo. Prospects are dim for any great change in Texas county government in the short run. Urban counties will continue to face many problems that have only a mild impact on rural counties and will have to seek solutions to their problems that do not involve the major structural changes home rule would bring. Improving the professionalism of the staff might prove difficult because each elected county official can hire his or her own people. In some counties, officials place great emphasis on professionalism. Other officials reward faithful campaign workers with appointments. In rural counties, these jobs are often well paid and much sought after by supporters.

CORE OBJECTIVE

Thinking Critically...

Identify some of the problems facing county governments. What solutions would you propose?

Special District Governments

special purpose district

Form of local government that provides specific services to citizens, such as water, sewage, fire protection, or public transportation

The biggest increase in government in Texas and the United States generally in the past 30 years or so has been in **special purpose districts** (not including school districts). Special purpose districts (also known as special purpose governments) have been referred to as shadow governments because they operate out of the view of most citizens. As the name implies, a special purpose district is a type of local government that is created to perform a specific set of duties or functions. Some districts are single function (e.g., fire) and others are multipurpose (e.g., water, sewer, street repair). Some special districts (such as metropolitan transit districts) cover several counties, and others (such as the municipal utility districts) are very small, covering only a few acres.

Texas has approximately 2,300 special purpose districts; only California and Illinois have more.[42] The primary reason special purpose districts are created is to provide services when no other unit of government exists to provide that service. Sometimes the need extends beyond the geographical boundaries of existing units of government. For example, flood control may transcend the municipal boundaries of any one city in particular, and the ability to coordinate among multiple city and county governments may be very difficult. Another good example is mass transportation. Dallas/Fort Worth, Houston, San Antonio, Austin, El Paso, and other metropolitan areas have created transit districts that serve several counties. Sometimes the service involves natural boundaries that extend over county lines.

In still other cases, the need for a service may be confined to a single county, but no government unit exists to provide the service. An excellent example of this is municipal utility districts (MUDs). These are multifunction districts generally created outside cities to provide water, sewage treatment, and other services. In Texas, these MUDs are created because county governments cannot provide these services. Finally, some districts are created for political reasons, when no existing unit of government wants to solve the service problem because of potential political conflicts. The creation of another unit of government to deal with a hot political issue is preferable. The Gulf Coast Waste Disposal Authority, created to clean up water pollution in the Houston area, is a good example.

Special purpose districts are often an efficient and expedient way to solve a problem, but they can also generate problems. One problem for citizens is keeping track of the many special districts that provide services to them. For example, a MUD, a soil and water conservation district, a flood control district, a fire protection district, a metropolitan transit authority, a hospital district, and a waste disposal district can govern a citizen living in the Houston suburbs. Most citizens have trouble distinguishing among a school district, a county, and a city. Dealing with seven or more units of government is even more complicated and can lead to a lack of democratic control over local governments.

The governing boards of special purpose districts in Texas are selected in two ways. Multicounty special purpose districts (such as DART in Dallas and METRO in Houston) are governed by boards appointed by the governmental units (cities, counties) covered by the district. Single-county special purpose districts (such as MUDs and flood control districts) usually have a board of directors elected by the voters.

Many special purpose districts have taxation authority and can raise local property taxes. The remoteness of these districts from the electorate, their number, and their potential impact on the lives of citizens raise questions of democratic control. The average citizen cannot be expected to know about, understand, and keep track of the decisions made by these remote governments. The alternatives are to consolidate governments, expand cities through the annexation of land, or expand the power of county governments. None of these alternatives is generally acceptable. Citizens demand and expect local governments to be decentralized. This is true even if they have only limited ability to watch and control the actions of local government and the government is ineffective. Big government is something most Texans want to avoid.

School Districts

Article 7 of the Texas Constitution vested in the legislature the authority to "establish and make suitable provision for the support and maintenance of an efficient system of public free school."[43] Although schools are subject to state control, especially in the areas of curriculum and financing, the administration of public

independent school district

School districts that are not attached to any other unit of government and that operate schools in Texas

education is largely the responsibility of the 1,000-plus school districts operating in the state. Officially, all but one of the school districts in Texas are **independent school districts** (ISDs), which means that they operate independently of any city or county.

School districts are governed by a board of trustees who are elected to staggered terms of office (varying from two, three, four, and six years) in nonpartisan elections. The board of trustees is made up of no more than seven members and, although school districts may choose under certain circumstances to have trustees elected from single-member districts, trustees in Texas school districts generally are elected at large. The trustees set policy for the district and approve the budget, set tax rates, make personnel decisions, and approve construction and renovation contracts. The board is also responsible for hiring the superintendent, who may serve on contract for no more than five years.[44]

The superintendent is the chief executive officer of the school district. The superintendent is responsible for planning, operation, evaluation of education programs, and annual performance appraisals of personnel. The superintendent reports to the board of trustees and is expected to provide policy and planning recommendations. The role of the school district superintendent is similar to the role of the city manager in the council-manager system of local government. Although the superintendent is the primary administrator who is responsible for the day-to-day operations of the district, he or she reports to elected officials.

School districts have a profound impact on all citizens and as expected, issues in education can be highly polarizing. Many school boards are politicized, which increases the pressure on the superintendent. Issues facing school districts are discussed in Chapter 11.

Conclusion

Although local governments do not generate the same degree of interest that national and state governments do, they have extremely important effects on the daily lives of citizens. Without the services provided by local governments, modern life would not be possible.

In Texas, city governments are the principal providers of local services. Council-manager governments govern most major cities, a system that has brought a degree of professionalism to city government that is often lacking in county and some other units of local government. In many respects, the contrast between county and city government is remarkable. County governments have resisted change and

seem content to operate under a form of government designed by and for an agrarian society. It is a paradox that council-manager city government and plural executive county government could exist in the same state, given the political culture. Economy, efficiency, and professionalism are not values supported by the traditionalistic political culture of the state, yet they are widely practiced in council-manager government. It has been suggested that strong support from the business community in the state is one reason for the acceptance of council-manager government. Business leaders see the economy and efficiency of this form.

Key Terms

at-large election systems
city manager
commissioner's court
commission form
council-manager form
county government
county sheriff

creatures of the states
cumulative voting
extra-territorial jurisdiction
general law city
home rule city
incorporation
independent school district

nonpartisan elections
preferential voting
single-member district
special purpose district
strong mayor form
weak mayor form

Notes

1 Federal Advisory Commission on Intergovernmental Relations, *State and Local Rates in the Federal System: A-88* (Washington, D.C.: US Government Printing Office, 1982), 59.

2 Terrell Blodgett, *Texas Home Rule Charters* (Austin: Texas Municipal League, 1994), 1.

3 *Vernon's Texas Statutes and Codes Annotated,* vol. 1, 5.001–5.003.

4 Texas Municipal League, *Handbook for Mayors and Councilmembers in General Law Cities* (Austin: Texas Municipal League, 1994).

5 *Vernon's Texas Statues and Codes Annotated,* "Local Government," vol. 1, 9.001–9.008.

6 Terrell Blodgett, *Texas Home Rule Charters* (Austin: Texas Municipal League, 1994), 113–114.

7 *Vernon's Texas Statutes and Codes Annotated,* "Local Government," vol. 1, 7.005.

8 David L. Martin, *Running City Hall: Municipal Administration in the United States* (Tuscaloosa: University of Alabama Press, 1990), 21–22.

9 Attorney General of Texas, Opinion GA–0737, https://www.oag.state.tx.us/opinions/opinions/50abbott/op/2009/pdf/ga0737.pdf.

10 Richard Stillman, *The Rise of the City Manager: A Public Professional in Local Government* (Albuquerque: University of New Mexico Press, 1974), 15.

11 James A. Svara, *Official Leadership in the City: Patterns of Conflict and Cooperation* (New York: Oxford University Press, 1990), chaps. 2 and 3.

12 Blodgett, *Texas Home Rule Charters,* 30–31.

13 Bradley Robert Price, *Progressive Critics: The Commission Government Movement in America, 1901–1920* (Austin: University of Texas Press, 1977), 12.

14 Ibid., 109.

15 Ibid., 85.

16 Ibid., 52.

17 *Tulsa City Charter,* June 1954, 6.

18 For a good discussion of electoral systems in American cities, see Joseph Zimmerman, *The Federal City: Community Control in Large Cities* (New York: St. Martin's Press, 1972), chap. 4.

19 Blodgett, *Texas Home Rule Charters,* 46–47.

20 Abigail Thernstrom. "Redisricting, Race, and the Voting Rights Act." *National Affairs.* Issue 3 (Spring 2010): http://www.nationalaffairs.com/publications/detail/redistricting-race-and-the-voting-rights-act

21 Ibid.

22 Joseph F. Zimmerman. "The Federal Voting Rights Act and Alternative Election Systems." *William and Mary Law Review.* Vol 19 Number 4 (Summer 1978): http://scholarship.law.wm.edu/cgi/viewcontent.cgi?article=2413&context=wmlr.

23 Svara, *Official Leadership in the City,* 136.

24 https://www.amaisd.org/index.php?hard=board/about.php.

25 https://www.amaisd.org/index.php?hard=board/about.php.

26 *Vernon's Texas Statutes and Codes Annotated,* "Elections," 41.003.

27 For a discussion of San Antonio, see David R. Johnson, John A. Booth, and Richard J. Harris, *The Politics of San Antonio: Community Progress and Power* (Lincoln: University of Nebraska Press, 1983).

28 Travis County Clerk, www.traviscountyclerk.org/eclerck/cotennt/images/election_results.

29 Dallas County Elections Department, www.http://www.dallascountyvotes.org/election-results-and-maps/election-results/historical-election-results/.

30 U.S. Department of Commerce, Bureau of the Census, 1997 *Census of Governments: Government Organization,* vol. 1, no. 1 (Washington D.C.: U.S. Government Printing Office, 1997), 18, Table 13.

31 *U.S. Census of Population 2010,* www.census.gov.

32 Gary M. Halter and Gerald L. Dauthery, "The County Commissioners Court in Texas," in *Governing Texas: Documents and Readings,* 3rd ed., eds. Fred Gantt Jr., et al. (New York: Thomas Y. Crowell, 1974), 340–350.

33 *Avery v. Midland County,* 88 S. Ct. 1114 (1968).

34 Robert E. Norwood and Sabrina Strawn, *Texas County Government: Let the People Choose,* 2nd ed. (Austin: Texas Research League, 1984).

35 Ibid., 24. Also see John A. Gilmartin and Joe M. Rothe, *County Government in Texas: A Summary of the Major Offices and Officials,* Issue No. 2 (College Station: Texas Agricultural Extension Service).

36 Texas Association of Counties, Oct. 2012, www.county.org/counties/desc_office/index.asp.

37 Ibid.

38 Norwood and Strawn, *Texas County Government,* 27.

39 Information supplied by the Texas Association of Counties, Austin.

40 Property tax records of the Brazos County Central Appraisal District, 1673 Briarcrest Dr., Bryan, TX.

41 For an extensive explanation of the county home rule efforts in Texas, see Wilborn E. Benton, *Texas: Its Government and Politics,* 2nd ed. (Englewood Cliffs, N.J.: Prentice Hall, 1966), 317–381.

42 U.S. Bureau of the Census, "Local Governments by Type and State, 2012," http://www2.census.gov/ govs/cog/2012/formatted_prelim_counts_23jul2012_2.pdf.

43 *Texas Constitution,* Article 7, sec. 1.

44 *Texas Education Code,* Chapter 11 School Districts, sec. 11.052.

CHAPTER 7

Voting and Political Participation in Texas

*Upon completing this chapter,
you will be able to...*

- **Identify the rights and responsibilities of citizens.**

One of the hallmarks of democratic life is people's ability to participate in politics. Voting is the most obvious way that citizens play a part in collective governance in a democracy. However, this is just one of many ways that people can participate in the public square. Most people choose not to engage in state and local politics, both here in Texas and around the country. So although men and women are certainly social beings, it might be too optimistic to argue—as the ancient Greek philosopher Aristotle did—that we are naturally political animals. This chapter explores the ways in which Texans participate in politics, with special emphasis on voting behavior. It also discusses why voter turnout in Texas is so low today and has been in years past.

Then Senate candidate Ted Cruz speaking with reporters during his campaign. Cruz defeated political powerhouse and sitting Lieutenant Governor David Dewhurst in the Republican primary, then went on to win the 2012 General Election. He assumed office in 2013 and is currently serving a 6-year term as the junior U.S. Senator from Texas.

187

Political Participation

political participation
All forms of involvement citizens can have that are related to governance

Political participation refers to taking part in activities that are related to governance. Table 7.1 lists some common forms of such participation and the percentage of adults who took part in them during a 12-month period, according to a recent national survey conducted by the Pew Research Center. (Note that a large proportion of survey respondents had not participated in any of these activities.)[1]

In addition to looking at involvement in specific activities, participation can also be conceptualized in terms of levels and types of activities. Sidney Verba and Norman H. Nie, in their book *Participation in America*,[2] divide the population into several groups based on the types of participation and the intensity of involvement that citizens can have in the political process (see Figure 7.1).

- Inactives, who take no part in politics
- Voting specialists, who confine their efforts to voting in elections
- Parochial participants, who become active in politics when the issue has a direct effect on them
- Campaigners, who like the activity and the controversial and competitive nature of political campaigns
- Communalists, who, while being active voters, avoid the combat and controversy of partisan campaigns and are attracted to other kinds of nonpartisan, noncontroversial community activity
- Complete activists, who get involved in all levels and kinds of activity, including voting, campaigning, lobbying officials, and participating in community affairs

TABLE 7.1

Civil and Political Participation in America

Activity	Percentage of Adults Surveyed Who Participated During the Previous 12 Months
Worked with fellow citizens to solve a problem in your community	35%
Attended a political meeting on local, town, or school affairs	22%
Signed a paper petition	22%
Contacted a national, state, or local government official in person, by phone call, or by letter about an issue	21%
Contributed money to a political candidate or party, or any other political organization or cause	16%
Been an active member of any group that tries to influence public policy or government, not including a political party	13%
Attended a political rally or speech	10%
Worked or volunteered for a political party or candidate	7%
Attended an organized protest of any kind	6%
Sent a letter to the editor of a newspaper or magazine	3%

Source: Pew Research Center's Internet & American Life Project, Civic Engagement Tracking Survey 2012. Based on an adult sample (n = 2,253). Margin of error is +/− 2%. Available online at http://www.pewinternet.org/datasets/august-2012-civic-engagement/.

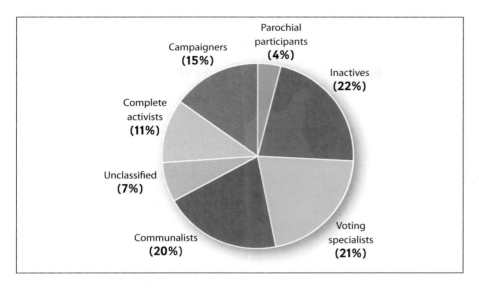

FIGURE 7.1   Types of Political Activists

SOURCE: Sidney Verba and Norman Nie, *Participation in America* (Chicago: University of Chicago Press, 1987), 79.

Voter Turnout in Texas

One of the most common forms of participation in politics is voting in elections. There are several ways to calculate **voter turnout,** or the proportion of people who cast ballots in an election.

One measure is the percentage of **registered voters** who cast a ballot. According to the U.S. Census Bureau, **voter registration** is "the act of qualifying to vote by formally enrolling on an official list of voters."[3] Most states make it very easy to register to vote, but there are drawbacks to using this way of assessing voter turnout. For example, ten states currently have no prior voter registration requirements, allowing "same-day" registration. (In addition, California has legalized same-day registration, but the law has not yet gone into effect.)[4] In these states, voters show up on election day, register on the spot (usually by providing identification and proof of residency), and are allowed to vote. Research has shown that **same-day voter registration** results in greater turnout; states that have implemented same-day registration have turnout levels above the national average.[5] North Dakota, for its part, has no voter registration whatsoever.[6] This makes it difficult to compare the turnout rates of registered voters across states. Furthermore, voter registration lists are not completely accurate and up to date; most contain "deadwood," or the names of individuals who are registered at a certain address but no longer live there.[7] This inaccuracy in the rolls distorts the count of registered voters in a precinct area.

A second measure is the percentage of the voting-age population that votes. **Voting-age population** (VAP) is defined as the number of people age 18 and over. To calculate turnout using VAP, the number of people casting votes in an election is divided by the number of residents 18 years of age and older.[8] VAP is generally the preferred measure (and the one most often used by political scientists) because it discounts variations in state voting and registration requirements and makes it easier to compare states. However, problems occur with using VAP to express voter turnout as well. The voting-age population includes a sizable number of people

voter turnout
The proportion of people who cast ballots in an election

registered voters
Citizens who have formally gone through the process of getting their names on the voter registration list

voter registration
The act of qualifying to vote by formally enrolling on an official list of voters

same-day voter registration
Voters are allowed to register on election day; no preregistration before the election is required

voting-age population
The number of people age 18 and over

Voters waiting in line to cast ballots

---

voting-eligible population

The voting-age population, corrected to exclude groups ineligible to vote, such as noncitizens and convicted felons

who have met the age requirement but are nonetheless unable to register and vote. Exclusions from voting include not being a U.S. citizen, having committed a felony, having been declared mentally incapacitated, or not having met the state and local residency requirements for registration.[9] Measuring turnout by using VAP is distorted because these ineligible persons are counted in the figure, even though it is impossible for them to vote.

The United States Election Project presents yet a third measure of voter turnout, based on the **voting-eligible population** (VEP). VEP is calculated by correcting VAP to eliminate ineligible groups, such as noncitizens and convicted felons.[10] Michael McDonald, one of the political scientists who pioneered the VEP measure, claims that "the most valid turnout rates over time and across states are calculated using voting-eligible population."[11] Using the VEP turnout rate (calculated by dividing the number of ballots cast for highest office by VEP), participation in recent presidential elections appears higher than previously determined using the VAP measure.[12] Some other political scientists also recommend the use of VEP turnout rates but acknowledge that VEP data is not universally available at this time.[13] Table 7.2 compares voter turnout rates calculated according to these three methods. Turnout rates using the percentage of registered voters who voted are higher than the other two methods; using the percentage of voting-age population who voted yields the lowest figures.

How does Texas fare in terms of voter turnout rates? In general, Texans are not avid voters. As shown in Table 7.3, Texas consistently falls below the national average in terms of percentage of the voting-eligible population participating in elections during the past 30 years. Texas also ranks low compared to other states in terms of voter turnout (see also Figure 7.2). In fact, for the 2010 congressional and statewide races, Texas had the lowest voter turnout of all 50 states. Data from the 2012 election suggests a continuation of this low-turnout trend. The Texas secretary of state reported that 7.9 million people, or 58.58 percent of registered voters, cast a ballot for president in 2012.[14] According to the U.S. Election Project, just less than half of the VEP voted. This represents a decrease in turnout from the previous presidential election in 2008, when over 8 million Texans cast a vote.[15]

It is also worth noting that voter turnout at the national level is lower in the United States than in most other industrialized nations. Moreover, participation in state politics is lower than at the national level and still lower at the local levels.

TABLE 7.2

Comparison of Percentage of Registered, Voting-Age, and Voting-Eligible Voters Voting in Texas Elections, 1988–2012*

Year	Percent of Registered Voters Who Voted	Percent of VAP Who Voted	VEP Highest Office Turnout Rate
Presidential Election Years			
1988	66.2	44.3	50.1
1992	72.9	47.6	54.2
1996	53.2	41.0	46.5
2000	51.8	44.3	49.2
2004	56.6	46.1	53.7
2008	59.5	45.6	54.1
2012	58.6	43.7	49.7
Congressional and Statewide Election Years			
1990	50.6	31.1	35.3
1994	50.9	33.6	37.5
1998	32.4	26.5	29.9
2002	36.2	29.4	34.2
2006	33.6	26.4	30.9
2010	38.0	27.0	32.1

*Data may differ slightly from those available online because of rounding.

Source: Texas Secretary of State, *Turnout and Voter Registration Figures* (1970–current). http://www.sos.state.tx.us/elections/historical/70-92.shtml; Michael P. McDonald, *United States 2012 Voter Turnout Rates* 1980–2012. (See http://elections.gmu.edu/voter_turnout.htm).

TABLE 7.3

Texas Rank as a Percentage of Voting-Eligible Population* in National Elections, 1988–2012

Year	Texas Rank	National Turnout	Texas Turnout
Presidential Election Years			
1988	37	52.8	50.1
1992	40	58.1	54.2
1996	43	51.7	46.5
2000	41	54.2	49.2
2004	48	60.1	53.7
2008	48	61.6	54.1
2012	47	58.2	49.7
Congressional/Statewide Election Only Years			
1990	41	38.4	35.3
1994	42	41.1	37.5
1998	47	38.1	29.9
2002	46	39.5	34.2
2006	48	40.4	30.9
2010	50	41.0	32.1

*Data compiled using the voting-eligible population instead of the more common voting-age population. Voting-eligible population excludes noncitizens, felons (depending on state law), and mentally incapacitated persons.

Source: Michael P. McDonald, *United States 2012 Voter Turnout Rates 1980–2012.* (See http://elections.gmu.edu/voter_turnout.htm)

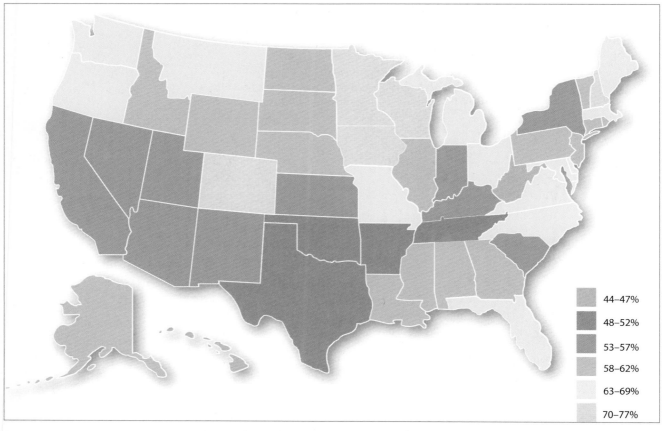

	44–47%
	48–52%
	53–57%
	58–62%
	63–69%
	70–77%

FIGURE 7.2   Percentage of Eligible Voters Voting in 2012 Presidential Election

SOURCE: Michael P. McDonald (2013). "2012 General Election Turnout Rates," United States Elections Project (accessed April 2014), http://elections.gmu.edu/Turnout_2012G.html.

CORE OBJECTIVE

Taking Personal Responsibility...

What activities do you engage in that are related to governance? Which forms of political participation do you think are the most effective?

Explaining Voter Turnout

How can we explain the relatively low levels of voting among Texans, even accounting for the fact that the state has a significant difference between its VAP and VEP that negatively exaggerates commonly cited turnout levels? Many factors are involved. The political culture discourages participation—there is a legacy of restricted access to the ballot for many groups, and other social, economic, and political factors play a role. Of course, many of the factors that impact voter turnout in Texas are also connected to turnout levels across the country, and even around the world.

Legal Restrictions Today

Like other southern U.S. states, Texas has a history of restrictive voter registration laws. In the past, these laws made it difficult to qualify to vote and limited avenues of political participation. Largely because of federal government intervention, most legal restrictions to voter registration have been lifted. However, some requirements do remain.

In Texas today, individuals who are at least 18 years of age (excluding noncitizens, convicted felons, and the mentally incapacitated) may vote, provided they register at least 30 days prior to an election. Citizens may mail in a voter registration form, with postage prepaid by the state. These applications are available at post offices, libraries, and many state offices as well as online. Applicants must provide either a driver's license number, personal identification number, or partial social security number. Barring this, another form of identification must be presented at the polls. After the application is processed, voters receive a voter registration card. This card is to be presented at the polling place on election day as proof of registration; without it, an affidavit must be signed and another form of identification provided. Voters are automatically sent a new card every two years; the post office is instructed not to forward it if an individual has moved. If the card cannot be delivered to the addressee at the address on the card, it is returned to the voter registrar, and the voter's name is removed from the registration list. Voters must re-register at their new address.[16]

Restrictions to registration vary greatly among the states. In states requiring preregistration, the amount of time varies from 10 to 30 days before the election. Although Texans can obtain an application for voter registration online, they must mail or present it to their local registrar's office for processing.[17] Nineteen states offer fully online voter registration, and four more have legalized but not yet implemented online systems.[18]

Thirty-four states, including Texas, have adopted voter ID legislation.[19] This legislation requires voters to present government-issued picture IDs when they go to vote. Even if voters are listed on the voter registration roll, they must still provide this identification. Advocates of voter ID laws argue that these requirements will reduce voting fraud, while opponents counter that the need to obtain proper identification effectively restricts the right to vote and imposes a burden on would-be voters and government officials. To participate in an election, Texans may present one of seven kinds of ID, including an election identification certificate (which is available free of charge from the Department of Public Safety for those who do not have any of the other six forms of ID).[20]

Texas passed its voter ID law in 2011. Under Section 5 of the Federal Voting Rights Act, certain states considered to be at high risk for discrimination could not change their voting laws without prior approval of either the U.S. Attorney General (Justice Department) or the U.S. District Court for the District of Columbia.[21] Texas, one of the states judged as having a history of discriminatory election practices, was subject to this provision. Therefore, Texas needed federal approval (or "preclearance") before its voter ID law could go into effect. In March 2012, the U.S. Justice Department denied preclearance of the Texas voter ID law because the data submitted by the state demonstrated minority groups would be adversely affected by the law. Texas Attorney General Greg Abbott appealed this decision, arguing there is no evidence of discrimination against minorities in Texas today and that Section 5 of the Voting Rights Act exceeded the enumerated powers of Congress and conflicted with both Article IV of the Constitution and the Tenth Amendment. However, the U.S. District Court for the District of Columbia denied the state's application for court reconsideration in August 2012.[22] Attorney General Abbott then filed a brief with the U.S. Supreme Court. On June 25, 2013, the Supreme Court declared Section 4 of the Voting Rights Act (which laid out the formula for identifying which states or jurisdictions would be subject to the preclearance requirement) unconstitutional. With this key portion of the Act struck down, Section 5 was rendered unenforceable. Texas no longer required federal approval for its voter ID law.[23] As a result, the voter ID law went into immediate effect.[24] The November 2013 election was the first in which Texans were required to show a photo ID in order to vote. Legal challenges have continued, and although the U.S. Supreme Court allowed the law to remain in effect for the 2014 election, this issue may be far from a final resolution.

There have been some attempts to make voting and registration easier in Texas. For example, in 1993, the U.S. Congress passed the National Voter Registration Act (also known as the "Motor Voter Act"), allowing people to register to vote when they apply for or renew their driver's license. Texas has since implemented this law. In addition, Texas allows early voting, either in person at a polling place (typically between 17 and 4 days before an election) or by mail. Individuals who will be away from their county of residence on election day (including military personnel) are encouraged to vote early by mail (sometimes called absentee voting), although an alternate process is also available to military and overseas voters.[25]

CORE OBJECTIVE

Thinking Critically...

How do you think the Texas voter ID law will impact voter turnout in Texas? Where do you stand on the issue? Explain why you favor or oppose voter ID laws.

The Legacy of Restricted Ballot Access in Texas

poll tax

In place from 1902 until 1966 in Texas, a tax citizens were required to pay each year between October and January to be eligible to vote in the next election cycle

The state's history of restricting access to voting is very much in keeping with its traditionalistic political culture. In 1902 the Texas legislature adopted, with voter approval, payment of a **poll tax** as a requirement for voting. This law primarily targeted the Populist movement, which had organized low-income white farmers into a political coalition that threatened the establishment within the Democratic Party.[26] This tax ($1.75) was a large amount of money for poor farmers in the early 1900s.[27] The poll tax also restricted ballot access for African Americans and Hispanics, who were disproportionately poor as a group. The poll tax had to be paid each year between October 1 and January 31 for a person to be allowed to vote in the next election cycle. Figure 7.3 shows an original poll tax receipt.

The poll tax was in effect in Texas for about 60 years. In 1964, passage of the Twenty-Fourth Amendment to the U.S. Constitution eliminated the poll tax as a requirement for voting in federal elections. However, Texas retained the poll tax as a requirement for voting in state elections.[28] In 1964–65, 2.4 million Texans still paid the tax. In 1966, the U.S. Supreme Court abolished the poll tax.[29] The very next election cycle proved how successful the poll tax had been in reducing the number

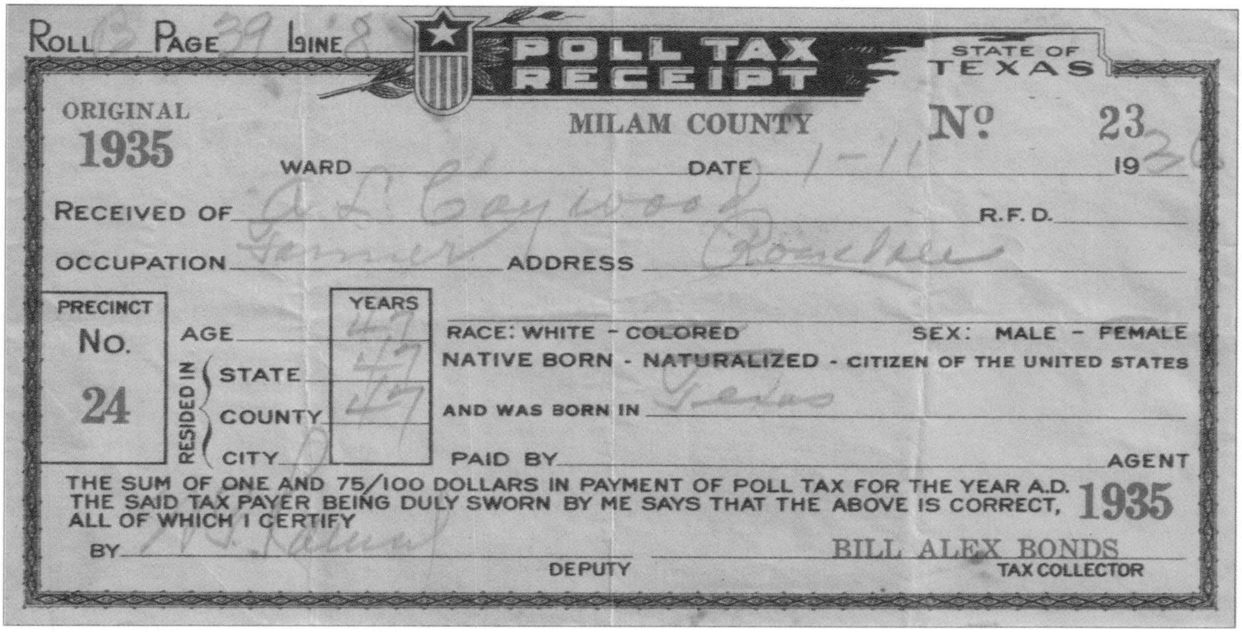
ROLL PAGE LINE
POLL TAX RECEIPT
STATE OF TEXAS
ORIGINAL
1935
MILAM COUNTY
No. 23
WARD ____ DATE ____ 19__
RECEIVED OF ____ R.F.D. ____
OCCUPATION ____ ADDRESS ____
PRECINCT No. 24
AGE ____ YEARS
RESIDED IN STATE ____ COUNTY ____ CITY ____
RACE: WHITE - COLORED SEX: MALE - FEMALE
NATIVE BORN - NATURALIZED - CITIZEN OF THE UNITED STATES
AND WAS BORN IN ____
PAID BY ____ AGENT
THE SUM OF ONE AND 75/100 DOLLARS IN PAYMENT OF POLL TAX FOR THE YEAR A.D. 1935
THE SAID TAX PAYER BEING DULY SWORN BY ME SAYS THAT THE ABOVE IS CORRECT,
ALL OF WHICH I CERTIFY
BY ____ DEPUTY
BILL ALEX BONDS
TAX COLLECTOR

FIGURE 7.3 Original Poll Tax Receipt

of qualified voters when, in 1968, voter registration rose to more than 4 million, an increase of about 41 percent.[30]

Even after the poll tax was eliminated in 1966, Texas retained a very restrictive system of voter registration. It had an **annual registration** system, meaning voters were required to register each year between October 1 and January 31. Individuals were required to register at the courthouse, where they had also been required to pay the poll tax. (In most Texas counties, even today, the county tax collector is also the voter registrar.) For minorities, the trip to the courthouse could be an intimidating experience, and many avoided it.

annual registration
A system that requires citizens to reregister to vote every year

Following a 1971 court decision prohibiting annual registration systems,[31] the Texas legislature passed a very progressive voter registration law that eliminated annual registration and replaced it with a permanent registration system. **Permanent registration** is a system that keeps citizens on the voter registration list without requiring them to reregister every year. Easy voter registration procedures have been shown to increase the number of registered voters. In 1972, the first year Texas used a permanent registration system, voter registration increased by almost 1.4 million.[32] All states now use some form of permanent registration.[33]

permanent registration
A system that keeps citizens on the voter registration list without their having to reregister every year

Another past practice used by many southern states, including Texas, to block participation by African Americans was the **white primary.** In 1923, the Texas legislature passed a law prohibiting African Americans from participating in Democratic Party primaries. The U.S. Supreme Court declared this law unconstitutional.[34] In 1927, the legislature granted the executive committee of each political party the right to determine voter eligibility for primaries, thereby allowing the Democratic Party to exclude African Americans.[35] In response, the U.S. Supreme Court again declared the legislature's role unconstitutional.[36] In 1932, bypassing the legislature entirely, the state Democratic Party convention adopted a resolution to hold a white primary.[37] This action prompted yet another U.S. Supreme Court challenge.[38] The

white primary
From 1923 to 1945, Democratic Party primary that excluded African Americans from participating

National Anti-Suffrage Association
Headquarters, 1911

issue before the Court at this point was whether a political party was an agent of the government or a private organization. The Supreme Court's 1935 ruling stated that political parties were in fact private organizations and therefore could decide who was permitted to participate in primary elections. This allowed the Democrats to exclude African Americans from participating in the party primary. Because, at this time, the Republicans presented no real competition in the general election, the primary effectively became the "general election." Thus, from 1932 until 1945, African Americans in Texas were denied the right to vote by the rules of the Democratic Party, rather than by state law.

In 1944 the U.S. Supreme Court outlawed all white primaries in southern states in *Smith v. Allwright,* a case that originated in Texas.[39] This ruling overturned earlier rulings that political parties were private organizations. In *Smith,* the Supreme Court held that political parties were agents of the state and therefore could not exclude people from participating in primary elections because of race. Thus, federal court actions finally ended the practice of the white primary after it had been used for two decades to deny the vote to African Americans.

As was common in many states, property ownership was also used to restrict the right to vote in Texas. These restrictions applied mostly to local elections, particularly bond elections. The reasoning behind using property ownership to restrict voting was that local governments are financed primarily with property taxes, and renters supposedly did not pay property tax. However, enforcement of the property ownership requirement was difficult. Property ownership requirements were eliminated in the 1970s when permanent registration took effect in Texas.

Women were also disfranchised in Texas. By 1914, 11 other states had granted women the right to vote.[40] In 1915, the Texas legislature considered granting women the right to vote, but the measure failed. In 1918, however, women were given the right to participate in primary elections, and in 1919, Texas became the first southern state to approve the Nineteenth Amendment to the U.S. Constitution, outlawing any citizen from being denied the right to vote because of their sex.[41]

All these restrictions combined to prolong the state's tradition of limiting or even discouraging participation in elections. Although past restrictions have been removed from law, and current access to voter registration is comparatively easy (and has increased the number of registered voters in the state), there are persistent and lingering effects of Texas's legacy of restricted ballot access. Texas still has low levels of participation in the political process. As shown in Table 7.3, Texas recently ranked at or near the bottom of all states on voter turnout in elections. In time, the residual effect of restrictive practices may decline, but there are other factors influencing voter turnout.

Social and Economic Factors

Rates of participation are also strongly affected by **socioeconomic factors,** such as educational level, family income, and minority status. High-income, well-educated people are more likely to vote than are lower-income, less well-educated people. People of higher socioeconomic status are likely to be more aware of elections and to perceive themselves as having a high stake in election outcomes; therefore, they are more likely to vote. They are also more likely to contribute financially to political campaigns and become actively involved in elections and party activity.

Age is another factor that contributes to turnout. Young voters are less likely to vote and become involved in politics. They often have other interests, are more mobile, and may not perceive themselves as having an important stake in political outcomes. Although still lower than the turnout rate for the population as a whole, youth voting rates have increased recently, including during the 2012 election.[42]

Race is yet another factor in voting. Minority groups in Texas now make up the majority of the state's population, but they tend to vote and register to vote in smaller proportions than Anglos or non-Hispanic whites. However, voting among African Americans has deviated from this pattern in recent years. In 2008, blacks both registered and voted at about the same level as whites. Because this is not normally the case, the higher levels of black registration and voting may have been attributable to President Obama being on the ballot. Black turnout remained relatively strong in the 2010 midterm elections (although as usual, absolute voting levels fell off compared to the numbers in a presidential election year). In the 2012 election, 63 percent of black citizens voted in Texas, surpassing the percentage of white non-Hispanics who voted (61 percent)[43] (see Figure 7.4). Again, this atypically high black turnout may have been due to President Obama's bid for reelection.

According to data collected by the U.S. Census Bureau on the 2012 election, both voter registration and turnout among Hispanics was significantly lower than the Anglo population. Only about 40 percent of voting-age Hispanics in Texas are

socioeconomic factors

Factors such as income, education, race, and ethnicity that affect voter turnout

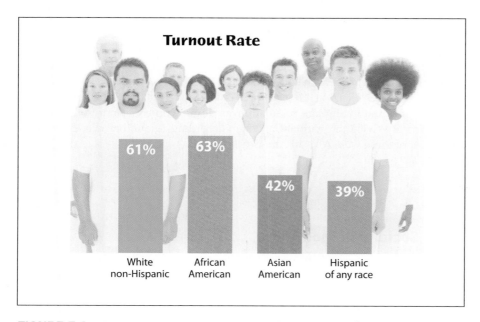

FIGURE 7.4   Voter Turnout in Texas in the 2012 Presidential Election, by Race

registered to vote. In the 2012 election, just over one-quarter (27.7 percent) of Hispanic Texans over the age of 18 cast a ballot. By comparison, about 60 percent of all Anglo Texans over the age of 18 voted in the same election. When considering only those who are citizens, the number of Hispanics in the state who voted increases to nearly 39 percent. Analysis of election data has shown that Hispanics constitute an increasing share of the national vote, and this is expected to be the case here in Texas in the future.[44] Currently, though, non-Hispanic whites and blacks in Texas are voting at much higher rates than Hispanics. Therefore, although Texas's Hispanic population continues to grow, Hispanics play a much smaller role in shaping the state's politics than their numbers might suggest. Turnout rates among Texans of Asian descent are also lower than those of Anglos and blacks. Although nearly 60 percent of Asian citizens are registered to vote, only 42.4 percent cast a ballot in the 2012 presidential election.[45]

Several socioeconomic factors contribute to lower voter turnout among Hispanics and Asians, including lower education levels and incomes. There are also compounding factors specific to each group. A national study by the Pew Hispanic Center found that a majority (55 percent) of Hispanics are not eligible to vote, compared to just under half of Asians, about a third of African Americans, and only one-fifth of whites.[46] This is especially true because Hispanic and Asian populations tend to be younger, but a higher proportion of Hispanics are noncitizens and therefore cannot vote in elections. Another reason for lower turnout among Hispanics and Asians in Texas is lower political interest. According to a May 2012 survey of Texas registered voters conducted by the University of Texas at Austin, 15 percent of Hispanics and 22 percent of Asians were "not very interested" or "not at all interested" in politics. This compares to only 7 percent of whites and 8 percent of African Americans who were disinterested in politics.[47] Table 7.4 provides a breakdown of voter turnout and voter registration rates by gender and ethnicity.

Felony Conviction and Voting

Most states limit the voting rights of persons convicted of a felony. Maine and Vermont are the only states that allow felons to vote, even while they are in prison.[48] Texas prohibits persons convicted of a felony, as well as those on probation or parole, from voting. However, felons in Texas may register to vote after they have served out their sentence and have completed their time on probation and parole.[49] According to U.S. Election Project, in 2012 there were 473,167 ineligible felons (2.5 percent of the voting age population) in Texas who could not vote.[50] This is approximately twice the national average; according to another account, nearly 30 percent of these were African Americans.[51]

Being Socially Responsible...

Considering the discussion on the socioeconomic factors that affect voter turnout, identify effective ways to increase civic knowledge in culturally diverse communities.

TABLE 7.4

Registration and Voter Participation by Race and Sex in Texas, 2012

	Total Voting Age Population (VAP)	Total Citizen Population	Total Registered	Percent Registered (Total)	Percent Registered (Citizen)	Total Voted	Percent Voted (Total)	Percent Voted (Citizen)
Total	18,642	16,062	10,749	57.7	66.9	8,643	46.4	53.8
Male	9,046	7,719	4,977	55.0	64.5	3,925	43.4	50.8
Female	9,596	8,344	5,772	60.1	69.2	4,719	49.2	56.6
White alone	15,029	12,989	8,643	57.5	66.5	6,900	45.9	53.1
White non-Hispanic alone	8,512	8,360	6,101	71.7	73.0	5,087	59.8	60.9
Black alone	2,213	2,144	1,569	70.9	73.2	1,352	61.1	63.1
Asian alone	900	506	299	33.2	59.1	214	23.8	42.4
Hispanic (of any race)	6,831	4,867	2,652	38.8	54.5	1,890	27.7	38.8
White alone or in combination	15,200	13,144	8,749	57.6	66.6	6,968	45.8	53.0
Black alone or in combination	2,293	2,207	1,606	70.0	72.8	1,380	60.2	62.5
Asian alone or in combination	909	515	305	33.5	59.2	220	24.2	42.8

VAP = Population 18 years and older, in thousands.

Source: U.S. Census Bureau. Voting and Registration in the Election of November 2012 Detailed Tables. Table 4b. Reported Voting and Registration by Sex, Race and Hispanic Origin, for States: November 2012. http://www.census.gov/hhes/www/socdemo/voting/publications/p20/2012/tables.html.

Party Competition

The lack of party competition in Texas for more than 100 years also contributes to the state's overall lower voter turnout. Studies have shown that party competition and the closeness of elections are important factors in voter turnout. (However, the effect of the latter is smaller in comparative perspective than one might think.)[52] When there is party competition in a district, voters believe that their votes will actually "count," so they are more likely to show up at the polls and to participate in grassroots political organizations. Moreover, in competitive districts, both parties have a big incentive to increase voter turnout.[53] Texans elected Republicans to all statewide offices in 2002, 2004, 2006, 2008, 2010, and 2012. The state is also solidly Republican in U.S. presidential elections. Furthermore, Texas has many noncompetitive seats, especially in the state legislature. It remains to be seen if this domination of state politics will be permanent. Although party competition has increased in recent years, the state has a long history of being a one-party state; consequently, voter turnout is lower than it might be with greater competition.

Other Factors Affecting Voter Turnout

Other factors can affect voter turnout in some elections. One is the timing of the election. Voter turnout is higher in November general elections than in off-year elections when we do not elect a president or other statewide or national offices. For the most part, turnout for primary elections is even lower than for general elections. Also, local elections for city councils and school boards are generally not held in conjunction with general elections; these are commonly held in May

Texas delegates at a convention

in Texas. However, efforts are currently being made to move these local contests to the fall. In 2012, Austin voters approved a proposition to move city elections from May to November.[54] Turnout in local elections is always lower than in other elections (despite the fact that the odds of being the marginal voter increase as the number of people voting goes down). There are several reasons for this: local elections are less visible and receive less attention by the media; voters do not perceive these elections as being important; and many of these races are not contested. In 1995 the Texas legislature proposed a constitutional amendment, which the voters approved, to change state law to allow cities and school boards to cancel elections if all races are uncontested. The governing body certifies the uncontested candidates as "winners." (Chapter 6 has more information on local elections.)

The day of the week can also affect voter turnout. Tuesday is the most common day for elections in the United States. This tradition dates back to 1845, when the U.S. Congress set the date for federal elections as the first Tuesday after the first Monday in November.[55] Local city and school board elections are often held on Saturday. Saturday might seem a better day than Tuesday, because many people are off work and have time to vote. However, Saturday is also a day to do other things, and people might forget to vote or might choose to use the day for other activities, such as recreation, that they believe will provide greater utility than participation in political life. Also, in the United States, elections are generally held on a single day, with the polls typically being open for 12 hours. Many European countries hold elections over an entire weekend.

Longer election periods, early voting opportunities, and other ways that voting (and registration) can be made easier (such as postal voting and more voting places) might increase voter turnout. As political scientist Andre Blais notes, "It makes sense to assume that people are more prone to vote if it is easy."[56] Empirical evidence generally supports this intuition. However, a recent University of Wisconsin study of early voting offers a caveat at least in this case. Kenneth Mayer, one of the authors of this study, notes that they found that early voting "actually causes voter turnout to go down."[57] It is not clear, though, whether this finding will be confirmed in other studies, because scholars have generally found the opposite impact when it comes to making voting easier.

Rationalist Explanations for Low Voter Turnout

A last reason for low voter turnout may be the realization by a number of voters that, at least in their individual cases, individual voting is irrational because (1) it does not meet the requirements of "strategic" or "instrumental" rationality (in the sense of voting being a purposeful act to influence an election) given the low probability of any individual being the "marginal" or "pivotal" voter in large-scale elections; and (2) the "consumption" or "expressive" value of voting does not outweigh the costs of participation (especially the time cost). In other words, duty doesn't call, nor is the act of voting all that valuable relative to the costs for some segment of the population.

There is a long tradition of literature in political science and economics, starting with the pathbreaking work of Anthony Downs, that makes these "rational choice" points. Scholars of voting often wonder, as Nobel Prize–winning economist Kenneth Arrow did, "Why an individual votes at all in a large election, since the probability that his vote will be decisive is so negligible."[58] But since so many do—thus creating the so-called paradox of voting—we may want to ask not why so many don't vote but why so many people do vote! This is undoubtedly a more complicated question than we can fully answer here. However, one answer might be that individuals, like people who clap at the end of a movie or cheer in a football stadium full of people, gain expressive value from the act of voting.[59] It simply makes them feel better to express their preference for one candidate (or against another). An individual may also, consciously or not, want to signal to others that he or she is a "good citizen" or a "serious person" by being seen voting or wearing the voting sticker we can only easily obtain at the voting facility. Or it could be that some individuals believe they have a real duty to participate in elections or to be concerned about the "social good," especially given the price they believe others have paid to secure that civil right.[60] Regardless, there could be any number of honestly good reasons why people might vote other than narrowly strategic ones. However, it is worth seriously considering that some people might choose not to vote for rational reasons. And it bears asking why individuals pay less attention to and vote less often in local elections where they have a statistically greater chance of influencing the election.

Another rational reason some people may not vote is that they are satisfied with (or alienated from) the political system in general and do not feel the need to express themselves in favor of (or against) any particular candidate. Last, an admittedly small number of eligible citizens may be principled nonvoters who do not want to provide legitimacy to what they believe is an illegitimate system.

CORE OBJECTIVE

Communicating Effectively...

Write a one-page summary of the rationalist explanations for low voter turnout.

Other Forms of Political Participation

Although voting in an election is the most common form of political participation, people participate in politics in many other ways. As noted at the opening of this chapter, participation types and the extent of involvement vary widely. In fact, one could be "involved" in politics quite intensely by becoming a candidate for public office or quite superficially by signing a petition or writing a short letter to the editor of the local newspaper. Other forms of participation seen in Texas and the rest of the country include donating money to a campaign, volunteering for a campaign, supporting an advocacy group, contacting an elected official, attending a rally or protest, or even using online social networks to support a candidate or group. A common feature of all these types of participation is the ultimate goal of affecting the decisions made by the government, either by electing certain people to office or by influencing those who are already in office.

A 2009 survey of Texas adults by the University of Texas at Austin (see Table 7.5) helps to shed more light on the ways in which Texans participate in politics. Although voting is far and away the most common form of political participation, just over half of respondents reported encouraging others to vote for a particular candidate. More than one-third of respondents reported supporting a candidate through such actions as displaying a bumper sticker, and the same number reported forwarding an email from a political candidate or group. Thirty percent reported contacting an elected official to express an opinion and 20 percent reported connecting with a candidate or political group through an online social network such as Facebook or Twitter. The least popular forms of political participation cited were attending a rally or protest (13 percent) and volunteering for a campaign (9 percent).[61]

Thanks to a greater reliance on the Internet by campaign fundraising efforts, donating to a campaign has become one of the easiest ways to participate in politics. About 22 percent of respondents to the University of Texas poll reported making a political donation. According to OpenSecrets.org, a website run by the Center for Responsive Politics that tracks political contributions, individual Texans contributed more than $68 million to presidential candidates during the 2012

TABLE 7.5

Popular Forms of Political Participation in Texas

"Please think back over the past year and indicate if you have done any of the following."

Political Activity	%
Voted in an election	80
Encouraged others to vote for a particular candidate	51
Publicly supported a political candidate (e.g., bumper sticker)	35
Forwarded an email from a political party, candidate, or interest group	35
Contacted an elected official to express an opinion	30
Donated money to a political candidate	22
Joined an online social network group supporting a political candidate	20
Attended a political rally, protest, or event	13
Volunteered for a political campaign	9

Source: University of Texas at Austin Department of Government, *N* = 800 Adults, Feb 24–Mar 6, 2009.

election.[62] This places Texas second in the nation for the amount of individual contributions to presidential campaigns. Republican candidates were the largest beneficiaries of these individual contributors, claiming about 78 percent of all political contributions.[63]

However, political participation as a whole is still relatively low in the United States, and especially in Texas. Why don't more people participate in politics? Political scientists Henry Brady, Sidney Verba, and Kay Schlozman answer, "Because they can't, because they don't want to, or because nobody asked."[64] Participation in politics requires free time, expendable income, and political interest. The time cost of participation, in particular, is a crucial constraint. Involvement in social networks such as civic associations and churches, which enable people to interact and mobilize, also promotes political participation. These kinds of social networks also help people to develop "civic skills," or the ability to communicate and organize, which are important to political activity. Many Americans lack some or all of these resources for political participation. As a result, they either "can't" or "don't want to" participate, or perhaps they would accept that they do not belong to a social network and so "nobody asked" them to participate.

Does low political participation threaten American democracy? Although turnout in presidential elections has experienced a slight increase in recent years, it is still much lower than in 1960. Other types of participation are also in decline. In his book *Bowling Alone,* Robert Putnam cites declining involvement in traditional civic associations as contributing to a loss of "social capital" in America. Social capital refers to the sense of shared purpose and values that social connection promotes, which Putnam and many others cite as necessary for a thriving democracy. Still others are less pessimistic. Russell Dalton, for example, argues that the decline in traditional civic associations is accompanied by a rise in other types of participation that reflect the changing values of a younger generation.[65]

Volunteers at campaign headquarters call voters on Election Day.

Conclusion

Political participation is affected by many factors. Some states, mostly southern and including Texas, have a legacy of restricting access to the ballot and discouraging voter participation. Despite the removal of these restrictions, participation has not immediately increased, suggesting political behavior can persist for generations (especially if there is a "habit component" to voting).[66] Social and economic factors also play a role

in participation, as do the rational calculations of individuals. Race, ethnicity, and the lack of party competition impact turnout and help explain lower turnouts in Texas. However, with increased party competition, voter turnout levels may change in the state. All these factors, combined with the traditionalistic political culture of Texas, help explain the low levels of participation in the political processes of the Lone Star State.

Key Terms

annual registration
permanent registration
political participation
poll tax

registered voters
same-day voter registration
socioeconomic factors
voter registration

voter turnout
voting-age population
voting-eligible population
white primary

Notes

[1] Pew Research Center, Internet & American Life Project Civic Engagement Tracking Survey 2012, http://www.pewinternet.org/datasets/august-2012-civic-engagement/.

[2] Sidney Verba and Norman H. Nie, *Participation in America* (Chicago: University of Chicago Press, 1987).

[3] U.S. Census Bureau, Voting and Registration—2012. http://www.census.gov/hhes/www/socdemo/voting/about/index.html

[4] National Conference of State Legislatures. Same Day Voter Registration. http://www.ncsl.org/research/elections-and-campaigns/same-day-registration.aspx.

[5] Ibid.

[6] North Dakota Secretary of State, North Dakota. . . . The Only State Without Voter Registration. https://vip.sos.nd.gov/pdfs/portals/votereg.pdf

[7] Michael P. McDonald, "Voter Turnout Frequently Asked Questions," *United States Elections Project*, 2012. http://elections.gmu.edu/FAQ.html#Permission.

[8] Thomas Holbrook and Brianne Heidbreder, "Does Measurement Matter? The Case of VAP and VEP in Models of Voter Turnout in the United States," *State Politics & Policy Quarterly*, 10:2 (Summer 2010): pp. 157–179.

[9] U.S. Census Bureau, *Current Population Survey (CPS—Definitions—2012*, http://www.census.gov/cps/about/cpsdef.html.

[10] Thomas Holbrook and Brianne Heidbreder, "Does Measurement Matter? The Case of VAP and VEP in Models of Voter Turnout in the United States," *State Politics & Policy Quarterly*, 10:2 (Summer 2010): pp. 157–179.

[11] Michael P. McDonald, "Voter Turnout Frequently Asked Questions," *United States Elections Project*, 2012, http://elections.gmu.edu/FAQ.html#Permission.

[12] Michael P. McDonald, "2008 General Election Turnout Rates," *United States Elections Project*, http://elections.gmu.edu/Turnout_2012G.html.

[13] Thomas Holbrook and Brianne Heidbreder, "Does Measurement Matter? The Case of VAP and VEP in Models of Voter Turnout in the United States," *State Politics & Policy Quarterly*, 10:2 (Summer 2010): pp. 157–179.

[14] Texas Secretary of State, Turnout and Voter Registration Figures (1970-current). http://www.sos.state.tx.us/elections/historical/70-92.shtml.

[15] Ciara O'Rourke, "Voter turnout down across Texas and Central Texas compared to 2008," *Austin American-Statesman*, November 7, 2012, http://www.statesman.com/news/news/local/voter-turnout-down-across-texas-and-central-texas-/nSzmQ/.

[16] Texas Secretary of State, *Texas Voting*, http://www.sos.state.tx.us/elections/pamphlets/largepamp.shtml.

[17] Ibid.

[18] National Conference of State Legislatures, Online Voter Registration. http://www.ncsl.org/research/elections-and-campaigns/electronic-or-online-voter-registration.aspx#table

[19] National Conference of State Legislatures, Voter Identification Requirements, http://www.ncsl.org/research/elections-and-campaigns/voter-id.aspx.

[20] Ibid., Texas Department of Public Safety, Election Identification Certificate (EIC), http://www.txdps.state.tx.us/driverlicense/electionid.htm.

[21] U.S. Department of Justice, The Voting Rights Act of 1965, http://www.justice.gov/crt/about/vot/intro/intro_b.php.

[22] For the court's opinion, see *State of Texas v. Holder*, available online at http://electionlawblog.org/wp-content/uploads/texas-voter-id.pdf.

[23] Adam Liptak, "Supreme Court Invalidates Key Part of Voting Rights Act," *New York Times*, June 25, 2013, http://www.nytimes.com/2013/06/26/us/supreme-court-ruling.html?pagewanted=all&_r=0; For the Supreme Court's ruling, see Shelby County, Alabama v. Holder, available online at http://www.supremecourt.gov/opinions/12pdf/12-96_6k47.pdf.

[24] Todd J. Gillman, "Texas voter ID law "will take effect immediately,' says Attorney General Greg Abbott," *The Dallas Morning News,* June 25, 2013, http://trailblazersblog. dallasnews.com/2013/06/texas-voter-id-law-could-start-now-attorney-general-greg-abbott.html/.

[25] Texas Secretary of State, Early Voting, http://votetexas.gov/voting/when#early-voting; Military and Overseas Voters. http://votetexas.gov/voting/.

[26] Calvert and DeLeon, *History of Texas,* 212.

[27] The state tax was $1.50. The county was permitted to add 25 cents, and most county governments did so. See Article 7, Section 3 of the Texas Constitution, 1902.

[28] Calvert and DeLeon, *History of Texas,* 387.

[29] *United States v. Texas*, 384 U.S. 155 (1966).

[30] *Texas Almanac and State Industrial Guide, 1970–1971* (Dallas: A.H. Belo, 1969), 529.

[31] *Beare v. Smith*, 321 F. Supp. 1100.

[32] *Texas Almanac and State Industrial Guide, 1974–1975* (Dallas: A.H. Belo, 1973), 529.

[33] *Book of the States*, 30:23, 5.6.

[34] *Nixon v. Herndon et al.*, 273 U.S. 536 (1927).

[35] Sanford N. Greenberg, "White Primary," *Handbook of Texas Online*, published by the Texas State Historical Association, accessed November 12, 2012, http://www.tshaonline.org/handbook/online/articles/wdw01.

[36] *Nixon v. Condon et al.*, 286 U.S. 73 (1932).

[37] Sanford N. Greenberg, "White Primary," *Handbook of Texas Online*, published by the Texas State Historical Association, accessed November 12, 2012, http://www.tshaonline.org/handbook/online/articles/wdw01.

[38] *Grovey v. Townsend*, 295 U.S. 45 (1935).

[39] *Smith v. Allwright*, 321 U.S. 649 (1944). Also, in *United States v. Classic*, 313 U.S. 299 (1941), the U.S. Supreme Court ruled that a primary in a one-party state (Louisiana) was an election within the meaning of the U.S. Constitution.

[40] George McKenna, *The Drama of Democracy: American Government and Politics,* 2nd ed. (Guilford, Conn.: Dushkin, 1994), 129.

[41] Wilbourn E. Benton, *Texas Politics: Constraints and Opportunities,* 5th ed. (Chicago: Nelson-Hall, 1984), 65.

[42] Stacy Teicher Khadaroo, "Youth vote decides presidential election – again. Is this the new normal?" *Christian Science Monitor.* http://www.csmonitor.com/USA/Elections/President/2012/1107/Youth-vote-decides-presidential-election-again.-Is-this-the-new-normal.

[43] U.S. Census Bureau, "Voting and Registration in the Election of 2012—Detailed Tables."Table 4b. Reported Voting and Registration by Sex, Race and Hispanic Origin, for States: November 2012, http://www.census.gov/hhes/www/socdemo/voting/publications/p20/2012/tables.html.

[44] Mark Hugo Lopez and Paul Taylor, "Latino Voters in the 2012 Election." http://www.pewhispanic.org/2012/11/07/latino-voters-in-the-2012-election/.

[45] U.S. Census Bureau, "Voting and Registration in the Election of November 2012 - Detailed Tables," Table 4b. Reported Voting and Registration by Sex, Race and Hispanic Origin, for States: November 2012. http://www.census.gov/hhes/www/socdemo/voting/publications/p20/2012/tables.html

[46] Pew Research Center, "A Record 24 Million Latinos Are Eligible to Vote, But Turnout Rate Has Lagged That of Whites, Blacks, October 1, 2012," http://www.pewhispanic.org/2012/10/01/a-record-24-million-latinos- are-eligible-to-vote/.

[47] See http://texaspolitics.laits.utexas.edu/11_1_0.html.

[48] National Conference of State Legislatures, Felon Voting Rights, http://www.ncsl.org/research/elections-and-campaigns/felon-voting-rights.aspx.

[49] Texas Secretary of State, Effect of Felony Conviction on Voter Registration. http://www.sos.state.tx.us/elections/laws/effects.shtml.

[50] United States Election Project, 2012 General Election Turnout Rates. http://elections.gmu.edu/Turnout_2012G.html

[51] See http://www.sentencingproject.org/map/map.cfm.

[52] See Andre Blais, "What Affects Voter Turnout?" *Annual Review of Political Science* 9 (2006), 119.

[53] See ibid., and G. Bingham Powell, Jr. "American Voter Turnout in Comparative Perspective," *American Political Science Review,* 80:1 (March 1986), pp. 17–43.

[54] City of Austin Communications and Public Information Office, "City Voters Approve Most Municipal Ballot Measures," November 7, 2012, http://austintexas.gov/news/city-voters-approve-most-municipal-ballot-measures.

[55] Peter Grier, "Election Day 2010: Why we always vote on Tuesdays," *Christian Science Monitor,* November 2, 2010, http://www.csmonitor.com/USA/DC-Decoder/Decoder-Wire/2010/1102/Election-Day-2010-Why-we-always-vote-on-Tuesdays

[56] Blais, 116.

[57] Julia Van Susteren, "Early Voting Has Little Effect." *Badger Herald,* October 2, 2012. Available online at http://badgerherald.com/news/2012/10/02/early_voting_has_lit.php.

[58] Kenneth Arrow, "The Organization of Economic Activity: Issues Pertinent to the Choice of Market versus Non-market Allocation," 1969. Available online at: http://msuweb.montclair.edu/lebelp/PSC643IntPolEcon/ArrowNonMktActivity1969.pdf. I first saw this quoted in a draft paper by David P. Myatt titled, "On the Rational Choice Theory of Voter Turnout." There is an enormous amount of research on this question, starting with key works such as Anthony Downs, *An Economic Theory of Democracy*

(New York: Harper and Row, 1957); Gordon Tullock, *Toward a Mathematics of Politics* (Ann Arbor: University of Michigan Press, 1967); and William Riker and Peter Ordeshook, "A Theory of the Calculus of Voting." *American Political Science Review* 62:1(1968): 25–42.

[59] For a review of the literature on "expressive" voting, see Alan Hamlin and Colin Jennings, "Expressive Political Behaviour: Foundations, Scope and Implications," *British Journal of Political Science* (2011).

[60] See Arrow.

[61] Texas Statewide Survey, University of Texas at Austin, *Texas Tribune*, March 2009.

[62] Center for Responsive Politics, Top States Funding Candidates. http://www.opensecrets.org/pres12/pres_stateAll.php?list=all

[63] Center for Responsive Politics, Fundraising By Party. http://www.opensecrets.org/pres12/states.php

[64] Brady, Verba, and Schlozman, "Beyond SES: A Resource Model of Political Participation," *American Political Science Review* 89:2 (June 1995).

[65] Russell Dalton, *The Good Citizen: How a Younger Generation Is Reshaping American Politics,* (Washington, D.C.: CQ Press, 2008).

[66] Many scholars have found this to be the case. See Blais, 123.

CHAPTER 8

Elections and Campaigns in Texas

Upon completing this chapter,
you will be able to...

- **Analyze the state and local election process in Texas.**

lections are the heart of any democratic system and perform a number of important functions that make government work. Elections bestow legitimacy upon government; without them, all actions of governments are questionable. Elections provide for an orderly transition of power from one group to another where, most importantly, the public perceives the newly elected government as legitimate. One of the great stabilizing forces in the American system of government has been this orderly transfer of power. Elections also allow citizens to express their opinions about public policy choices. By voting in elections, citizens express what they want the government to do. Elections are still the most essential element of any democracy, despite the fact that many citizens do not participate in them.

Delegates to the Texas GOP Convention cheer for Gov. Rick Perry after his speech in Fort Worth, Texas on Thursday, June, 5, 2014. In his address, the longest-serving governor in the state's history focused more on the future and national issues than his political legacy at home.

Elections occur at regular intervals as determined by state and federal laws. All states conduct elections on two-year cycles. The date established by federal law for electing members of the U.S. Congress and the president is the first Tuesday after the first Monday in November of even-numbered years. States must elect members of Congress and vote for the president on this date. Most states also use this November date to elect governors, state officials, state legislators, and some local offices.

Texas holds **general elections** every two years. During nonpresidential years, voters elect candidates to statewide offices: governor, lieutenant governor, attorney general, land commissioner, agricultural commissioner, comptroller, some members of the Texas Railroad Commission and the Texas State Board of Education, and some members of the Texas Supreme Court and the Court of Criminal Appeals.[1] Before 1976, all nonjudicial officeholders served two-year terms. In 1977 the state constitution was amended, and in 1978, four-year terms were first used.

general elections
Regular elections held every two years to elect state officeholders

Every two years, voters also elect all 150 members of the Texas House of Representatives (for two-year terms), one-half of the members of the Texas

Senate (for four-year terms), many judges to various courts, and local county officials.

Ballot Form

ballot form

The forms used by voters to cast their ballots; each county, with approval of the secretary of state, determines the form of the ballot

party column format

Paper ballot form where candidates are listed by party and by office

office block format

Ballot form where candidates are listed by office with party affiliation listed by their name; most often used with computer ballots

Each county in Texas decides the **ballot form** and method of casting ballots. The method used to cast votes must be approved by the secretary of state's office. Some systems are precleared by the secretary of state's office, and counties can choose any of these systems.

Texas counties formerly used paper ballots with a **party column format**, where candidates were listed by party and by office. The party that holds the governor's office was the first party column on the ballot. Being first on the ballot is an advantage—voters often choose the first name when all candidates are unfamiliar to them. The party column ballot also encouraged straight ticket voting and was advocated strongly by the Democratic Party for many years. In recent years, straight ticket voting has worked to the advantage of the Republicans in some elections, especially judicial offices.

Since the 2008 election, all 254 counties in Texas have used electronic voting systems. These systems were purchased with federal funds provided by the Help America Vote Act. The secretary of state must approve all electronic voting systems before counties can purchase them. Three systems are currently approved by the secretary of state's office: The Premier Election System (formerly called Diebold) is used by six counties in Texas; the Electronic Systems Software (ESS) is used by 148 counties; and the Hart e-slate systems are used by 100 counties.

Most computer ballots are in **office block format** (see Figure 8.1). This ballot form lists the office (e.g., president), followed by the candidates by party (e.g., Republican: Mitt Romney, Democrat: Barack Obama). The ballot for each county system in Texas can be found on individual county websites or the Texas Secretary of State website prior to each election.

The office block format is often advocated as a way of discouraging straight ticket voting, the impact of which is discussed in Chapter 9. However, Texas law allows computer-readable ballots to enable voters to vote a straight ticket. By marking a single place on the ballot, the voter can vote for all candidates for that party. The voter can then override this by voting in individual races. For example, a voter could vote a straight Republican ticket, but override this and vote for the Democratic candidate for selected offices.

Ballot Access to the November General Election

To appear on the November general election ballot, candidates must meet criteria established by state law. Each state has its own unique set of requirements. These criteria prevent the lists of candidates from being unreasonably long. The Texas Election Code specifies three ways for names to be on the ballot, which are discussed in the following sections.

Independent and Third-Party Candidates

To run as an independent, a candidate must file a petition with a specified number of signatures. For statewide office, signatures equal to 1 percent of the votes cast for governor in the past general election are required. For example, in the 2010

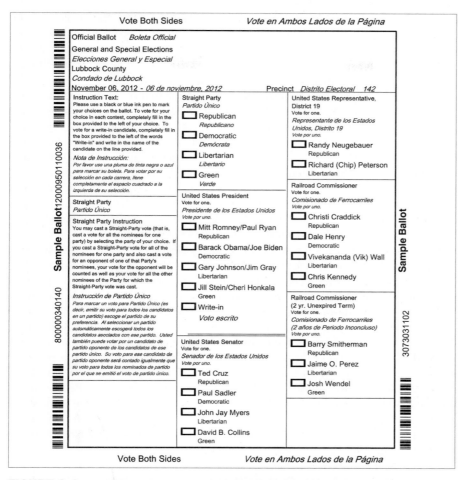

FIGURE 8.1   A Sample Texas General Election Ballot in Office Block Format

governor's race, a total of 4.9 million votes were cast. An **independent candidate** for statewide office in 2012 would have to collect 49,000 signatures. For multicounty offices, such as state representative, signatures equal to 5 percent of the votes cast for that office in the past election are needed. On the average, 30,000 to 40,000 votes are cast in house races.[2] For county offices, signatures equal to 5 percent of votes cast for those offices are needed. This might seem like a large number of signatures, but the process is intended to weed out people who do not have a serious chance of being elected. Few candidates file for statewide office as independents. However, it is not uncommon to have independents for house and senate races. In 1996, 13 people filed by petition as Libertarians and 2 filed as independents for the 150 Texas house seats. In 1998, only 3 people filed as independents for these house seats.[3] In 2000, the Libertarian Party had candidates in 22 of 150 house seats and 1 senate seat. In 2002, the Libertarian Party fielded 12 candidates for the state senate and 29 for the state house. Even if these candidates declare a party, such as Libertarian, they may still be considered independents under the state election code.

Obtaining signatures on a petition is not easy. Each signer must be a registered voter and must not have participated in the primary elections of other parties in

independent candidate

A person whose name appears on the ballot without a political party designation that electoral cycle. For example, persons who voted in either the Democratic or the Republican Party primary in 1996 were not eligible to sign a petition to have Ross Perot's Reform Party placed on the 1996 ballot. Signing the petition is considered the same as voting. This provision of state law makes it all the more difficult for independents to gather signatures and be placed on the ballot.

The 2006 governor's race in Texas was an exception to this. Carole Keeton Strayhorn, the then Comptroller, and Kinky Friedman, a country-western singer and mystery writer, qualified for positions on the ballot as independents. Friedman and Strayhorn suffered the same fate as most independent and minor party candidates: they did not win, but they pulled enough votes away from the Democratic candidate to upset the election outcome. Governor Perry won with a plurality of 38.1 percent while Friedman had just 12.6 percent and Strayhorn 18 percent. Chris Bell, the Democratic candidate, did better than expected with 30 percent. The role of these independent candidates was to help reelect the governor who, after six years in office, managed to capture less than 40 percent of the votes.

Candidates who were defeated in the primary election may not file as independents in the general election for that year. This is the **"sore loser" law**. Write-in candidates are sometimes confused with people who file and are listed on the ballot as independents. The process of filing as a write-in candidate is a separate procedure. To be "official" **write-in candidates**, individuals must file their intention before the election. This is true for all elections, including local, city, and school board elections. If a person does not file before the election, votes for that person are not counted. For some state offices, a filing fee may be required to have a person's name listed on the ballot as a write-in candidate. The amount varies from $4,000 for statewide office to as little as $300 for local justices of the peace. People sometimes write in things such as "Mickey Mouse" and "None of the above." These are recorded but not counted. In 1990, nineteen write-in candidates filed for governor. Bubbles Cash, a retired Dallas stripper, led the pack with 3,287 out of a total of 11,700 write-in votes.[4]

"sore loser" law

Law in Texas that prevents a person who lost the primary vote from running as an independent or minor party candidate

---

write-in candidate

A person whose name does not appear on the ballot; voters must write in that person's name, and the person must have led a formal notice that he or she was a write-in candidate before the election

---

CORE OBJECTIVE

Thinking Critically...

Explain the challenges that hinder minor party candidates from succeeding in statewide elections.

---

minor party

A party other than the Democratic or Republican Party; to be a minor party in Texas, the organization must have received between 5 and 19 percent of the vote in the past election

---

party caucus

A meeting of members of a political party that is used by minor political parties in Texas to nominate candidates

Party Caucus

The state election code defines a **minor party** (sometimes called a *third party*) as any political organization that receives between 5 and 19 percent of the total votes cast for any statewide office in the past general election. In the past 50 years, there have been four minor parties: the Raza Unida Party in South Texas in the 1970s,[5] the Socialist Workers Party in 1988, as well as the Libertarian Party and the Green Party in the 1990s and 2000. Parties that achieve minor-party status must nominate their candidates in a **party caucus** or convention and are exempt from the petition requirement discussed previously. Currently, only the Libertarian Party and the Green Party qualify as minor parties.

The Texas Election Code defines a *major party* as any organization receiving 20 percent or more of the total votes cast for governor in the past election. Only the Democratic and Republican parties hold this status today. By law, these party organizations must nominate their candidates in a **primary election**.

Texas has an **open primary system**, by definition (though this will be challenged in a moment). Open primaries allow the voter to vote in any primary without a party declaration. The voter can vote as a Democrat and attend the Republican precinct convention or participate in any activity of the opposite party.

A **closed primary system** is currently used in 14 states. This system requires voters to declare their party affiliation when they register to vote. They may vote only in the primary of their party registration. Most of these states have a time limit after which a voter may not change party affiliation before the election.

There are several important variations of open and closed primaries (see Table 8.1). A **semi-closed primary system** allows voters to register or change their party registration on election day. Independents may vote in the primary of their choice, but otherwise, registered members are required to vote in their party's primary. In a **semi-open primary system**, the voter may choose to vote in the primary of either party on election day. After they request a specific party ballot, however, voters are considered "declared" for the party in whose primary they vote. If you vote in the Republican Party primary, you are in effect declaring that you are a member of that party. You may not participate in any activity of any other party for the remainder of that election year. For example, if you vote in the Republican primary, you may not attend the precinct convention of the Democratic Party. This also limits the voter in other ways.

Texas is, perhaps confusingly, also commonly labeled as having a semi-open system (see Table 8.1). While Texas does have an open primary system, the state also restricts voters to a certain degree (though, not to the extent of a more by-the-book semi-open system). Voters in Texas do not have to declare a party, but when attending a primary, they must choose a ticket and only pick from the candidates in that party. Once the primary is over, however, voters can cross party lines. In addition, when the next

Former gubernatorial candidate Bill White campaigning He served three full terms as the 60th Mayor of Houston (2004–2010). Previously, he served as the U.S. Deputy Secretary of Energy from 1993 to 1995 under President Bill Clinton.

primary election
An election used by major political parties in Texas to nominate candidates for the November general election

open primary system
A nominating election that is open to all registered voters regardless of party affiliation

closed primary system
A nominating election that is closed to all voters except those who have registered as a member of that political party

semi-closed primary system
A nominating election that is open to all registered voters, but voters are required to declare party affiliation when they vote in the primary election

semi-open primary system
Voter may choose to vote in the primary of either party on election day; voters are considered "declared" for the party in whose primary they vote

TABLE 8.1

Primary Systems Used in State Elections

Closed Primary: Party Registration Required before Election Day

Alaska	Maine	New York
Connecticut	Nebraska	Oklahoma
Delaware	Nevada	Pennsylvania
Florida	New Jersey	South Dakota
Kentucky	New Mexico	

(continued)

(continued)

Semi-closed Primary: Voters May Register or Change Registration on Election Day		
Arizona	Massachusetts	Utah
Colorado	New Hampshire	West Virginia
Iowa	North Carolina	Wyoming
Kansas	Oregon	
Maryland	Rhode Island	
Semi-open Primary: Voters Required to Request Party Ballot		
Alabama	Mississippi	Virginia
Arkansas	Ohio	
Georgia	South Carolina	
Illinois	Tennessee	
Indiana	Texas	
Open Primary: Voters May Vote in Any Party Primary		
California	Missouri	
Hawaii	Montana	
Idaho	North Dakota	
Michigan	Vermont	
Minnesota	Wisconsin	
Nonpartisan: Voters May Switch Parties between Races		
Louisiana	Washington	

Source: John R. Biddy and Thomas M. Holbrook, "Parties and Elections," in *Politics in the American States: A Comparative Analysis*, 8th ed., edited by Virginia Gray and Russell L. Hanson (Washington, D.C.: Congressional Quarterly Press, 2004). Reprinted by permission.

year begins, voters receive a new registration card and are free to vote however they so choose. Texas might be best labeled as having a (semi-) open system.

In the past, three states, Alaska, California, and Washington, used a **blanket primary**. This system allowed voters to switch parties between offices. A voter might vote in the Republican primary for the races for governor and U.S. House, and in the Democratic primary for the U.S. Senate race. These have been ruled unconstitutional by the U.S. Supreme Court. Alaska currently uses a closed primary with voter registration by party, whereas California has adopted an open primary system. Washington has adopted Louisiana's system of a nonpartisan primary for all statewide and U.S. House and Senate races. Under this system, all candidates are listed on the ballot by office. The voter can choose one candidate per office. If no person receives a majority, the top two candidates face each other in a runoff. This can result in two candidates from the same party facing each other in a runoff election.

blanket primary system

A nominating election in which voters could switch parties between elections

Political Differences between Open and Closed Primary Systems

The primary system used in a state may affect the party system in the state. Advocates of the closed primary system say that it encourages party identification and loyalty and, therefore, helps build stronger party systems. Open primary systems, they say, allow participation by independents with no loyalty to the party, which weakens party organization. There is no strong evidence that this is the case.

Open primaries do allow **crossover voting**. This occurs when voters leave their party and vote in the other party's primary. Occasionally voters in one party might vote in the other party's primary in hopes of nominating a candidate from the other party whose philosophy is similar to their own. For example, Republicans have been accused of voting in the Democratic primary in Texas to ensure that a conservative will be nominated. This occurred in the 1970 U.S. Senate race when Republicans voted for the more conservative Lloyd Bentsen over the liberal Ralph Yarborough. Many voting precincts carried by Bentsen in the Democratic primary voted for Republican George H. W. Bush in the general election.

From 1996 to 2002, more Texans voted in the Republican primaries than in the Democratic primaries. Republicans claimed that this was evidence that their party was the majority party. Democrats suggest that these differences in turnout are explained by the low levels of opposition in the Democratic primaries. For instance, President Clinton did not have any opposition in his primary election, whereas Bob Dole and Pat Buchanan were still actively seeking the Republican nomination. Some Democratic Party leaders claim that many traditional Democratic Party voters, therefore, crossed over and voted in the Republican primary in an attempt to affect the Republican outcome. As it turned out, the Democrats' explanation may be the more accurate.

Party raiding is difficult to orchestrate. Party raiding occurs when members of one political party vote in another party's primary. What distinguishes party raiding from crossover voting is that whereas crossover voting may be genuine (another party's candidate appeals to voters), party raiding is intentional and designed to nominate a weaker candidate or split the vote among the strongest contenders. Although there are often accusations of such behavior during primary elections, it is difficult to prove. Additionally, although there have been attempts to organize party raids, it is unclear whether they are effective. A notable example during the 2008 primary is Operation Chaos, in which popular conservative talk radio host Rush Limbaugh encouraged Republicans to vote in Democratic primaries for Hillary Clinton in order to weaken then-candidate Obama.[6] More recently, in 2012, voters in Michigan attempted to disrupt the Republican primary by voting for Rick Santorum over frontrunner Mitt Romney.[7] In both cases, efforts were ineffective in changing the outcome.

Runoff Primary Elections

Runoff primaries are held in 11 states: Alabama, Arkansas, Georgia, Louisiana, Mississippi, North Carolina, Oklahoma, South Carolina, South Dakota, Texas, and Vermont.[8] A **runoff primary** is required if no candidate receives a majority in the first primary. Until recently in the South, winning the Democratic Party primary was the same as winning the general election, and the runoff primary became a fixture, supposedly as a way of requiring the winner to have "majority" support. In reality, voter turnout in the runoff primary is almost always lower than in the first primary, sometimes substantially lower. The "majority" winner often is selected by a small percentage of the electorate—those who bother to participate in the runoff primary.

The Texas Election Code specifies that voters who voted in the primary election of one party may not participate in the runoff primary of the other party. Occasionally in the past decade, there have been charges that this has happened, as in a 1992 Democratic primary congressional race in Houston. The Houston congressional district had been drawn to "ensure" that a Mexican American could be elected, but the primary was won by an Anglo, Gene Green. His opponent, Ben T. Reyes,

crossover voting
Occurs when voters leave their party and vote in the other party's primary

party raiding
Occurs when members of one political party vote in another party's primary in an effort to nominate a weaker candidate or split the vote among the top candidates

runoff primary
Election that is required if no person receives a majority in the primary election; primarily used in southern and border states

charged that Republicans had "raided" the primary and voted for Green. There was some evidence that this had happened, but it had not changed the results of the election. The current system of recordkeeping and the difficulty of checking voter lists make it almost impossible to prevent such raiding or crossover voting from occurring in runoff primaries. A reform might be to require voters to sign a statement saying they had not voted in the opposition party's primary election. Another suggestion is to have computerized records at each polling place that election workers can check.

The Administration and Finance of Primary Elections

In the past, primary elections were considered functions of private organizations, and the state did not regulate them. As we discussed in Chapter 7, courts have ruled that political parties are not private organizations, and their functions are subject to control by state law. The Texas Election Code governs primary elections. It specifies the time and method of conducting primary elections. Runoff elections are usually held 30 days later.

filing fee

A fee or payment required to get a candidate's name on the primary or general election ballot

Persons wanting to file for an office in the primary election must pay a **filing fee**. In 1970, court cases forced Texas to alter its filing fee system because the cost of filing for county offices had increased substantially. For example, the cost of filing for a countywide race in Dallas County was $9,000 in 1970. In constant dollars, this would be $54,000 in 2012. In 1972, the state of Texas assumed part of the cost of financing primary elections. Filing fees are still required, but they are lower. Currently, the cost for filing for a statewide office is $4,000. For countywide races, the fee is $500. Anyone who cannot pay the filing fee can still be placed on the primary ballot by filing a petition. For statewide office, about 45,000 signatures are required; for district or local office, signatures equal to 3 percent of the votes cast for that office in the past election are required. Some candidates file a petition as a campaign tactic to show they have broad support. Occasionally, petitioners also pay the filing fee just to play it safe and prevent a challenge to the validity of the petition.

Technically, primary elections are administered by the local party county chair and executive committee and by the state party officials at the state level. However, the Texas Election Code and the secretary of state oversee the administration of elections to ensure that the rules are followed, and the party has only limited discretion in the conduct of these elections. The secretary of state keeps a hotline open on election day so that citizens can report problems with an election, such as workers instructing voters how to vote.

Special Elections

Another kind of election is the special election. By Texas law, elections may be held in January, May, August, and November. Any election that takes place in January, May, or August is considered a special election. There are three types of special elections. The most common special election in Texas is selection of city council members and mayoral elections if they are not held in November. Most Texas cities hold municipal elections in May, but a few, including Houston, hold theirs in November. Additionally, all school board elections in Texas are held in May.

A second type of special election may be called to decide on amendments to the state constitution. In the past 20 years, it has been common for the state legislature to arrange Texas constitutional amendment elections for January and August, when no other elections are usually held. As a general rule, election turnout for constitutional amendment elections held in January, May, and August are substantially lower than such elections held in November.

A third type of special elections occurs when only one contest is on the ballot. These special elections are called by the governor to fill a vacancy caused by the death or resignation of a member of the Texas Legislature or a Texas member of the U.S. House of Representatives or the U.S. Senate. Such special elections have played a very important role in Texas political history. For example, the death of Senator Morris Sheppard in 1941 led to a special election that pitted Governor W. Lee "Pappy" O'Daniel against Congressman Lyndon Johnson—an election that Johnson lost because of election fraud committed by O'Daniel supporters. In 1960, Senator Lyndon Johnson was reelected to the senate and elected to the Vice Presidency of the United States. Johnson resigned his senate seat and in a special election the next year, John Tower became the first Republican to win a statewide office in Texas since Reconstruction, elected in part by liberal Texas Democrats.

Phil Gramm was elected in a special election to his U.S. House seat in 1981. Oddly, he had just resigned from the seat after being elected to it in 1980. Gramm was originally elected to the House as a Democrat but fell out with his party. After becoming a Republican, Gramm resigned his seat and ran again in 1981 as a Republican. Following Gramm's resignation, Governor William Clements, the first Texas Republican governor since Reconstruction, called for an election 30 days later. This gave the Democrats no time to mount a serious campaign, and Gramm easily won. Finally, Senator Lloyd Bentsen resigned in late 1992 after accepting nomination as secretary of the treasury by president-elect Clinton. Texas Democratic Governor Ann Richards had the authority to appoint a temporary successor. Still unhappy with her 1990 Democratic primary opponent, Jim Mattox, she passed over the well-known Mattox and selected the less-known Robert Krueger, who later ran a lackluster campaign against Kay Bailey Hutchinson, who defeated him in the regular election in 1994.

The Federal Voting Rights Act

In 1965, under the leadership of President Lyndon Johnson, the U.S. Congress passed the Voting Rights Act. As previously mentioned in Chapters 6 and 7, this Act has had extensive effects upon the state of Texas and the conduct of elections. After being passed in 1965 and extended to Texas in 1975, the **Voting Rights Act** required preclearance by the U.S. Justice Department of all changes in the election procedures – including such things as ballot reform, the time and place of an election, and the method of electing legislators.[9]

Voting Rights Act
A federal law aimed at preventing racial discrimination in the operation of voter registration and elections at the state level

Until 2013, the Voting Rights Act allowed the federal government to oversee the operation of elections at a state level. The greatest impact had been felt in southern states, where racial and ethnic minorities were formerly barred from participating in elections (see Chapter 6.). When the U.S. Supreme Court struck down Section 4 of the Voting Rights Act in late June 2013, the primary method of enforcement of Section 5 was rendered useless. Section 4 had targeted specific states with known disenfranchising tactics and, in those states, Section 5 required federal oversight. Texas was one of those states, and pushed to legislate

Voter ID laws for several years without success. Once Section 4 died, however, Texas immediately passed its Voter ID laws into effect. They applied to the November 2014 election, though their constitutionality is still very much in question as can be seen by recent activity in the courts (see Chapter 7).

The other sections of the Voting Rights Act are still functioning. It continues to require Texas to use a bilingual ballot for all elections in counties that contain more than 20 percent Spanish-speaking residents. Ballots are printed in both English and Spanish for all elections – federal, state, and local.

CORE OBJECTIVE

Communicating Effectively...

Do you think the Voting Rights Act requirement that Texas provide a bilingual ballot in counties with more than 20 percent Spanish speakers increases voter turnout? Construct an argument in favor or against this provision of the Voting Rights Act.

Absentee and Early Voting

absentee voting
A process that allows a person to vote early, before the regular election; applies to all elections in Texas; also called early voting

All states allow some form of **absentee voting**. This practice began as a way to allow members of the U.S. armed services who were stationed in other states or overseas to vote. In all but a few states, it has been extended to other individuals. In most states, persons who will be out of the county on election day may file for absentee voting.

In Texas before 1979, to vote absentee, voters had to sign an affidavit saying they would be out of the county and unable to vote on election day. They could also file for an absentee ballot to be sent to them if they were living out of state or confined to a hospital or nursing home. In 1979, the state legislature changed the rules to allow anyone to vote absentee without restrictions. In Texas this is called "early voting." Early voting now begins 17 days before an election and closes 4 days before the election. During that period, polls are open from 7 A.M. to 7 P.M. Voters simply go to an early voting polling place and present their voter registration cards or, as of 2012, a government-issued ID; then they are allowed to vote.

The Changing Nature of Elections

If you go back 30 to 40 years, you will find that social issues were rarely a facet of state and national politics. The civil rights movement was an exception. Today, such issues as abortion, gay rights, women's rights, gun control, the environment, and health care dominate elections. All these issues excite passions in the minds of voters. To some degree, this is why politics have become so partisan. Many people have very strong feelings about these issues and maintain their positions on these issues throughout their lives. Some individuals believe that their views are endorsed by God; often these "value voters" consider people who don't agree with them to be valueless. Other individuals feel strongly that human rights should never be dictated by religion or majority opinion. Most of the time, neither side will compromise on such wedge issues. For example, in the 2004 presidential election, 14 states had antigay marriage propositions on the ballot. This turned out an impressive number of so called "value voters" and infuriated supporters of gay rights.

Three other changes in elections are also worth noting. First, labor unions have declined in the United States as a voice in elections because of manufacturing jobs being shipped overseas and southern states that have antiunion (right to work) statutes, including Texas. Second, the Catholic and male votes, which used to be overwhelmingly Democratic, have migrated over to the Republican party because of such issues as abortion and gay rights. Many Catholics have formed alliances with Christian fundamentalist groups, and many traditional old-line males have gravitated further to the right. Third, changes in the media have had an enormous impact on politics. Influential 24-hour news networks such as CNN and Fox News, as well as email campaigns and political activity through social networking websites, have changed the way election campaigns are run and often have undue influence on the outcome of elections.

Campaigns

Campaign activity in Texas has changed considerably in the past two or three decades. These changes are not unique to Texas but are part of a national trend. Norman Brown, in his book on Texas politics in the 1920s, describes the form of political campaigning in the state as "local affairs."[10] Candidates would travel from county seat to county seat and give "stump" speeches to political rallies arranged by local supporters. Brown devotes special attention to the campaigns of governors Jim and Miriam Ferguson ("Pa" and "Ma" Ferguson). Jim Ferguson, when campaigning for himself and later for his wife, would travel from county to county, telling each group what they wanted to hear—often saying different things in different counties. Brown contends that Ferguson and other candidates could do this because of the lack of a statewide press to report on these inconsistencies in such political speeches.

The Role of the Media in Campaigns and Elections

In modern-day Texas, the media play a significant role in political campaigns. Reporters often follow candidates for statewide office as they travel the vast expanses of Texas. Political rallies are still held but are most often used to gain media attention and convey the candidate's message to a larger audience. Candidates hope these events will convey a favorable image of them to the public.

Heavy media coverage can have its disadvantages for the candidates. For instance, in 1990 Clayton Williams, the Republican candidate for governor, held a media event on one of his West Texas ranches. He and "the boys" were to round up cattle for branding in a display designed to portray Williams as a hardworking rancher. Unfortunately for Williams, rain spoiled the event and it had to be postponed. Resigned to the rain delay, Williams told the reporters, "It's like rape. When it's inevitable, relax and enjoy it." The state press had a field day with this remark, and it probably hurt Williams's chances with many voters. The fact that his opponent was a woman (Ann Richards) helped to magnify the significance of the statement.[11]

The Republican incumbent for District 45 (Blanco and Hays counties), Texas State Representative Jason Issac returns home with his wife Carrie for campaign season leading up to the November 2014 gubernatorial election.

Similarly, in 1994, George W. Bush was the Republican candidate for governor running against incumbent Ann Richards. In Texas, the opening day of dove season is in September, and the event marks the beginning of the fall hunting season. Both Bush and Richards participated in opening-day hunts in an attempt to appeal to the strong hunting and gun element in the state. Unfortunately for Bush, he shot a killdeer by mistake rather than a dove. Pictures of Bush holding the dead bird appeared in most state papers and on television. He was fined for shooting a migratory bird. A Texas Democratic group in Austin produced bumper stickers reading: "Guns don't kill killdeer. People do." In 1998, Governor Bush did not have a media event for the opening day of dove season. He was so far ahead in the polls that even opening the issue could result in nothing but a painful reminder.

Most campaign events are not as disastrous as the cattle-branding and dove-hunting incidents. Some gain attention and free media coverage for the candidate; however, free media attention is never enough. Candidates must purchase time on television and radio and space in newspapers. In a state as large as Texas, this can be quite costly. Candidates try to make the most of the expensive time they purchase by conveying simple messages. This has led to the *sound-bite commercial,* a 30-second message that, it is hoped, will be remembered by the voters. This is not unique to Texas but occurs nationwide.

These sound bites can be classified into at least five types. The *feel good spot* lacks substance or issues and is designed to make the public feel good about the candidate or the party. In 1984, Ronald Reagan told viewers it was "morning in America." The commercial featured scenes of a "middle America" town filled with happy people. In 1988, President George H. W. Bush saw "a thousand points of light." Others promise "fresh, bold leadership" or claim to have "common sense and uncommon courage." Still others, including Clayton Williams, say, "Share my vision." In 1998, Governor George W. Bush ran a number of TV spots that asked voters to support his effort to have every child read and become a productive member of society.

Sainthood spots try to depict the candidate as having saintly qualities:[12] "Senator Smith is a Christian family man, Eagle Scout, Little League coach, Sunday school teacher, involved, concerned, committed, community leader who fights the people's fights. Let's keep him working for us."

Good ol' boy (or "good ol' girl") spots are testimonials from other citizens about the candidate. In a staged "person on the street" interview, the citizen says something like, "Senator Smith is the most effective leader this state has seen since Sam Houston. He's so effective it's frightening. He is committed to his job, and we need him to fight the coming battles with the liberals." In Texas, cattle and horses in the background provide a down-to-earth backdrop for ranchers' good ol' boy testimonials.

NOOTS ("No one's opposed to this") commercials are also common. In these ads, candidates take courageous stands on issues everyone supports: sound fiscal

Social media outreach has become increasingly important to modern political campaigns. Facebook, YouTube, Twitter and other popular platforms allow politicians to connect with a massive online audience.

management, planned orderly growth, good schools, open government, getting tough on crime, no new taxes, and so on.

Basher spots play on voters' emotions by painting their opponent in a very unfavorable light. If your opponent is a lawyer, you can point out that he or she defends criminals. You can also "play the gay card" by pointing out that your opponent received money from gay rights organizations. Governor Rick Perry, running for secretary of agriculture in 1990, defeated Democratic incumbent Jim Hightower. In one of his commercials, Perry claimed that Hightower had once visited the home of Jane Fonda. Fonda is often used as a symbol for the radical war protesters of the 1960s because of her visit to Hanoi during the Vietnam War. When pressed for details on the visit, Perry said that Hightower had visited Los Angeles, and that Los Angeles was the home of Jane Fonda.

Basher spots have developed into a fine art. Newt Gingrich, former speaker of the U.S. House of Representatives, extended the art when he used his GOPAC political action committee to help "train local Republican candidates." In 1990, GOPAC mailed a glossary of 131 words to more than 4,000 state Republican candidates. This glossary included a list of "optimistic positive governing words" that Republican candidates should use to describe themselves and a list of "contrasting negative words" they should use to describe their opponents. Republicans are described as having common sense and Democrats as big-spending liberals.

These types of advertisements are used because most often they work to the advantage of the candidate. Occasionally, basher spots can backfire. These ads plant a simple message in the voters' minds that they carry into the voting booth. Most citizens do not spend much time studying issues or candidates' backgrounds. They are often entirely dependent upon advertisements for information. Although the news media (which receives most of the money spent in campaigns) often denounce such ads, they do not refuse to run them.

By typing "campaign commercials" into YouTube, you can see a wide variety of these ads. You might want to contrast recent ads with those for the Eisenhower presidential campaign to see how political ads have changed.

CORE OBJECTIVE

Being Socially Responsible...

What responsibility do you think the media have in covering campaigns and elections? Are the media living up to your expectations?

Political Consultants

The use of professional campaign consultants is common in almost all races. Most candidates find it necessary to have such professionals help run their campaigns. If their opponents use professionals, candidates might be disadvantaged by not having one. Professional campaign consultants use many techniques. They take public opinion polls to measure voter reaction to issues so the candidate knows what stands to take. They run **focus groups** where a panel of "average citizens" is asked to react to issues or words. Consultants also help the candidate in the design

focus groups

Panel of "average citizens" who are used by political consultants to test ideas and words for later use in campaigns of written and visual advertisements and generally "package" the candidate to the voters. In 2002, David Dewhurst filmed a TV spot for his consulting firm, praising its effectiveness in making him look professional.

Money in Campaigns

Using media advertisement, professional consultants, and a full-time paid campaign staff increases the cost of running for state office. The cost can run into the millions, even for a race for the Texas House of Representatives.

The amount of money spent in campaigns is increasing each election cycle. Most of this money comes from political action committees (PACs). Table 8.2 shows the increase in the total amount of money contributed by PACs 2002 to 2012. Only at the start of the new decade was there any decrease and that only in the ideological sector. The business sector continues to increase and makes up a significant majority of total PAC campaign contributions.

As shown in Table 8.3, statewide races can be quite costly, and costs have continued to increase. Most of the money is coming from PACs, which obviously want something from government for their contributions. A few candidates, such as Tony Sanchez in 2002, are able to self-finance their campaigns. In that year, Sanchez self-financed $27 million (89 percent of the total) and received campaign contributions totaling $3.5 million.[13] In that same election year, Governor Rick Perry raised $31,402,362 from political action committees.[14]

Money in campaigns has increased dramatically in recent years. With the 2010 Supreme Court decision in *Citizens United v. Federal Election Commission,* campaign advertising by corporations and labor unions cannot be prohibited or restricted at the federal level.[15]

Money supplied by PACs obviously has an impact on elected officials. At the least, PAC money buys the group access to the official. At the worst, PAC money buys the vote of the elected official. Distinguishing between the two is almost impossible. Most states, including Texas, have passed laws designed to regulate campaign finances. Many other states have passed laws limiting the amount of money that could be spent on campaigns, but these laws have been invalidated by the U.S. Supreme Court (see Chapter 10 on interest groups).

Candidates sometimes loan themselves money that they can later repay with what are often called "late train" contributions. Special interest groups seldom will retire the debt of losers. The law limits the amount of money that a candidate can

TABLE 8.2

Total PAC Money in State Campaigns from 2002 to 2012

Sector	2002 Cycle	2004 Cycle	2006 Cycle	2008 Cycle	2010 Cycle	2012 Cycle	'2010–'2012 Growth
Business	$48,000,676	46,088,137	$57,034,732	$ 62,741,376	$ 68,235,849	$ 70,399,948	3%
Ideology	$33,466,788	$17,789,167	$37,003,210	$ 50,403,265	$ 57,847,226	$ 47,292,862	−18%
Labor	$ 3,776,290	$ 4,512,391	$ 5,116,613	$ 6,307,456	$ 7,032,134	$ 8,173,262	16%
Unknown	$ 76,473	$ 514,829	$ 13,099	$ 109,764	$ 330,977	$ 501,388	51%
Totals	$85,320,226	$68,904,524	$99,167,654	$119,561,860	$133,446,187	$126,267,460	−5%

Source: Texas PACs: 2012 Election Cycle Spending. See (www.tpj.org).

TABLE 8.3

Total Contributions Raised by Major Party Candidates by Office

Office	Loser Total	Primary Loser Total	Winner Total	Candidates
Governor	$26,298,865	$16,565,395	$39,328,540	8
Attorney General	$ 910,779	NA	$ 5,828,869	2
Comptroller	NA	NA	$ 2,716,730	1
Land Commissioner	$ 98,758	$ 2,270	$ 863,307	3
Lieutenant Governor	$ 949,944	$ 56,772	$10,635,480	4
Texas House	$15,367,175	$ 5,328,930	$56,155,371	271
Texas Senate	$ 110,780	$ 897,362	$10,951,410	44

Texans for Public Justice, Money in PoliTex: A Guide to Money in the 2010 Texas Elections, (http://info.tpj.org/reports/politex2010/Introduction.html).

collect to retire personal campaign debts for each election (primary, runoff, general) to $500,000 in personal loans. In 2002, several candidates far exceeded this amount in personal loans. The leaders were gubernatorial candidate Tony Sanchez with $22,262,662 in personal loans and Lieutenant Governor-elect David Dewhurst with $7,413,887 in outstanding debt.[16]

Today the regulation of campaign finances in Texas is limited to requiring all candidates and PACs to file reports with the Texas State Ethics Commission. All contributions over $50 must be reported with the name of the contributor (see Map 8.1). An expenditure report must also be filed. These reports must be filed before and after the election. The idea behind the reporting scheme is to make public the sources of the funds received by candidates and how the candidates spend their funds. Sometimes these reports are examined closely by the news media and are given significant media coverage, but this is not common. The best source for Texans' funds is Texas for Public Justice (www.tpj.org). For the most part, citizens are left to find out such information on their own, which is difficult for the average citizen. Texas has no limit on the amount of money candidates can spend on their statewide races.

CORE OBJECTIVE

Taking Personal Responsibility...

If you choose to contribute to a candidate's campaign, to what extent is the candidate obligated to you as a contributor? Should your contribution influence public policy? What about corporate contributions?

Impact of Citizens United Decision

The 2010 decision in *Citizens United v. Federal Election Commission* established that the federal government cannot prohibit or limit direct spending on campaign advertising by corporations or labor unions. Although the case applied to federal elections, it did leave the question unresolved as to the status of 24 states that have

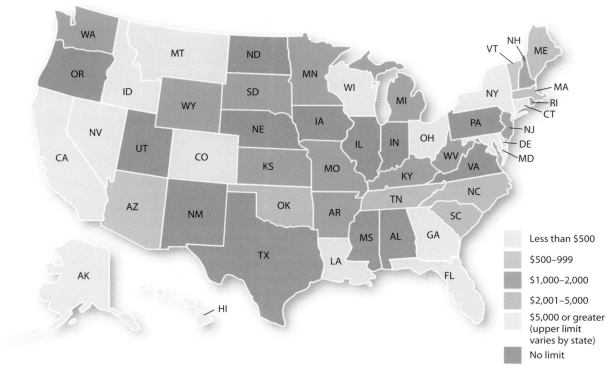

MAP 8.1   Limitations on Campaign Contributions in Statewide Races

laws prohibiting such spending by corporations and labor unions.[17] For example, the Supreme Court ruled in 2012 that Montana's law limiting corporate contributions in support of a candidate or a political party was unconstitutional. Eight other states have repealed laws limiting or prohibiting such spending. Texas's election code provides that "a corporation or labor organization may not make a political contribution or a political expenditure that is not authorized by this subchapter."[18] The Texas legislature amended section 253.094 of the election code pertaining to corporate contributions in 2011. The amendment removed the ban on political expenditures and solely regulated direct campaign contributions.

Conclusion

Elections and campaigns are essential to any democracy. The rules governing the conduct of elections have an impact on who gets elected and on the policies enacted by government. For reasons discussed in Chapter 7, active involvement in politics in Texas is limited to a small number of citizens. The electoral process is dominated by the Anglo population, which controls a disproportionate share of state offices. Most citizens choose not to participate in elections or the activities of political parties. As in other states, campaigns in Texas have become media affairs dominated by political consultants, sound bite ads, and money.

Key Terms

absentee voting
ballot form
blanket primary
closed primary system
crossover voting
filing fee
focus groups
general elections

independent candidate
minor party
office block format
open primary system
party caucus
party column format
party raiding
primary election

runoff primary
semi-closed primary system
semi-open primary system
"sore loser" law
Voting Rights Act
write-in candidate

Notes

[1] The office of treasurer was also a statewide elected office. In 1996, the voters abolished this office by constitutional amendment. The functions of this office have been taken over by the state comptroller and other state agencies.

[2] Texas Secretary of State home page http://www.sos.state.tx.us.

[3] Ibid.

[4] James A. Anderson, Richard W. Murray, and Edward L. Farley, *Texas Politics: An Introduction,* 6th ed. (New York: HarperCollins, 1992), 34.

[5] The Raza Unida Party did not receive enough votes to qualify as a minor party but challenged this in court. The federal court sustained the challenge, and they were allowed to operate as a minor party.

[6] *Rush Limbaugh Show,* transcript March 12, 2008, "Rush the Vote: Operation Chaos," http://www.rushlimbaugh.com/daily/2008/03/12/rush_the_vote_operation_chaos.

[7] Maggie Haberman, Politico, "Romney also said he voted in Dem primaries to influence the race (Updated)," February 2014, accessed October 2012. http://www.politico.com/blogs/burns-haberman/2012/02/romney-also-said-he-voted-in-dem-primaries-to-influence-115774.html.

[8] National Conference of State Legislatures, "Primary Runoffs," (May 2014), http://www.ncsl.org/research/elections-and-campaigns/primary-runoffs.aspx, October 2014.

[9] A court case in 1971 ended the early registration procedures in Texas (*Beare v. Smith,* 31 F. Supp. 1100).

[10] Norman D. Brown, *Hood, Bonnet, and Little Brown Jug: Texas Politics, 1921–1928* (College Station: Texas A&M University Press, 1984).

[11] *The New York Times,* "Texas Candidate's Comment About Rape Causes Furor, " March 26, 1990, accessed November 2012. http://www.nytimes.com/1990/03/26/us/texas-candidate-s-comment-about-rape-causes-a-furor.html.

[12] Bowman and Kearney, *State and Local Government,* 166. The "feel good" and "sainthood" classifications were adopted from this source.

[13] Texans for Public Justice, "Tony Sanchez's War Chest: Who Gives to a $600 Million Dollar Man?" www.tpj.org/docs2002/10reports/sanchez/page3.html.

[14] Texans for Public Justice, "Governor Perry's War Chest: Who Said Yes to Governor No?" www.tpj.org/docs/2002/10/reports/perry/page3.html.

[15] *Citizens United v. Federal Elections Commission* 558 U.S. 310 (2010).

[16] Lobby Watch, "Texas Loan Stars Incurred $48 Million in Political Debts," www.tpj.org/lobby_Watch/latetrain.html.

[17] National Conference of State Legislatures, "Life After Citizens United," August 2011, accessed October 2014. http://www.ncsl.org/legislatures-elections/elections/citizens-united-and-the-states.aspx.

[18] *Texas Election Code,* Title 15, Chapter 253, sec. 253.094.

CHAPTER 9

Political Parties in Texas

Upon completing this chapter, you will be able to...

- **Evaluate the role of political parties in Texas.**

Political parties are integral to government and politics in the nation and states, even though they are not mentioned in either the U.S. Constitution or the Texas Constitution. Furthermore, the Founding Fathers did not favor parties, calling them "factions," because they saw these entities as pursuing special parochial interests instead of the interests of the country as a whole. Yet today, our representative government would not function without political parties.

A **political party** is an organization that acts as an intermediary between the people and government, with the goal of having its members elected to public office. Traditionally, parties have vetted candidates, run campaigns, informed the populace on policy issues, and organized their members who are serving in office to ensure a measure of accountability.[1] As political scientists frequently note, parties play an important role in aggregating and articulating the preferences of citizens.

> **political parties**
> Organizations that act as an intermediary between the people and government with the goal of getting their members elected to public office

U.S. political parties have never been strongly centralized. Throughout history, parties in the United States have consisted of coalitions of state parties. The most powerful party leaders arose from leadership positions in important states. Today, Texas and the United States do not have strong parties, although partisan polarization has been increasing. Most candidates within parties self-select to run for office; once elected, they tend to toe the party line, as evidenced by their voting patterns. In Texas, neither party has a strong party organization or a strong grassroots organization. Candidates can act quite independently of either party.

Fifty States, Fifty Party Systems

The United States does not have strong national parties; it has 50 state party systems. The lack of national offices is a factor that weakens national parties and shifts emphasis to the state parties. President and vice president are the only offices that are elected on a nationwide basis. In fact, even the presidential and vice presidential elections are essentially state elections, with voters in the states electing members of the Electoral College, who in turn elect the president and vice president. The only time we see anything resembling a national party organization is when

Democrats and Republicans hold conventions every four years to nominate their candidates for president. In addition to conventions during a presidential election year, both major parties hold odd-year national conventions, but these receive little notice from the news media, and the average citizen is generally unaware of them. Each of the 50 state party organizations can act independently of the others and of the national party organization.

A clear distinction exists between federal and state office holders. At the federal level, Texas elects 2 U.S. senators and 36 U.S. representatives. These members of Congress spend most of their time in Washington, focusing on national, not state, policy. At the state level, Texans elect 31 state senators and 150 representatives to the state legislature. These state legislators focus on state issues. Occasionally, federal and state legislators might come together on common ground, but most often they have different interests, agendas, and priorities. Thus, although state-elected officials might carry the Democratic or Republican label, little interaction occurs between state and national parties or officials.

Years ago, V. O. Key, Jr., observed this about the state party system:

> The institutions developed to perform functions in each state differ markedly from the national parties. It is an error to assume that the political parties of each state are but miniatures of the national party system. In a few states that condition is approached, but . . . each state has its own pattern of action and often it deviates markedly from the forms of organization commonly thought of as constituting party systems.[2]

Professor Key's observation is as valid today as it was in the 1950s. State party systems vary widely, and often the only common link is the name *Democrat* or *Republican*.

The Strength of State Party Organizations

States can be classified according to the strength of party organization within the state. In Texas and other southern states, the Democratic Party dominated state politics from Reconstruction in the 1870s until the 1960s. Few Republicans placed their names on the ballot. Essentially, the Republican Party was absent, but for a few occasions. However, the Republican Party in Texas has been gaining strength for the past 50 years. It now controls both houses of the Texas legislature, and it has captured the governor's office without interruption since 1994. Today, Republicans hold all statewide elected offices.

party ideology
Basic belief system that guides the party

The Democratic and Republican party labels do not necessarily indicate ideology. **Party ideology** is the basic belief system that guides the party. The Democratic Party in one state can be quite different ideologically from the Democratic Party in another state. For many years in Texas, the Democratic Party had very strong conservative leanings. The Democratic Party in Massachusetts, on the other hand, has a strong liberal orientation. The conservatism of Texas Democrats shows in voter support for presidential candidates. Since the end of World War II, Texans have most often supported Republican candidates. Texas supported Dwight Eisenhower in 1952 and 1956, Richard Nixon in 1972, Ronald Reagan in 1980 and 1984, George Bush in 1988 and 1992, Bob Dole in 1996, George W. Bush in 2000 and 2004, John McCain in 2008, and Mitt Romney in 2012. In the past 16 presidential elections, Texas has voted Democratic only four times; in two of these cases, a native-son Democrat was on the ballot. Texans voted Democratic in 1960 and 1964 for Lyndon Johnson, and for Hubert Humphrey, vice president under Johnson, in 1968.

Texans supported Jimmy Carter in 1976, in part because he was a southerner and in part because of the backlash from the Watergate scandal. This strong support for Republican presidential candidates results from ideological differences between the more conservative Texas Democratic Party and the more liberal national Democratic Party organization.

CORE OBJECTIVE

Taking Personal Responsibility...

Examine your political values and compare them to the expressed values of both parties. Do your ideas about the role of government, politics, and policy align with one particular party?

Evolution of Political Parties in Texas

For most of its history as part of the United States, Texas has been a one-party state. It was one-party Democratic from 1845–1865, one-party Republican from 1870–1873, one-party Democratic from 1873 to 1978, and one-party Republican from 1994 until the present.

Politics of the Republic of Texas

Interestingly, the politics of the Texas Republic were highly competitive, but parties as we know them did not exist at the time. The politics and government of the Republic were dominated by two men, Sam Houston and Mirabeau Buonaparte Lamar. Houston advocated for annexation and peaceful relations with the Native American tribes of Texas, whereas Lamar envisioned a Texas empire stretching to the Pacific and initiated hostilities against the Native tribes. During the years of the Republic, Houston, Lamar, and their supporters competed for control of the Texas government. Elections revolved around the personalities of the two men and their surrogates because the Republic's Constitution did not permit presidents to serve consecutive terms. During this time, Texas politics was dominated by strong political leaders instead of issues and public policy differences. This characteristic is still present today.

Annexation and the Civil War Era

Texas's state politics after U.S. annexation and until the end of the Civil War clearly established Democratic Party dominance. The Anglo settlers of pre-Civil War Texas were from the U.S. South; they were slave holding or slave supporting, distrustful of the federal government, and convinced of the legitimacy of state sovereignty. In this period, Texas experienced a substantial expansion of its slave plantation economy.[3]

As a rule, Texas Democratic officeholders supported the southern position on the issues dominating the United States during the Civil War era, with the conspicuous exception of Sam Houston, who represented Texas in the U.S. Senate from 1846 to 1859 and served as governor from 1859 to 1861 as a Union Democrat.

Sam Houston, Governor of Texas, 1859–1861; U.S. (Democratic) Senator from Texas, 1846–1859; President of Texas, 1836–1838, 1841–1844; Texas House of Representatives, 1839–1841; Governor of Tennessee, 1827–1829; U.S. Representative from Tennessee, 1823–1827

Houston voted for establishing Oregon as a free territory in 1848, and he argued successfully for the Boundary Act, a part of the Compromise of 1850, whereby Texas sold its right to territory now in New Mexico, Oklahoma, Kansas, Wyoming, and Colorado to the United States.

Houston's opposition to slavery deepened the cleavages between pro- and anti-Houston groups in the Texas Democratic Party that had existed since the early 1850s. Two factions arose in Texas: the pro-Houston faction, or "Jacksonians," and the newer, radical anti-Houston faction who called themselves the Constitutional Democrats. By 1857, the latter completely controlled the party. Houston ran for governor and lost that year, but in 1859 he ran for governor as an independent and won in an attempt to build up a Union Party. Houston campaigned against secession, but the people of Texas voted for it by more than a 3 to 1 margin in a popular referendum. Houston refused to take the oath of allegiance to the Confederacy, and the convention declared the governorship vacant and appointed the lieutenant governor to replace him. The Democratic Party would remain the sole party in Texas for the duration of the Civil War.

The only period of one-party Republican politics in Texas before the 1990s was during Reconstruction under Edmund J. Davis's governorship. Davis, a native of Florida, moved to Texas in 1848 and was one of the few to oppose secession in 1861. Davis was elected governor in 1869 and took office in January 1870 in an election that saw less than 50 percent of registered white citizens voting because of federal Reconstruction laws and the boycott by Conservative Democrats.[4] The party was divided between the Conservative Republicans and the Radicals under Davis. It was Davis's rule, not that of the U.S. military (1866–1869), that embittered most Texans and left them hostile to the Republican Party. V. O. Key, Jr. observed that following the Civil War and the experiences of Reconstruction, southerners felt a very strong resentment toward the rest of the nation and the party that dominated it after the Civil War. This resentment bonded the South together as a unit, and they voted against all Republicans.[5]

The One-Party Democratic Era in Texas

From the end of Reconstruction in Texas in 1874 until the 1960s, Texas was a one-party Democratic state. When Reconstruction ended, the switch from Republican control to Democratic control was almost immediate and absolute. From 1874 until 1961, no Republican was elected to statewide office, and only a few were elected to other offices. In 1928, the state did vote Republican, casting its Electoral College votes for Herbert Hoover. President Hoover's opponent was Al Smith, a Roman Catholic, and the vote was more anti-Catholic and anti-New Yorker than pro-Republican.

Other factors were influential in deflecting Republican challenges and allowed the Democratic Party to dominate. Several second-party movements developed during the last three decades of the nineteenth century, and the conservative Democrats who controlled the party effectively destroyed all opposition.

In 1877, the Greenback Party (initially, Greenback clubs) formed in the South and West in reaction to declining farm prices. In Texas, the Greenbackers were recruited from the more radical farmers. They demanded currency expansion ("greenbacks") to drive up agricultural prices, an income tax, the secret ballot, direct election of U.S. senators, better schools, and reduced railroad freight rates.

In 1878, Greenbackers won 12 seats in the Texas legislature and even won a U.S. House seat. In 1880, the Greenback Party received about 12 percent of the vote in the governor's race and reelected its member to the U.S. Congress.[6] However, the party was already in decline. By 1886, the organization had faded out of existence and its reform agenda was taken up by the People's Party, or "Populists"—a party that fused these different groups together and ultimately had a large impact on U.S. politics. Also formed at this time was the Texas Farmers' Alliance, which became known as the Grange. This organization also represented small farmers and made an uneasy alliance with African Americans, who were the primary supporters of the Republican Party in Texas and in the rest of the South.[7]

The People's Party—or Populists—had a large impact on the national Democratic Party (as depicted in the picture) and the U.S. system as a whole, despite its short life. Formed in the early 1890s from the remnants of other agrarian reform groups, the Populists were primarily a farm movement but expanded its membership to include urban labor voters. The Populists were anti-elite and stood for bimetallism, a graduated income tax, direct election of senators, an eight-hour work day, and government ownership of the railroad.[8] In Texas, the Populists were a "coalition of Anglo small farmers, blacks, and labor," and currency issues predominated.[9] The national party had its greatest electoral success in the presidential election of 1892, when Populist candidate James B. Weaver of Iowa won four states and 22 Electoral College votes. Weaver and Texas gubernatorial candidate Thomas Nugent won about a quarter of the vote in the state. Despite its successes early in the decade, Populism waned as an independent force in the country and in Texas, as the Democratic Party swallowed many of its planks and the national economy improved.[10] In 1896, the Populists supported the Democratic Party presidential nominee William Jennings Bryan, and as one historian put it, "in effect, abolished themselves."[11] It also did not help that William Jennings Bryan was defeated in successive presidential elections by Republican William McKinley.

Swallowed! Political cartoon showing python with head of William Jennings Bryan, as the Populist Party, swallowing the Democratic Party donkey, 1900

As the Populists waned, the Progressives waxed as the key reform movement. Despite its differences with the Populists, the Progressive movement did take up some Populist causes and carried them across the goal line in the early twentieth century. However, the Progressives did not share the anti-elitism and anti-centralism of the Populists. In fact, the Progressives embodied "a faith that educated and civilized individuals can, through the use of reason, determine what is best for society as a whole."[12] Thus it is not surprising that the Progressives favored elite (and national) management of government and the economy to lead the country forward. More specifically, Progressive causes included both political and economic reforms, such as women's suffrage, prohibition, direct election of Senators, anti-monopoly efforts and greater regulation of business, as well as progressive taxation and other egalitarian reforms.[13] One could argue that this activist government view came to dominate American politics for much of the twentieth century, especially in the presidencies of Republican Theodore Roosevelt and Democrats Woodrow Wilson and Franklin D. Roosevelt. However, in Texas, it met with limited favor owing to the state's basic conservatism. Prohibitionism, though, did strike a chord with certain segments of the Texas population, and the state eventually ratified the prohibition amendment to the federal Constitution and passed a state prohibition amendment.[14]

Texas's large landowners and businesses controlled the state Democratic Party and successfully destroyed these party movements. This alliance between landowners and merchants allowed the Democratic Party to dominate state politics from the late 1880s until the 1960s. There was no effective challenge to their dominance, except for a brief period during the Great Depression of the 1930s when the more liberal faction of the party successfully elected some state officials.

Party Realignment in Texas

From 1940 to 1960, political conflicts and competition were confined to the Democratic Party. Writing about Texas political parties in 1949, V. O. Key, Jr. observed: "In Texas the vague outlines of a politics are emerging in which irrelevancies are pushed into the background and the people divided broadly along liberal and conservative lines." This division, according to Key, was due to "personal insecurity of men suddenly made rich who are fearful lest they lose their wealth. . . . The Lone Star State is concerned about money and how to make it, about oil and sulfur and gas, about cattle and dust storms and irrigation, about cotton and banking and Mexicans."[15]

Until the late 1960s, Texas politics revolved almost exclusively around personality and economic issues. Race issues, which dominated many southern states, were less important in Texas.[16] The period from 1940 to 1960 might even be characterized as an era of nonpartisan politics, with domination by the conservative business community. Factional issues within the party, between liberals and conservatives, were driven by economics. Business people, oilmen, wealthy farmers, and cattle ranchers formed the backbone of the conservative element.

Voting Democratic was a habit, and the lack of competition from Republicans made that habit easier to continue. November general elections were pointless because there was little to no competition from Republicans. Party primary elections decided the races. On the few occasions when Republicans did challenge Democrats in November, most Texans still voted for Democrats.

The Beginning of Change

In the 1952 and 1956 presidential elections, however, many Yellow Dog Democrats (individuals who strongly identify as Democrats regardless of the party's ideological position) broke with tradition and voted for the Republican presidential candidate, Dwight D. Eisenhower. The leader of this movement was Governor Allan Shivers, the leader of the conservative faction of the Texas Democratic Party. This faction chose to dissociate from the New Deal/Fair Deal element of the national Democratic Party and from any candidate it might put forward.

In the fall of 1952, at the state Democratic Party convention, Governor Shivers persuaded the state delegates to endorse Eisenhower. The Texas Republican Party convention also nominated Shivers and most statewide Democratic candidates as the Republican nominees. Thus, Shivers and most statewide office seekers were candidates for *both* political parties in 1952. This group became known as the "Shivercrats." The liberal faction of the Texas Democratic Party, still aligned with the national party, became known as the "Loyalists."[17]

This action, and a similar action in 1956, began the Texas tradition of supporting Republican presidential candidates while retaining Democratic Party dominance over state offices. Presidential politics in 1952 broke the tradition of voting a straight ticket, at least for the top offices on that ticket.

Allan Shivers, Governor of Texas, 1949–1957

The Election of John Tower

In 1960, Lyndon Johnson, the senior senator from Texas, ran as the Democratic candidate for U.S. Senate and won. But he was also John F. Kennedy's running mate. Johnson's presence on the Democratic ticket temporarily stayed the movement toward the Republican Party. After the Kennedy-Johnson victory, in a special election in 1961, John Tower was elected to the U.S. Senate to fill Johnson's seat. He was the first Republican statewide officeholder in Texas since the 1870s, winning 41 percent of the vote in the first election and claiming victory with a slight majority in the runoff election.

Tower's election seemed to herald the beginning of a new era of two-party politics in the state. In the 1962 elections, Republicans managed to field candidates for many statewide, congressional, and local races. There were, for a variety of reasons, few successes. Some of these candidates were

Elect

JOHN G.

TOWER

For U. S. Senator

For Truly Texan
Representation
In Washington

Campaign literature from Tower's election.

very weak, and some proved an embarrassment for the Republicans. Tower won reelection in 1966, 1972, and 1978, but it would be 17 years after Tower's first victory before a different Republican won statewide office.

The Election of Bill Clements

Republicans had some success in electing legislators and local officeholders. The election of Republican Bill Clements as governor in 1978 marked the real beginning of two-party politics in Texas. Governor Clements used his power to make appointments to boards, commissions, and judgeships, and to recruit people who would publicly declare their Republicanism. Some referred to these new converts as "closet Republicans" who had finally gone public. These appointments helped build the Republican Party in Texas and begin party realignment.

Clements's 1982 loss to Democrat Mark White was a blow to the Republicans because the party also had little success in gaining other statewide offices. In that year, the Democrats elected Ann Richards as state treasurer, Jim Hightower as agriculture commissioner, Gary Mauro as land commissioner, and Jim Mattox as attorney general. Republican fortunes improved in 1986 with Clements's return to the governor's office. He defeated White in what many termed a "revenge match," and he used his return to the office to resume building the Republican Party in Texas.

The "Conversion" and Election of Phil Gramm

In 1983, John Tower announced he would not seek reelection to the U.S. Senate in 1984. Phil Gramm, the Democratic representative from the sixth congressional district, used Tower's retirement to advance from the U.S. House to the Senate. Gramm was first elected as a Democrat in 1978. By early 1981, Gramm had gained some national prominence by helping President Reagan "cut the federal budget."[18] Gramm, who served as a member of the House Budget Committee, was accused of leaking Democratic strategy to the White House Budget Office. David Stockman, budget director under Ronald Reagan, confirmed that Gramm had in fact done this.[19] Because of his disloyalty to the party and because of House rules, Gramm was not reappointed to another term on the Budget Committee.

In a smart political move, Gramm used the loss of his committee seat as an excuse to convert to the Republican Party. In 1983 Gramm resigned his seat in the U.S. House. Outgoing Republican Governor Clements called a special election, which was held one month after Gramm's resignation, to fill Gramm's seat. Because no other candidate could possibly put together a successful campaign in so short a time and due to the fit between his views and the state's conservative

Former Senator Gramm, with wife Wendy by his side

majority, Gramm easily won reelection to the same seat he had just vacated, this time as a Republican. In 1984, "fully baptized" as a Republican, Gramm won election as U.S. Senator, pulled along on the coattails of President Ronald Reagan. This allowed the Republican Party to retain the U.S. Senate seat previously held by John Tower. Gramm easily won reelection in 1990 and 1996, but chose not to run for reelection in 2002, thus ending a long career in Texas politics.

The Move toward Parity with the Democrats

In 1988, the Republicans made significant gains, aided by Bill Clements's 1987 return to the governor's mansion and George H. W. Bush's election to the presidency. The party won four statewide offices. Three Republicans won election to the Texas Supreme Court, and Kent Hance was elected to the Texas Railroad Commission.

In 1990, Republicans captured the offices of state treasurer and agricultural commissioner and another seat on the state supreme court. The big setback for the Republicans in 1990 was the loss of the governor's office. Bill Clements did not seek reelection. Clayton Williams, a political newcomer, used his considerable wealth to win the Republican nomination. His campaign for governor was something of a disaster, and he lost to Democrat Ann Richards. Williams's loss, in a way, aided George W. Bush's 1994 gubernatorial and 2000 presidential victories. If Williams had won and served two terms, Bush could not have been elected governor until 1998, and this would have made it less likely for him to make a legitimate bid for president in 2000.

In 1992, Democrat Lloyd Bentsen, after serving as U.S. senator from Texas for 20 years, resigned to become secretary of the treasury under President Clinton. His resignation allowed Republicans to capture their second seat in the U.S. Senate with the election of Kay Bailey Hutchison. In 1996, Phil Gramm was elected to a third term as U.S. Senator from Texas.

Ann Richards, Governor of Texas, 1991–1995

In 1994, the Republicans captured all three seats on the Railroad Commission and a majority of the seats on the state supreme court, and they retained control of the agriculture commissioner's office. Republicans also captured three additional seats on the state board of education, for a total of eight. In addition, George W. Bush was elected governor. When the dust cleared, Republicans controlled a total of 23 statewide offices. These wins, coupled with additional seats in the Texas House and Senate, substantially changed Texas party politics.

One-Party Republican Dominance in Texas

The 1994 election marked the year that Texas went from its brief two-party system to a one-party Republican system. After the 1998 elections, the Republicans held all but one statewide office. After the 2000 elections, Republicans held all statewide offices and were in the majority in both the Texas House and Senate. Today the state is as solidly one-party Republican as it had been one-party Democratic (see Table 9.1).

The state Democratic Party today has less factional fighting because the vast majority of conservative Democrats have stampeded to the Republicans. There are liberal and moderate wings, which are distinguished more by personalities than policies. There is probably a tendency for liberal Texas Democrats to support the national party candidates more than the moderates, but within the state, the Democrats have failed to field candidates in all 254 counties.

TABLE 9.1

Total Offices Held by Republicans, by Year 1974–2014

Year	U.S. Senate	U.S. House	Statewide Office	Texas Senate	Texas House	County Office	State Board of Education[*]
1974	1	2	0	3	16	53	—
1976	1	2	0	3	19	67	—
1978	1	4	1	4	22	87	—
1980	1	5	1	7	35	166	—
1982	1	5	0	5	36	270	—
1984	1	10	0	6	52	377	—
1986	1	10	1	6	56	504	—
1988	1	8	5	8	57	608	5
1990	1	8	6	8	57	717	5
1992	1	9	7	13	58	814	5
1994	2	11	13	14	61	900	8
1996	2	11	13	17	68	950	8
1998	2	11	18	16	71	973	9
2000	2	11	18	16	71	1,231	9
2002	2	15	27	19	88	1,327	10
2004	2	22	27	19	87	1,390	10
2006	2	22	27	19	81	1,410	10
2008	2	22	27	19	76	1,345	6
2010	2	26	27	19	101	1,356	6
2012	2	23	27	19	100	n/a	11
2014	2	25	27	20	98	n/a	10

[*]State Board of Education was not elected until 1988.

Wendy Davis, flanked by Julian Castro (left) and Joaquin Castro (right)

In an effort to revitalize their standing in the state, Democratic Party operatives recently launched an initiative called "Turn Texas Blue." (The name plays on the common media reference to Republican-dominated states as "red" states and Democratic states as "blue" states.) This Democratic movement is alternatively known as "Battleground Texas" and refers to efforts to return Texas to Democratic dominance. Wendy Davis's 2014 campaign for governor was seen as key to that effort. Even if she was unlikely to win against heavily favored Greg Abbott, Davis's candidacy was seen as critical to the long-term Democratic Party effort, given her ability to raise money and inspire the grassroots.[20] Both of these activities, in addition to building party infrastructure, will be important for the long-term success of this initiative.

Democrats have long viewed demographic realities in the state cutting in their favor, particularly the relative increase in the size of the Hispanic population. *Texas Monthly* recently explained this logic:

> Demography is the driver of this runaway freight train. The 2010 census found that the state's population had increased by 4.3 million over the previous decade and that more than 3.3 million of the new inhabitants were minorities. Of these, an astounding 2.8 million were Hispanic, historically a reliable constituency for Democrats. These numbers conveyed a new reality: the Texas political landscape was getting friendlier for Democrats and tougher for Republicans.[21]

Moreover, the Democrats have two talented young Hispanic politicians to add to Davis's efforts: the Castro brothers. Former San Antonio mayor and Obama administration Secretary of the Department of Housing and Urban Development, Julián Castro, and his twin brother, Congressman Joaquín Castro, are likely to be key players in the future of the Democratic Party in Texas and in Washington. Democrats could also benefit from the influx of in-migrants from other states that could change the state's political culture (though these migrants may also consider themselves "refugees" from more liberal states).

However, there are a few caveats to a Democratic destiny that some see as inevitable. First, some liberal Democrats—including Davis herself, given her strong support of abortion rights—may not be attractive to the more socially

Governor Greg Abbott

conservative Hispanics. This can be seen in Davis's inability to perform well in many parts of south Texas during the 2014 primary.[22] Second, as the *New Republic* argues, "Latinos in Texas are disproportionately ineligible to vote. Too many either aren't citizens or are too young to upend the state in the next few election cycles."[23] Third, the Republican Party also gets a vote in this war for the future. More specifically, the Republicans aren't likely to hold pat and allow Texas to turn blue without a fight. They have already begun greater outreach efforts toward minorities. Moreover, the success of the current Republican majority to help maintain Texas's general economic growth as well as opportunities for the Hispanic community in particular could impact future voting patterns. However, it is unclear if the state's Republicans can be successful in attracting Hispanics to their cause, especially if national Republican policies cut against those efforts.

If the Democrats are successful in turning Texas "blue," the national political ramifications could be huge. Indeed, it could cinch Democratic dominance at the Presidential level and perhaps beyond. As recent U.S. Trade Representative and former Dallas mayor Ron Kirk noted back in 2010: "When Texas turns blue, this country's going to turn blue and it's going to stay blue."[24] Republican Ted Cruz was even more dour about the future of the Republican Party if Texas goes Democratic, arguing: "No Republican will ever again win the White House. . . If Texas turns bright blue, the Electoral College math is simple . . . The Republican Party would cease to exist."[25] Clearly, the success or failure of these efforts will have big national and state ramifications.

The Republican Party in Texas, like most dominant parties, is currently characterized by multiple, sometimes overlapping, factions with differing agendas. Two of the primary factions are the social conservatives and the more pro-market, libertarian Republicans. However, traditional establishment and pro-business conservatives (some of whom might be more accurately called moderates in contemporary Texas politics), such as Speaker of the House Joe Straus, are also well-represented in the diverse Republican caucus.

Traditionally, pro-business conservatives have been at the core of the Texas establishment. Their priorities were to keep spending and taxes low while limiting state government regulation of the economy. Their goal has been to foster a pro-business climate, even when that has meant compromising a general free-market outlook by active government support of business. This has meant support for government spending on infrastructure, such as roads, highways, and port development and maintenance. But it has also meant more active efforts, such as special subsidies for companies such as the Texas Enterprise Fund and the Texas Emerging Technology Fund.[26] Of course, some due consideration is also given to the basic economic liberalism shared by the pro-market, libertarian Republicans. This economic liberalism is centered on belief in the existence of an efficient, largely self-regulating market that functions best when government strongly defends property rights. But either because of the power of special interests or a principled position that sometimes the business climate needs a helping hand, these pro-business establishment Republicans are not generally too particular about maintaining a strict allegiance to the creed of economic liberalism. This, in turn, drives the more pure free-market libertarian Republicans to call some of the pro-business efforts "crony capitalism," inconsistent with true capitalism.[27]

The social conservatives focus on "culture war" issues and are troubled by a perceived decline of morality in Texas and the United States generally. These conservatives stress their pro-life stance against abortion, oppose gay civil rights (including gay marriage), support prayer in public schools (although this is not a consensus view even among social conservatives), and have pushed for teaching alternatives to evolution (such as creationism or intelligent design) in the public schools. The strength of these conservatives was seen in the Texas Republican primary in July 2012, when Tea Party and social conservative candidate Ted Cruz defeated the pro-business conservative and establishment candidate Lieutenant Governor David Dewhurst by 57 percent to 43 percent. Dewhurst's defeat was also a defeat for Governor Rick Perry, who supported Dewhurst.

There is also a rising force in the GOP—the more pro-market, libertarian Republicans who are as committed to personal liberty as they are to economic freedom and who challenge both the party establishment and the social conservatives. Indeed, Wayne Slater of the *Dallas Morning News* argues that the "real divide within the Texas GOP is between Christian conservatives who have been dominant in recent years and 'liberty' groups with a more secular view—those who believe government should set a moral agenda and those who want as little government as possible."[28] Some, including supporters of Kentucky Senator and possible Republican presidential candidate Rand Paul (son of long-time Texas Republican Congressman Ron Paul) believe at the national level that these libertarian types represent the future of the Republican Party if it is to compete with the Democrats. It is unclear whether they can make serious inroads in the still relatively conservative Texas GOP or find a way to live together with more socially conservative Republicans in a "fusionist" party that somewhat mirrors the one that Ronald Reagan put together in the 1980s.[29]

Finally, it should be noted that the "Tea Party" includes both some of the pro-market libertarian Republicans and the social conservative Republicans. Indeed, some members fuse in more or less consistent ways both the libertarian freedom agenda with a number of social conservative positions. The group also includes a fair number of anti-establishment or more populist tenants who rage against the many problems they see coming from the political and cultural power centers on both coasts.

CORE OBJECTIVE

Being Socially Responsible...

What impact, if any, do factions have on enhancing or diminishing civic engagement?
In your opinion, do factions promote acceptance of diverse opinions?

Party De-alignment

Many argue that **party de-alignment** occurred at the national level in roughly 1968 and hit Texas a decade or so later. There are many indicators for such de-alignment since the late 1960s nationally and the early 1980s in Texas. First, voters have increasingly engaged in split-ticket voting—that is, they will vote for candidates from

party de-alignment
View that a growing number of voters and candidates do not identify with either major political party but are independents

straight ticket voting
Casting all your votes for
candidates of one party

different parties for different offices during the same election. In the past, **straight ticket voting**, in which voters selected candidates for all the offices from the same party in the same election, was much more prevalent, and it was an indication of party strength.

Second, candidates distance themselves from the parties and try to establish themselves as brand names so as to have a direct connection to the voters. Many party candidates do not put their party name on their billboards, yard signs, and campaign literature. Now they want voters to recognize their name, not the party.

Third, the number of Texans who identify themselves as Democrats has declined. In 1952, 66 percent of Texans identified themselves as Democrats; in 1983, only 39 percent did so.[30] By 2009, that number had dropped to 22 percent.[31]

Fourth, voter turnout is low. When then-Governor George W. Bush was reelected with a landslide 67 percent of the popular vote in 1996, only 18 percent of registered voters had voted for him. Almost three-quarters of the eligible voters did not participate in the election. However, this lack of participation might be expected in a one-party state with a traditionalistic political culture.

Fifth, since the early 1970s, we have seen a rise in media, specifically mass media, campaigning. Candidates now spend the lion's share of their campaign budgets on 30- and 60-second television and radio spots. A majority of Texans and U.S. voters in general obtain most of their information about candidates from these very short mass media advertisements. Media campaigning has contributed to the increased independence of candidates, increased split-ticket voting, and the decreased strength of parties.

According to the most recent data from Gallup (an independent national polling firm), in 2013, 42 percent of Texans identified as either Republican or leaning Republican, whereas 38 percent identified as Democratic or leaning Democratic.[32] This is consistent with 2012 polling conducted by the University of Texas and the *Texas Tribune*, which found the state split about evenly in terms of identification with the two major parties.[33] These newer figures suggest that the Democratic Party may be gaining steam in Texas and that the ranks of the independents are thinning. However, in terms of the latter, it is questionable whether most self-identified independents were ever truly free of party leanings in the first place. Indeed, political scientists and journalists have suspected for some time that so-called independents actually harbor allegiance to one party or the other.[34]

Traditional Party Functions in the United States

Labor-Intensive Politics

In the past, political parties in the United States were stronger in part because they performed multiple functions. From the 1790s until roughly the 1970s, parties relied on members and volunteers to perform a number of tasks. These traditional party functions are sometimes described as *labor-intensive politics* because, historically, the lack of communication and printing technologies (such as radio, television, the photocopier, and the personal computer) meant that parties had to enlist a lot of people or expend a lot of labor to accomplish these tasks.

First, the parties selected candidates for office. Party leaders (usually, but not always, elected officials) would decide who would be put forward as candidates.

The infamous Tammany Hall was the first urban party organization that successfully selected candidates for office. In reality, Tammany was the executive committee of the New York City Democratic Party, which put together slates of candidates for city and county offices. The organization was so powerful that it not only controlled New York City elections but also (due to the city's large population) influenced state and national elections from 1790 until well into the twentieth century. Tammany leaders through the years represented a Who's Who of important political figures, such as Aaron Burr and "Boss" William Tweed. A competing Whig-Republican machine in upstate New York was headed by Thurlow Weed from the early 1830s to the late 1860s. In Illinois, the Cook County Democratic Party slated candidates for city and county offices and was influential in determining statewide Democratic candidates from the 1930s until the present. Richard J. Daley served as both mayor of Chicago and Chair of the Cook County Democratic Party machine. These offices led to his dominance of both city and county and had a great effect on Illinois and even national politics by his selection of candidates and his "get out the vote" ability. The Texas Establishment, led by such luminaries as Colonel Edward M. House, dominated the selection of candidates from the turn of the previous century until quite recently.

A second traditional party function was organizing candidates' campaigns. In the past, candidate campaigns were completely controlled by the parties, which sent party workers into neighborhoods to inform potential voters about the candidates and issues. Many times, the entire party slate would share the platform and speak at the same event. Third, parties could raise money directly and then distribute it to their different candidates' campaigns. By controlling the purse strings, the party could keep its candidates in line and under control. Fourth, the party organized campaign rallies to facilitate candidate and voter interaction. Before candidates campaigned for themselves, the party would produce campaign literature, arrange speakers on behalf of the candidates, and, from the early 1900s on, arrange speaking tours for the candidates.

Fifth, inconceivable as it may be today, the parties, not local governments, printed election ballots. Sixth, starting in the 1930s, parties hired pollsters to conduct survey research for their candidates. Candidates were beholden to the party for such poll data. Seventh and last, the parties ran the governments to which their candidates were elected, especially after the introduction of the spoils system (giving government jobs to party members). When Andrew Jackson won the presidency in 1828, government positions were filled by recognized party members; the higher the office, the more important the party member chosen to fill it.

Capital-Intensive Politics

Recently, there has been a shift from labor-intensive politics, dominated by political parties, toward more capital-intensive politics. These are activities for which campaigns must use money (or capital) to purchase "non-human resources" (such as information and communication technology and media services) to reach voters.[35] The importance of broadcast media began with radio in the 1930s, and that importance substantially increased with the introduction of television in most U.S. homes by the early 1960s. By the 1970s, broadcast media advertisements accounted for approximately 80 percent of the increase in campaign costs since the mid-1950s. Mass communication replaced candidate rallies as a way to communicate with voters. In fact, some rallies were staged so they could be filmed and edited to meet the needs of television.

Polling or survey research has also become ubiquitous in campaigns. Survey workers ask potential voters questions about party affiliation, candidate preferences, issue preferences (pro-choice or pro-life, for example), and issue salience or intensity (the relative importance of an issue to a voter). With the information obtained from polling data, phone banking can be set up. This involves calling targeted groups and asking for a donation or other form of support for a candidate, such as displaying yard signs. During early voting and on Election Day, phone bank callers remind people who identified themselves as supporting a particular candidate to go to the polls.

Capital-intensive politics also includes direct mail. Using information from survey research, specific campaign literature is mailed to targeted likely voters. For example, if a person answered a telephone survey question by saying that education was the most important issue for her, a direct-mail piece about education would be sent to her. This process of using poll data to isolate subsets within subgroups within groups to target campaign and candidate messages sometimes is called "salami-slicing the electorate."

The newest element of capital-intensive politics is the use of the Internet to communicate directly with likely voters. Successful campaigns have learned how to utilize email and websites to drive down the cost of communicating their message to voters, because electronic communication is substantially cheaper than direct mail. However, there still exists what Stanford University researchers have called a "digital divide"—the finding that higher-income households are much more likely to own computers and have Internet access than are lower-income households.[36] Therefore, campaigns that rely too heavily on such communication risk ignoring substantial numbers of the potential electorate.

Professional campaign companies have replaced the parties when it comes to running campaigns. Many times, these companies have different departments or sections that are able to produce television and radio advertisements, direct mail pieces, phone banking, email communication and web design, and write and conduct polls. Sometimes the campaign companies will contract out some or all of the services associated with capital-intensive campaigns, providing the large themes and overall campaign direction while reserving the right to veto or modify any of the campaign products being developed by these specialized companies. Polling is the most likely service to be contracted out to an independent company. Excellent poll data is absolutely essential to campaigns today. Because of the more specialized skill sets necessary for professional polling, many campaign companies are more comfortable contracting out their polling needs to a company whose sole function is to construct and conduct polls. Without good polling data, a modern campaign might have difficulty gaging the effectiveness of its message or the mood of the electorate.

Political Reforms and the Weakening of Political Parties

In general, parties are weaker today than they have been during their entire history. Nothing suggests this trend of weaker parties is going to reverse itself anytime soon. Political reforms are responsible for much of this party weakening, although often it is an unintentional result.

The secret or "Australian" ballot was first introduced in a few other states in the 1880s. Prior voting systems (some of which involved vocally announcing one's candidate preference in public) had made it easy for party members to intimidate or coerce voters. In addition, where printed ballots were used, the parties themselves printed them. As a result, parties had devised a variety of techniques to identify how a ballot was cast or otherwise influence voters. With the Australian ballot, voters could mark and submit their choice in private. Governments also began to print ballots, relieving parties of that responsibility and leading to more standardized formats. Therefore, ballot reforms decreased the influence of political parties on the voting process.[37]

Another way parties had consolidated their power was the appointment, by elected officials, of faithful party members to government jobs. Civil service reform gained wide support in the United States in the wake of the assassination of President James A. Garfield in 1881. Garfield was shot by a disappointed office seeker who had previously campaigned on Garfield's behalf, and the president's wounds ultimately led to his death.[38] The Pendleton Act of 1883 established a class of federal government positions that would be filled as a result of competitive examinations instead of political appointments.[39] Under the Pendleton Act, a rather small percentage of government positions were designated as civil service (nonpartisan) jobs. But Chester A. Arthur, the Republican vice president who succeeded to the presidency at the death of Garfield, added more positions to the civil service rolls, as did each president thereafter through the end of the nineteenth century. By 1900, a majority of federal government positions were protected by the Pendleton Act. As the civil service system replaced the patronage system, it undermined the connection the parties had with party workers.

In the Progressive Era (1901–1920), reformers were very concerned about the power of large urban political machines, which were led by powerful men who controlled government jobs, contracts, and regulations. In an attempt to reduce the power of the machines, the reformers helped to reduce the strength of the political parties. The reformers pushed for nonpartisan local elections to remove municipal policy from political considerations, and they championed the manager-council form of municipal government in which professional city managers, not mayors, would administer the departments and employees of the cities. (See Chapter 6 for a fuller discussion of this form of city government.) In the past, city governments were a breeding ground for the development of talent for the political parties. Grover Cleveland began his career in elected politics by being elected mayor of Buffalo, New York, and Theodore Roosevelt began as police commissioner of New York City.

Another reform established during this era and having far-reaching consequences was the introduction of the direct primary. Primaries were designed to allow voters, rather than party bosses, to select candidates for office; initially only a small number of primaries were held. But in the wake of the disastrous 1968 Democratic National Convention in Chicago (characterized not only by party divisiveness but also outright violence between protestors and police), the Democratic Party instituted substantial reforms. The Republican Party soon followed suit, and by 1972, the vast majority of delegates to party presidential nominating conventions were picked as a result of primary election totals. Party primaries are now used to select the nominees of all elected government positions, from justice of the peace to U.S. Senator. As a general rule, Democratic Party delegates are selected on a proportional system based on the popular vote of the party's presidential candidates listed on the primary ballot. Some states use a caucus system to determine party nominations, rather than conducting a primary. A caucus is a gathering at which party members publicly declare which candidate they will support and select delegates who will attend the nominating convention. In Texas, the

Democratic Party holds both a primary and a caucus. On Election Day, Democrats can go to the polls to vote in the primary, then return in the evening to participate in the caucus. About two-thirds of delegates are determined by results of the primary, while the remaining third is determined by caucuses.[40]

It is worth noting that campaign finance laws have also harmed parties, albeit without achieving their intended goal of dampening the role of money in elections.

CORE OBJECTIVE

Communicating Effectively...

Explain how political reforms have weakened political parties.

Third-Party Movements

Although the story of Texas politics is generally one of two major political parties, it should be noted that from time to time third-party movements develop in Texas. Some are national, whereas others have been state based. At a national level, segregationist George Wallace used the American Independent Party to run for president in 1968 and managed to gain 18 percent of the Texas vote.[41] In the 1970s, the **Raza Unida** (United Race) Party ran candidates for several state and local offices, especially in south Texas. As a Raza Unida candidate, Ramsey Muniz managed to gain 7.2 percent of the vote for governor in 1972.

The Libertarian Party has put forth candidates for statewide office in Texas for many years. It adheres to the principles of respect for individual rights, constitutionalism and the rule of law, personal responsibility, and limited government.[42] In general, Libertarian Party (LP) candidates do not receive more than a small percentage of the vote, especially because many Republicans also espouse the same principles. It is also the case that not all philosophical libertarians belong to the LP, and some of these are principled non-voters. Nobel Prize-winning economist Milton Friedman, for example, famously noted he was a small l-libertarian and a large-R Republican—meaning his party of choice was the Republican Party even though his principles were largely libertarian. The most successful Libertarian candidate for governor of Texas was Jeff Daiell, who received 3.3 percent of the vote in 1990.[43] The LP has consistently maintained its status as a minor party in Texas and guaranteed its candidates' appearance on the ballot by garnering at least 5 percent of total votes cast in the previous election.[44] Currently, Libertarians hold four elected offices in Texas: three city council seats and a town mayorship, and the party had 132 candidates for statewide and local offices on the ballot in 2014.[45] Despite its staying power, it is highly unlikely the LP will ever be a major electoral force in the state.

Texas industrialist Ross Perot ran as an independent candidate for president in 1992; he received about 22 percent of the statewide vote in Texas (see Table 9.2) as well as an impressive 19 percent of the national vote. In 1996, the Natural Law Party gained enough signatures to have its name placed on the ballot in Texas. This organization promoted the idea of transcendental meditation as a way to reduce

Raza Unida (United Race)
Minor party that supported election of Mexican Americans in Texas in the 1970s

TABLE 9.2

Texas General Election Results for President, 1992–2012

Year	Candidate	Percentage of Vote
1992	**Republican** George Bush/Dan Quayle	40.56%
	Democrat Bill Clinton/Al Gore	37.07%
	Independent Ross Perot/James Stockdale	22.01%
	Libertarian Andre Marrou/Nancy Lord	0.32%
1996	**Republican** Bob Dole/Jack Kemp	48.75%
	Democrat Bill Clinton/Al Gore	43.83%
	Independent Ross Perot/James Campbell	6.74%
	Libertarian Harry Browne/Jo Jorgensen	0.36%
2000	**Republican** George W. Bush/Dick Cheney	59.29%
	Democrat Al Gore/Joe Lieberman	37.98%
	Green Ralph Nader/Winona LaDuke	2.15%
	Libertarian Harry Browne/Art Olivier	0.36%
2004	**Republican** George W. Bush/Dick Cheney	61.08%
	Democrat John F. Kerry/John Edwards	38.22%
	Libertarian Michael Badnarik/Richard V. Campagna	0.52%
2008	**Republican** John McCain/Sarah Palin	55.45%
	Democrat Barack Obama/Joe Biden	43.68%
	Libertarian Bob Barr/Wayne A. Root	0.69%
2012	**Republican** Mitt Romney/Paul Ryan	57.16%
	Democrat Barack Obama/Joe Biden	41.38%
	Libertarian Gary Johnson/Jim Gray	1.10%
	Green Jill Stein/Cheri Honkala	0.30%

Source: Office of the Secretary of State, 1992-Current Election History, See: (http://elections.sos.state.tx.us/elchist.exe).

crime and strongly supported environmental protection, clean energy, and health issues. This party is no longer active in Texas.[46] However, the Green Party of Texas, which advocates social justice, ecological sustainability, nonviolence, and political reform (including public financing of election campaigns), has been more active in recent years (see Table 9.3).[47] It, too, is unlikely to occupy a prominent place in state politics.

TABLE 9.3

Texas Election Results for Governor, 1998–2014

Year	Candidate	Percentage of Vote
1998	**Republican** George W. Bush	68.23%
	Democrat Garry Mauro	31.18%
	Libertarian Lester R. "Les" Turlington, Jr.	0.55%
2002	**Republican** Rick Perry	57.80%
	Democrat Tony Sanchez	39.96%
	Libertarian Jeff Daiell	1.46%
	Green Rahul Mahajan	0.70%
2006	**Republican** Rick Perry	39.02%
	Democrat Chris Bell	29.78%
	Independent Carole Keeton Strayhorn	18.11%
	Independent Richard "Kinky" Friedman	12.44%
	Libertarian James Werner	0.60%
2010	**Republican** Rick Perry	54.97%
	Democrat Bill White	42.29%
	Libertarian Kathie Glass	2.19%
	Green Deb Shafto	0.39%
2014	**Republican** Greg Abbott	59.25%
	Democrat Wendy R. Davis	38.91%
	Libertarian Kathie Glass	1.41%
	Green Brandon Parmer	0.39%

Source: Office of the Secretary of State, 1992–Current Election History. See: (http://elections.sos.state.tx.us/elchist.exe).

To date, third parties have not had much impact on Texas politics. The rules governing elections in Texas, as in many other states, do not make it easy for third parties to gain access to the ballot. Even if third parties do gain access to the ballot, they still face an uphill battle to gain the financial resources necessary to run a successful high-dollar media campaign. Often the best a minor party can hope to do is to have its ideas picked up by a major party. Ross Perot is credited with focusing on the need to balance the federal budget in his 1992 campaign. Few other good examples of third-party movements that have had an impact on state or national policy can be found in the last several decades of the twentieth century. Instead, we have seen groups like the "Tea Party" emerge and try to influence the major parties. Indeed, the Tea Party has explicitly tried to fight within the Republican Party in order to reshape or focus the party on its policy preferences. This strategy has met with mixed electoral results, but it has certainly led to a fight on "the Right" about the future of conservatism and the Republican brand. The most recent manifestation of this fight occurred in Virginia where a relatively obscure Tea Party-backed candidate (David Brat) defeated the incumbent U.S. House majority leader (Eric Cantor) in a primary race.

A number of reasons have been suggested to explain the failures of third parties in the United States at the federal and state levels. First, some scholars point to the political cultural consensus in our country and state. The United States operates within a narrower ideological range than has most of the world in the past couple of centuries. Our political range is rather limited, and most people agree on the foundations of our political order. Second is the issue of voter identification. Most people grew up with the two major parties. They know them and identify themselves politically in reference to those parties.

Third is the lack of proportional representation in our state and national legislatures. Many countries elect representatives by the percentage of the national and provincial (state) vote that the parties receive. For example, if in Germany 35 percent of the votes are cast for a Christian Democratic candidate, then 35 percent of the seats in the national or provincial/state legislature will be held by Christian Democrats. In the United States, we have single-member districts. A candidate is elected if he or she receives more votes than any other candidate, regardless of any other election outcome. Therefore, if people vote for a candidate who comes in third, their votes do not lead to any seats in a legislature.

Another factor hurting third parties is allowing candidates to be elected to office by a plurality (winning the most votes, not necessarily more than 50 percent) rather than a majority (winning with more than 50 percent of the votes). Currently, Texas law requires that to win a primary election, a candidate must win a majority of the vote. But candidates in general elections for positions in the executive, judicial, and legislative branches in the United States and Texas need to win only a plurality of the vote. If a majority was required, it is possible that would increase the bargaining leverage of third parties and their candidates, thereby raising the profile of both and leading to increased support and interest in those third parties.

The difficulty of third parties in single-member districts with plurality election rules is not surprising given Duverger's Law. This scientific law tells us that the electoral system strongly conditions the type of party system that will result. Therefore, an electoral system in which candidates in single-member districts only need to win a plurality incentivizes parties to develop broad pre-election coalitions and disincentivizes more narrow parties that cannot win a large vote share (and thus consistently fail to win any elections). Likewise, in proportional representation systems, there is little disincentive for smaller parties, because they can win seats without winning pluralities or majorities and even play a key role in coalition governments.

A fifth reason is that the two major parties legally limit access to the ballot. Republicans and Democrats are automatically on the ballot, but other parties need petitions signed by 5 to 10 percent of registered voters who did not vote in any of the primaries. Third parties must spend large amounts of money merely to qualify their candidates for the ballot. The two major parties have no such costs, so they are free to spend more money on the actual campaigns. Finally, the perception of third-party failure also contributes to the weakness of third parties. Many people think that a vote for a third party is wasted. Past failures reinforce the belief in future failures. No third-party candidate has ever won the U.S. presidency or the Texas governorship.

CORE OBJECTIVE

Thinking Critically...

On average, about 1 in 3 Texans identify themselves as independents, suggesting that they do not align with either the Republicans or the Democrats. What measures might be taken to level the playing field for third parties and improve their competitiveness in elections?

---

permanent party organization
Series of elected officials of a political party that keep the party organization active between elections

Party Organization in Texas

Political parties in all states have both formal and informal organizations (see Figure 9.1). Their organizational structure is partly determined by state law, but parties have some discretion in deciding specific arrangements. Additionally, rules established by the national Democratic and Republican Party organizations might dictate state party actions in selected areas, such as the number of delegates to the national convention and how those delegates are selected.

The Texas Election Code decides many aspects of party activity, especially the conduct of primary elections. Earlier we discussed the white primaries in Texas, which excluded African Americans from voting in Democratic Party primary elections and which were eventually outlawed by the U.S. Supreme Court. This is a good example of party activity being restricted by national or state laws. Parties are not free agents or purely private organizations, but quasi-public agents.

Permanent Party Organization

The **permanent party organization** consists of elected party officers. At the lowest level is the precinct chair. Each county in Texas is divided into voting precincts or polling places. Each voting precinct contains about 2,000 voters, although rural areas may have as few as 100 voters in a precinct. Statewide there are about 9,000 voting precincts. When voters register, they are assigned to a precinct-based polling place near their home. Polling places are normally located in public buildings (schools, city halls, churches) but may be located in private homes when no public building is available.

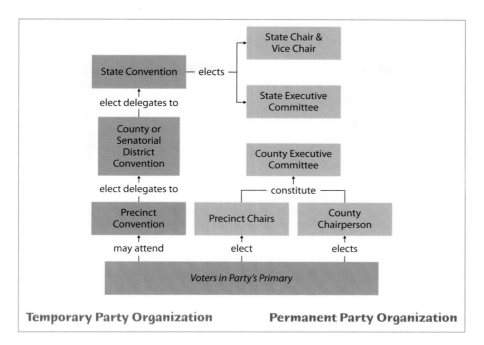

FIGURE 9.1   Temporary and Permanent Party Organization

SOURCE: http://www.laits.utexas.edu/txp_media/html/part/features/0603_01/slide1.html

The Precinct Chair

The **precinct chair** is elected for a two-year term during the party's primary election, which is normally held in March of even-numbered years. Any registered voter may file for precinct chair, and his or her name will be placed on the ballot. Occasionally these races are contested, but more often the precinct chair is unopposed. Write-in votes are allowed with no preelection filing notice required. It is not uncommon for a person to win election by writing in his or her name. In 1976, Paul Van Riper, a professor of political science at Texas A&M, was elected precinct chair in Brazos County with one write-in vote, his own. In 1978, his name appeared on the ballot, and he was reelected with three votes.

Ideally, the role of the precinct chair is to organize the precinct, identify party supporters, make sure they are registered to vote, turn out voters on Election Day, and generally promote and develop the interests of the party at this level. In the one-party Democratic era in Texas, few precinct chairs performed these duties; generally their only duty was to serve as election judge during primary and general elections. As Texas develops into a two-party state, the role of the precinct chair may change from election judge to party organizer at the grassroots level. In some counties this already has occurred, but neither party is well organized at the grassroots level.

The County Chair

The next office in the party hierarchy is **county chair**. This position is also filled during the primary election, and the person elected serves a two-year term. Any registered voter may file for the office. In large urban counties, this office is usually contested. The role of the county chair is similar to that of the precinct chair, but at the county level. Informally, the county chair's duties consist of representing the

precinct chair
Party official elected in each voting precinct to organize and support the party

county chair
Party official elected in each county to organize and support the party

party in the county, serving as the official spokesperson for the party, maintaining a party headquarters (in some counties), and serving as a fundraiser. Formally, the county chair is responsible for receiving formal filings from persons seeking to have their names placed on the party's primary election ballot, conducting the primary election, filling elected judge positions, and officially counting the ballots in the primary election.

In large urban counties, the county chair is often a full-time employee whose job is to organize the party at the county level. This involves voter registration, fundraising, candidate recruitment and education, and aiding in the election of candidates in the general election.

The County Executive Committee

county executive committee
Committee made up of a county chair and all precinct chairs in the county; serves as the official organization for the party in each county

The **county executive committee** is the next level in the permanent party organization. It is composed of all precinct chairs and the county chair. The degree of organization of this committee varies greatly from county to county. In some counties, the executive committee is an active organization that works to promote the party's interests. In many counties, especially in rural areas, this committee is more a paper organization that fulfills the formal duties of canvassing the election returns and filling vacancies in party offices when they occur. Occasionally, the committee might be called upon to fill a vacancy on the general election ballot if a nominee has died or has become ineligible to run between the time of the primary and the general election.

Many large metropolitan counties use, instead of the county executive committee, a district executive committee for some functions. This is an organizational convenience because these counties have such large county committees. District committees are organized around the state senatorial districts. In Harris, Dallas, Tarrant, and Bexar counties, there are several state senate districts.

The State Executive Committee

state executive committee
Committee made up of one man and one woman elected from each state senatorial district that functions as the governing body of the party

The next level of permanent party organization is the **state executive committee**. From each of Texas's 31 senatorial districts, the Democrats elect one man and one woman to serve on the state executive committee. The Republicans use congressional districts and also elect one man and one woman to the state executive committee. Their election usually occurs during the state convention, which traditionally is held in June of even-numbered election years. Delegates to this convention caucus by senatorial or congressional district and elect their representative to the state executive committee; the state convention, as a whole, ratifies these choices.

Being selected to serve on the state executive committee is considered an honor, usually reserved for those who have strong political ties and who have supported the party for many years. Occasionally a maverick group will surface and take control of the party, electing its people, who might not be the longtime party faithful.

The State Party Chair

state party chair
Heads the state executive committee and provides leadership for the party

The state convention also elects a **state party chair** and vice chair; one must be a woman and one must be a man. Traditionally in the Democratic Party, the state chair and vice chair were chosen by the governor or gubernatorial candidate, and the state chair office was often filled by the governor's campaign manager. With the rise of the Republican Party and the election of three GOP governors, the state chair is not the automatic choice of the governor; however, the party candidate for governor still has influence in deciding who the state party chair will be.

At the state level, the functions of the party chair and the executive committee are very similar to those of the county chair and county executive committee. They have similar informal duties of organizing the party and formal duties of conducting primary elections. Both parties in Texas have permanent, full-time, paid professional staffs that do most of the work at the state level. The state chair and executive committee are policy-making positions. One of their main functions is to provide leadership for the party.

Temporary Party Organization

The **temporary party organization**, for both parties, consists of a series of conventions (caucuses) held in even-numbered years. The precinct convention is held on the same day as the party primary, usually the second Tuesday in March. Any voter who has voted in that party's primary is eligible to attend the precinct convention. The polls usually close at 7:00 P.M., and the precinct convention begins shortly thereafter, typically at 7:30 to 7:45 P.M. The precinct chair acts as temporary chair of the convention, checking to see that attendees have voted in that party's primary election, calling the meeting to order, and directing the election of permanent officers. Sometimes, especially during presidential-election years, control of the convention's officers becomes an issue. In non-presidential-election years, attendance is usually very low, and control of the convention is generally not an issue.

> **temporary party organization**
> Series of meetings or conventions that occur every two years at the precinct, county, and state levels

After officers are elected, the most important function of the convention is the selection of delegates to the county convention (or the district convention, in large metropolitan counties). This convention is held two weeks after the precinct convention. The number of delegates a precinct sends to the county convention is based on party support in the precinct; the higher the party support, the larger the number of delegates. For years, Democrats have awarded one county convention seat for every 25 votes cast for the party's candidate for governor in the past election. During presidential election years, many people are interested in attending the county convention, and the seats can be hotly contested. In odd years, finding enough volunteers to attend the county convention is often difficult. Precinct conventions may also adopt resolutions in hopes of having them included in the party platform.

The county convention (or district convention) is a replay of the precinct convention. Selection of delegates to the state convention is its most important function. Again, the number of delegates a county sends to the state convention depends on the county's support for the party's gubernatorial candidate in the previous election.

Democratic Party Convention in 2008

In most election years, few people attend the precinct conventions. In 2008, the situation was quite different. Hillary Clinton and Barack Obama were in a very tight race for delegates. The precinct conventions were attended by thousands of people statewide. Most caucus chairs were overwhelmed by the crowds of participants. Sign-in sheets, used to show candidate support, were in short supply. In a few cases, campaign signs were used to register attendees.

News reports described the meetings as attended by rowdy mobs. Often the size of the rooms was inadequate to hold the large crowds. In a few cases, police were called in. Many meetings lasted until late in the evening. Most attendees had never attended a precinct meeting before and were unaware of why they were there and what the meeting would accomplish. The news reports had described the activity as a chance to vote twice, and many showed up thinking they were going to vote again.

Democratic presidential candidates Barack Obama and Hillary Clinton debate before the Texas primary in March 2008. The Texas primary was widely anticipated and closely watched, with Clinton winning the popular vote, yet Obama winning the majority of the state's precinct convention delegates.

presidential preference primary

Elections held every four years by political parties to determine the preferences of voters for presidential candidates

The county and district conventions held two weeks after the precinct meetings were equally well attended, and some were almost as disorganized as the precinct conventions. Many attendees were first-timers and did not know the rules. Some were suspicious that those running the convention were somehow not playing fairly. Often these meetings ran from noon to late in the evening. Many attendees left the meeting before it ended. Some suggested that the whole process proved the old saying by Will Rogers, "I am not a member of any organized political party. I am a Democrat."

The state convention is normally held in June of even-numbered years. Generally, the convention is held in a major city. At the state convention during presidential election years, the most important event is the selection of delegates to the national convention that nominates the party's candidate for president. In presidential election years, Texas has used a **presidential preference primary**, held in March. The primary decides the presidential preference of most, but not all, of the delegates from Texas at the national conventions. Without presidential preference primary elections, all delegate preferences would be decided at the state convention.

In addition to the state party officers chosen at these conventions, during presidential election years the conventions also elect the representatives (electors) who will serve in the Electoral College if their party candidate wins the popular vote in Texas. By tradition, Texas Democratic delegates caucus by senatorial districts at the state convention and choose their elector. Republicans caucus by U.S. congressional districts. These decisions are ratified by the conventions as a whole. Those chosen to serve in the Electoral College are generally longtime party supporters. The electors of the party winning the popular vote meet in Austin, in the senate chamber, at 2 P.M. on the first Monday after the second Wednesday in December following the election and cast their vote.[48]

Both parties hold national conventions every four years. These conventions attract national media attention and are usually covered from gavel to gavel. They are perhaps the best-known American party institution. Although the main purpose of these conventions is to nominate a candidate for president, they also elect the Democratic or Republican national executive committee. This body acts as a policy-making group for the national party, as the state executive committee does for the state. Service is considered a great honor, usually reserved for the longtime party faithful.

Caucus and Primary Delegate Selection Systems

As described previously, Texas has used a primary system to determine most of the state delegates to the national convention for presidential elections. In states without presidential preference primaries, such as Iowa, precinct conventions (also called caucuses) take on greater significance. Delegates selected at the precinct level go to the county level and, eventually, to the state and national conventions. A well-organized group can take control of these caucuses. In 2008, Arkansas Governor Mike Huckabee used his organization and worked with local churches to win more delegates than any other candidate in the Iowa caucuses. Churches are used as a rallying point before the evening caucus. Potluck dinners, child-care services, and church buses that help deliver voters to precinct conventions produce a turnout that exceeds the candidate's actual support among the voting population.

Thus, a caucus system can be an effective way to win delegates to conventions. However, it requires an organization of active volunteers to produce results. Win enough delegates to enough precinct conventions, and you can take over the county. Win enough counties, and you control the state. Control the state, and you select the delegates to the national convention. Control enough states, and you might win the nomination for president.

If Texas were to change from the current system to using caucuses exclusively, different campaign organization and strategies would be required. Preference primaries are mass media events that require big money and professional organizations. Caucus systems require grassroots organizations and dedicated volunteers. This again shows how important electoral rules are in impacting political behavior and outcomes. In Texas Republican state conventions since 1996, some Christian organizations have called for an end to preference primaries and a shift to a caucus system of selecting delegates to the national convention. Obviously, the caucus system is in their best interest and would allow them to control most of the delegates to the national convention. If the Texas caucus were held early enough in the election process, it might affect the direction of the Republican presidential race, or at least give the winner some early exposure.

Conclusion

In the past, the state executive committees of both parties were likely to be part-time organizations with limited staff. Today, both parties have permanent headquarters, full-time paid professional staffs, and financial resources to help party development. They are actively engaged in organizing and building the party through voter identification and registration, candidate recruitment, candidate education, get-out-the-vote drives, and supporting candidates during the general election.

The average citizen has little awareness of party organization at the state and local levels. Control of this element of American politics is left to the few active elite of the party; however, it is not very difficult to become part of this group. Any citizen with a little time can become active in precinct, county, and state party activities. Most of these are not paid positions. Individuals must be willing to contribute their time and money to serving the party.

Although Texas remains today a solid Republican state, both major parties are well established, and although political parties are not nearly as strong today as they were in the past, they still play a vital role in our democracy.

Key Terms

county chair
county executive committee
party de-alignment
party ideology
permanent party organization

political parties
precinct chair
presidential preference primary
Raza Unida
state executive committee

state party chair
straight ticket voting
temporary party organization

Notes

[1] Theodore J. Lowi, Benjamin Ginsberg, Kenneth A. Shepsle, and Stephen Ansolabehere, *American Government: Power and Purpose,* brief 12th ed. (New York: W.W. Norton Company, 2012), 354.

[2] V. O. Key Jr., *Politics and Pressure Groups,* 4th ed. (New York: Thomas Y. Crowell, 1958), 331.

[3] T. R. Fehrenbach. *Lone Star: A History of Texas and the Texans* (New York: American Legacy Press, 1968), pp. 279, 275–278.

[4] Dale Baum, "Chicanery and Intimidation in the 1869 Gubernatorial Race," *Southwestern Historical Quarterly* 97 (April 1994), 34–54.

[5] V. O. Key Jr., *Southern Politics in State and Nation* (New York: Knopf, 1949), 7.

[6] Texas State Historical Association, "Greenback Party," http://www.tshaonline.org/handbook/online/articles/wag01.

[7] Robert A. Calvert, Arnoldo De León, and Gregg Cantrell, *History of Texas* (Wheeling, Ill.: Harlan Davidson, 2002), 201–207.

[8] Jack M. Balkin, "Populism and Progressivism as Constitutional Categories—Part II," *Yale Law Journal* (1995).

[9] Donna A. Barnes, "People's Party," Handbook of Texas Online, http://www.tshaonline.org/handbook/online/articles/wap01.

[10] Ibid.

[11] Paul Johnson, *A History of the American People* (New York: Harper Collins, 1997), 599.

[12] Jack M. Balkin, "Populism and Progressivism as Constitutional Categories—Part II," *Yale Law Journal* (1995), http://www.yale.edu/lawweb/jbalkin/articles/popprog2.htm.

[13] John Halpin and Conor P. Williams, *The Progressive Intellectual Tradition in America,* Center for American Progress (April 2010), http://americanprogress.org/issues/progressive-movement/report/2010/04/14/7677/the-progressive-intellectual-tradition-in-america/.

[14] Lewis L. Gould, "Progressive Era," Handbook of Texas Online, http://www.tshaonline.org/handbook/online/articles/npp01; K. Austin Kerr, "Prohibition," Handbook of Texas Online, http://www.tshaonline.org/handbook/onlline/articles/vap01.

[15] V. O. Key Jr., *Southern Politics in State and Nation,* 225.

[16] James R. Soukup, Clifton McCleskey, and Harry Holloway, *Party and Factional Division in Texas* (Austin: University of Texas Press, 1971), 8.

[17] Douglas O. Weeks, *Texas Presidential Politics in 1952* (Austin: University of Texas, Institute of Public Affairs, 1953), 3–4.

[18] The budget actually increased during this time period.

[19] David A. Stockman, *The Triumph of Politics: How the Reagan Revolution Failed* (New York: Harper & Row, 1986).

[20] Manny Fernandez, "For Wendy Davis, Filibuster Goes Only So Far in Race to Be Governor of Texas," *New York Times,* June 28, 2014, http://www.nytimes.com/2014/06/29/us/for-davis-filibuster-goes-only-so-far-in-race-to-be-governor-of-texas.html.

[21] Robert Draper, "The Life and Death (and Life?) of the Party," *Texas Monthly,* August 2013, http://www.texasmonthly.com/story/life-and-death-and-life-party?fullpage=1.

[22] Manny Fernandez, "For Wendy Davis, Filibuster Goes Only So Far in Race to Be Governor of Texas," *New York Times,* June 28, 2014, http://www.nytimes.com/2014/06/29/us/for-davis-filibuster-goes-only-so-far-in-race-to-be-governor-of-texas.html.

[23] Nate Cohn, "These Eight Charts Explain Why 'Blue Texas' Won't Happen," *New Republic,* August 11, 2013, http://www.newrepublic.com/article/114145/blue-texas-eight-charts-show-why-it-wont-happen.

[24] Alexander Burns, "Democrats Launch Plan to Turn Texas blue," *Politico,* http://www.politico.com/story/2013/01/democrats-launch-plan-to-turn-texas-blue-86651_Page2.html.

[25] Tim Wigmore, "The Republicans' Worst Nightmare: Losing Texas and Becoming Extinct. Could It Really

Happen?" *The Telegraph,* May 23, 2013, http://blogs. telegraph.co.uk/news/timwigmore/100218460/ the-republicans-worst-nighmare-losing-texas-and-becoming-extinct-could-it-really-happen/.

[26] Erica Grieder, "The Revolt Against Crony Capitalism," *Texas Monthly,* February 18, 2014, http://www.texasmonthly.com/story/ revolt-against-crony-capitalism?fullpage=1.

[27] Ibid.

[28] Wayne Slater, "Texas GOP Splits between Social Conservatives, Libertarians," *Dallas Morning News,* June 7, 2014, http://www.dallasnews.com/news/ politics/headlines/20140607-texas-gop-splits-between-social-conservatives-libertarians.ece.

[29] Frank S. Meyer, *In Defense of Freedom,* (Indianapolis: Liberty Fund, 1996).

[30] James A. Dyer, Arnold Vedlitz, and David B. Hill, "New Voters, Switchers, and Political Party Realignment in Texas," *Western Political Quarterly, 41:*156, March 1988.

[31] Earl Survey Research Laboratory, Texas Tech University, Spring 2009, http://www.orgs.ttu.edu/ earlsurveyresearchlab/data.php.

[32] Gallup, "State of the States," http://www.gallup.com/ poll/125066/State-States.aspx) This is consistent with 2012 polling conducted by the University of Texas and the *Texas Tribune,* which found the state split about evenly in terms of identification with the two major parties.

[33] University of Texas at Austin, Texas Politics, Texas Party Identification and Ideology (October 2012), http://www.laits.utexas.edu/txp_media/html/poll/ features/201210_partyid/slide1.html).

[34] For example, see Bruce E. Keith, David B. Magleby, Candice J. Nelson, Elizabeth A. Orr, Mark C. Westlye, and Raymond E. Wolfinger, *The Myth of the Independent Voter* (Berkeley: University of California Press, 1992); Alan I. Abramowitz, "The Myth of the Independent Voter Revisited," *Sabato's Crystal Ball,* August 20, 2009, http://www.centerforpolitics.org/crystalball/articles/ aia2009082001/); and Amy Walter, "The Myth of the Independent Voter," *Cook Political Report,* January 15, 2014, http://cookpolitical.com/story/6608).

[35] The University of Texas at Austin, Texas Politics, Changes in Technology, http://texaspolitics.laits. utexas.edu/5_4_3.html).

[36] Stanford University, "The Digital Divide," http://cs.stanford.edu/people/eroberts/ cs201/projects/digital-divide/start.html; Jim Jansen, "Use of the Internet in Higher-Income Households," Pew Research Center, http://www.pewinternet.org/2010/11/24/ use-of-the-internet-in-higher-income-households/).

[37] Jamie L. Carson and Jason M. Roberts, "The Politics of Congressional Elections Across Time: Adoption of the Australian Ballot and the Direct Primary," https:// www.princeton.edu/csdp/events/Congress/ CarsonRobertsHoC.pdf).

[38] The White House, "James Garfield," http://www. whitehouse.gov/about/presidents/jamesgarfield).

[39] Carolyn Feibel, "A Guide to Texas' Electoral Two-step," Houston Chronicle, March 1, 2008, http://www. chron.com/news/politics/article/A-guide-to-Texas-electoral-two-step-1653159.php).

[40] Pendleton Act (1883), http://www.ourdocuments.gov/ doc.php?doc=48.

[41] James E. Anderson, Richard W. Murray, and Edward L. Farley, *Texas Politics: An Introduction* (New York: Harper & Row, 1989), 70.

[42] Libertarian Party of Texas, https://www.lptexas.org/).

[43] Ross Ramsey, "Analysis: Democrats Found Candidates, if Not Voters," *Texas Tribune,* June 4, 2014, http://www.texastribune.org/2014/06/04/ analysis-democrats-found-candidates-if-not-voters/).

[44] Texas Secretary of State, 1992 – Current Election History, http://elections.sos.state.tx.us/elchist.exe.

[45] Libertarian Party, Elected Officials, http://www.lp.org/ candidates/elected-officials; Libertarian Party, 2014 Candidates, https://lptexas.org/candidates).

[46] Natural Law Party, Main Issues, http://www.natural-law.org/platform/index.html).

[47] Green Party of Texas, Green Party of Texas State Platform, http://web.txgreens.org/platform).

[48] Benton, *Texas Politics,* 80–81.

CHAPTER 10

Interest Groups and Lobbying in Texas

*Upon completing this chapter,
you will be able to...*

- **Evaluate the role of interest groups in Texas.**

Chapter 7 discussed various forms of participation in the political process. Being an active member of an interest group is yet another form of political participation and a way to exert influence on the government. Chapter 7 also demonstrated that voter participation in Texas is relatively low. This lack of citizen involvement in elections leads to a corresponding increase in the importance and influence of interest groups in Texas politics. Indeed, it is frequently not the individual, or even the more broadly defined "public opinion," that influences government, but rather these interest groups that have the ear of public officials. However, interest groups are not necessarily "others" but are often "us" as we act in concert with like-minded or similarly interested citizens.

An **interest group** is an organization of individuals sharing common goals that tries to influence governmental decisions. This term is often used interchangeably with the term "lobby group," although lobbying is a specific activity or technique (discussed later) whereby interest groups attempt to influence legislation. Sometimes the term **political action committee (PAC)** is also used to refer to interest groups. PACs are organizations that collect and distribute money to candidates and, as such, are a more specialized kind of interest group. Often, broad-based interest groups have PACs associated with them.

Interest groups play an important role in a democratic society. They are capable of exerting both positive and negative effects on political processes and outcomes. Public attention is often drawn to the negative influences; however, interest groups and their activities are protected by the First Amendment to the U.S. Constitution, which provides for the people's right "peaceably to assemble, and to petition the Government for a redress of grievances."

Early observers of American politics realized the importance of these political associations. In 1787, James Madison, writing under the name Publius in *Federalist No. 10,* predicted that interest groups or factions would play a significant role in American politics. Madison believed that the diversity of economic and social interests in an "extended republic" would be so great, and so many factions would form, that no one group would be able to dominate. Madison's observation regarding

interest group
An organization of individuals sharing common goals that tries to influence governmental decisions

political action committee (PAC)
Spin-offs of interest groups that collect money for campaign contributions and other activity

James Madison, c. 1821

membership organizations
Interest groups that have individual citizens or businesses as members, such as the National Rifle Association

nonmembership organizations
Interest groups that represent corporations and businesses and do not have broad-based citizen support

government organizations
Interest groups that represent state and local governments; also called SLIGs, for state and local interest groups

the diversity of national interests applies to most individual states as well—especially large and populous states such as Texas. Alexis de Tocqueville, writing in 1835, commented on the formation of interest groups in American politics and their importance in increasing individual influence.[1] De Tocqueville's observation to some degree confirmed Madison's predictions.

Interest Group Typology

Considering the great diversity of economic and social interests in the country and the state, it would not surprise Madison that a vast array of interest groups exists throughout the United States and in Texas. Interest groups may be formed for any reason and may represent any interest. Many of these groups have both national and state organizations. The National Rifle Association (NRA), the U.S. Chamber of Commerce, Mothers Against Drunk Driving (MADD), and the National Education Association (NEA) are all examples of groups that are active on both the national and state levels.

The diversity of interest groups applies not just to the range of topics they address, but also to their form of organization and other characteristics. For instance, some groups are permanent organizations with full-time, well-financed professional staffs; others are temporary organizations that fade out of existence after their issue is resolved. Groups advocating property tax reform, insurance reform, and amendments to state constitutions are examples of such temporary groups. Groups can represent a single person, a large number of people, a private company, an entire industry, or even government employees and officials.

There are three broad categories of interest groups (see Table 10.1.) **Membership organizations** are private groups whose members are individual citizens or businesses. **Nonmembership organizations** represent individuals, single corporations, businesses, law firms, or freelance lobbies; they do not have broad-based citizen support. **Government organizations** represent local government (city, county, school board, special districts) as well as state and federal agencies. Membership in these organizations ranges from local elected officials (such as mayors and council members) to government employees (police officers, firefighters, and federal and state employees).[2] This type of group is also called a state and local interest group, or SLIG, and will be discussed later in the chapter.

Membership Organizations

Membership organizations within the state are devoted to a wide range of both economic and noneconomic interests. Peak business associations are interest groups that represent statewide business interests. These groups primarily try to promote their members' interests. They also present a united front against policies that do not promote a "good business climate" in the state. Examples include the state Chamber of Commerce, the Texas Association of Manufacturers, and the National Federation of Independent Business Owners. Such groups are often most active at the state level and are generally well financed.

Trade associations differ from peak business associations in that they represent more specific business interests. Texas has many such groups. Two trade associations often considered among the more powerful are the Mid-Continent Oil and Gas Association, representing oil and gas producers, and the Good Roads Association, which represents highway contractors.

trade associations
Interest groups that represent more specific business interests

TABLE 10.1

Interest Group Typology

Type	Examples
Membership Organizations	
Business/Agriculture	
Peak business organizations	State Chamber of Commerce
	State Federation of Businesses
Trade associations	Oil and Gas Producers Association
	Good Roads Association
Agricultural trade groups	Commodity groups
	Texas Farm Bureau
Retail trade associations	Texas Apartment Association
	Texas Automobile Dealers Association
Professional Associations	
Private sector organizations	Texas Medical Association
	Texas Trial Lawyers Association
Public sector organizations	Texas State Teachers Association
	Association of Texas Professional Educators
Organized Labor Unions	Texas AFL-CIO
Noneconomic Membership Organizations	
Racial and ethnic groups	NAACP
	League of United Latin American Citizens
Religious groups	Christian Coalition
	Interfaith Alliance
Public interest groups	MADD
	American Civil Liberties Union
	AARP
	MoveOn.org
Nonmembership Organizations	
Representing individuals or single businesses	Halliburton Industries
	Bank of America
	El Chico Corporation
Government Organizations	
State and local interest groups (SLIGs)	Texas Municipal League
	Texas Association of Police Chiefs

Source: Charles Wiggins, professor emeritus of political science at Texas A&M University, class handout, 1999.

CORE OBJECTIVE

Thinking Critically...

Review Table 10.1. Are you a participant in a membership organization? If so, how does the organization represent your interests? If not, how are your interests represented at the state and federal levels of government?

Given the importance of agriculture to the Texas economy, it is not surprising that there are multiple types of agricultural interest groups. First are those that represent general farm interests. The Texas Farm Bureau represents large agricultural producers in the state, whereas the Texas Farmers Union represents family farms and ranches. Second are organizations that represent commodity groups, such as cotton growers, cattle raisers, chicken raisers, and mohair producers. The third type of agricultural interest group represents suppliers to the above-mentioned producers. These groups include, for example, cotton ginners, seed and fertilizer producers, and manufacturers and sellers of farm equipment.

retail trade associations
Organizations seeking to protect and promote the interests of member businesses involved in the sales of goods and services

Retail trade associations are another type of trade group. The primary goal of these groups is to protect their trades from state regulations that the groups deem undesirable and to support regulation favorable to the groups' interests (what some would consider "rent seeking" behavior, as we discuss later in the chapter). Examples of retail trade groups are the Texas Apartment Association, the Texas Automobile Dealers Association, the Texas Restaurant Association, and the Association of Licensed Beverage Distributors.

professional associations
Organizations promoting the interests of individuals who generally must hold a state-issued license to engage in their profession

Professional associations differ from trade associations in two ways: (1) members typically hold a professional license issued by the state, and (2) the state regulates their scope of practice. These groups represent professionals such as physicians (the Texas Medical Association) and attorneys (the Texas Trial Lawyers Association). In addition, other organizations represent the interests of architects, landscape architects, engineers, surveyors, plumbers, accountants, librarians, barbers, hairdressers, cosmetologists, funeral directors, dentists, nurses, chiropractors, optometrists, pharmacists, podiatrists, clinical psychologists, veterinarians, and many other professions.

Although medical, legal, and other aforementioned professions generally fall under the private sector, public school educators (who, ultimately, are government employees) are part of the public sector. There are multiple interest groups related to education. One such group (which is also the largest professional group in the state) is the Texas State Teachers Association (TSTA). Affiliated with the National Education Association, TSTA is well organized and generally considered to be politically liberal. The group's cohesiveness varies; TSTA members sometimes present a united front, but at other times have been known to fight among themselves. The Association of Texas Professional Educators (ATPE) is a more conservative organization representing some teachers in the state. It was formed to counter the TSTA and has strong associations with the Texas Republican Party.

The Texas High School Coaches Association (THSCA) is an example of a specialized "educational" association. In a state where football is a Friday night tradition, this organization has some political clout. In 1984, Texas enacted the "no-pass/no-play" law, requiring students to pass their classes or be barred from participating in athletic and other extracurricular events.[3] The THSCA formed a PAC to combat this rule, earning them the moniker "Flunk-PAC."[4]

In other states, groups representing state and local employees are classified as public-sector labor unions. However, Texas does not give public employees the right to bargain collectively. **Collective bargaining** is a process of negotiation "between an employer and a group of employees so as to determine the conditions of employment."[5] If collective bargaining existed in Texas, organizations representing government workers would be able to force the government to enter into such negotiations and reach an agreement. Because Texas lacks collective bargaining, public-sector employee organizations are merely professional associations rather than labor unions.

collective bargaining
Negotiations between an employer and a group of employees to determine employment conditions, such as those related to wages, working hours, and safety

In many industrialized states, organized labor unions have traditionally been important and powerful interest groups, although their influence has declined in recent years. In Texas, private sector labor unions do exist; however, they are not powerful and represent only a small fraction of workers. Except in a few counties on the Texas Gulf Coast, where organized labor represents petrochemical workers and longshoremen, organized labor in Texas is very weak. According to the Bureau of Labor Statistics, 4.8 percent of wage and salaried employees in Texas belonged to labor unions in 2013.[6] As in most of the South, strong antiunion feelings are very much a part of the traditionalistic/individualistic political culture.

Texas is one of 24 states with **right-to-work laws**.[7] According to these laws, "a person cannot be denied employment because of membership or nonmembership in a labor union or other labor organization."[8] Among other things, these laws prohibit union shops where all workers are required to join the union within 90 days of beginning employment as a condition of keeping their jobs (see Map 10.1). Compare this map with the political culture map in Chapter 1.

As previously stated, interest groups are not limited to focusing on economic interests; they can address social issues as well. One type of noneconomic organization relates to the special interests of minorities or ethnic groups. These groups are primarily concerned with advancing civil rights, ending discrimination, improving government services, and gaining economic and political equality for those they represent. The two most active ethnic groups in the state of Texas are Hispanics and African Americans. Hispanics are represented by a variety of groups that are sometimes at odds with each other. The **League of United Latin American Citizens (LULAC)** is the largest such group in the state. Other organizations include Mexican American Democrats (MAD), the Mexican American Legal Defense and Education Fund (MALDEF), and the Political Association of Spanish-Speaking Organizations (PASSO). The National Association for the Advancement

right-to-work laws
Legislation stipulating that a person cannot be denied employment because of membership or nonmembership in a labor union or other labor organization

League of United Latin American Citizens (LULAC)
Largest organization representing Latinos in Texas

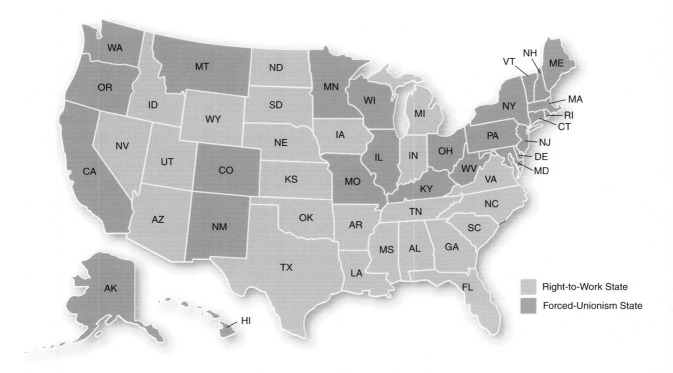

MAP 10.1   States with Right-to-Work or Antiunion Laws

of Colored People (NAACP) and the Congress of Racial Equality (CORE) represent African Americans in Texas and throughout the United States.

Another type of social interest group is religious groups. These groups have a long history in Texas. In the nineteenth century, fundamentalist Protestants in Texas, believing alcohol consumption to be immoral, supported the nationwide temperance movement to prohibit the production and sale of alcohol.[9] These religious groups advocated the passage of local option laws, allowing communities to vote on whether alcohol sales would be legal in their area. These local option elections persist to this day, and 11 Texas counties are currently completely "dry," not permitting alcoholic beverage sales anywhere in the county.[10]

In recent years, too, fundamentalist Christian groups have been quite visible on the national stage as well as in Texas. Organizations such as the Christian Coalition attempt to promote antiabortion campaigns, abstinence-based sex education, home schooling, a school voucher system, and prayer in schools, among other issues. These groups have had some success at using government to promote their agenda. The Texas State Board of Education, which oversees some aspects of school policy statewide, including textbook selection and curriculum, is composed of 15 elected members. Within the past decade, Christian fundamentalists were thought to control a majority of seats on the board. In fact, in 2009 and 2010, the board generated controversy by approving changes to the science and social studies curricula consistent with more conservative or religious views. However, by 2011, the number of "conservative Christians" on the board had declined to six.[11] Fundamentalist groups are also active within the state Republican Party.

Over the past several decades, the Catholic Church has become active in Texas state politics. This activity, primarily among Hispanic Catholics, is motivated by concerns about economic advancement, local services, and abortion. In San Antonio, the Catholic Church was a driving force behind the creation of Communities Organized for Public Service (COPS). This organization successfully challenged the Good Government League, which had dominated city elections for decades.[12] In the Rio Grande Valley, the Catholic Church was a driving force in the formation of the Interfaith Alliance. In the El Paso area, the Interreligious Sponsoring Organization was created to advance Hispanic interests. In the summer of 2012, the Catholic Church sued the federal government over the Affordable Care Act (also called "ObamaCare"), alleging the new health care law violates religious freedom by mandating coverage of contraceptives and other drugs.[13] Several dioceses in Texas were among those filing suit.

Public interest groups represent causes or ideas rather than economic, professional, or governmental interests. Many of these Texas organizations have national counterparts—for instance, Mothers Against Drunk Driving (MADD), the National Organization for Women (NOW), the National Right to Life Committee, the Sierra Club, the American Civil Liberties Union (ACLU), the Institute for Justice (IJ), Common Cause, the League of Women Voters, and Public Citizen. These groups usually limit their support or opposition to a narrow range of issues.

Demonstrators gather outside the Capitol building to protest the passage of President Barack Obama's health care reform bill. With the Democratic Party in control after the 2008 election, conservatives became more outspoken in exercising their right to protest.

Nonmembership Organizations

Nonmembership organizations (which do not have active members but rather represent a single company, organization, corporation, or individual) form the largest category of interest groups. Even a cursory glance at the list of organizations registered with the Texas Ethics Commission in Austin reveals hundreds of these groups. For example, Chili's Grill and Bar in Dallas, El Chico Corporation, and H. Ross Perot are all registered as interest groups with the Ethics Commission. Many law firms, including Locke Lord, also can act as "hired guns" available to represent a variety of interests in the state.

Government Organizations

In this typology, government organizations are considered separately from membership groups, even though some government organizations have active members. The members of these **state and local interest groups (SLIGs)** are government employees and officials; however, the interest groups represent the organization, not the interests of individual members.

The goal of these groups is to protect local government interests from actions of the state legislature, the governor, and state agencies. Examples include the Texas Municipal League, the Texas Association of Police Chiefs, the Combined Law Enforcement Association of Texas, the Texas Association of Fire Fighters, the City Attorneys Association, the Texas Association of County Officials, and the Texas School Board Association.

Techniques Used by Interest Groups

Member of the ACLU

state and local interest groups (SLIGs)
Interest groups that represent state and local governments, such as the Texas Association of Counties

lobbying
The practice of attempting to influence the legislature, originally by catching members in the lobby of the capitol

For interest groups to accomplish their goals, they must have an influence on government and public policy decisions. How do they exert this influence? Interest groups use a variety of techniques to further their agendas; the type of technique employed depends on the type of group and the resources available to that group.

Lobbying

Perhaps the best known and most common technique used by interest groups is **lobbying** the state legislature. Lobbying is the practice of trying to influence members of the legislature. The term "lobbying" originated from the fact that commonly, in the past, legislators did not have their own private offices; their workspace was a desk on the floor of the house or senate chamber. Because access to the chamber floor was limited to members of the legislature, those wanting to speak with legislators had to catch them in the lobby of the capitol building. Thus, the term "lobbying" grew out of this practice of waiting in the lobby of the legislative chamber.

Today, lobbying involves much more than this ambush-style meeting. The following activities, all aimed at convincing legislators to promote an interest group's agenda, are included in lobbying efforts:

- Contacting members of the legislature before the session begins
- Convincing members of the legislature to file a bill favorable to the group
- Testifying before a committee, informing legislators of the effect a bill will have on their district
- Keeping group members informed about legislative activities
- Asking members of the group to contact legislators (email or phone campaigns)
- Issuing press releases and buying newspaper and television ads
- Presenting written material to members of the legislature[14]

This last activity serves a particularly important function in Texas politics. Interest groups often provide research findings to members of the legislature and their staffs. This information can obviously be self-serving, but it is often accurate and can be an important resource for state legislators. An interest group that produces good, high-quality research and information can have a positive impact on public policy. Over the years, several business-sponsored groups in Texas have developed a reputation for providing quality research and information to the Texas legislature. A Texas lobbyist recently confided to one of this book's authors just how important such a reputation is and how well it must be guarded. This desire to maintain integrity acts as a much-needed self-check on lobbyists' behavior.

Lobbying efforts take place throughout the year, although there are periods of particularly intense activity. Because the Texas legislature meets every two years for 140 days, most lobbying efforts are concentrated during the regular legislative session. However, lobbying does not stop when the legislature adjourns. All legislatures, including the one in Texas, perform some activities between regular sessions, and interest groups attempt to influence interim committees and other special activities of the legislature. Lobbyists also try to build knowledge and political capital between sessions. As two Texas lobbyists, Jim Grace and Luke Ledbetter, recently noted in the *Houston Lawyer*, "The session is simply too busy to build long-standing relationships while it is in progress. Only through continued hard work in the interim can you understand the personalities of the members, the unique needs of the constituents in their districts, and the issues about which they are passionate."[15] Moreover, most legislation requires the governor's signature. Persuading the governor either to sign or to veto a bill is an important part of lobbying activity. See Table 10.2 for Grace and Ledbetter's advice to fellow lobbyists.

A good example of interest groups convincing the governor to veto a bill occurred during the 2009 session. Small retail merchants worked to pass a bill requiring online companies to collect sales taxes for their sales (thereby eliminating

---

TABLE 10.2

Grace and Ledbetter's Rules and Tricks of the Lobbying Trade

1. NEVER lie to a member of the legislature.
2. Preparation. Preparation. Preparation.
3. Know what you don't know and be willing to admit it.
4. There are some things you can't control.
5. Information is the currency of the realm.
6. "Only speak when it improves the silence."[16]
7. Don't write it down (and especially don't put it in an email) unless you are comfortable waking up and seeing it as the headline on the front page of the *Houston Chronicle*.
8. The "Reply to All" button is not your friend.
9. Be prepared to forge strange alliances.
10. Compromise when you can; hold firm when you must.
11. Never ask members for a vote you know they can't take back to the district.
12. Be ever-present at the Capitol during session.
13. Know the calendar rules better than anyone else.
14. Money will never buy you a vote.
15. Treat everyone with respect.
16. Legislation (like water) takes the path of least resistance: do everything possible to make a staffer's life easier.
17. And finally, remember that "[n]o man's life, liberty, or property are safe while the legislature is in session."[17]

Source: Jim Grace and Luke Ledbetter, "The Lobbyist," *Houston Lawyer* (September/October 2009), 10. Available online at http://www.thehoustonlawyer.com/aa_sep09/page10.htm.

an advantage online companies had over local "brick and mortar" stores). The governor vetoed the bill, leading to accusations that he was being influenced by the big online retailers, but he countered that he was against raising taxes. In 2012, the Texas comptroller reached an agreement with Amazon.com about collecting taxes for its online sales. This still leaves many small businesses at a disadvantage to online sales companies, but few consumers complain about the lower prices.

Once the governor signs a bill, an administrative agency will need to enforce the applicable law. Lobbying can also be directed toward administrative discretion in law enforcement. Interest groups expend great effort to influence how agencies interpret and enforce laws. If individuals friendly to the interest group are appointed to governing boards and commissions, enforcement of the law can be eased considerably.

Lobbyists can be classified into five types: (1) Contract lobbyists are hired to represent a client. Most represent more than one client. It is estimated that this group constitutes about 15 to 25 percent of all lobbyists. (2) In-house lobbyists are employees of businesses or associations and lobby as part of their job. They constitute 40 to 50 percent of all lobbyists. (3) Governmental lobbyists and legislative liaisons work for a governmental organization and lobby as part of their job. They might not be required to formally register as lobbyists. One estimate is that they constitute about 25 to 35 percent of all lobbyists. (4) Citizen or volunteer lobbyists are nonpaid volunteers representing citizen groups and organizations. A good example is volunteers for Mothers Against Drunk Driving (MADD). This type constitutes about 10 to 20 percent of all lobbyists. (5) Finally, there are private individuals, usually with a pet project or issue. Sometimes called "hobbyists," these individualists act on their own behalf and do not officially represent any organizations. They constitute less than 5 percent of all lobbyists.[18]

Lobbying is often looked down upon by people worried about special interests overwhelming the general interest. This is not a new sentiment, as evidenced by Supreme Court Justice Noah Swayne's remark in *Trist v. Child* (1874) about such "infamous" employment: "If any of the great corporations of the country were to hire adventurers who make market of themselves in this way, to procure the passage of a general law with a view to the promotion of their private interests, the moral sense of every right-minded man would instinctively denounce the employer and employed as steeped in corruption, and the employment as infamous."[19]

CORE OBJECTIVE

Taking Personal Responsibility...

Socrates suggested, "know thyself," and Shakespeare's Hamlet admonished "to thine own self be true." It is important to know what your interests are and how they are represented in government. Consider what you have read in this chapter and determine how interest group efforts align with your personal interests. If they do not, what can you do to ensure that government addresses your interests or the interests of those who share similar values?

Electioneering

In addition to lobbying political leaders, interest groups devote considerable time and effort trying to influence the outcome of elections. This type of activity is called **electioneering**. In pursuit of electioneering, an interest group's most important

electioneering
Various activities in which interest groups engage to try to influence the outcome of elections

resource is money, usually funneled to candidates through PACs. Some interest groups prefer to give money to other groups who, in turn, funnel the money to campaigns. At the national level, PACs are required to register with the Federal Election Commission at the time they are formed, and traditionally there have been limits on how much money PACs can receive and distribute in a single year or election cycle.[20] See Table 10.3 for the amount of money contributed by the major PACs in Texas during recent election cycles. Note that the total amount of money spent by general purpose PACs in the 2006 spending cycle was double the amount spent in 1998. During that period, PAC spending grew from $51 million to $99 million.[21] Table 10.4 shows PAC spending broken down by major interest category.

TABLE 10.3

PAC Spending from 1998 to 2012

Election Cycle	No. of Active PACs	PAC Spending	Spending Increase from Previous Cycle	Percent Spending Increase
1998	893	$ 51,543,820	$ 8,461,274	20%
2000	865	$ 53,996,975	$ 2,453,155	5%
2002	964	$ 85,320,226	$31,323,251	58%
2004	850	$ 68,904,524	($16,415,702)	(19%)
2006	1,132	$ 99,167,646	$30,263,122	44%
2008	1,209	$119,561,861	$20,394,215	21%
2010	1,302	$133,466,187	$13,904,326	12%
2012	1,364	$126,367,460	($ 7,098,727)	(5%)

Source: Texans for Public Justice, "Texas PACs: 2008 Cycle Spending," April 2009 (http://info.tpj.org/reports/txpac08/chapter1.html); Texans for Public Justice, "Texas PACs: 2010 Election Cycle Spending," August 2011 (http://info.tpj.org/reports/pdf/PACs2010.pdf); Texans for Public Justice, "Texas PACs: 2012 Election Cycle Spending," October 2013 (http://info.tpj.org/reports/pdf/PACs2012.pdf).

TABLE 10.4

PACs by Interest Category

Interest Category	No. of Active 2012 PACs	2012 PAC Spending	Share of 2012 Spending	'10-'12 Change
Agriculture	27	$ 2,381,509	2%	−10%
Communications/Electronics	23	$ 2,504,530	2%	−9%
Construction	96	$ 7,057,173	6%	−5%
Energy/Nat'l Resources/Waste	79	$ 11,889,587	9%	14%
Finance	37	$ 5,829,265	5%	6%
Health	75	$ 9,932,355	8%	5%
Ideological/Single Issue	597	$ 47,292,862	37%	−18%
Insurance	28	$ 3,685,814	3%	23%
Labor	153	$ 8,173,262	6%	16%
Lawyers & Lobbyists	53	$ 11,233,116	9%	0%
Miscellaneous Business	65	$ 4,094,964	3%	25%
Other/Unknown	57	$ 501,387	<1%	51%
Real Estate	41	$ 9,210,139	7%	−7%
Transportation	33	$ 2,581,497	2%	1%
TOTALS	1,364	$126,367,460	100%	−5%

For Public Justice, "*Texas PACs*: 2012 Election Cycle Spending," October 2013 (http://info.tpj.org/reports/pdf/PACs2012.pdf).

CORE OBJECTIVE

Communicating Effectively...

Review the data presented in Table 10.4. Identify the interest group category that spent the most money in 2012. Discuss the impact that PAC spending has on government.

For an in-depth look at money in state politics, go to the website www.followthemoney.org, where data are available on how much money is given in each of the 50 states. The organization behind these data is Money in State Politics. Compare Texas with other states.

Money may be the most important tool for interest groups trying to influence an election, but it is by no means the only tool. The process of electioneering begins with candidate recruitment. Interest groups work to recruit candidates for office many months before an election. They encourage individuals who will be sympathetic to their cause to seek nominations in party primaries. This encouragement takes the form of promises of support and money in both the primary and general elections. Some interest groups might encourage both Democratic and Republican candidates to seek nomination in their respective parties. This covers their bets. Regardless of which candidate wins, the interest group will likely have access and influence.

Some writers have observed that PAC money has undermined party loyalty and weakened political parties in this country. Candidates no longer owe their loyalty to the party that helped elect them but to interest groups that funded them.

What point does this cartoon make about the nature of 2008 political campaign contributions?

Political action committees buy access in "an intricate, symbiotic relationship involving trust, information exchange, pressure and obligations. The inescapable fact is that resources, and especially money, are at least three-fourths of the battle in building and maintaining good relations and in securing the other essential elements that lead to access and influence."[22]

There is little doubt that the power of money in state politics will continue to increase. This can involve running television and newspaper ads explaining the records of officials or the virtues of a nonincumbent, or working in voter registration drives and get-out-the-vote campaigns. Interest groups might also aid candidates by helping to write speeches and organize rallies and by staging political events such as fundraisers. Some groups keep track of legislators' voting records and circulate "good guy/bad guy score cards" to members of the organization, instructing members to vote for or against candidates.

Public Education and Public Relations: Grassroots Lobbying

Interest groups also attempt to influence public policy through public relations activities. The goal of these efforts is to create a favorable public image for the group. Obviously, much information disseminated in this fashion can be very self-serving and might even be called propaganda. Not all such information is wrong, but some filtering of the information by the public is necessary. Some interest groups might counter the information provided by a competing interest group. In a mass media society, characterized by constant public scrutiny, an interest group's credibility with the public can be compromised if the group provides inaccurate or misleading information.

Aside from efforts to present a favorable opinion of themselves to the public, interest groups also try to curry favor with public officials. Inviting public officials to address organizational meetings is one technique utilized to advance the group's standing in the eyes of these officials. Giving awards to officials at such gatherings, thanking them for their public service, is also a common technique.

Another note is warranted here regarding the attempts of interest groups to curry favor with public officials: Interest group tactics have changed in recent years. In the past, the process was described primarily as "booze, bribes, and broads." Although there is much less of that today, entertaining members of the legislature remains very much a part of the process. "As for making women 'available' to interested male lawmakers, a veteran lobbyist reported in 1981 that 'I got hit up for the first time this session by a member wanting me to get him a woman. I told him I have trouble enough getting my own dates.'"[23] Interest groups today are more likely to rely on the other tactics previously discussed.

Regulation of Interest Groups

Most states have laws regulating two activities in which interest groups engage: lobbying and making financial contributions to political campaigns (also known as "campaign finance"). In terms of lobbying regulations, organizations that have regular contact with legislators are generally required to register and file reports on their activities. Often these reporting requirements are weak, and the reports generated might not reflect the true activities of the organization.

Texas required registration of interest groups for the first time in 1907. The relevant statute prohibited "efforts to influence legislation 'by means other than appeal to reason' and provided that persons guilty of lobbying were subject to fines and imprisonment."[24] However, the statute was never enforced. In 1957, a new law was passed requiring lobbyists to register and disclose information about their activities; this law had many loopholes and was ineffective. In 1973, yet another law called for more stringent reporting. This act was amended in 1983.

According to Chapter 305 of the current Government Code, an individual "who crosses either a compensation or expenditure threshold" while engaged in lobbying efforts must register as a lobbyist with the **Texas Ethics Commission**. In other words, a person who receives more than $1,000 per quarter-year as pay for lobbying must register. Alternatively, persons must register if they spend more than $500 per quarter on gifts or other paid expenses for a state official or employee or the official's or employee's immediate family. The code stipulates that these activities must involve "direct communication" with a member of the executive or legislative branch, the goal of which is to influence legislation.[25] The official list of registered lobbyists for 2014 included 1,479 individuals.[26] Government employees who lobby in an official capacity (as part of their jobs) are exempt from registration, as are owners and employees of news media outlets.[27] Also, some lawyers do not register because they claim they are representing clients and are not lobbying. Thus, the total number of persons who actually lobby the legislature is much higher than reported.

Texas Ethics Commission
State agency responsible for enforcing requirements for interest groups and candidates for public office to report information on money collected and activities

Regarding campaign finance, most states require some formal registration of PACs. PACs must register with the Texas Ethics Commission, designate a treasurer, and file periodic reports. These reports must provide the full name and address of persons who donate more than $50 in total to a campaign.[28] PACs are also prohibited from making a contribution to members of the legislature during the period beginning 30 days before the start of a regular session and ending 20 days after the regular 140-day session. Although corporations and labor unions are prohibited from making campaign contributions, Texas law does not limit the amount individuals or PACs can contribute to candidates for statewide or legislative office.[29]

In 2010 the U.S. Supreme Court, in *Citizens United v. Federal Election Commission*, removed previous restrictions by the federal government on PACs' ability to spend money on election campaigns. The case stated that "political spending is a form of protected speech under the First Amendment."[30] Therefore, the government cannot prohibit corporations and unions from spending money, via PACS, on "electioneering communications," such as television ads for or against a particular candidate.[31] This ruling opened the door to a greatly expanded role for PACs in future elections. Since Texas law currently prohibits campaign contributions by unions and corporations, the Citizens United decision may lead to revision, repeal, or nonenforcement of the state's law (at least with regard to funding of advertising).[32]

The Texas Ethics Commission does not have the resources to be effective. It has never been adequately funded by the legislature and has a small staff. Although the reporting system for lobbyists has improved, it is still difficult to find and summarize information on interest group activities. The group Texans for Public Justice (TPJ.org) has organized the commission's data and issues regular reports. Their website makes much of this data more accessible.

The ethics of interest group activity varies from state to state, dictated by the political culture of each state. What is considered acceptable in a traditionalistic/

individualistic state such as Texas may be viewed as corrupt in a state with a moral-istic political culture. The late Molly Ivins, a well-known Texas newspaper writer and observer of Texas politics, once said that in the Texas legislature, "what passes for ethics is if you're bought, by God, you stay bought."[33] Despite Ms. Ivins's deprecating humor, her comment reflects the evolution of Texas lobbying activity over time.

Factors Influencing the Strength of Interest Groups

Interest groups have a variety of resources available to them. Their resource base depends on the type of group, the number of members in the group, and who those members are. For example, the Texas State Teachers Association (TSTA) has strength because it has so many members (hence voters). On the other hand, the Texas Municipal League (TML), which represents Texas city officials, has very little money and fewer members than the TSTA. However, the TML's member-ship includes influential public officials, such as mayors and council members. The TML has lists of representatives and senators keyed with local officials. The TML contacts local officials, asking them, in turn, to contact representatives and senators regarding legislation. Local elected officials can easily contact legislators, and those legislators will listen, even if they do not always agree.

It is important to note, though, that some groups have difficulty recruiting mem-bers (or money) to their cause due to the "free-rider problem." All interest groups provide benefits, and individuals may derive benefits from an interest group's efforts regardless of whether they participate in the group's activities. Thus, it is rational for some people not to contribute to or work on the group's behalf because they will still benefit.[34] This can lead to an underprovision of a collective good. The larger the group and the more diffuse the possible benefits, the greater the possibil-ity of the free-rider problem undermining the group's cause. On the other hand, smaller groups that seek more concentrated benefits are less likely to suffer from this problem.[35]

The status and size of an interest group are important determinants of power. Obviously, the presidents of large banks and corporations in Dallas, due to their status, can command the ear of most state senators and state represen-tatives from the Dallas area. Groups with many members can use their numbers to advantage by inciting a barrage of telephone calls and mes-sages to legislators regarding legislative actions.

The total number of interest groups representing a particular inter-est may not be an indication of strength. For example, in recent years the number of groups representing business interests has multiplied dramatically, whereas the number of groups representing the inter-ests of local government has grown very little. One might take this as a sign that business groups have grown in influence relative to governmental groups. However, numbers do not necessarily indi-cate increased influence. Instead they may indicate the increased diversity of economic interests in Texas over the past several decades. Except for special districts, the number of local governments has not changed in the past 40 years, which explains the more constant number of governmental inter-est groups. Factors other than sheer numbers, such as leadership, organization, geographic distribution of its membership, and money, determine the strength of

Dallas teachers protest against an extended school day. The Texas State Teachers Association, the largest professional group in Texas, represents teachers but lacks the right to collective bargaining under Texas law.

an interest group. Other authors point to additional factors (economic diversity, party strength, legislative professionalism, and government fragmentation) to help explain an interest group's power.[36]

Leadership and Organization

Leadership quality and organizational ability can be important factors in the power of interest groups. Many interest groups hire former legislators to help them. Some groups are decentralized, with a loose-knit membership, making mobilization difficult. Other groups, like the Texas Municipal League, are highly organized, monitor legislation being considered, and can easily contact selected members to influence bills while they are still in committee. Even before the legislative session begins, the TML has a legislative committee that recommends positions on legislation likely to be considered. At an annual meeting, the TML membership adopts stands on key items. This action gives the leadership a firm basis on which to act, and constant contact with all members is not necessary. Key members are contacted only when quick action is required.

Geographic Distribution

Some groups have more influence than others because they have members in all geographic areas of the state and therefore can command the attention of many more legislators. The Texas Municipal League, for example, has city officials in the district of every senator and representative. Texas bankers and lawyers are located throughout the state as well. Legislators might not listen to citizens from other areas of the state, but they certainly will listen to citizens from their own district. Legislators will also listen to local elected officials. Thus, having members that are geographically distributed across the state is a key advantage for interest groups. Obviously, some groups cannot have **geographic distribution**. For instance, commercial shrimp fishermen are limited to the Gulf Coast region of Texas.

geographic distribution
A characteristic of some interest groups in that they have members in all regions of the state

CORE OBJECTIVE

Being Socially Responsible...

How can geographic distribution of interest groups improve political awareness between culturally diverse populations?

Money

As one might guess, interest groups need money to fund their lobbying, electioneering, and public relations efforts. Money is also an important resource for other, less obvious reasons. Interest groups that can afford to hire full-time staff and travel to meet with legislators have more influence than those dependent on volunteers and part-time staff. As indicated earlier, some groups have no active members per se, but instead represent individuals, corporations, or businesses. With enough money, groups do not need dues-paying or contributing members

astroturf

A political term for an interest group that appears to have many grassroots members but in fact does not have individual citizens as members; rather, it is sponsored by an organization such as a corporation or business association

to have an impact on government policy. Some of these groups do a very good job of mobilizing nonmember citizens to their cause. For example, through the use of television ads, newspaper ads, and "talk radio," one such group, the Coalition for Health Insurance Choices (CHIC), managed to mobilize opposition to President Clinton's health care proposal. One writer has referred to such nonmembership groups, which lack a grassroots (spontaneous, community-based) organization, as "**astroturf** organizations."[37]

Economic Diversity

The economic diversity of a state can impact the strength of an interest group operating within that state. Highly industrialized states with a variety of industries generally have a multitude of interest groups. Because of the diversity and complexity of the state's economy, no single industry or group can dominate. The many interests cancel each other out, as Madison predicted they would in *Federalist No. 10*. In other states, a single or a few industries dominate the economy. For example, in Alaska, oil is still dominant. Coal mining dominates Wyoming's economy, providing much of the state's revenues. Copper mining was once the most prominent industry in Montana, and lumbering is still the primary industry in Oregon.

In the past, the Texas economy was dominated by a few industries: cotton, cattle, banking, and oil. Today, the Texas economy is more diversified, and the number of interest groups has grown accordingly. It is much more difficult for one or a few interests to dominate state politics. Nonetheless, the traditional industries still wield a lot of power.

Political Party Competition

The strength of political parties in the state can influence the strength of interest groups. States with two strong, competitive parties that recruit and support candidates for office can offset the influence of interest groups attempting to put their own candidates forward. Legislators in competitive party states might owe their election to, and therefore be more loyal to, their political party and be less influenced by interest groups. In Texas, a history of weak party structure has contributed to the power of interest groups.

Professionalism of the State Legislature

In Chapter 3, we defined a professional legislature as being characterized by higher legislative pay, longer sessions (such as no limits on the length of regular sessions), and more staff support.[38] In theory, well-paid legislators with professional staffs are less dependent upon information supplied by interest groups, and the information exchange between lobbyist and legislator is reduced. The Texas legislature has improved staff quality in recent years; most members have full-time staff in Austin and their local offices. In addition, committee staff has increased. The Texas legislature now provides more money than any other state for staff salaries. The Texas Legislative Council also provides excellent staff assistance in research and information. This increased level of support has led to a rise in legislative professionalism in Texas; whether this has resulted in a corresponding decrease in the power of interest groups remains to be seen. However, there are potential costs, too; it is not automatically better to have a professional legislature rather than a citizen legislature.

Fragmented Government Structure

As previously stated, interest groups expend much effort trying to influence the administration of state laws. The degree to which interest groups succeed in this endeavor depends on the structure of state government. If the government is centralized under a governor who appoints and removes most department heads, interest groups will find it necessary to lobby the governor directly and the agencies indirectly. Texas has a **fragmented government structure**. The governor of Texas makes few significant appointments of agency heads. Therefore, each interest group tries to gain access to and influence the state agency relevant to its cause. Often these agencies are created to regulate the industry that the interest group represents. For example, the Texas Railroad Commission, an agency originally created to regulate railroads, also oversees the state's oil industry. Historically, oil industry lobby groups have had great influence over the agency's three commissioners and their decisions.[39] In 1971, the Texas Almanac contained a full-page ad, paid for by the Texas Independent Producers and Royalty Owners Association and the American Association of Oil Well Drilling Contractors, thanking the Railroad Commission. The ad read: "Since 1891, The Texas Railroad Commission Has Served the Oil Industry." Following public outcry over the impropriety of a state regulatory agency "serving" a private industry, the revised ad in the 1974 edition of the Almanac read as follows: "Since 1891 The Texas Railroad Commission Has Served Our State."[40] In truth, similar relationships exist between many state agencies and interest groups.

The members of most state licensing boards (such as the Texas State Bar, Texas Medical Board, and State Board of Morticians) are professionals in those fields (and may also be members of a relevant interest group). These licensing boards were ostensibly created to "protect the public interest," but they often spend most of their time protecting the profession by limiting the number of persons who can be licensed and by creating rules favorable to the group.

For example, in Texas a person cannot be cremated until the deceased has been dead for 48 hours. However, if the person is not buried within 24 hours, the body must be embalmed or refrigerated.[41] Supposedly, the reason for embalming before cremation is to protect the public from the spread of diseases. Others have suggested the procedure is unnecessary and merely protects the profit margin of morticians doing the embalming. In this way, members of a profession or interest group can control rule making that affects the group, thereby influencing how much money members of the group can make. Another term for this type of practice is **rent seeking**. Rent seeking occurs when individuals or groups try to secure benefits for themselves through political means.[42] Rent-seeking behavior can lead to great costs to society, not only in the obvious senses but also because of the opportunity cost associated with people using scarce resources (time, energy, human capital, money, etc.) to capture political benefits rather than for "productive endeavors."[43]

When the relationship between a state agency and an interest group becomes very close, it is referred to as **capture**. In other words, the interest group has "captured" the agency. However, capture of the agency by the interest group is probably more the exception than the rule. Often, competing interest groups vie for influence with the agency and reduce the likelihood of capture by a single interest group. (The creation of the Public Utility Commission is a good example of this.)

In practice, policy is created through the combined efforts of interest groups, the state agency, and the legislative committee (with oversight of the agency). This process is called the "Iron Triangle." (See Figure 10.1)

fragmented government structure
A government structure where power is dispersed to many state agencies with little or no central control

rent seeking
The practice of trying to secure benefits for oneself or one's group through political means

capture
The situation in which a state agency or board falls under the heavy influence of or is controlled by its constituency interest groups

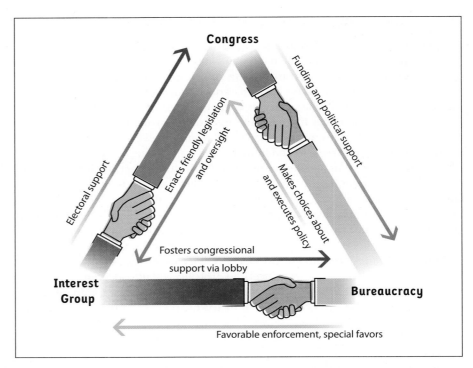

FIGURE 10.1   Often, a close relationship exists between the state agency created to regulate an industry, the legislative oversight committee, and interest groups. This relationship is sometimes called the "Iron Triangle."

Conclusion

Though often criticized (and sometimes rightly so), interest groups play a very important role in state politics. The First Amendment to the U.S. Constitution protects free speech and association, and interest groups are a necessary part of the political process. Efforts by government to control interest groups are, and should be, limited. Knowing the tactics these groups use to influence government helps us understand how politics operate.

There is little doubt that the influence of interest groups, especially PACs, will continue to grow in the years ahead—especially if the size, scope, and budget of government continue to expand, thereby offering greater enticement for getting a piece of the pie or capturing a regulatory agency. In some campaigns, PAC money has essentially replaced the political party as a nominating and electing agent.

The recent U.S. Supreme Court decision in *Citizens United v. Federal Election Commission,* by lifting a previous ban on direct PAC funding of certain types of political communication, has given PACs even more freedom to participate in election campaigns. In a mass-media age, little can be done to suppress the influence of interest groups.

Given the low levels of voter turnout and other forms of political participation in Texas, interest groups will likely continue to dominate state politics. The traditionalistic/individualistic political culture also supports such dominance. The present decentralized administrative structure in the state enhances the ability of interest groups to control state agencies. Because a reorganization of state agencies into a centrally controlled administration seems unlikely, this situation will persist for many years to come.

Key Terms

astroturf
capture
collective bargaining

electioneering
fragmented government
      structure

geographic distribution
government organizations
interest group

League of United Latin American
    Citizens (LULAC)
lobbying
membership organizations
nonmembership organizations

peak business organizations
political action committee (PAC)
professional associations
rent seeking
retail trade associations

right-to-work laws
state and local interest groups
    (SLIGs)
Texas Ethics Commission
trade associations

Notes

[1] Alexis de Tocqueville, *Democracy in America,* trans. George Lawrence, ed. J. P. Mayer (Garden City, N.J.: Anchor Books, 1969), 190–191.

[2] Adapted from a typology developed by Charles Wiggins, Professor of Political Science, Texas A&M University, College Station, 1999 (unpublished class handout).

[3] Texas State Library and Archives Commission, "Modern Texas." https://www.tsl.state.tx.us/governors/modern/page2.html&#White.

[4] "Flunk-PAC," *Washington Post,* National Weekly Edition, 30 December 1985, 22.

[5] Cornell University Law School Legal Information Institute, "Collective Bargaining," http://www.law.cornell.edu/wex/collective_bargaining.

[6] U.S. Department of Labor, Bureau of Labor Statistics, "Union Affiliation of Employed Wage and Salary Workers by State," 2013, http://www.bls.gov/news.release/union2.t05.htm.

[7] National Right to Work Legal Defense Foundation, Inc., "Right to Work States," 2014, http://www.nrtw.org/rtws.htm.

[8] Attorney General of Texas Greg Abbott, "Right-to-Work Laws in Texas," 2012, https://www.oag.state.tx.us/agency/righttowork.shtml.

[9] Texas State Historical Association, "Prohibition," 2012, http://www.tshaonline.org/handbook/online/articles/vap01.

[10] Texas Alcoholic Beverage Commission, "Wet and Dry Counties," 2014, http://www.tabc.state.tx.us/local_option_elections/wet_and_dry_counties.asp.

[11] Gail Collins, "How Texas Inflicts Bad Textbooks on Us," *The New York Review of Books* 21 (June 2012), http://www.nybooks.com/articles/archives/2012/jun/21/how-texas-inflicts-bad-textbooks-on-us/?pagination=false.

[12] Robert Lineberry, *Equity and Urban Policy: The Distribution of Urban Services* (Newbury Park, Calif.: Sage, 1977).

[13] Terry Baynes, "U.S. Catholic Groups Sue to Block Contraception Mandate," Reuters, 21 May 2012, http://www.reuters.com/article/2012/05/21/us-usa-healthcare-contraception-idUSBRE84K19R20120521.

[14] Adapted from Ronald Hrebenar, Melanee Cherry, and Kathanne Green, "Utah: Church and Corporate Power in the Nation's Most Conservative State," in *Interest Group Politics in the American West,* ed. Ronald Hrebnar and Clive S. Thomas (Salt Lake City: University of Utah Press, 1987), 117.

[15] Jim Grace and Luke Ledbetter, "The Lobbyist," *Houston Lawyer* (September/October 2009), 10. Available online at http://www.thehoustonlawyer.com/aa_sep09/page10.htm.

[16] Chris Mathews, *Hardball: How Politics Is Played Told by One Who Knows the Game* (Touchstone Press, 1988), 133.

[17] *Final Accounting in the Estate of A. B.,* 1 Tucker 248 (N.Y. Surr. 1866).

[18] Clive S. Thomas and Ronald J. Hrebenar, "Interest Groups in State Politics," in *Politics in the American States,* ed. Virginia Gray, Herbert Jacob, and Robert Albritton, 5th ed. (Glenview, Ill.: Scott Foresman/Little, Brown, 1990), 150–151.

[19] As cited in Luigi Zingales, *A Capitalism for the People: Recapturing the Lost Genius of American Prosperity* (New York: Basic Books, 2012), 183.

[20] Center for Responsive Politics, "What is a PAC?" https://www.opensecrets.org/pacs/pacfaq.php.

[21] Texans for Public Justice, "Texas PACs: 2008 and 2011 Cycle Spending," www.tpj.org/reports/txpacs02total.html.

[22] Clive S. Thomas and Ronald J. Hrebenar, "Interest Groups in State Politics," in *Politics in the American States,* ed. Virginia Gray, Herbert Jacob, and Robert Albritton, 5th ed. (Glenview, Ill.: Scott Foresman/Little, Brown, 1990), 154.

[23] Keith E. Hamm and Charles W. Wiggins, "The Transformation from Personnel to Information Lobbying," in *Interest Group Politics in the Southern States,* ed. Ronald J. Hrebenar and Clive S. Thomas (Tuscaloosa: University of Alabama Press, 1992), 170.

[24] Keith E. Hamm and Charles W. Wiggins, "The Transformation from Personnel to Information Lobbying," in *Interest Group Politics in the Southern States,* ed. Ronald J. Hrebenar and Clive S. Thomas (Tuscaloosa: University of Alabama Press, 1992), 152.

[25] Texas Ethics Commission, "Lobbying in Texas: A Guide to the Texas Law," August 29, 2013, http://www.ethics.state.tx.us/guides/LOBBY_guide.htm#COMPENSATION AND REIMBURSEMENT THRESHOLD.

[26] Texas Ethics Commission, "2014 List of Registered Lobbyists," June 6, 2014, http://www.ethics.state.tx.us/tedd/2014_Lobby_List-Lobbyist_Only.htm.

[27] Texas Ethics Commission, "Lobbying in Texas: A Guide to the Texas Law," 28 September 2011, 2012, http://www.ethics.state.tx.us/guides/LOBBY_guide.htm.

[28] Texas Ethics Commission, "Title 15, Election Code, Regulating Political Funds and Campaigns,"

http://www.ethics.state.tx.us/statutes/09title15. html#254.001.

[29] National Conference of State Legislatures, "State Limits on Contributions to Candidates," http://www.ncsl. org/Portals/1/documents/legismgt/Limits_to_ Candidates_2012-2014.pdf.

[30] SCOTUSblog, *Citizens United v. Federal Election Commission,* http://www. scotusblog.com/case-files/cases/ citizens-united-v-federal-election-commission/.

[31] Cornell University Law School Legal Information Institute, Supreme Court, http://www.law.cornell. edu/supct/html/08-205.ZS.html.

[32] National Conference of State Legislatures, Life After Citizens United. http://www.ncsl.org/research/ elections-and-campaigns/citizens-united-and-the- states.aspx.

[33] Molly Ivins, *Molly Ivins Can't Say That, Can She?* (New York: Random House, 1991), 58.

[34] Tyler Cowen, "Public Goods," *Library of Economics and Liberty,* 2012, http://www.econlib.org/library/Enc/ PublicGoods.html.

[35] Mancur Olson, *The Logic of Collective Action,* (Cambridge, MA: Harvard University Press, 1971).

[36] Thomas R. Dye, *Politics in States and Communities,* 7th ed. (Englewood Cliffs, N.J.: Prentice Hall, 1991), 112–113.

[37] Molly Ivins, "Getting to the Grass Roots of the Problem," *Bryan-College Station Eagle,* 13 July 1995, A4. Copyright Molly Ivins. Reprinted by permission.

[38] Peverill Squire, "Measuring State Legislative Professionalism: The Squire Index Revisited," *State Politics & Policy Quarterly* 7:2 (Summer, 2007), 211–227.

[39] David F. Prindel, *Petroleum Politics and the Texas Railroad Commission* (Austin: University of Texas Press, 1981).

[40] Richard H. Kraemer and Charldean Newell, *Texas Politics,* 2nd ed. (St. Paul: West, 1984), 79. Also see *The Texas Almanac and State Industrial Guide, 1970–71* (Dallas: A.H. Belo, 1970), 425; and *The Texas Almanac and State Industrial Guide, 1974–75,* (Dallas: A.H. Belo, 1974), 19.

[41] Texas Administrative Code, Department of State Health Services, http://www.statutes.legis.state.tx.us/Docs/ HS/pdf/HS.716.pdf; http://info.sos.state.tx.us/pls/ pub/readtac$ext.ViewTAC? tac_view=4&ti=25&pt= 1&ch=181.

[42] David R. Henderson, "Rent Seeking," *Library of Economics and Liberty,* 2012, http://www.econlib. org/library/Enc/RentSeeking.html. Also see the pioneering works by Gordon Tullock and Anne Krueger, especially the latter's "The Political Economy of the Rent-Seeking Society," *American Economic Review* 64 (1974), 291–303.

[43] Tyler Cowen and Alex Tabarrok, "The Opportunity Costs of Rent Seeking," http://mason.gmu.edu/ atabarro/TheOpportunityCostsofRentSeeking.pdf. Also see Kevin M. Murphy, Andrei Scheifer, and Robert W. Vishny, "Why Is Rent-Seeking So Costly to Growth?" AEA Papers and Proceedings (May 1993).

CHAPTER 11

Public Policy in Texas

*Upon completing this chapter,
you will be able to...*

- **Analyze issues and policies of Texas.**

What is public policy? This seems like a simple question. However, political scientists have wrestled with it and offered a variety of answers. Thomas Dye, in one of the most popular books on **public policy**, defines it quite simply as, "Whatever governments choose to do or not to do." Scholars Marc Eisner, Jeffrey Worsham, and Evan Ringquist are even more minimalist, defining public policy as "patterns of governmental action and inaction." A scholar outside the field of political science, psychiatrist and crime victim rights advocate Dean Kilpatrick, provides one of the more detailed definitions, arguing that public policy is "a system of laws, regulatory measures, courses of action, and funding priorities concerning a given topic promulgated by a governmental entity or its representatives."[1]

Each of these three definitions offers a useful perspective on what the realm of public policy involves. But they all imply that the public policy world is fairly huge and touches nearly all aspects of our lives. Our state and local governments here in Texas impact us from the time we wake up in the morning until we go to bed at night. They affect us when we turn on the lights (utility regulation), when we take a shower (water policy), when we get in the car and drive to work or school (the Department of Motor Vehicles, among others), when we are at the office or the university (education policy and business regulations), and so on throughout the day. In this chapter, we examine some of the most important areas of governmental action at the state and local levels. These include regulatory policy, welfare policy, education policy, criminal justice, social policy, water policy, and policies affecting immigrants and veterans. But first we discuss the steps involved in the policy-making process and how Texas compares to other states in terms of its overall policy ideology.

> **public policy**
> "Whatever governments choose to do or not to do."
> —Thomas Dye

Steps in the Policy-Making Process: The "Policy Cycle"

Political scientists have for some time been interested in explaining the process by which public policy is formulated and implemented. In his book *Public Policymaking*, James Anderson published one of the first comprehensive attempts to define policy making as a process. In particular, he refers to this process as a "policy cycle."[2] He outlined the primary stages of the policy cycle as follows: problem identification and agenda setting; policy formulation; policy adoption; policy implementation; and policy evaluation (see Figure 11.1).

Of course, not all policy-making efforts include each step in the process. The cycle, instead, represents the ideal. In actuality, there is often no policy evaluation, which consists of an attempt to assess effectiveness after a policy has been implemented and then to make possible adjustments. Often policies are passed with no consideration of this need for review and change in the future. In some cases, reversing a policy would be quite costly, requiring funding that would put pressure on the budget (and necessitate either cuts elsewhere or tax increases). For example, the Texas state legislature has decided to fund less and less of the cost of education. It is not likely that this policy will be reversed unless tax revenues increase substantially, because reversing this policy would probably require a tax increase.

The policy formulation stage may also lack critical analysis of the impact of the proposed policy or any alternatives (not to mention failure to consider the likely unintended consequences of any policy proposal). This is due in part to the nature of legislative work: constituents complain and legislators react. Indeed, responding to constituent complaints is a time-honored role for legislators—and something that many citizens expect of state and local decision makers. In some cases, legislators may propose legislation to correct a perceived problem based on anecdotal evidence from a single constituent. Legislators may react, not with great forethought, but instead because they know their constituents expect them to take some action. This is not a recipe for careful policy design, especially in moments of crisis when the urge to "do something, do anything" is strong. However, the Texas legislature's biennial sessions help to mitigate somewhat the problem of reacting under pressure without thinking.

In some cases, the policy implementation stage of the policy cycle is skipped altogether because the new policy is largely symbolic. Some would argue that state bans on gay marriage are examples of such policies, because these laws require little substantive implementation when the state already restricts marriage to heterosexual

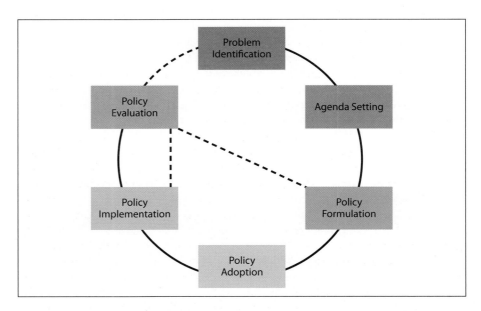

FIGURE 11.1   The Policy-Making Cycle

couples. Instead, these laws often are ways for some legislators to show symbolic support for the conservative and religious beliefs of their key constituencies.

CORE OBJECTIVE

Taking Personal Responsibility...

How can you impact public policy decisions? At what point in the policy cycle could you voice your preferences?

Policy Liberalism Index

"Policy liberalism" is a common measure of state policy ideology that can be used to compare the 50 states. Political scientists have identified policy liberalism as a key component underlying variation in state policy. In other words, policy differences in the American states are understood to reflect differences in ideology that run along a left-right, or liberal-conservative, spectrum. Policy liberalism also tracks well with public opinion ideology. However, as political scientists Jason Sorens, Fait Muedini, and William Ruger have cautioned in their own recent study of state policy ideology, "It is also important to recognize that most policy variation in the states is not a reflection of mere ideological differences." Instead, a variety of factors specific to each state accounts for a lot of the policy differences we see. These include the fact that each state has specific policy problems it is trying to solve (and policies that will reflect those particular conditions and needs) as well as different historical "legacies" and institutional arrangements.[3]

However, rigorous policy liberalism indices have been developed that help us measure how liberal or conservative a state is on some state policies and compare the 50 states in terms of those policies. Despite possible connotations of the term "policy liberalism," these indices are not judgments about state policies from a particular political stance or ideology. Instead, they are simply scientific measures that help us understand state policy and how the states compare to each other along a liberal-conservative dimension. Most of these indices utilize only a few policies but are still able to construct accurate and informative measures that capture the underlying concept. For example, political scientist Virginia Gray has constructed a policy liberalism index using five policy indictors: gun control laws, abortion laws, conditions for receiving Temporary Assistance to Needy Families (TANF) benefits, tax progressivity, and right-to-work laws.[4] However, Sorens, Muedini, and Ruger's "State Policy Index" (SPI) contains a **policy liberalism index** constructed from more than 170 different policies in the fiscal, regulatory, and social policy realms.

Table 11.1 shows how the states ranked in the SPI (2006) and what their scores were for that year. Despite the different constructions, the Gray and SPI indices are remarkably consistent in their findings for many of the states. For example, New York, California, and New Jersey were the most liberal and in the top three in both SPI and Gray (2011); likewise, many of the same states were the most conservative in both indices. Differences between the two are likely due to the greater range of policies examined in the SPI index as well as policy changes over time.

policy liberalism index
A measure of how liberal or conservative a state is on some state policies

TABLE 11.1

State Rankings on Policy Liberalism

State	SPI Policy Liberalism Ranking (2006)	SPI Policy Liberalism Score (2006)	Gray Policy Liberalism Index (2005)	Gray Policy Liberalism Index (2011)
New York	1	11.15647	3	2
New Jersey	2	10.54791	5	3
California	3	9.07802	1	1
Massachusetts	4	9.056458	8	11
Maryland	5	8.072636	11	7
Rhode Island	6	6.958129	10	8
Hawaii	7	6.495414	2	6
Connecticut	8	6.293627	6	5
Illinois	9	4.376863	13	18
Maine	10	3.808599	9	10
Vermont	11	3.710918	4	4
Oregon	12	3.093124	7	9
Washington	13	2.674887	18	15
Ohio	14	2.327857	26	28
Delaware	15	2.059649	16	21
Minnesota	16	0.69509	14	12
Michigan	17	0.428525	25	22
Florida	18	0.312584	40	46
Colorado	19	0.170392	28	23
New Hampshire	20	0.099858	23	19
Wisconsin	21	0.013047	21	13
Alaska	22	−0.43976	17	20
Pennsylvania	23	−0.59078	20	24
Montana	24	−0.94488	12	14
Nevada	25	−1.18756	30	31
Arizona	26	−1.61638	35	38
New Mexico	27	−1.89614	15	16
North Carolina	28	−1.93916	37	30
Iowa	29	−1.95767	24	25
West Virginia	30	−2.3277	19	17
Nebraska	31	−2.76732	29	33
Virginia	32	−2.78202	38	36
Louisiana	33	−3.03234	36	49
Kentucky	34	−3.15325	27	26
Indiana	35	−3.19559	33	35
Kansas	36	−3.20814	31	29
Idaho	37	−3.2982	42	42
Missouri	38	−3.41958	22	27
Georgia	39	−3.50983	46	32
South Carolina	40	−3.59032	32	34
Utah	41	−3.60315	39	37
South Dakota	42	−3.90715	49	44
Arkansas	43	−4.10305	43	50
Oklahoma	44	−4.23185	45	43
Tennessee	45	−4.30366	34	39

Texas	46	−4.42573	41	48
Wyoming	47	−4.79034	50	45
North Dakota	48	−5.41306	48	40
Alabama	49	−5.69125	44	41
Mississippi	50	−6.10423	47	47

Sources: Jason Sorens, Fait Muedini, and William Ruger, "U.S. State and Local Public Policies in 2006: A New Database," *State Politics and Policy Quarterly* 8:3 (Fall 2008): 309–326; Virginia Gray, "The Socioeconomic and Political Context of States," in *Politics in the American States: A Comparative Analysis*, 9th ed., ed. Virginia Gray and Russell Hanson (Congressional Quarterly Press, 2008); Virginia Gray, "The Socioeconomic and Political Context of States," in *Politics in the American States: A Comparative Analysis*, 10th ed., ed. Virginia Gray, Russell L. Hanson, and Thad Kousser (Congressional Quarterly Press, 2011).

It is important to note that some states rank high on some particular indicators of policy liberalism and near the bottom on others. For example, Vermont is one of the states with the most laissez-faire gun laws in the country, despite being a relatively liberal (in the modern sense) state on many other issues. In the Gray index (2011), Washington state ranks second on abortion rights and sixth in terms of fewest conditions for receiving TANF benefits, but ranks at the bottom on regressivity of taxes and near the middle on gun control. Some states (especially those that are more liberal on social policies such as civil unions but economically more conservative) fit the standard left-right, liberal-conservative pattern less well than others.

Texas ranks as one of the most conservative states in the country. It comes in at #46 in the SPI ranking and #48 in the most recent version of Gray's policy liberalism index. In terms of the Gray index, Texas ranks roughly in the middle on gun laws (which might surprise many Texans) while generally conservative on abortion, tax progressivity, and access to TANF (see Map 11.1). Both rankings provide accurate

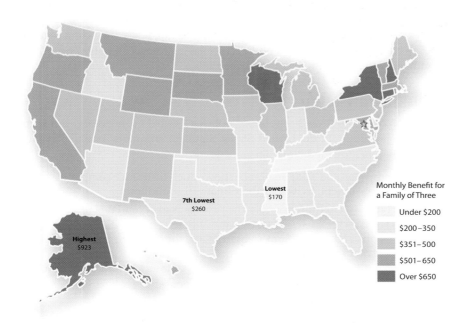

MAP 11.1   Monthly TANF Benefits by State

SOURCE: Ife Finch & Liz Schott, "TANF Benefits Fell Further in 2011 and Are Worth Much Less Than in 1996 in Most States," *Center on Budget and Policy Priorities*, Nov. 2011 (http://www.cbpp.org/files/11-21-11pov.pdf).

reflections of the political culture of Texas. Texans oppose gun control, are more often than not pro-life/anti-abortion, and favor regressive consumer taxes. The states ranked near or below Texas are, as one might expect, either Western or Southern states—thus passing a "smell test" of sorts in terms of the validity of the rankings.

These policy liberalism indices can also provide some insight into the kind of policies that can be expected to pass the legislature and be advocated by the governor and other state agencies. They are not intended as critiques of conservative states like Texas, or their policies, but rather as one way of explaining why things are the way they are. Texas ranks in the high 40s in both indices because it has very conservative policies, such as relatively limited regulation (for example, right-to-work/anti-union laws), a strict criminal justice system, a very regressive tax structure (meaning that, as economist Dwight Lee notes, such taxes "take a larger percentage of income from those with less income"), and laws limiting some aspects of abortion.[5] The average Texan likely agrees with these policy positions, especially if we assume that legislators are responsive to public opinion (especially the opinion of the average voter!).

Public Policy Areas in Texas State Government

Despite the ever-expanding range of issues over which the federal government has assumed control in the past half-century or so, states still play an important role in legislating in certain policy areas and implementing a wide array of policies set at both the state and federal levels. As we saw in the discussion of state policy liberalism, states vary quite a bit in terms of policy output and outcomes. The next chapter focuses specifically on tax policy at the state level, an area in which states differ dramatically and meaningfully. The remainder of this chapter examines a number of other important policy areas in the state of Texas, including regulatory policy, welfare policy, education policy, criminal justice, social policy, water policy, and policies affecting immigrants and veterans.

Regulatory Policy

First, let us consider Texas's regulatory policies toward business and put them in national perspective. In the United States, state governments regulate a range of activities that include the following:

- Life, property, and auto insurance (how much insurance companies can charge consumers, as well as their financial soundness)
- The court system (how friendly the process is to defendants or plaintiffs, often covered by the term "tort reform")
- Professions and occupations (requirements for obtaining and maintaining licenses to practice)
- Public utilities (electricity, natural gas, telecommunications, and cable)
- Labor law (minimum wage, workers' compensation, collective bargaining between unions and employers, and so on)
- The environment, including land use (whether and how land can be developed or taken for a public purpose)

Texas's regulatory policies are usually considered pro-business. For instance, *Chief Executive Magazine* rated Texas the best state for business in 2012 and fifth in the "Taxation and Regulation" category.[6] In some policy areas, that reputation is well-deserved.

For instance, Texas labor law tends to be antiunion and pro-employer. Texas has a right-to-work law that prohibits collective bargaining agreements between employers and unions from including clauses that require employees to pay agency fees to the union as a condition of employment. (See Map 10.1 for all right-to-work states.) Right-to-work laws tend to reduce the power of unions because many employees prefer to opt out of paying the agency fees, while still receiving the benefits of collective bargaining. (Agency fees and union dues are slightly different. As one teachers' group explains: "An agency fee is a percentage of dues that the union determines is the amount it costs the union to represent you before your employer in the areas of bargaining, contract administration, and grievances.")[7] Another example that supports Texas's pro-employer reputation is that it is the only state that does not mandate that employers purchase workers' compensation insurance in case of employees' injuries. Employers are allowed to opt for a "tort" model instead, in which injured employees can sue their employers for damages. Texas's labor laws have both benefits and costs. They probably raise business investment and levels of employment, but they also reduce the wages of those workers who would otherwise be represented by stronger unions.

Texas is also considered to be pro-business because of what the state and local governments do to actively support and attract businesses. Foremost among these are tax abatements and programs for special corporate subsidies, such as the Texas Enterprise Fund and the Texas Emerging Technology Fund. The Texas Enterprise Fund, which was created to attract businesses (and the jobs that come with them) to the state and for business expansion projects, has provided companies with more than $560 million in incentives since its inception in 2003. The Office of the Governor notes that this program "provides the state's leaders with a 'deal closing fund' that has the flexibility and financial resources to help strengthen the state's economy."[8] Meanwhile, the Texas Emerging Technology Fund aims to help "early-stage tech companies grow their ideas from the laboratory into the marketplace" and has dispersed over $220 million.[9]

Former Governor Rick Perry holds a sign boasting of Texas's favorable business climate.

This amalgamation of pro-business policies has drawn the ire of both liberal Democrats and free-market, libertarian Republicans. The former complain that the subsidy programs are, at best, funnels for "corporate welfare" and, at worst, "political slush-funds" for Republican politicians.[10] The latter criticize them on the grounds that they are examples of "crony capitalism" and inconsistent with true capitalism. As Erica Grieder of *Texas Monthly* explained, these skeptics "argue that such subsidies aren't even good for business, because they amount to the government 'picking winners and losers,' thereby distorting potentially efficient markets: companies with a bad product may be artificially buoyed by the grants, and those that might otherwise succeed struggle to outlast their well-funded competitors."[11] Critics also point out that there isn't enough transparency in the incentive rewarding process.[12] Given that Governor Perry was a strong advocate of these programs, it will be interesting to see if the new governor (Abbott has said he wants the government "out of the business of picking winners and losers") or a left-right "purple" coalition will unite to scale back these programs, or whether pro-business forces and concentrated interests will continue to prevail in the name of jobs and economic development.[13]

Texas is one of the least regulated states in the country on land use. The state and most localities within the state place comparatively few restrictions on landowners' ability to subdivide and build on their property. The city of Houston remains the only city in the country without zoning, a type of land-use regulation that segregates residential and commercial uses for land. (However, Houston's municipal code regulates land use significantly.) The most recent national study of state and local land-use regulations was conducted by researchers at the University of Pennsylvania's Wharton School of Business. The "Wharton Residential Land-Use Regulation Index" rates Texas as the twenty-first least-regulated state, with many rural states somewhat less regulated. However, Dallas, Fort Worth-Arlington, San Antonio, and Houston are all in the top 10 least-regulated metropolitan areas in the country.[14] A benefit of low land-use regulation is a high supply of housing and therefore low home prices and rents, perhaps the biggest reason Texas has attracted so many new residents in recent years.[15] The costs of few restrictions on development include loss of natural habitat and lower quality of life for residents who oppose development.

Texas has also placed more restrictions on the use of eminent domain than most other states. Eminent domain is the process whereby the government can take private land for a public purpose with compensation. The U.S. Supreme Court case *Kelo v. City of New London* (2005) established that local governments may use eminent domain to transfer private property to other private parties so long as the government envisions public benefits from doing so. This decision was highly unpopular across the country, and many state legislatures rushed to place legal restrictions on this use of eminent domain. In most states, those reforms were mostly symbolic and left significant loopholes. Texas, however, enacted one of the more far-reaching reforms, and according to the Sorens, Muedini, and Ruger study, which includes an index of eminent domain reform, Texas is tied for eighth among the states in the strictness of its restrictions on private-to-private eminent domain transfers.[16]

In other regulatory policies, however, Texas is comparatively less friendly to business. For instance, occupational and professional licensing regulations can be a barrier to small business formation. Strict requirements in education, examinations, and fees for obtaining a license to become a contractor, nurse, hair stylist, or even an interior designer in some states reduce competition, economic opportunities for working-class people, and affordability for consumers, but they are often justified on grounds of public health or ensuring higher quality for the consumer.[17] Recent data collection shows that Texas licenses slightly fewer occupations than average, requires slightly higher fees than average, and requires slightly less education and fewer examinations than average for those occupations it does license.[18] Occupational licensing remains a controversial issue for interest groups, even as the general public rarely pays attention. For instance, nurse practitioners want to be allowed to open independent practices (in Texas they are not allowed to do so, but they are in many other states), but physicians have often opposed this reform because it would increase competition and reduce their incomes and, they argue, reduce the quality of medical services. Similar battles go on between dentists and dental hygienists at statehouses around the country.

Another area where Texas is not so pro-business is its court system. The U.S. Chamber of Commerce rates states on the business friendliness (and, therefore, plaintiff unfriendliness) of their civil liability systems. In the latest survey from 2012, Texas scored thirty-sixth, indicating that the state is comparatively friendly to plaintiffs who sue businesses for, say, product-liability claims.[19]

Welfare Policy

States are responsible for administering many federally legislated programs providing income support and in-kind benefits to the poor, unemployed, and disabled. In some cases, states have considerable leeway to determine eligibility for these programs. For instance, Medicaid, the public health insurance program for the poor, is run entirely by state governments, but the federal government encourages states to fund the program generously by offering matching grants. Still, because Medicaid expenditures are such a large item in state budgets (looking across all 50 states, Medicaid accounted for nearly one-quarter, or 22.3 percent, of total state spending in 2010[20]), there is significant variation in benefit levels and eligibility requirements among the states, as some states try to keep costs down.

As of July 2011, 15.3 percent of Texas's population was enrolled in Medicaid, compared to a national average of 18.3 percent.[21] Because Texas has a relatively high poverty rate (18.5 percent of Texas's 2011 population lived in households with incomes below the federal poverty threshold, compared with the national average of 15.9 percent below the poverty line[22]), these figures suggest that Texas's eligibility and benefit standards for Medicaid are relatively strict. Also in 2011, Texas had the highest total number of people participating in the Supplemental Nutrition Assistance Program (SNAP, formerly known as "food stamps") of all 50 states. SNAP recipients made up 15.5 percent of the state's population, compared to 14.3 percent of the population participating in SNAP nationwide. However, the average monthly benefit per person was $125.57 in Texas, slightly lower than the national average of $133.85.[23] Other evidence bolsters the idea that Texas tends toward more stringent rules regarding qualification for benefits. In 2013, the state legislature passed a bill requiring drug testing of some applicants for unemployment, but implementation of that law has been delayed.[24] Only two other states have passed similar legislation.

When it comes to income support expenditures classified by the census bureau as "public welfare and veterans' services," Texas's state and local governments spent $29.1 billion in fiscal year 2010. That figure amounts to 3.1 percent of the state economy (measured in personal income), one of the lowest figures in the country. Texas spent 13.3 percent of all state and local spending on public welfare, below the national average of 14.7 percent. Nevertheless, "welfare policy" might be thought more broadly to include all spending on health, hospitals, housing, community development, and unemployment insurance in addition to income support. If we add all those categories together, they total $54.8 billion for Texas in 2010, or 25.2 percent of all state and local spending. The national average for these categories is 28 percent. Thus, no matter how one slices the data, Texas spends less than most other states on welfare programs, not just as a share of the economy but as a share of state and local budgets.

Health Care Policy

The Affordable Care Act (ACA, also known as "ObamaCare") was passed by Congress and signed into law by President Obama in 2010 as an effort to reform health care and expand coverage. After weathering multiple legal challenges (the state of Texas was among those who sued the Obama administration), most of the ACA was ultimately upheld by a 5-4 vote of the U.S. Supreme Court in 2012.[25] The court ruled that while Congress's passage of an individual mandate to buy health insurance could not be justified under the Commerce Clause of the Constitution, it could be upheld as part of Congress's taxing power. However, the court rejected the portion of the law involving expansion of Medicaid eligibility by arguing that this expansion would unduly "coerce" the states. As a result, states have discretion over whether to expand Medicaid benefits to individuals and families with higher income levels than those previously specified.

Under the ACA, insurance companies cannot place an annual or lifetime limit on benefits, nor can they deny coverage to someone with a preexisting condition. Individuals can maintain coverage under their parents' insurance until age 26, and certain preventive services are available at no cost to the insured. A major provision of the law is the requirement—known as the "individual mandate"—that every individual purchase and maintain health insurance coverage satisfying certain minimum standards; uninsured individuals are assessed what the IRS calls an "individual shared responsibility payment," or what less officially is called a "fee" or tax.[26] To implement this provision and assist uninsured individuals in finding coverage, a health insurance marketplace was devised. Like many other federal programs, these marketplaces, or exchanges, were expected to be administered by the states. According to the law, state governments can opt to run their own exchange, share an exchange with other states, or operate an exchange jointly with the federal government.[27] However, if a state refuses to set up an exchange, the federal government will step in and establish one. As of March 2014, only 14 states and the District of Columbia were operating their own exchanges.[28] Texas has declined to run its own exchange, meaning that Texans shopping for health insurance in the online marketplace use a federally run exchange.[29]

According to the U.S. Census Bureau, in 2011–2012, Texas had the highest percentage of uninsured people of all 50 states, at roughly 24 percent of the state's population.[30] Proponents of the ACA anticipate the law will reduce the number of uninsured, therefore guaranteeing access to health care for a greater number of people, and drive down the cost of coverage. Opponents argue the law represents an overreach of federal authority that violates individual rights protected by the U.S. Constitution. Furthermore, they point out that compliance with the law will be very expensive, thus stressing state budgets, and that the federal government has not provided clear information about how the system will work.[31] Governor Perry denounced the health care law, calling its provisions "brazen intrusions into the sovereignty of our state."[32] He indicated Texas has no plans to develop its own exchange or implement other provisions of the law, including the expansion of Medicaid coverage. Interestingly, the decision whether or not to set up a state-run exchange has generally aligned with party affiliation: the majority of states defaulting to a federally run exchange are led by Republican governors, whereas most states with their own exchanges are governed by Democrats.[33]

Primary and Secondary Education in Texas

School District Financing

Just as it does with higher education (see the Higher Education in Texas section later in this chapter), the state of Texas pays for part of the cost of public K–12 (also referred to as primary and secondary) education. Over the past 20 years, the state's share of the cost of education has declined, and local school districts have been forced to pick up a larger part of the cost. For the 2011–2012 school year, the state of Texas paid about 35 percent of the cost of public education; the federal government picked up another 10 percent; and local districts provided the rest through taxes, bonds, and other means.[34] Because the primary source of local funding is the property tax, some school districts have been better able than others to absorb the higher local share. Some school districts have a high per-pupil property tax base (so-called rich districts) and others have a low per-pupil property tax base (so-called poor districts). Although the state does show preference to poor districts with increased funding, this support does not completely alleviate the disparities that exist in the amount of money available to school districts on a per-pupil basis.

These funding disparities became a statewide issue in 1968 when parents in the Edgewood school district in San Antonio filed a lawsuit challenging the financing of schools in Texas (*Rodriguez v. San Antonio Independent School District*). The U.S. Supreme Court found the system of school financing to be unfair but deemed it a state problem and said that resolution should rest with the state. Because of this case, the state did increase aid to poor school districts. However, severe differences continued. In 1984 another lawsuit brought education finance to the forefront in Texas (*Edgewood v. Kirby*). This case was filed in state district court, and because of the efforts of the Mexican American Legal Defense and Education Fund and the Equity Center in Austin, the Texas Supreme Court ruled the state's system of school finance unconstitutional in 1989.

Data used in this court case indicate the disparities among school districts. The critical variable is the par value. This is an index of the per-pupil/student value of property in a district compared with the statewide average, with an index of 100 being average. If a district is above 100, it has more wealth per pupil; below 100, it has less wealth per pupil. Changes in state law have decreased these disparities, but they have not disappeared. Although state aid makes up for some of these differences, most aid is aimed at providing the basic foundations of education. Rich districts can still provide funds for so-called enrichments.

In an attempt to correct these funding disparities, the state legislature in 1991 consolidated property taxes within 188 units called county education districts. These districts collected property taxes to be used for school operations and distributed it to the school districts in their jurisdiction on a per-student basis. This system became known as the **Robin Hood Plan** and was subsequently challenged in court by some high per pupil property tax districts. The courts ruled that the plan violated the Texas Constitution. Although the state legislature proposed a

---

Robin Hood Plan
System for funding the state's primary and secondary public school education whereby rich districts send money to the state, which then distributes those funds to poor school districts

constitutional amendment to make the system legal, voters rejected this amendment in May 1993 by a large margin (63 percent against).[35]

Incidentally, rejection of this system had political implications for the governor's race at the time. According to the *Dallas Morning News,* the Republican National Committee spent $400,000 to help defeat this amendment and to promote negative views about the Democratic governor, Ann Richards, by linking her to the amendment in ads.[36] Richards was defeated by George W. Bush in 1994.

Following the defeat of this amendment, the legislature passed a new law, this one accepted by the courts, giving the so-called rich districts several options. Under this plan, a school district's property tax wealth per pupil is capped at a certain amount. For 2012–2013, that level of property wealth per student was $319,500.[37] When a district meets or exceeds that cap (and a final determination is made, based on a few other factors, that it must reduce and equalize its wealth), a district has several choices. It may send its excess wealth to the state, which will send the money to poor districts. Alternatively, the district can combine its wealth with another specific district, educate nonresident students from another district, or detach property from the district. Most districts opt to send money to the state. Of the school districts in Texas, 90 percent are "poor districts." Only 10 percent must give money to the state. This system was also labeled a Robin Hood plan.

CORE OBJECTIVE

Being Socially Responsible...

To what extent should Texas be responsible for ensuring equal funding for wealthy school districts and poor school districts?

Teachers at the Texas capitol protest proposed cuts to the education budget.

High Stakes Test

Local school districts are required to follow guidelines set by the State Board of Education (SBE) and the Texas Education Authority (TEA). In effect, the TEA is the enforcement body for the SBE and the state in general. According to the TEA's website, its organization is responsible for "assessing public school students on what they have learned and determining district and school accountability ratings."[38] To that end, basic mandatory standardized testing is administered to measure student and school performance. The Texas Assessment of Knowledge and Skills (TAKS) testing was the standard until 2012, when it was replaced by the State of Texas Assessment of Academic Readiness (STAAR) exam. STAAR is given to students starting in third grade and continuing throughout students' public school education. Elementary and middle school students are assessed in the areas of reading, math, writing, science, and social studies, and high school students take end-of-course (EOC) tests in English, math, science, and social studies.[39] Performance is classified as either advanced, satisfactory, or unsatisfactory, and to graduate, students must achieve a cumulative score reflecting satisfactory performance in each subject area. Students are allowed to retake EOC exams for any reason.

Anecdotal evidence suggests that teachers "teach to the test" because of the central role that test scores play in the evaluation of public school districts.

Controversial Curriculum

In school board elections in Texas and across the nation, three curriculum issues have stirred up controversy: sex education, creation science (creationism), and bilingual education. Sex education (see page 296 for more information on this) and creationism are issues driven by "social conservatives," including the Christian Right, which has representatives on the state board of education and is attempting to elect school board members locally. These candidates often run as "stealth" candidates, not openly revealing their agenda during the campaign. Their goal is to limit sex education to abstinence-based programs and to require teaching of creationism as an alternative to evolution or along with evolution. The extent to which these groups have managed to control school boards is unknown. Some of the state school board's authority has been reduced by the legislature over the past 10 years.

Bilingual education has been a controversial issue dating back to the early twentieth century, when Germans and Czechs in Texas wanted to teach their native languages in the schools. Following World War I, anti-German sentiment in the state killed these efforts, and in the 1920s the legislature prohibited the teaching of languages other than English. There is an old story in the lore of Texas politics claiming that when Governor "Ma" Ferguson signed the bill prohibiting teaching in any language other than English, she reportedly said, "If English was good enough for Jesus Christ, it's good enough for the school children of Texas."

Currently the bilingual issue revolves around teaching in both Spanish and English to Hispanic children in elementary schools. Many Anglo Texans object to the use of tax dollars for bilingual education. Some take the inconsistent position that everyone should speak English, but no tax money should be spent to ensure that they can. Governors Bush and Perry both helped soften the resistance to these education programs and reached out to Hispanic voters in the state.

Higher Education in Texas

Like other populous states, Texas has a large number of public higher educational institutions serving a diverse population of students. According to the Texas Higher Education Coordinating Board, Texas's public higher education system is composed of "a vast network of nine health science centers, 38 universities (or general academic teaching institutions), 50 community college districts, three state colleges, and four state technical colleges."[40] These schools received $17.5 billion in total funds in fiscal year 2013 while enrolling more than 1.3 million students.[41]

Tuition and Fees

For many years the cost of college tuition and fees in Texas was very low and affordable for most people. In fact, nonresidents of Texas often found it cheaper to come to Texas and pay a small out-of-state fee than to attend college in their own state. In the 1970s, the legislature began to gradually increase tuition, tying the amount students paid to the number of semester hours taken. For most of the 1970s, the cost was $4.00 per semester hour (about $12.00 per course) with a few fees for labs attached to certain courses. Although this cost was very low, most students did not realize what a bargain it was.

State universities approached the legislature for more money during the 1980s and 1990s. For most of this time the legislature prohibited universities from setting their own tuition rates but did allow them to charge additional fees for student services. Such services included computer access, recreation, and transportation.

Texas A&M and the University of Texas at Austin approached the legislature about allowing the two "flagship" universities to charge higher tuition. ("Flagship" is a term used by the University of Texas and Texas A&M to denote their claimed status as the lead universities in the state.) This request to charge higher tuition rates encountered considerable opposition in the legislature, especially from legislators who had graduated from "non-flagship" universities. Nonetheless, Texas A&M and the University of Texas continued to press the issue, and during the 2003 legislative session, the newly installed Republican majority and then-Republican Speaker Craddick passed a new policy of **"deregulated" tuition** for all state universities. Deregulating tuition allowed individual colleges and universities to set the tuition rate they charged their students. Because the legislature faced a $10 billion revenue shortfall at the time, increasing tuition seemed an easy way to increase revenue.

In the fall of 2003, the average cost of tuition and fees for 15 credit hours was $1,934. In the spring of 2004, after tuition deregulation took effect, the cost per semester increased to $2,032. Thereafter, from fall 2003 to fall 2011, average tuition charges at Texas public universities jumped 90 percent, to an average of $3,671 per semester.[42] After the policy changed, constituents began to complain to legislators about the increases.

Much of the state budget is fixed by the state constitution and state and federal law. In other words, the legislature has very little discretion regarding how the money is spent. However, operating funds for higher education are not part of this **budget fix**. Education funds come from the nonrestricted area of the budget and thus can be reduced. Even as tuition costs have risen, the proportion of educational costs covered by state funding (on a per-pupil basis) has gone down. The Texas comptroller's office reported that "from fiscal years 2002 to 2007, the Texas state budget was cut in terms of real dollar, per-student funding for universities by 19.92 percent."[43] Therefore, the cost of higher education has been funded increasingly with tuition and fee hikes, and the burden of paying for higher education has increasingly shifted to the individual student and parents. (In a similar fashion, the cost of elementary and secondary education has been increasingly funded by local property taxes, which now equal almost half the total taxes collected at the state and local levels in Texas.) In the spring of 2012, the University of Texas at Austin voted to hold tuition rates steady for two years.[44] In the fall of 2012, Governor Rick Perry proposed that state universities offer incoming freshmen a four-year tuition freeze, thus guaranteeing students a level tuition rate during the time they are pursuing a degree.[45] While parents and students continue to exert pressure on universities to keep costs down, others express concern that educational quality will suffer due to cost-cutting measures. On the other hand, some suggest the costs of education are rightly borne by those who utilize the service and benefit the most, rather than taxpayers in general.

"deregulated" tuition

A decision by the state legislature to allow state colleges and universities to set the rate of tuition charged to students

---

budget fix

State laws and constitutional amendments that set aside money to be spent on specific items; the best example is the state gasoline tax being committed to state highways.

TABLE 11.2

2013-2014 Tuition Costs among Major Public Universities (First-Year Tuition and Fees for Undergraduates)

University	Residents ($)	Nonresidents ($)
University of Illinois at Urbana-Champaign	15,258	29,640
University of Michigan, Ann Arbor	13,819	40,496
University of California, Los Angeles	12,696	35,574
University of Arizona	10,391	27,073
University of Texas at Austin	9,816	33,976
Colorado State University	9,313	25,166
University of Alabama	9,200	22,950
Texas A&M University	8,506	25,126
University of North Carolina at Chapel Hill	8,340	30,122
State University of New York at Buffalo	7,989	18,609
Iowa State University	7,726	20,278
University of Florida	6,263	28,541

Sources: The University of Texas at Austin, Tuition Dollars & Sense, Historical Tuition Costs, http://www.utexas. edu/tuition/attach/tf_undergrad_fall13.pdf; U.S. News & World Report, National University Rankings, http:// colleges.usnews.rankingsandreviews.com/best-colleges/rankings/national-universities

Tuition increases over the years have helped Texas schools stay competitive with institutions in other states. See Table 11.2 for a look at how tuition at these two Texas schools compares with the costs of other state universities. It is worth remembering that there are many Texas state colleges and universities with lower costs than the University of Texas and Texas A&M.

Curriculum and Degree Requirements

In recent years the Texas legislature has been more active in making laws and rules that impact the curriculum choices of students, faculty, and university officials. The following are a few examples of these decisions.

According to state law, all state universities are required to offer a set number of courses in what is called the core curriculum. As of 2013, the core will consist of 36 hours of fundamental component areas identified by the Higher Education Coordinating Board (which includes 6 hours of political science and 6 hours of history) plus an additional 6 hours identified by each institution, provided they justify that the courses meet at least 4 core objectives. Students must complete these courses in order to graduate.

The total number of hours required for degree completion is limited to 120 hours for most degrees. Prior to this change (which went into effect in fall 2008), most degrees required at least 128 hours. The justification for this policy change was cost cutting: the legislature wants students to graduate more quickly, thereby reducing the state's cost for higher education. In addition, if a student takes more than 120 hours, the university does not receive any state funding for these extra hours.

Students can receive a rebate of $1,000 if they graduate within three credit hours of the total number of hours required for their degree. The legislature forced this policy on universities but did not appropriate any money to cover the cost. Therefore, rebates are most likely funded by fees.

Undergraduate students pay in-state tuition rates up to a certain number of total hours in their undergraduate degree. Once they have exceeded this number of credit hours (set by the legislature), a student must pay the out-of-state tuition rate.

Transferring courses from one university to another has been a source of controversy. If a student earns a "D" in a course at one school, other state schools have to accept this course as transfer credit. Although this benefits students in their ability to transfer credits, some of the major schools object to transfers of such low grades.

Higher Education Funds

Permanent University Fund (PUF)
The PUF is money set aside in the state constitution to benefit the University of Texas at Austin and Texas A&M University.

Operating budgets for institutions of higher education are part of the regular state budget, but higher education in Texas has other funds available for capital projects. (A capital project is a "long-term investment project requiring relatively large sums" of money, such as constructing a new building on campus.[46]) The **Permanent University Fund (PUF)** was established by the Texas Constitution of 1876 to support the University of Texas and Texas A&M University systems. The original endowment began in 1839 when the Republic of Texas set aside 221,400 acres of land, the income from which was designated to fund higher education. This land was located in East Texas and was rather good farmland. Because this land was so valuable for agricultural purposes, the state legislature later transferred the endowment to approximately 2 million acres of land, thought to be of less value, primarily in West Texas. Ironically, in the early part of the twentieth century, oil was discovered on these new lands, and the income they generated became substantial over time.[47] As of June 30, 2012, the PUF had a market value of $13.1 billion and a book value of $11.6 billion.[48] The University of Texas and some of its branch campuses receive two-thirds of the money generated by the PUF's investments, and Texas A&M, its branches, and divisions receive the remaining one-third.[49]

According to this policy, other colleges and universities in the state did not receive any portion of these funds, and other universities began to pressure the Texas legislature for a share of the PUF fund. In 1984, the legislature proposed an amendment to the state constitution (subsequently approved by the voters) creating the **Higher Education Assistance Fund (HEAF)**. Beginning in 1985, the legislature set aside annual appropriations of $100 million for this fund. This amount was later increased to $175 million. Today this fund provides about $275 million each year for colleges and universities not supported by the PUF.[50]

Higher Education Assistance Fund (HEAF)
The HEAF is money set aside for use by those universities not benefiting from the PUF.

The authors of the Texas Constitution of 1876 saw a need for higher education in Texas and responded by creating the PUF. Later sessions of the legislature wanted to fund other institutions of higher learning and created the HEAF. The establishment of these funds is an example of public policy with regard to education. Although tuition costs have increased and may continue to do so, at least part of the cost of higher education is constitutionally protected and covered by the state.

Access to Higher Education

From the 1950s to the 1970s, access to state colleges and universities in Texas was governed by "open enrollment." In other words, all Texas residents who had graduated from high school were automatically admitted without consideration of high school standing or standardized test scores. Nearly all students could enroll in the university of their choice. In the 1980s many schools, particularly Texas A&M and the University of Texas, began to impose higher standards for admittance, using mainly SAT scores and high school class standing to make that determination.

Higher enrollment standards conflicted to some degree with the aim of increasing minority enrollment at state colleges and universities. At the time, Hispanics and African Americans were a growing minority of the state's population, but only about 20 percent were enrolled in colleges and fewer still in the top two state universities. Minority students were also underrepresented in law and other professional schools.

Many colleges and universities began affirmative action programs in an attempt to increase minority enrollment in colleges and universities. These programs prompted a lawsuit regarding admission of minority students to the University of Texas law school. In 1996, the federal court ended affirmative action practices at the University of Texas law school in the **Hopwood Decision**.[51] Texas Attorney General Daniel Morales, himself a beneficiary of affirmative action programs while a student in Texas, applied the *Hopwood* decision to all state colleges and universities and effectively eliminated affirmative action admission policies across the state. Morales found that ". . . Hopwood's restrictions would generally apply to all internal institutional policies, including admissions, financial aid, scholarships, fellowships, recruitment and retention, among others."[52] Thus, under Morales' interpretation, *Hopwood* was extended to prevent race from being considered in areas beyond admissions. *Hopwood* was overturned in 2003 by a case originating in Michigan. The U.S. Supreme Court, in *Grutter v. Bollinger,* 539 U.S. 306 (2003), ruled that the U.S. Constitution does not prohibit tailoring standards to use race as an admission decision or policy.

Prior to *Grutter v. Bollinger,* the Texas legislature, in an attempt to solve the problems of minority representation and unequal opportunity, changed admission standards at Texas universities and established that admissions decisions and financial awards could not be based primarily on standardized test scores such as the SAT, ACT, or GRE. Under the new policy, any student graduating in the top 10 percent of his or her high school class was granted automatic admission to any state college or university, without consideration of other factors such as SAT scores. This ruling had the greatest impact on the University of Texas, where 81 percent of the 2008 freshman class was admitted under the 10 percent rule.[53]

Hopwood Decision

Decision by federal courts to end affirmative action in Texas schools; these programs had provided for special treatment for minority students in being accepted to colleges and professional schools.

This cartoon suggests a number of the factors that colleges consider when making admissions decisions. Why is membership in a minority group controversial, whereas other factors—such as the ability to play a certain sport or being the son or daughter of a graduate—are not? In the future, how can colleges achieve the goals of a diverse campus and a fair admissions process?

This 10 percent rule was expected to increase minority enrollment by allowing students from inner-city high schools to attend the top schools in the state. Some evidence suggests that the 10 percent rule has in fact increased minority enrollment, especially at the University of Texas and to a lesser degree at Texas A&M. However, the policy has created a problem for some high-performing students at better high schools in the state. It is not unusual for students at a competitive high school not to place in the top 10 percent of their graduating class, even with a 1500 or higher score on the SAT. Therefore, these students are not guaranteed admission to a Texas institute of higher education under the 10 percent rule. Conversely, some students from small rural schools, who have very low SAT scores, are able to gain admission via the same policy.

In 2013, the Supreme Court revisited the issue of race and university admissions in Texas. In *Fisher v. University of Texas*, the Court ruled that universities can use affirmative action in their admissions policies only if there is no other way to achieve diversity among the student body.[54] This ruling did not change the University of Texas's admissions policy, but the case was sent back to a lower court for consideration of whether the university had met this standard.[55]

Criminal Justice and Social Policy

Criminal Justice

Texas has a reputation as a "tough on crime" state. That reputation is well deserved. One example of this is Texas's use of the death penalty. From 2011 to 2013, 44 prisoners were executed in Texas, compared to 81 total in the rest of the country. Since the U.S. Supreme Court removed a moratorium on the death penalty in 1976, Texas has executed 515 prisoners, nearly five times as many as Oklahoma, the next highest state on the list.[56] Thirty-two states in the U.S. currently have the death penalty.

Texas's strict criminal-justice policies can also be observed in incarceration and arrest rates. According to the Bureau of Justice Statistics, Texas's incarceration rate in 2010 was 648. The incarceration rate represents the number of prisoners with longer than one-year sentences who are under the jurisdiction of state and federal correctional authorities, per 100,000 residents. Texas's incarceration rate is tied with Alabama for fourth highest in the country. At the other end of the spectrum, Maine's incarceration rate was 148.

However, Texas's incarceration rate is high in part because the state's crime rate is high. Texas had the fifteenth-highest violent crime rate in the country in 2010. Ruger and Sorens employ a method for adjusting the incarceration rate for the violent crime rate using a statistical technique called *regression analysis*. The "residuals" of the regression analysis tell us how many more people were incarcerated than would be expected given a state's incarceration rate. They argue that the adjusted measure of incarceration more accurately measures the strictness of a state's sentencing policies, as well as systematic differences in likelihood of conviction, than the raw incarceration rate. Texas's adjusted incarceration rate was seventh in the country in 2010, implying that its sentencing policies and prosecutorial success were well above average in their strictness.

Ruger and Sorens also have a way of measuring how the police in different states prioritize drug crimes versus other crimes. They divide arrests for drug violations by the number of people in the state who report using illegal drugs in the past year in surveys conducted by the Substance Abuse and Mental Health Services Administration, a federal agency. The resulting variable is called the "drug enforcement rate." A low percentage on this measure indicates that fewer people involved with drugs were actually arrested, whereas a high percentage indicates more people involved with drugs were arrested. In 2010 this figure ranged from 1.1 percent in Hawaii to 16.7 percent in Illinois. In Texas, the drug enforcement rate was 7.6 percent, higher than the national average of 5.7 percent. Thus, in Texas, police departments tend to prioritize arresting people involved with the illegal drug trade more than police in most other states. Texas has not adopted policies such as a medical marijuana exception that would also reduce arrest rates for drug offenses.[57]

As noted previously, Texas's reputation as a "tough on crime" state is well-deserved. However, Texas has recently witnessed some fairly significant reform efforts and gained national attention as a leading criminal justice reform state. These reforms included increased use of drug courts, which channel nonviolent drug offenders into treatment programs rather than jail, changes to its juvenile justice system, and shutting down prisons.[58] Perhaps surprisingly, these reforms have been supported by conservative Republicans, such as Governor Rick Perry and state legislator Jerry Madden, as well as conservative groups such as the Texas Public Policy Foundation (with its "Right on Crime" initiative) and the Texas Association of Business. They were allied with Democrats such as State Senator John Whitmire. Although more elevated motives may be at play, the daunting price tag and impact on labor markets of having a high incarceration rate and being so tough on crime has not failed to escape the attention of conservative reformers.[59]

Firearms Policies

As a relatively conservative state, Texas has tended to have fewer gun laws than more liberal states. On the other hand, as a "tough-on-crime" state, Texas has retained more restrictions on the right to carry firearms than other states such as Alaska, New Hampshire, and Vermont. For instance, in Texas an initial permit to carry a concealed firearm costs about $260 including training costs, more than most other states. In addition, Texas has extensive limitations on where concealed firearms are permitted, and it forbids outright the open, unconcealed carry of loaded handguns. Still, Texas has fewer overall restrictions on guns than does the average state.

Gay Rights

Texas was one of the last states to maintain antisodomy laws, which banned particular private sex acts between consenting adults (and were largely aimed at homosexuals). At one time all states had antisodomy laws, but by 2003, when the Supreme Court declared these laws unconstitutional in the case *Lawrence v. Texas*, only Texas and 13 other states still had such laws on the books.[60] Today, though most Americans agree that antisodomy laws were rightly invalidated, whether same-sex marriages should enjoy the same legal status as opposite-sex marriages is still controversial.

Public opinion has been changing rapidly on the issue of same-sex marriage, and the legal landscape regarding this issue looks very different than it did just a few years ago. In January 2013, only 9 states and the District of Columbia allowed same-sex couples to marry; as of October 2014, 24 states and the District of Columbia allowed same-sex marriage.[61] Texas is currently one of 26 states with either a constitutional or statutory ban on gay marriage. Many of these bans follow the language of the federal Defense of Marriage Act (DOMA), passed by the U.S. Congress in 1996, which defined marriage as the union of one woman and one man and denied federal recognition of same-sex unions. In June 2013, in the case *United States v. Windsor,* the U.S. Supreme Court struck down a portion of DOMA and declared that the federal definition of marriage was unconstitutional.[62] Although this ruling did not necessarily guarantee same-sex couples the right to be married (because individual states regulate marriage within their borders), it opened the door for state laws or constitutional provisions banning same-sex marriage to be challenged in court. At the time of this writing, such challenges were making their way through the court system in all states where same-sex marriage is not allowed (see Map 11.2).

Texas amended its state constitution in 2005 to prohibit same-sex marriage; the ban was initially proposed in the legislature and overwhelmingly approved by voters. In February 2014, the ban was struck down by a federal judge.[63] That decision is currently pending appeal by the state.[64] Therefore, gay and lesbian couples are still unable to marry legally in Texas. There is also no provision for same-sex civil unions or domestic partnerships in the state.[65] Individuals, however, are allowed to adopt children without consideration of their sexual orientation. Therefore, gays and lesbians can adopt children in Texas; because only one partner in a same-sex couple can be listed on the child's birth certificate,[66] these adoptions tend to be single-parent adoptions and may be followed by a second adoption by

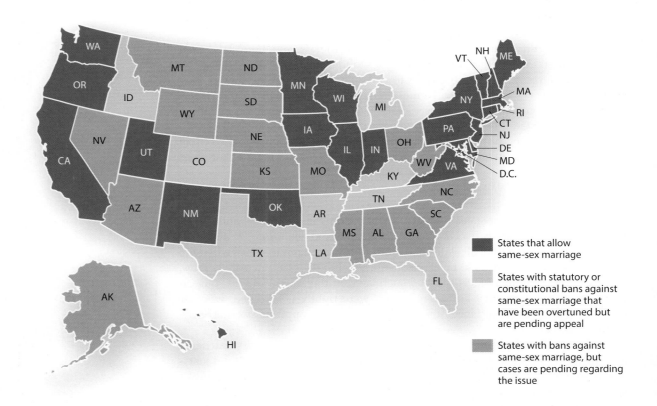

MAP 11.2   State Marriage Laws

SOURCE: National Conference of State Legislatures, "Defining Marriage: State Defense of Marriage Laws and Same-Sex Marriage," October 2014, http://www.ncsl.org/research/human-services/same-sex-marriage-overview.aspx.

a same-sex partner. Some Texas courts have recognized same-sex second parent adoptions, such as in *Hobbs v. Van Stavern* (2006) and *Goodson v. Castellanos* (2007).[67] Finally, there is no state antidiscrimination law specifically protecting members of the LGBT community. However, some local governments in Texas have passed such laws.

Abortion Policies

In the 1973 case ***Roe v. Wade***, the U.S. Supreme Court ruled that the Texas law banning abortions was unconstitutional.[68] The ruling limits what states can do to prevent a woman from having an abortion. Ever since the ruling, however, states have tried in a variety of ways to limit and restrict abortions. Texas is no exception.

Some abortion-related regulations already on the books in Texas include a requirement that abortions be performed by a licensed physician, specify a gestational limit banning late-term abortions (with life and health exceptions as required by the Supreme Court), and include requirements that young women under 18 obtain parental consent before having an abortion (with a judicial bypass required by the Supreme Court). In addition, there is a 24-hour waiting period for abortion, and women must receive an ultrasound from their physician before an abortion can be performed.[69] Texas also prohibits public funding of abortions except in cases of rape, incest, or life endangerment.[70] In 2013, Texas enacted controversial abortion legislation considered strict in comparison with other states. The new law bans abortion after the twentieth week of pregnancy, requires abortion clinics to meet the same standards as surgical centers, and requires doctors to have hospital admitting privileges near where they perform abortions. Senate deliberation of the bill was marked by intense Democratic opposition, including an 11-hour filibuster by state senator Wendy Davis that initially killed the bill during a special session. However, Governor Perry called another special session for the bill to be reconsidered, and it was subsequently approved (although the filibuster had gained wide media attention and vaulted Ms. Davis to statewide and national prominence).[71] The law continues to generate controversy and has been the subject of multiple court challenges and appeals, with a final resolution yet to be determined.[72]

Roe v. Wade
Texas court case that limits what states can legally do to prevent abortions

Public debate over abortion was not settled by the Supreme Court's 1973 decision in *Roe v. Wade*. Here, a group from Texas demonstrates their pro-life position at a march in Washington, D.C. In the other photo, abortion rights supporters express their dissatisfaction with new legal restrictions inside the State Capitol.

CORE OBJECTIVE

Communicating Effectively...

Summarize the legislation that Texas has passed on abortion. Discuss the advantages and disadvantages of state involvement in this policy issue.

Sex Education

Sex education is frequently a controversial component of public school curricula. In their 2009 study of sex education in Texas school districts, Wiley, Wilson, and Valentine found that 94 percent of Texas school districts taught abstinence-only when providing instruction on human sexuality. Their review of actual materials used in classrooms indicated that 2 percent of school districts skipped over sexual education entirely, and only the remaining 4 percent provided information on STD and pregnancy prevention, including contraception. These researchers concluded that "Abstinence-only programs have a stranglehold on sexuality education in Texas public schools."[73] Indeed, the state accepts no federal funding for sex education programs that promote anything beyond celibacy.[74]

Discussions of sexuality are often glossed over because of a desire to avoid controversy.[75] For example, many Texans believe it is not the role of public schools but rather that of parents to provide sex education. These parents express concern that giving students information about sex will encourage them to engage in sexual activity. Nonetheless, these parents believe that if schools are going to venture into this realm, they should teach total abstinence. Other parents favor teaching sex education as a necessary part of health education as well as a way of empowering young people to make good choices about an important aspect of life. Attitudes about these issues have implications not just for education but also for public health initiatives.

At the beginning of the 2007 legislative session, Governor Rick Perry issued an executive order requiring all Texas schoolgirls to be vaccinated against the human papillomavirus (HPV), a common sexually transmitted infection that can cause cervical cancer.[76] Several members of the house and senate introduced legislation preventing these vaccinations from taking place. They reasoned that if young women were vaccinated, they would be more likely to engage in promiscuous sex owing to the reduced risk of cancer later in life. Other members were skeptical that teen decision making about sex involved such rational considerations. Still others accused Perry of being influenced by donations from the vaccine manufacturer[77] or questioned his attempt to mandate government intervention in the private health care decisions of parents for their daughters, a seemingly inconsistent position for a conservative Republican governor. In the end, the legislature overturned Perry's executive order, and the governor allowed the legislation to stand. Nonetheless, this controversy trailed Perry into his unsuccessful presidential bid in 2011–2012.[78]

Immigration Policy

Immigration is a significant issue in Texas. During the period from 2008 to 2012, 16.3 percent of the state's population was composed of foreign-born persons.[79] Although the Census Bureau counts people who are present both legally and illegally, it is important to distinguish between the two types of immigrants. Legal immigrants go through a process to become legal permanent residents, also known as Green Card holders. The process for becoming a legal permanent resident (LPR) differs depending on whether the individual is outside or inside the U.S. at the time of application, but it generally requires being sponsored by a family member or employer, submitting forms, paying fees, and sometimes even attesting that an individual will have adequate financial support when he or she is in the country.[80] Certain categories of immigrants must first obtain an immigrant visa; the number of immigrant visas issued each year is limited by Congress. Upon approval, permanent residents have permission from the federal government to live and work in the U.S. permanently.[81] LPRs can subsequently apply for U.S. citizenship, or naturalization. In 2012, 95,557 people in Texas obtained legal permanent resident status, and 57,762 people were naturalized.[82] Illegal immigrants, on the other hand, are those who have entered or remain in the country without having government permission; these individuals may also be referred to as unauthorized or undocumented. In January 2012, the number of unauthorized immigrants in the United States was estimated at 11.4 million, with 1.8 million of that population living in Texas.[83]

This large illegal immigrant population impacts the state in many ways. According to a 2006 report by the Texas state comptroller, state revenue generated by undocumented immigrants (primarily from sales tax and other government fees) outweighed what the state spent on services for this population. However, the report acknowledged that local governments and hospitals bear a disproportionate share of the cost of educating, incarcerating, and providing health care for illegal immigrants—costs for which localities are not compensated. Although illegal immigrants are not eligible for TANF, food stamps, or public housing in Texas, they are eligible for K-12 education, emergency medical care, and other health services.[84] In fiscal year 2009, the Texas Health and Human Services Commission (a state agency) estimated the cost of providing services to illegal immigrants at $96 million. During fiscal year 2008 (the most recent year for which data are available), public hospitals in Texas provided care for undocumented immigrants at an estimated cost of $717 million.[85]

In the 1981 case *Plyler v. Doe* (which originated in Tyler, Texas), the U.S. Supreme Court ruled that denying any individual the right to an education violated the Equal Protection Clause of the U.S. Constitution. Therefore, all states are required to provide K-12 education for undocumented immigrants and their children.[86] In 2001 the state legislature passed House Bill (HB) 1403, also known as the Texas DREAM Act (which stands for Development, Relief and Education of Alien Minors). This law allows children born in Texas to illegal immigrant parents to pay the in-state college tuition rate, as long as the student promises to apply for legal resident status as soon as possible.[87]

Recent federal policy on immigration has primarily been to enforce existing immigration laws by apprehending and deporting people who are in the country illegally. Although border security is mainly the responsibility of the federal government, state and local agencies in Texas have partnered with the federal government to strengthen enforcement along the state's more than 1,200-mile border with Mexico. Texas programs relevant to border security include the following:

- Operation Linebacker (2005) provides county funding for local law enforcement to develop tools and resources to prevent border crime and deter illegal immigration.

- Operation Border Star (2006) coordinates efforts between local and federal law enforcement to aid in inspection efforts at the Texas–Mexico border.[88]

Members of the U.S. Army install part of the fence along the border near Puerto Palomas, Mexico. The federal government is building a 745-mile fence along the U.S.–Mexico border to reduce the flow of illegal migrants into the United States.

Although the number of unauthorized or illegal immigrants in Texas had remained fairly constant for several years, there has been a recent surge of illegal immigrants entering the state. From October 2013 to June 2014, Border Patrol in the Rio Grande Valley picked up an estimated 160,000 unauthorized immigrants—more than 52,000 of whom were children traveling by themselves—a greater number than agents had detained during the previous 12 months.[89] The resultant overcrowding in federal detention centers, along with poor health conditions in those centers, precipitated what was called a "humanitarian crisis" and led to the transportation of illegal immigrants caught in Texas to facilities in other states.[90] In response, state leaders increased funding to the Texas Department of Public Safety to enhance border security, at a price tag of $1.3 million per week.[91] The ability of states to influence this matter is limited, given the federal government's control over immigration policy, and it remains to be seen how this matter will be resolved.

Water Policy

A snapshot of water use in Texas is necessary to understand the state's water policies. The Texas population is projected to grow 82 percent from 2010 to 2060, from 25.4 million in 2010 to 46.3 million in 2060.[92] For purposes of allocating water rights, water is measured in "acre feet," which equals the amount of water needed to cover one acre of land in one foot of water.[93] Employing this unit of measure, total water use in Texas from 2010 until 2060 will increase from approximately 18 million acre feet to approximately 22 million acre feet, representing a jump of 22 percent.[94]

These statistics suggest something puzzling: namely, that water demand will grow at just over one-fourth the rate of population growth. Part of the explanation for this apparent discrepancy concerns how water is used in different sectors of the economy. State policy makers break down the demand for water into six categories: municipal (residential and commercial demand in cities); manufacturing; mining; steam-generated electricity; livestock production; and crop irrigation.[95] Of these categories, between 2010 and 2060, municipal, manufacturing, and steam electricity uses are expected to increase.[96] At the same time, however, livestock and irrigation uses are expected to decline. Geographically, the Dallas-Fort Worth, Austin, San Antonio, and Lower Rio Grande urban areas will experience the greatest increase in demand.[97]

Texas relies on both surface and groundwater to satisfy its tremendous demand for water. The state's fresh water derives from 1 natural lake, 200 man-made reservoirs, 14 major rivers, 3,700 streams, and 30 underground aquifers (a naturally formed underground reservoir) of varying sizes throughout the state.[98] The central region of the Edwards Aquifer, for example (approximately 180 miles long from Del Rio, Texas, to south of Austin, Texas) is one of the state's largest bodies of underground water.[99] Groundwater currently provides approximately 59 percent of the state's water demand; surface water totals 41 percent.[100]

The broadest way to categorize water law relates to quantity and quality: one set of laws and policies determines who has the right to use a given quantity of water. A second set of laws and policies exists to keep water uncontaminated and suitable for human use.

Water rights in Texas are governed by a complex system of laws: both statutes the legislature has enacted and law that courts have created on a case-by-case basis. Taken together, these laws regulate surface and groundwater in different ways. With respect to surface water, the state of Texas owns the water, but citizens can obtain exclusive rights to use a certain quantity of water, expressed in acre feet. Landowners with property adjoining a river have so-called riparian rights to withdraw limited quantities of water. Otherwise, the procedure for obtaining water rights in publicly owned surface water is called "prior appropriation" or "first in time, first in right," the same system used in most of the western United States.[101] The first person to claim water in a stream can obtain a right ("usufruct") over a quantity of water that no one else can use without purchasing the right from the first owner. The person who claims the right to use the water first then "perfects" the right by registering it with a state agency called the Texas Commission on Environmental Quality (TCEQ), which maintains records of who owns how many acre feet of water in different rivers, streams, and lakes of the state.[102] Surface water rights have been perfected for at least 98 percent of the total available water in the state. Individuals, local governments, and businesses now sell surface water rights to one another in a burgeoning market.[103]

Even though the majority of groundwater is connected with bodies of surface water such as rivers or reservoirs, Texas treats groundwater as if it were a separate source, subject to its own rules. Whereas surface water is publicly owned, Texas treats the water underneath a landowner's property as private property.[104] This leads to strange results. For example, the law would define water in a river as publicly owned, but when the same body of water flows underground, the law defines it as privately owned. A significant percentage of the water in the Edwards Aquifer flows to the surface to feed major springs and rivers, for example.[105] The so-called "rule of capture" provides that, even before the landowner removes the water from the ground, it is private property. Any law that limits the landowner's property-right interest in groundwater could be construed as a regulatory taking for which a unit of government might have to provide compensation.[106]

Despite the legal definition of groundwater as private property, the Texas legislature has made efforts to regulate groundwater in various ways. On the local level, groundwater conservation districts have limited powers over such issues as the spacing of wells and monitoring the quantity of water pumped.[107] In response to problems that excessive groundwater pumping has caused in particular regions of the state, the legislature has created larger groundwater districts with more authority limited to a specific geographic area. Examples include preventing land subsidence and property damage in the Galveston area,[108] or keeping groundwater levels sufficient to prevent the intrusion of contaminated water into the water supply of roughly 3 million Texans, or preserving habitat for federally endangered plant and animal species.[109] Texas has now created a statewide groundwater planning process under the Texas Water Development Board (TWDB).[110]

The TWDB also oversees a statewide water planning process for surface and groundwater every five years.[111] The state is divided into 16 regions, each of which has the responsibility for developing a comprehensive plan detailing the total estimated water needs of the region for the next five years and the total water supply from all sources for that region. The regional plans compare their cumulative water demand to a water supply equivalent to the severe drought of the 1950s to plan for contingencies. At the end of each five-year regional water planning cycle, the TWDB synthesizes the 16 regional water plans and other sources to create the State Water Plan. The governor, lieutenant governor, and state legislature then review the final adopted plan and approve it for use in the following five-year planning period.[112]

The second broad category of water law deals with water quality. The TCEQ carries out the Federal Clean Water Act and Safe Drinking Water Act, as well as state water quality statutes, to eliminate water contamination from many sources.[113]

Texas faces a number of water-related challenges in the coming decades. Severe drought conditions in recent years have dealt a blow to surface water supplies. Declining river levels deprive coastal estuaries of fresh water they must have to support multibillion-dollar commercial fishing and tourism industries. Texas water policy makers continue to seek solutions to such problems.[114]

CORE OBJECTIVE

Thinking Critically...

Given the water-related challenges facing Texas, what measures would you recommend to ensure all Texans have access to water? What might be some negative or unintended consequences of your recommendations?

Veteran Policy

Texas has one of the largest veteran populations of any state, with an estimated 1,667,740 former members of the armed forces living within its borders as of 2013.[115] The main public agency responsible for veterans' issues in the state is the Texas Veterans Commission (TVC), established in 1927. The TVC assists veterans in filing claims for disability benefits and represents them in matters involving the

U.S. Department of Veterans Affairs (VA).[116] In addition to traditional public programs for welfare-related assistance, service-connected disability compensation is available for qualified veterans, as are non-service-connected pensions for qualifying veterans with low or no income. In 2009, Governor Rick Perry directed the TVC to establish a Claims Processing Assistance Team to reduce the number of cases pending in the state's disability and claims system.[117]

The TVC also provides employment and education services through Veterans Employment Services and the Veterans Education Program. Veterans Employment Services addresses such issues as translating military skills to civilian employment, providing career guidance, and connecting veterans with employers. In addition, the TVC oversees delivery of a number of federal programs providing education benefits to veterans in the state of Texas; for example, the Montgomery and Post-9/11 GI Bills both provide financial support for veterans pursuing vocational training or higher education. The Hazlewood Act (also known as the Hazlewood Exemption) is a state program providing exemption from tuition and certain fees (for qualified veterans, spouses, and some children) at higher education institutions in Texas.[118]

The Texas Veterans Leadership Program, established in 2008 under the Texas Workforce Commission, focuses on veterans of the Iraq and Afghanistan wars. It provides resources and referrals for those veterans for services ranging from employment to educational and healthcare needs. Another program established in partnership with the Texas Workforce Commission, the College Credit for Heroes Program, allows institutions of higher education to give veterans college credit for experience, knowledge, and skills earned during their service. In addition, the Texas legislature has provided that qualified veterans, spouses, and children receive veterans' employment and retention preference in state agencies.[119]

Texas provides a range of other policies and programs for veterans. For example, the Veterans Land Board (VLB), established in 1946, has established Texas State Veterans Homes that provide long-term nursing care, including specialized Alzheimer's units, to veterans and qualified veterans' families. The VLB also provides various types of land, home, and home-improvement loans to veterans. In 2009, HB 8 and HB 3613 were enacted to minimize property appraisal costs and increase exemptions for disabled veteran homeowners.[120] Qualified veterans are able to obtain various state-issued licenses and passes at reduced fees, such as the Texas Parklands Passport[121] for entry and discounts within the state park system; various hunting and fishing licenses, such as the Texas Resident Active Duty Military "Super Combo" Hunting and All-Water Fishing Package[122]; and free driver's licenses.[123]

Conclusion

As this chapter shows, state and local government policy decisions impact a wide range of issues and areas of life. For good or bad, the Texas state government is actively involved in regulating business activity, providing welfare and educational services, attempting to manage natural resource and land use, and restricting certain behaviors or protecting certain rights. Whether or not you are interested in public policy, public policy is interested in you! The legislature, the governor, and many state agencies, including the board of regents of your public college or university, can have a direct effect on your life (including your education). Hopefully, by reading this book, you are more aware of how the government of Texas impacts your life and the community in which you live.

Key Terms

budget fix
"deregulated" tuition
Higher Education Assistance
    Fund (HEAF)

Hopwood Decision
Permanent University Fund
    (PUF)
policy liberalism index

public policy
Robin Hood Plan
Roe v. Wade

Notes

[1] See Thomas R. Dye. *Understanding Public Policy*, 7th ed. (Englewood Cliffs, N.J.: Prentice-Hall.1992), 4; Marc Allen Eisner, Jeff Worsham, and Evan J. Ringquist, *Contemporary Regulatory Policy* (Boulder, Colo.: Lynne Reinner, 2000); Dean G. Kilpatrick, "Definitions of Public Policy and the Law," http://www.musc.edu/vawprevention/policy/definition.shtml/.

[2] For his earliest attempt to do so, see James E. Anderson, *Public Policy-making* (New York: Praeger Publishing, 1975). The most recent edition is James E. Anderson, *Public Policymaking: An Introduction*, 7th ed. (Boston: Wadsworth, Cengage Learning, 2010).

[3] Jason Sorens, Fait Muedini, and William Ruger, "U.S. State and Local Public Policies in 2006: A New Database," *State Politics and Policy Quarterly* 8:3 (Fall 2008), 318, 319, and 321.

[4] Virginia Gray, "The Socioeconomic and Political Context of States," in *Politics in the American States: A Comparative Analysis*, 10th ed., ed. Virginia Gray, Russell L. Hanson, and Thad Kousser (Congressional Quarterly Press, 2011).

[5] Dwight Lee, "Redistribution," *The Concise Encyclopedia of Economics*, http://www.econlib.org/library/Enc/Redistribution.html.

[6] "How CEOs Grade the Best/Worst States: 2012," Chief Executive.net, http://chiefexecutive.net/how-ceos- grade-the-states-2012.

[7] http://www.ctenhome.org/faq.htm.

[8] Office of the Governor Rick Perry, "Texas Enterprise Fund," http://governor.state.tx.us/priorities/economy/investing_for_growth/texas_enterprise_fund/.

[9] Office of the Governor Rick Perry, "Economic Development," http://governor.state.tx.us/initiatives/economic_development.

[10] Forrest Wilder, "The Future of 'Corporate Welfare' in Texas after Rick Perry," *The Texas Observer*, April 24, 2014, http://www.texasobserver.org/future-corporate-welfare-texas-rick-perry/; and see Dana Liebelson, "Rick Perry's $487 Million Corporate Slush Fund Doesn't Need Your Stinkin' Audit," *Mother Jones*, March 20, 2013, http://www.motherjones.com/politics/2013/03/rick-perry-texas-enterprise-fund-audit.

[11] Erica Grieder, "The Revolt Against Crony Capitalism," *Texas Monthly*, February 18, 2014, http://www.texasmonthly.com/story/revolt-against-crony-capitalism?fullpage=1.

[12] Jess Fields (January 2014) "An Overview of Local Economic Development Policies in Texas," Texas Public Policy Foundation, http://www.texaspolicy.com/sites/default/files/documents/2014-01-PP06-OverviewLocalEconomicDevelopmentPoliciesinTexas-CLG-JessFields.pdf.

[13] Alexa Ura, "Future of Texas Enterprise Fund Uncertain Under New Governor," *Star-Telegram*, January 3, 2014, http://www.star-telegram.com/2014/01/03/5458599/future-of-texas-enterprise-fund.html.

[14] Joseph Gyourko, Albert Saiz, and Anita Summers, "A New Measure of the Local Regulatory Environment for Housing Markets: The Wharton Residential Land Use Regulatory Index," *Urban Studies* 45 (March 2008), 693–729.

[15] Edward L. Glaeser and Kristina Tobio, "The Rise of the Sunbelt," NBER Working Paper No. 13071, April 2007, http://www.nber.org/papers/w13071.

[16] Jason Sorens, Fait Muedini, and William Ruger, "U.S. State and Local Public Policies in 2006: A New Database." *State Politics and Policy Quarterly* 8:3 (Fall 2008), 309–326.

[17] Morris M. Kleiner, *Licensing Occupations: Ensuring Quality or Restricting Competition?* (Kalamazoo: W.E. Upjohn Institute for Employment Research, 2006).

[18] See data from William Ruger and Jason Sorens at http://www.statepolicyindex.com/the-research/.

[19] http://www.instituteforlegalreform.com/states/texas.

[20] National Association of State Budget Officers, 2010 State Expenditure Report, http://www.nasbo.org/sites/default/files/2010%20State%20Expenditure%20Report.pdf.

[21] U.S. Department of Health and Human Services, 2011 Medicaid Managed Care Enrollment Report, http://www.medicaid.gov/Medicaid-CHIP-Program-Information/By-Topics/Data-and-Systems/Downloads/2011-Medicaid-MC-Enrollment-Report.pdf.

[22] U.S. Census Bureau, "Poverty: 2010 and 2011," http://www.census.gov/prod/2012pubs/acsbr11-01.pdf.

[23] U. S. Department of Agriculture Food and Nutrition Service, Supplemental Nutrition Assistance Program State Activity Report, Fiscal Year 2011 (December 2012), http://www.fns.usda.gov/sites/default/files/2011_state_activity.pdf.

[24] David Barer, "Drug Testing for Unemployment Benefits Postponed," *Dallas Morning News*, January 31, 2014, http://trailblazersblog.dallasnews.com/2014/01/

drug-testing-for-unemployment-benefits-postponed.
html/.

[25] U.S. Department of Health and Human Services,
http://www.hhs.gov/healthcare/rights/law/index.
html.

[26] HealthCare.gov, "The Fee You Pay if You Don't Have
Health Coverage," https://www.healthcare.gov/
what-if-i-dont-have-health-coverage/.

[27] National Conference of State Legislatures, "State
Actions to Address Health Insurance Exchanges,"
http://www.ncsl.org/research/health/state-actions-
to-implement-the-health-benefit.aspx.

[28] Ibid.

[29] Sarah Kliff, "It's Official: The Feds Will Run Most
Obamacare Exchanges," *Washington Post,* February 18,
2013, http://www.washingtonpost.com/blogs/
wonkblog/wp/2013/02/18/its-official-the-feds-will-
run-most-obamacare-exchanges/.

[30] U.S. Census Bureau, Income, Poverty, and Health
Insurance Coverage: 2012 - Tables & Figures,
"Number and Percentage of People Without Health
Insurance Coverage by State Using 2- and 3-Year
Averages: 2009-2010 and 2011-2012," http://
www.census.gov/hhes/www/hlthins/data/
incpovhlth/2012/tables.html.

[31] Robert Pear, "Most Governors Refuse to Set Up Health
Exchanges," *New York Times,* December 14, 2012,
http://www.nytimes.com/2012/12/15/us/most-
states-miss-deadline-to-set-up-health-exchanges.html.

[32] Manny Fernandez, "Perry Declares Texas' Rejection of
Health Care Law 'Intrusions,'" *New York Times,* July 9,
2012, http://www.nytimes.com/2012/07/10/
us/politics/perry-says-texas-rejects-health-law-
intrusions.html.

[33] Sarah Kliff, "It's Official: The Feds Will Run Most
Obamacare Exchanges," *Washington Post,* February 18,
2013, http://www.washingtonpost.com/blogs/
wonkblog/wp/2013/02/18/its-official-the-feds-will-
run-most-obamacare-exchanges/); Drew Desilver,
"Most Uninsured Americans Live in States That
Won't Run Their Own Obamacare Exchanges," Pew
Research Center, September 19, 2013, http://www.
pewresearch.org/fact-tank/2013/09/19/most-
uninsured-americans-live-in-states-that-wont-run-
their-own-obamacare-exchanges/.

[34] Susan Combs, "Public Education Funding in Texas,"
Financial Allocation Study for Texas (FAST), http://
fastexas.org/about/funding.php.

[35] Secretary of State, State of Texas, *Votes on Proposed
Amendments to the Texas Constitution,* 1875–November
1993 (Austin: Secretary of State, 1994), 73.

[36] *Dallas Morning News,* January 12, 1994, 1A.

[37] Texas Education Agency Office of School Finance,
"School Finance 101: Funding of Texas Public
Schools," January 2013, SF101manual_Jan2013.pdf.

[38] Texas Education Agency, "Testing & Accountability,"
http://www.tea.state.tx.us/index.aspx?id=
2147495410&menu_id=660&menu_id2=
795&cid=2147483660.

[39] Texas Education Agency, STAAR Resources, http://
www.tea.state.tx.us/student.assessment/staar/.

[40] http://www.thecb.state.tx.us/index.cfm?
objectid=26AEABDA-D2CC-4D37-
5AB48345339DFCE1.

[41] Texas Higher Education Coordinating Board, "2014
Texas Public Higher Education Almanac: A
Profile of State and Institutional Performance and
Characteristics," http://www.thecb.state.tx.us/index.
cfm?objectId=CE293EED-DD31-BCDE-51EB322FF8B8
56A8&flushcache=1&showDraft=1.

[42] Texas Higher Education Coordinating Board,
"Overview: Tuition Deregulation," September 2012,
http://www.thecb.state.tx.us/.

[43] Texas Comptroller of Public Accounts, "Texas Where We
Stand," http://www.window.state.tx.us/comptrol/
wwstand/wws0512ed/.

[44] Ralph K.M. Haurwitz, "Regents Freeze In-State
Tuition for Two Years at UT-Austin," *Austin
American-Statesman,* May 3, 2012, http://www.
statesman.com/news/news/local/regents-
freeze-in-state-tuition-for-two-years-at-1/
nRnTP/.

[45] "Perry Pushing Tuition Freeze, $10,000 Degrees," *Austin
American-Statesman,* October 1, 2012, http://www.
statesman.com/news/news/state-regional-govt-
politics/perry-pushing-tuition-freeze-10000-degrees/
nSQ8b/.

[46] "Capital Project," BusinessDictionary.com, http://www.
businessdictionary.com/definition/capital-project.
html.

[47] Vivian Elizabeth Smyrl, "Permanent University Fund,"
Handbook of Texas Online, published by the Texas State
Historical Association, http://www.tshaonline.org/
handbook/online/articles/khp02.

[48] UTIMCO, "Permanent University Fund: Report on
Certain Specified Data as Required by Art. 4413
(34e) of the Civil Statutes, June 30, 2012," http://
www.utimco.org/Funds/Endowment/PUF/
PUFSemiAnnual201206.pdf.

[49] State Constitution, art. 7, sec. 18.

[50] www.thecb.state.tx.

[51] *Hopwood v. Texas,* 78 F.3d 932 (5th Cir. 1996), *cert. denied,
Texas v. Hopwood,* No. 95–1773 (July 1, 1996).

[52] Ibid.

[53] "81% of U.T.'s Admissions Offers Go to Top 10%
Graduates," *Houston Chronicle,* March 20, 2008, p. i.

[54] Amy Howe, "Finally! The Fisher Decision in
Plain English," SCOTUSblog, June 24, 2013,
http://www.scotusblog.com/2013/06/
finally-the-fisher-decision-in-plain-english/.

[55] Manny Fernandez, "Texas University's Race Admissions
Policy Is Debated Before a Federal Court," *New York
Times,* November 13, 2013, http://www.nytimes.
com/2013/11/14/us/texas-universitys-race-
admissions-policy-is-debated-before-a-federal-court.
html).

[56] Death Penalty Information Center, Number
of Executions by State and Region Since
1976, http://www.deathpenaltyinfo.org/
number-executions-state-and-region-1976.

[57] William P. Ruger and Jason Sorens, *Freedom in the 50
States: An Index of Personal and Economic Freedom*

(Arlington, Va.: Mercatus Center at George Mason University), forthcoming.

58 Editorial Board, "Texas Leads the Way in Needed Criminal Justice Reforms," *Washington Post*, January 28, 2014, http://www.washingtonpost.com/opinions/texas-leads-the-way-in-needed-criminal-justice-reforms/2014/01/28/83919b72-879d-11e3-916e-e01534b1e132_story.html; Office of the Governor Rick Perry, "Drug Courts," http://governor.state.tx.us/priorities/security/public_safety/drug_courts/; Olivia Nuzzi, "Prison Reform Is Bigger in Texas," *The Daily Beast*, April 12, 2014, http://www.thedailybeast.com/articles/2014/04/12/prison-reform-is-bigger-in-texas.html.

59 Bill Hammond, "Why Texas Businesses Back Reforming the State's Criminal Justice System," *Dallas Morning News*, January 19, 2014, http://www.dallasnews.com/opinion/latest-columns/20140119-why-texas-businesses-back-reforming-the-states-criminal-justice-system.ece.

60 Erwin Chemerinsky, *Lawrence v. Texas*, Duke Law, http://web.law.duke.edu/publiclaw/supremecourtonline/commentary/lawvtex.

61 National Conference of State Legislatures, "State Same-Sex Marriage Laws: Legislatures and Courts," December 2012, http://www.ncsl.org/issues-research/human-services/same-sex-marriagelaws.aspx; National Conference of State Legislatures, "Defining Marriage: State Defense of Marriage Laws and Same-Sex Marriage," October 2014, http://www.ncsl.org/research/human-services/same-sex-marriage-overview.aspx.

62 Supreme Court of the United States, *United States v. Windsor*, http://www.supremecourt.gov/opinions/12pdf/12-307_6j37.pdf.

63 Manny Fernandez, "Federal Judge Strikes Down Texas' Ban on Same-Sex Marriage," *New York Times*, February 26, 2014, http://www.nytimes.com/2014/02/27/us/texas-judge-strikes-down-state-ban-on-same-sex-marriage.html#.

64 Edgar Walters, "State Files Notice of Appeal on Gay Marriage Ruling," *Texas Tribune*, February 26, 2014, http://www.texastribune.org/2014/02/26/federal-judge-rules-texas-gay-marriage-ban-unconst/.

65 National Conference of State Legislatures, "Civil Unions and Domestic Partnership Statutes," http://www.ncsl.org/research/human-services/civil-unions-and-domestic-partnership-statutes.aspx)

66 Texas Department of State Health Services, "Adoption: Frequently Asked Questions," http://www.dshs.state.tx.us/vs/reqproc/faq/adoption.shtm#question 4.

67 National Center for Lesbian Rights, "Legal Recognition of Lesbian, Gay, Bisexual, and Transgender (LGBT) Parents in Texas," http://www.nclrights.org/wp-content/uploads/2013/07/TX_custody_pub_FINAL.pdf.

68 Tex. Code Crim. Proc. arts. 1191–94, 1196.

69 Texas Department of State Health Services, Woman's Right to Know, http://www.dshs.state.tx.us/wrtk/.

70 Guttmacher Institute, "State Facts About Abortion: Texas," http://www.guttmacher.org/pubs/sfaa/texas.html.

71 John Schwartz, "Texas Senate Approves Strict Abortion Measure," *New York Times*, July 13, 2013, http://www.nytimes.com/2013/07/14/us/texas-abortion-bill.html?_r=0.

72 Erik Eckholm, "Court Panel Upholds Texas Law on Abortion," *New York Times*, March 27, 2014, http://www.nytimes.com/2014/03/28/us/court-panel-upholds-texas-law-on-abortion.html#.

73 David Wiley, Kelly Wilson, and Ryan Valentine (2009), *Just Say Don't Know: Sexuality Education in Texas Public Schools*, Texas Freedom Network Education Fund, http://www.tfn.org/site/DocServer/SexEdRort09_web.pdf?docID=981.

74 Gail Collins, "Gail Collins on Texas's Abstinence Sex Education Problems," *The Daily Beast*, June 4, 2012, http://www.thedailybeast.com/articles/2012/06/04/gail-collins-on-texas-s-abstinence-sex-education-problems.html.

75 David Wiley, Kelly Wilson, and Ryan Valentine (2009). *Just Say Don't Know: Sexuality Education in Texas Public Schools*, Texas Freedom Network Education Fund, http://www.tfn.org/site/DocServer/SexEdRort09_web.pdf?docID=981.

76 Centers for Disease Control and Prevention, "Genital HPV Infection—Fact Sheet," http://www.cdc.gov/std/hpv/stdfact-hpv.htm.

77 Dan Eggen, "Rick Perry and HPV Vaccine-maker Have Deep Financial Ties," *Washington Post*, September 13, 2011, http://www.washingtonpost.com/politics/perry-has-deep-financial-ties-to-maker-of-hpv-vaccine/2011/09/13/gIQAVKKqPK_story.html.

78 Kate Alexander, "Perry Calls HPV Vaccine Mandate a Mistake," *Austin American-Statesman*, Aug. 15, 2011, http://www.statesman.com/news/news/state-regional-govt-politics/perry-calls-hpv-vaccine-mandate-a-mistake/nRdY7/.

79 United States Census Bureau (2012), United States Census Bureau State & County QuickFacts Texas, U.S. Department of Commerce, http://quickfacts.census.gov/qfd/states/48000.html.

80 U.S. Department of State, "The Immigrant Visa Process," http://travel.state.gov/content/visas/english/immigrate/immigrant-process.html.

81 Randall Monger and James Yankay (2013), "U.S. Legal Permanent Residents: 2012," Department of Homeland Security, https://www.dhs.gov/sites/default/files/publications/ois_lpr_fr_2012_2.pdf.

82 Office of Immigration Statistics (July 2013), 2012 Yearbook of Immigration Statistics, Department of Homeland Security, http://www.dhs.gov/sites/default/files/publications/ois_yb_2012.pdf.

83 Bryan Baker and Nancy Rytina (2013), Estimates of the Unauthorized Immigrant Population Residing in the United States: January 2012. Department of Homeland Security, http://www.dhs.gov/sites/default/files/publications/ois_ill_pe_2012_2.pdf.

84 Carole Keeton Strayhorn, (December 2006), "Undocumented Immigrants in Texas: A Financial Analysis of the Impact to the State Budget and Economy," http://www.cpa.state.tx.us/specialrpt/undocumented/undocumented.pdf)

[85] Strategic Decision Support (2010), *Update to the 2007 Report on Services and Benefits Provided to Undocumented Immigrants,* Financial Services Division, Texas Health and Human Services Commission, http://www.hhsc.state.tx.us/reports/2010/Rider59 Report_2010.pdf.

[86] *Plyler v. Doe,* 457 U.S. 202 (1982).

[87] Texas Higher Education Coordinating Board, Overview: Residency and In-State Tuition, September 2008. http://www.thecb.state.tx.us/reports/PDF/1528. PDF.

[88] Office of the Governor Rick Perry (2012), *Border Security,* Office of the Governor, http://governor.state.tx.us/initiatives/border/.

[89] Jennifer Medina, "Protesters in California Delay Transfer of Migrants," *New York Times,* July 2, 2014.

[90] Alexa Ura, "Health Officials: Immigrant Surge is a Medical Crisis," *Texas Tribune,* June 24, 2014, http://www.texastribune.org/2014/06/24/health-officials-docs-raise-concerns-about-immigra/; Gilad Edelman, "Abbott, Cruz Blame Obama for 'Humanitarian Crisis,'" *Texas Tribune,* June 23, 2014, http://www.texastribune.org/2014/06/23/abbott-cruz-blame-obama-humanitarian-crisis/.

[91] Juan Aguilar, "DPS Addresses New Border Operation," *Texas Tribune,* June 19, 2014, http://www.texastribune.org/2014/06/19/states-leadership-instructs-dps-increase-patrols-b/.

[92] www.twdb.state.tx.us/publications/state-water-plan/2012/03.pdf.

[93] www.merriam-webster.com/acrefoot.

[94] www.twdb.state.tx.us/publications/state-water-plan/2012/03.pdf.

[95] www.twdb.state.tx.us/publications/state-water-plan/2012/03.pdf.

[96] www.twdb.state.tx.us/publications/state-water-plan/2012/03.pdf.

[97] www.twdb.state.tx.us/publications/state-water-plan/2012/03.pdf.

[98] Ibid.

[99] Ibid.

[100] www.twdb.state.tx.us/publications/state-water-plan/2012/07.pdf.

[101] www.texaswater.tamu.edu/water-law.edu.

[102] www.tceq.texas.gov/permitting/water_rights.html.

[103] www.texaswatermatters.org/pdfs/articles/powerful_thirst.pdf.

[104] *Edwards Aquifer Authority v. Day,* 389 S.W.3d 814 (Tex. 2012).

[105] Edwardsaquiferauthority.net/.../san-marcos-and-barton-springs-connection.org.

[106] See Private Real Property Rights Preservation Act, www.oag.tx.us/AG_Publications/txts/propertyguide2005.shtml.

[107] Chapter 36, Texas Water Code. See also "Spotlight on Groundwater Conservation Districts," (Environmental Defense, Austin, Texas), www.texaswatermatters.org.

[108] www.hgsubsidence.org.

[109] www.edwardsaquifer.org/display_authority_m.php?pg=mission. See also Louis Rosenberg, Nohl P. Bryant, Cynthia Smiley et al., *Essentials of Texas Water Resources,* ed., Mary Sahs (State Bar of Texas 2012) pp. 4–20 through 4–23.

[110] Louis Rosenberg, Nohl P. Bryant, Cynthia Smiley et al., *Essentials of Texas Water Resources,* ed., Mary Sahs (State Bar of Texas 2012) pp.4–11 through 4–19.

[111] www.twdb.state.tx.us/WRPI/swp/swp.asp.

[112] www.twdb.state.tx.us/WRPI/swp/swp.asp.

[113] www.tceq.gov/agency/water_main.html.

[114] www.mysanantonio.com/news/article/Texas-part-of-growing-drought-in-U.S.-that-rivals-3711733; www.cbbep.org.

[115] U.S. Department of Veterans Affairs, "Veteran Population," National Center for Veterans Analysis and Statistics, http://www.va.gov/vetdata/veteran_population.asp.

[116] Texas Veterans Commission, "Welcome to the Texas Veterans Commission," http://www.tvc.state.tx.us/Home.aspx.

[117] Office of the Governor Rick Perry (Nov. 12, 2009), *Gov. Perry Announces Initiative to Reduce Federal Claims Backlog for Veterans in Waco and Houston,* Office of the Governor Rick Perry, http://governor.state.tx.us/news/press-release/13928/.

[118] Texas Veterans Commission, "My Education Benefits," http://www.tvc.texas.gov/tvc/Education-Home.aspx.

[119] Texas Government Code, "Title 6, Public Officers and Employees. Subtitle B. State Officers and Employees. Chapter 657. Veteran's Employment Preferences," http://www.statutes.legis.state.tx.us/Docs/GV/htm/GV.657.htm.

[120] Office of the Governor Rick Perry (July 9, 2009), "Gov. Perry: Appraisal Reform Legislation Makes Progress Toward Slowing Pace of Increasing Property Appraisal Rates," http://governor.state.tx.us/news/press-release/13190/.

[121] Texas Parks and Wildlife (n.d), "Texas Parklands Passport," Texas Parks and Wildlife, http://www.tpwd.state.tx.us/state-parks/texas-parklands-passport.

[122] Texas Parks and Wildlife (n.d.), "Licenses: Frequently Asked Questions," Texas Parks and Wildlife, http://www.tpwd.state.tx.us/faq/business/license/.

[123] Texas Department of Public Safety, "Veteran Services," http://www.txdps.state.tx.us/driverlicense/VetServices.htm.

CHAPTER 12

Financing State Government

Upon completing this chapter,
you will be able to...

- **Analyze issues and policies of Texas.**

A fundamental question in the realm of political science is, "What should government do?" Individuals answer this question in many ways depending on their **political values**, a set of beliefs about political processes and the role that government should play in our society. Any action taken by government requires an expenditure of resources—whether it is measured as an expense or by the time it takes to reach a decision. Today much attention is focused on federal spending, but few citizens realize that state governments also spend large sums of money to supply services to their citizens. In 2011, state and local governments combined spent $3.4 trillion.[1] Some money spent by state and local governments comes from the federal government as grants, but on average, state and local governments generate roughly three-quarters of their revenue from their own sources. Texas generates about 66 percent of its revenue.

political values
A set of beliefs about political processes and the role that government should play in our society

Because the Texas legislature meets in regular sessions every other year (biennially), it approves budgets for two-year periods (biennial budgets). In May 2013, the legislature approved a budget of $200.4 billion for the fiscal years 2014 and 2015. Thirty-four percent of that budget comes from federal funds, most of which (60 percent) is allocated to health and human services (welfare and Medicare).

Why Do Governments Provide Services to Citizens?

Most citizens agree that some form of government is necessary, if only for the protection of life, liberty, and property. Generally, governments also provide many other goods and services. These come in a variety of different types. Certain goods or services are known as **public goods** and have two special features: **"nonexcludability"** and **"nonrivalrous consumption."**[2] Nonexcludability is the most important and means that it is not practical to exclude people from receiving or enjoying the good or service due to nonpayment (to separate payers from nonpayers). Suppose, for instance, that a city tried to charge a fee for fire protection, and the occupant of one-half of a duplex

public goods
Goods or services characterized by the features of nonexcludability and nonrivalrous consumption; they are often provided by governments

nonexcludability
The inability to practically prevent people from receiving or enjoying a good or service due to nonpayment

nonrivalrous consumption
Situation in which the use or enjoyment of a good or service by a person or persons does not diminish the availability of that good or service for others to use or enjoy

collective benefit
Goods that are provided with no charge because there is a broader public benefit associated with the good

redistributive goods
Those goods where government takes money from one group of citizens and gives it to other citizens; welfare is a good example

regulatory goods
Good, activity, or resource that the government regulates to prevent overuse; an example is pumping water from a commonly owned aquifer

house paid for fire protection and the occupant of the other half refused to pay. The city could not deny fire protection to the person who had not paid because protecting the occupant who had paid could require preventing or putting out any fire in the half of the house occupied by the nonpayer. The same is true for national defense and some other government services such as lighthouses, which are commonly thought to exhibit the nonexcludability feature.[3]

Nonrivalrous consumption holds when the use or enjoyment of a good or service by a person or persons does not diminish the availability of that good or service for others to use or enjoy. Street lamps offer a good example. Some also call this feature "nonexhaustion," which has been defined by one scholar as holding when "Any number of people can consume the same good at the same time without diminishing the amount of good available for anyone else to consume."[4] For example, one person's consumption of national security provided by nuclear deterrence does not exhaust or diminish another person's ability to receive protection (assuming they are both in the same country).

Thus, governments frequently provide a good or service when it is not practical to exclude people for nonpayment and when the use of a service does not diminish others' ability to use the service. Although this explains some government services, it does not explain them all. For example, in public education, it would be easy to separate payers and nonpayers. Children whose parents did not pay could be excluded; however, we do not exclude any child from education for nonpayment. In fact, most states, including Texas, require students to attend school until they reach a certain age. Why do states do this? Because it is believed that there is a broader public purpose or benefit to having an educated populace. Thus, some government services are provided without charge because there is a benefit to society as a whole—a **collective benefit**. Some believe that without government involvement public goods and collective benefits would not exist or would be underprovided by the market or the collective action of individuals and social groups. Others disagree. For example, economist and *New York Times* columnist Tyler Cowen has noted, while discussing some examples of public goods that do require government provision, "Many other problems, though, that are often perceived as public-goods problems are not really, and markets handle them reasonably well."[5]

For many other government goods, such as toll roads or utilities (e.g., water, sewer, and electricity), people are often excluded for nonpayment. Usually there are private-sector counterparts to what some think are "public goods" but that nonetheless do not actually fit the definition. However, governments may or may not also provide such goods for a variety of reasons.

Still other government expenditures do not fall into these categories. For some goods, government involvement is not due to the failure of markets to allocate resources (through pricing structures) but rather for redistributive purposes—**redistributive goods**. Expenditures for social welfare purposes are a good example. Government, in effect, redistributes wealth in an effort to see that all members of society have a minimum standard of living, sometimes referred to as the poverty line. In Texas, most redistributive funds are from the national government. Very few such funds are from taxes raised at the state level. Also, as we will see later, Texas's tax structure is regressive, meaning lower income earners pay more in terms of percentage of income earned. A progressive state tax structure, in which higher income earners pay more as a percentage of income earned, is necessary in order to redistribute wealth. The provision of redistributive goods is frequently controversial.

Last, in another class of government-provided goods, the state regulates an activity or use of a resource or other common pool good—**regulatory goods**. An example is the pumping of water from aquifers. Without government involvement, there is no practical way to exclude people from drilling wells, taking water, and exhausting the resource (the aquifer). In Texas, the Edwards Aquifer supplies water to San Antonio, Austin, and many other cities in that area of the state. State government has intervened to regulate the amount of water withdrawn from the aquifer. Similar examples exist in the Houston area, where, when water is withdrawn, the land sinks and the possibility of flooding increases in low-lying areas. (See Chapter 11 for more on Texas water policy.) Regulatory goods deal with what is often called a common pool resource, namely something that can be difficult to exclude but rivalrous and thus easy to exhaust or diminish. Fishery exhaustion and traffic jams on public roads show what can happen when governments or other groups fail to properly design institutions to protect such commons.

As we can see, governments provide services for many reasons. Although some think the government provides too many services to far too many citizens, attempts to reduce services often result in protests from those affected. As we all know, everyone favors cutting budgets (and taxes), but no one wants his or her favorite program cut. Despite what services one would think could be cut, all services must be paid for (eventually), either with tax money or from service charges and fees.

CORE OBJECTIVE

Thinking Critically...

What goods and services do you think state government should provide? Consider the consequences of your answer. What would the possible impact to society be, given your position?

Sources of State Revenue

To pay for the many services a state government provides, revenue must be raised from many sources. For state governments, the primary source of revenue is taxes paid by citizens, not money derived from service charges or fees. The amount of tax money available for any given state depends on the wealth of the citizens of that state. Some states, like some individuals, have a higher income capacity than others. The measure of a state's potential to tax is called its **tax capacity**. This measure is an index of all states, with 100 being the average tax capacity. States above 100 have a higher tax capacity, and states below 100 have a lower tax capacity.[6] Texas had a tax capacity index of 104 in 2011, meaning that it was just above the national average.[7] Map 12.1 groups the 50 states by per capita tax capacity in 2011.

Whereas a state's tax capacity measures its potential to tax, a state's **tax effort** measures its level of taxation. Ideally, a state's tax effort will equal its tax capacity. The tax effort in Texas is around 87, meaning that the State of Texas taxes below its capacity. Thus, overall, Texas is a low-tax state; however, it is a high-tax state in terms of its dependency on sales and property tax when compared to other states on these taxes.

Per Capita Taxes

Another measure of state taxes is **per capita tax**. This is a simple measure obtained by taking the total taxes collected and dividing by the number of citizens in the state. Although this might be useful to know, it is not very informative about how

tax capacity
A measure of the wealth of a state or its ability to raise revenues relative to all other states

tax effort
A measure of how close a state comes to using its tax capacity

per capita tax
The total taxes raised in a state divided by the number of residents

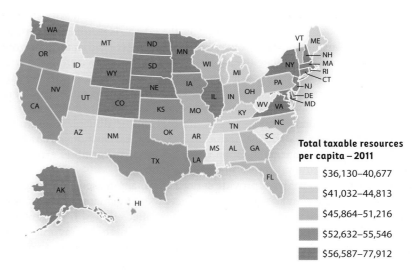

MAP 12.1 Total Taxable Resources per Capita, 2011

SOURCE: U.S. Department of the Treasury, Resource Center, "2013 Total Taxable Resources Estimates" (http://www.treasury.gov/resource-center/economic-policy/taxable-resources/Pages/Total-Taxable-Resources.aspx).

tax exporting

The shifting of taxes to citizens in other states; a good example is Wyoming coal, which is exported to Texas to generate electricity

much citizens actually pay in taxes. The primary point missed by the per capita tax measure is **tax exporting**. Sometimes taxes are exported to out-of-state residents.

Alaska and Wyoming rank near the top on per capita tax burden. However, much of this tax is from oil in Alaska and coal in Wyoming and is exported to residents of other states—tax exporting.[8] Anyone who has ever observed a coal train hauling Wyoming coal to Austin, San Antonio, or Houston has seen tax burden being exported to Texas from Wyoming. This coal is used to generate electricity, and consumers pay the tax when they pay their utility bills. Thus, per capita tax is not a true measure of the tax burden on the citizens living in the state unless tax exporting is taken into account. For example, Texas receives about $1 billion in taxes on oil production and natural gas each year. However, much of the final product is exported to other states, and the tax paid is exported with the oil and gas and other petrochemical products.

Thus, if you do a ranking of all states on per capita revenues, the data does not tell us much about the actual taxes paid by residents living in the state. A somewhat better measure is to compare the 15 most populous states on the amount of revenue raised per $1,000 of personal income. This still does not overcome the issues of tax exporting, but at least it compares the larger states' taxes as a percentage of income. By this comparison, Texas is the second to lowest tax state. (see Table 12.1).

State Taxes in Texas

consumer taxes

Taxes that citizens pay when they buy goods and services—sales taxes

The most common, single sources of revenue for state governments are **consumer taxes**, such as sales and excise taxes on gasoline, tobacco, and liquor. Figure 12.1 shows the breakdown for Texas state tax revenue in 2014–2015, which totals $98.7 billion for the two-year period. As the figure shows, most revenue comes from consumer taxes paid by individuals when they make purchases. More than 80 percent of all tax revenue comes from consumer taxes (sales, motor vehicle sales, motor fuels, alcoholic beverages, tobacco taxes).

Because of high sales taxes, most of the taxes in Texas are paid by consumers and not by businesses. Business taxes are limited, taking the form of a corporate franchise tax. When compared to taxes on consumers, business taxes in Texas pale to insignificance. This point is discussed later in this chapter.

TABLE 12.1

State Tax Revenue for 15 Most Populous States, 2012

State	Per $1,000 of Personal Income	Per Capita	As % of State-Local Tax 2011
New York	$70.18	$3,655.84	46.9
Massachussetts	$62.75	$3,431.41	61.6
New Jersey	$57.75	$3,097.29	51.1
California	$65.67	$2,953.94	63.0
Illinois	$63.15	$2,830.06	51.4
Pennsylvania	$59.19	$2,581.57	58.0
Washington	$56.27	$2,555.41	61.3
Michigan	$64.68	$2,425.16	65.2
North Carolina	$62.87	$2,329.08	66.4
Ohio	$57.16	$2,245.63	55.4
Virginia	$47.06	$2,215.72	54.1
Arizona	$55.02	$1,979.67	56.6
Texas	**$44.97**	**$1,864.85**	**47.5**
Florida	$42.34	$1,708.13	49.9
Georgia	$45.32	$1,671.07	51.4
U.S Average	**$59.29**	**$2,531.17**	**56.8**
Texas as % of U.S.	**75.84%**	**73.70%**	**83.70%**

Source: Texas Legislative Budget Board. *Fiscal Size-up 2014-15 Biennium*, February 2014, p. 53.

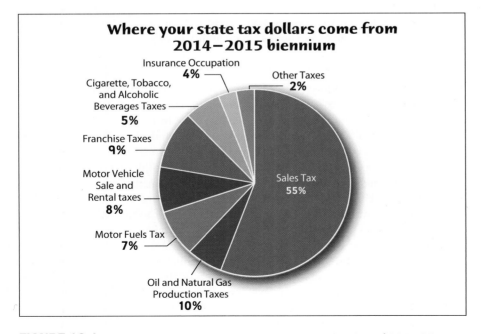

FIGURE 12.1   Total Tax Revenue in Texas, 2014–2015 Biennium: $98.7 billion.

SOURCE: Texas Legislative Budget Board. *Fiscal Size-up 2014–15 Biennium*, February 2014, p. 27.

Equity in Taxes

benefit-based taxes
Taxes for which there is a relationship between the amount paid in taxes and services received; motor fuel taxes are a good example

ability to pay
Taxes that are not based on the benefit received but the wealth, or ability to pay, of an individual

The question of who should pay taxes raises many issues. Should those who benefit from public services pay taxes (**benefit-based taxes**), or should those who can most afford it pay the taxes? Some taxes are based more on the benefit a person receives, and others are based more on the **ability to pay**. For example, the excise tax on gasoline is an example of a tax based on benefit received rather than on ability to pay. A large portion of the gasoline tax is earmarked for highway construction. The more gasoline people buy, the more tax they pay, and the more benefit they receive from using the streets and highways.

For most taxes, other than the gasoline tax, showing direct benefit is problematic. Benefit received is more applicable to service charges and fees than to taxes. Sometimes the service charge covers the actual cost of providing the service, such as for garbage collection. In other cases, the service charge might cover only part of the cost of providing the service. College students receive most of the benefit from attending classes, and they pay tuition and fees to attend. In state-supported universities and colleges, however, not all of the cost of a college education is covered by tuition and fees paid by students. Some of the cost is still paid by taxpayers.

Generally, when individual benefit can be measured, at least part of the cost of the service is paid in the form of fees. People using a public golf course pay a greens fee, hunters pay for hunting licenses, and drivers pay a driver's license and tag fee. Often these funds go directly to the government unit providing the service. Taxpayers may pick up part of the cost through money paid in taxes. For example, greens fees paid by golfers often do not cover the total capital and operating costs of running a golf course. The difference is paid from revenue from other sources, typically from property tax revenues.

Other taxes, such as the federal income tax, are based more on ability to pay. The higher your net income, the higher your income tax bracket, and the higher the percentage of your net income you pay in federal income taxes. Most taxes, especially at the state level, are not based on ability to pay.

Regressive and Progressive Taxes

regressive taxes
Taxes that take a higher percentage of income from low-income persons

progressive taxes
Taxes that take a higher percentage of income from high-income persons

proportional taxes
Taxes that take the same percentage of income from all citizens

Using the criterion of ability to pay, taxes can be ranked as regressive or progressive. A **regressive tax** takes a higher percentage of income from low-income people, and a **progressive tax** takes a higher percentage from higher-income people. Economists also talk about **proportional taxes**, in which the tax paid is a fixed percentage of each person's income. Examples of proportional taxes are difficult to come by but, in theory, are possible. Perhaps the best example of a proportional tax is the tax on earned income for Medicare. One might argue that some state income taxes that tax each person the same percentage of income are proportional. No taxes in Texas can be described as proportional. The key to understanding this is not the total dollars paid but the percentage of income taken by the tax.

Texas has one of the most regressive tax structures of all the states (see Table 12.2). The Institute for Taxation and Economic Policy, a Washington, D.C., advocacy group, issued a report that ranked the 50 states on the degree of progressivism or regressivism of their tax systems. Texas made the "Terrible Ten" list.[9] It is worth noting that 5 of the 7 states that do not have a personal income tax are among the top 10 states with the most regressive tax systems. Figure 12.2 shows the percentage of income taken in Texas by income group in 2010, and Figure 12.3 shows the U.S. average percentages for each income group. As the

TABLE 12.2

The 10 Most Regressive State Tax Systems (2013)

Taxes as Shares of Income for Non-elderly Residents

	Taxes as a Percent of Income		
Income Group	Poorest 20%	Middle 60%	Top 1%
Washington	16.90%	10.50%	2.80%
Florida	13.20%	8.30%	2.30%
South Dakota	11.60%	8.20%	2.10%
Illinois	13.80%	11.10%	4.90%
Texas	**12.60%**	**8.80%**	**3.20%**
Tennessee	11.20%	8.60%	2.80%
Arizona	12.90%	9.70%	4.70%
Pennsylvania	12.00%	9.80%	4.40%
Indiana	12.30%	10.70%	5.40%
Alabama	10.20%	9.40%	3.80%

Source: Institute on Taxation & Economic Policy, *Who Pays? A Distributional Analysis of the Tax Systems in All 50 States,* January 2013 (http://www.itep.org/pdf/whopaysreport.pdf), 4.

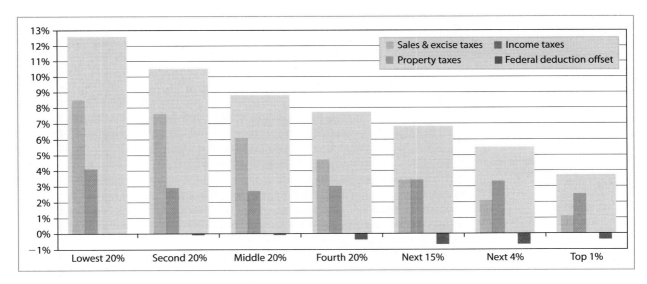

FIGURE 12.2   State and Local Taxes in Texas, 2010 State and local taxes imposed on residents as share of income.

SOURCE: Institute on Taxation and Economic Policy, "Who Pays? A Distributional Analysis of Tax Systems in All 50 States," January 2013 (http://www.itep.org/pdf/whopaysreport.pdf), 3–6. Reprinted by permission.

figure shows, a Texas family in the lowest 20 percent of income will be paying about 12 percent of their income in taxes, while the national average for such a family is slightly less.

Figures 12.2 and 12.3 show that, although all state tax structures are regressive, the tax structure in Texas is more regressive than average. States such as Texas that have no personal income tax have the most regressive tax systems. These states also have the lowest taxes on the rich.[10]

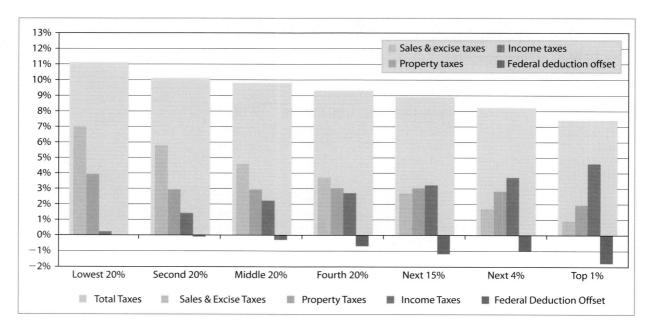

FIGURE 12.3 **State and Local Taxes, All States, 2010** State and local taxes imposed on residents as share of income.

SOURCE: Institute on Taxation and Economic Policy, "Who Pays? A Distributional Analysis of Tax Systems in All 50 States," January 2013 (http://www.itep.org/pdf/whopaysreport.pdf), 128. Reprinted by permission.

tax base

The items that are subject to tax; for example, the items subject to sales tax

The degree to which taxes are regressive or progressive depends upon many factors. Regressivity and progressivity are affected not only by the mix of taxes used in a state (income, sales, excise, property), but also by taxation rates and what is subject to tax. What is subject to taxation is called the **tax base**. For example, some states tax only unearned income (stock dividends and interest) instead of earned income (wages and salaries). Others do the opposite. Some states have a proportional rate for state income tax rather than a progressive tax rate.

With the sales tax, the tax base—what is subject to sales tax—is an important factor. If food and medicine are subject to a sales tax, the tax is more regressive because these are commonly consumed goods for which lower-income earners would pay a higher percentage of their income in order to pay the tax. Only 17 states exempt food items, 44 exempt prescription drugs, and 11 exempt nonprescription drugs. By exempting services used predominantly by the wealthy, such as legal and accounting fees, from sales tax, the tax is less progressive.

Some argue that taxes based on consumption are the "best taxes" because citizens have a choice to consume or not to consume. The less you consume, the smaller your tax burden. The degree to which this is true depends upon what is subject to tax. If many necessities of life, such as food, clothing, and medicine, are subject to tax, the range of choice will be very limited, especially for low-income people who spend most of their income on such items. If, on the other hand, necessities are excluded and nonessentials are included, the choice theory has some validity. For example, if golf course fees, country club fees, accounting services, and legal fees are excluded, the argument that choice is a factor takes on a hollow ring. Table 12.3 shows rates of state and local sales taxes in the 15 most populous states.

TABLE 12.3

Comparison of State Tax Rates: 15 Most Populous States, 2013

State	Retail Sales Tax (Percentage)	Cigarette Tax Rate (Per Pack)	Gasoline Tax Rate (Per Gallon)
Arizona	6.6	$2.00	$0.19
California	7.5	$0.87	$0.43
Florida	6	$1.34	$0.17
Georgia	4	$0.37	$0.20
Illinois	6.25	$1.98	$0.20
Massachusetts	6.25	$2.51	$0.21
Michigan	6	$2.00	$0.19
New Jersey	7	$2.70	$0.15
New York	4	$4.35	$0.27
North Carolina	4.75	$0.45	$0.38
Ohio	5.75	$1.25	$0.28
Pennsylvania	6	$1.60	$0.31
Texas	**6.25**	**$1.41**	**$0.20**
Virginia	5	$0.30	$0.18
Washington	6.5	$3.03	$0.38

Source: Federation of Tax Administrators in Legislative Budget Board, *Fiscal Size-Up 2014–15*, p. 56, Figure 69.

CORE OBJECTIVE

Being Socially Responsible...

Texas taxes prepared food items, but does not tax unprepared food items (e.g., raw meats and fresh produce). If, as it was noted earlier in this chapter, individuals can be excluded from receiving services, such as electricity, because of the inability to pay, how does taxing prepared food impact our state's poorest citizens?

Tax Shifting

Another tax issue is the question of who actually pays the taxes, or **tax shifting**. Some taxes can be shifted from the apparent payer of the tax to others who become the true payers, or the **incidence**, of the tax. For example, a business may respond to a tax rate increase in three general ways: (1) by shifting the tax onto the consumer through increased prices; (2) by shifting the tax onto workers in the form of lower wages or fewer benefits; and (3) by absorbing the cost of the tax through lower profits to its owners or, in the case of publicly traded companies, in lower returns to investors.[11] No matter the approach, the goal of shifting the tax burden is achieved.

Students renting apartments near their campus and who never receive a property tax bill provide another example of tax shifting. The landlord pays the tax each year; however, the landlord will try to pass along the property tax as part of the rent. Market conditions will determine when 100 percent of the tax is passed along to the renter and when the landlord has to lower prices and absorb part of the tax in lower profits.

Except for personal income tax, all taxes can be shifted to others. Market conditions will decide when taxes are shifted. People sometimes argue against business

tax incidence
The person actually paying the tax

tax shifting
Passing taxes on to other citizens

tax increases by advancing the argument that such increases will "simply result in higher prices to the customer." If taxes on businesses could always be shifted forward to customers as higher prices, no business would object to tax increases. Except for the inconvenience of collecting the tax and forwarding it to the government, there would be no cost involved. Obviously, taxes cannot always be shifted to the customer as higher prices, and businesses resist tax increases.

Local Taxes

In addition to taxes collected at the state level, local governments in Texas also collect taxes from two primary sources—property tax and local sales tax. Almost all units of local government collect property tax. For school districts, the property tax is the single largest source of revenue, exceeding state contributions. For so-called rich school districts, all of the cost of running local schools may come from the property tax. The property tax is also an important source of revenue for cities and counties. In addition, most cities, many counties, and all local transit authorities collect a local sales tax. In Texas, the local sales tax is fixed by state law at no more than 2 percent of the value of sales. Thus, in most urban areas in Texas, there is a 6.25 percent state sales tax plus a 2.0 percent local tax, for a total of 8.25 percent total sales tax.

There is effectively no state-level property tax in Texas. All but a small portion of 2000 property tax revenue, the most recent year for which data are available, goes to local governments. In recent years, property taxes have increased dramatically. In 2011, a total of 3,764 local governments in Texas assessed a property tax. The total property tax levy was $40.6 billion, an increase of about 13 percent since 2007, and 28 percent since 2003.[12] Table 12.4 shows this change. Texas local governments, especially school districts, have become more dependent upon the property tax. Texas is not a low-property-tax state. Table 12.5 shows the comparison with the 15 most populous states. Among the top 15 states, Texas has the ninth-highest property tax per $1,000 of personal income. Among the 50 states, Texas ranks thirteenth in property tax.

Comparison of State and Local Tax Revenues

Local taxes are often lost in the focus on state revenues and expenditures. Over the past several decades, the legislature has paid for less and less of the cost of local government services, especially school districts. Figure 12.4 shows the total state and local tax revenue picture for the State of Texas in 2014–15. As the figure shows, property taxes in Texas are almost half of all state and local revenues collected (44 percent). If the local sales tax is added to the local property tax, local

TABLE 12.4

Property Tax Collections by Local Governments in Texas, in Millions

Type of Government	2003	2005	2007	2009	2010	2011
School Districts	$17,264.2	$20,194.9	$18,874.2	$21,780.1	$21,558.30	$22,001.60
City Governments	$ 4,415.2	$ 5,323.0	$ 5,890.3	$ 6,593.8	$6,755.40	$6,810.00
County Governments	$ 4,121.8	$ 5,339.6	$ 5,837.0	$ 6,526.7	$6,567.10	$6,742.90
Special Districts	$ 3,092.3	$ 3,609.6	$ 4,513.1	$ 5,133.8	$5,394.70	$5,038.70
Total Property Tax	$28,893.4	$ 33,479	$35,114.6	$40,034.4	$40,275.50	$40,593.20

Source: Comptroller of Public Accounts in Legislative Budget Board, *Fiscal Size-Up 2014–15*, p. 42, Figure 50.

TABLE 12.5

Comparison of Property Tax Rates per $1000 of Personal Income: 15 Most Populous States, 2013

State	Revenue	Rank among 50 states
Arizona	$28.71	28
California	$25.47	35
Florida	$31.08	22
Georgia	$26.43	33
Illinois	$37.50	12
Massachusetts	$34.32	14
Michigan	$32.38	18
New Jersey	$16.99	3
New York	$39.54	8
North Carolina	$22.91	40
Ohio	$31.26	21
Pennsylvania	$28.14	29
Texas	**$39.03**	**9**
Virginia	$27.30	31
Washington	$28.88	27
U.S. Average	**$30.83**	
Texas as % of U.S.	$126.60	

Source: U.S. Census Bureau in Legislative Budget Board, *Fiscal Size-Up 2014–15*, p. 54, Figure 68.

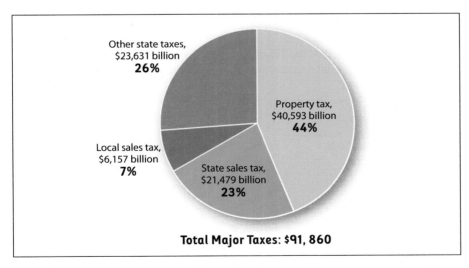

Total Major Taxes: $91, 860

FIGURE 12.4   State and Local Sales and Property Tax as a Percentage of Major Taxes in Texas in 2014–2015 Biennium (numbers in millions)

SOURCE: Texas Comptroller Office in Legislative Budget Board, *Fiscal Size-Up 2014–15*.

tax revenues constitute 50.9 percent of total taxes collected in the state. Thus, local governments collect and pay just over a half the total cost of government in Texas. If the current trend of the state spending less continues, local governments will be picking up a greater share of the cost of providing services to the citizens of the state.

The fact that local governments collect over half of state and local revenues combined in Texas is an indication of the declining role of the state government in funding services, especially schools. This has been a trend in school financing for several decades and the root cause of much of the objection to property tax increases.

Nontax Revenue Sources

nontax revenue

Governmental revenue derived from service charges, fees (tuition), lottery, and other sources

Service charges and fees are another source of **nontax revenue** for state governments. Governments often charge service charges and assess fees when a person can be excluded from receiving the service for nonpayment. When this exclusion is not possible, tax revenue usually finances the service. Figure 12.5 shows nontax revenue by source for the State of Texas in 2014–15. Nontax revenue sources make up about 34 percent of state revenue. Whereas state governments obtain only a small percentage of their revenue from service charges and fees, some local governments, especially cities, are heavily dependent upon service charges and fees to finance their services. Cities usually impose service charges or fees for water, sewer, and solid waste collection. Seventy-two cities in Texas also operate an electrical system and receive revenue for providing this service. The largest cities with electrical systems are San Antonio, Austin, Lubbock, Brownsville, Garland, Bryan, and College Station.

The trend in recent years has been to increase service charges and fees as a way to increase revenue and avoid raising taxes. All students attending state colleges and universities in Texas have experienced these increases as higher tuition and service charges (see Chapter 11). In terms of total dollars in the state budget, the various service charges and fees provide 15 percent of total state revenue.

The state lottery and interest income generates about 1.5 percent of all (total) state revenue. Even though the Texas Lottery has been the most successful lottery in history in terms of total dollars raised, it contributes only a small portion of the

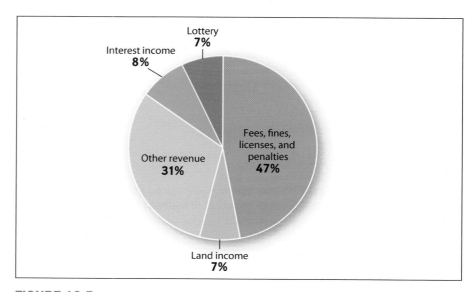

FIGURE 12.5   Total Nontax Revenue for Texas 2014–2015 Biennium: $35,481.8 Million

SOURCE: Texas Comptroller Office in Legislative Budget Board, *Fiscal Size-Up 2014–15*, p. 27, Figure 39.

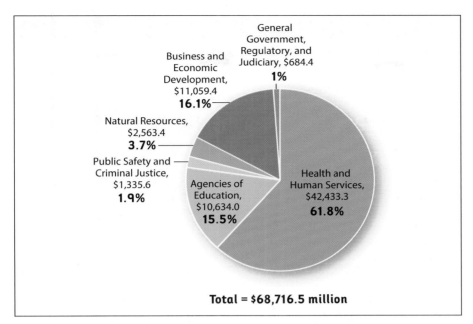

FIGURE 12.6   **Total Federal Funds by State Function 2014–2015 Biennium.**

SOURCE: Legislative Budget Board, Fiscal Size up 2014–15, p. 6, Figure 9.

state's total budget and will never be a significant player in providing revenue. In recent years, revenue from the lottery has declined.

Federal aid makes up about 35.5 percent of the Texas 2014–2015 biennial budget. As shown in Figure 12.6, the largest part (61.8 percent) of these federal funds goes to health and human services for Medicare or Medicaid payments and welfare payments. About 15.5 percent of these funds goes to education, and about 16 percent goes to business and economic development. The remainder is divided between various other federal programs.

The Budget "Fix"

The legislature is limited in the amount of discretion it has in spending money. Much of the revenues are **earmarked** for specific items, called fixed revenues. Revenues are fixed in three ways: by constitutional or statutory provisions, by funding formulas, and by federal government rules. Although the legislature could change the statutory and funding formula rules, these are often politically fixed by past actions and, except in extraordinary circumstances, are not changed. Interest groups have a strong attachment to these appropriations and will fight to maintain them. Table 12.6 shows how much is fixed in these various categories. These "fixes" primarily are the results of funds being earmarked for specific programs (see Chapter 2). For example, the proceeds from the state lottery go to education. Motor fuel tax goes primarily to state and local road programs.

The earmarking of revenues obviously limits the ability of the legislature to change budget priorities or to react to emergency situations. If one fund is short, movement of money from another fund may not be possible. Last year's budget becomes the best predictor of next year's budget. Changes in the budget occur incrementally, in small amounts, over a long period of time.

earmarked revenue

Tax revenue set aside for specific purposes; in Texas about 80 percent of revenue is earmarked

TABLE 12.6

Restricted Appropriations from General Revenue Funds and General Revenue—Dedicated Funds, 2014–15 Biennium

In Millions

Function	Appropriation	Percentage of Total Appropriation
Appropriations or allocations of revenue dedicated by constitutional or statutory provisions	$ 45,753.4	44.7%
Appropriations influenced by federal law, regulation, or court decisions	$ 27,213.7	26.6%
Appropriations influenced by formulas	$ 11,602.8	11.3%
Total Restricted Appropriations	**$ 84,551.9**	**82.7%**
Nonrestricted appropriations	$ 17,555.4	17.2%

Source: Legislative Budget Board, *Fiscal Size-Up 2014–15*, p. 9, Figure 16.

CORE OBJECTIVE

Communicating Effectively...

Consider Table 12.6, which illustrates how specific appropriations are restricted. What percentage of funds is not restricted? How does restricting funds impact budget flexibility?

Table 12.6 indicates that most funds in Texas are fixed. Only 17.2 percent of the moneys in the general fund are nonrestricted and available for change. This does not give the legislature much leeway in making changes in the budget. Similar patterns are also found in most state budgets. (For more detail on this, check the Legislative Budget Board's website.) Funding for state universities is not in an earmarked category, but is part of the 17.2 percent **discretionary funding**. This may help explain why student tuitions have been increasing in recent years.

discretionary funding
Those funds in the state budget that are not earmarked for specific purposes

Expenditures: Where the Money Goes

The pattern of expenditures for Texas differs little from most states in terms of the items funded. In most states, three items consume most of the state budget—education, health and welfare, and transportation. In recent years, an increase in the prison population has greatly increased the amount spent for public safety, which includes prison operations. After these items, everything else pales in comparison. Figure 12.7 shows the major expenditure items in the State of Texas 2014–2015 biennial budget.

Although education takes the lion's share of the state budget (about 37 percent), local school districts contribute about 60 percent of the funds for local schools. The state currently finances about 40 percent of the cost of elementary and secondary education. This is a decline in state contributions from a decade ago. The state's contribution has been steadily decreasing, and school districts have been forced to pick up a greater share of the cost of local education, which they are covering by assessing higher local property taxes.

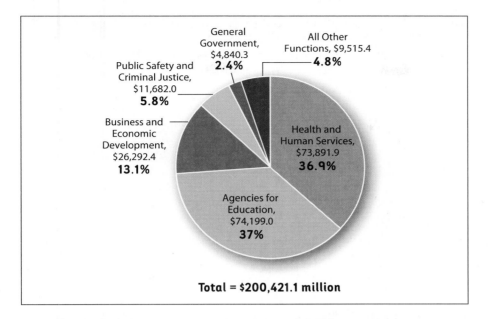

Total = $200,421.1 million

FIGURE 12.7   **Total Appropriations by Function, 2014–2015 Biennium,**

SOURCE: Legislative Budget Board, *Fiscal Size up 2014–15*, p. 6, Figure 2.

Health and human services accounts for about 37 percent of the state budget and is funded primarily with federal grants to the state. The State of Texas contributes less than most states to the cost of providing these services. The Texas Constitution prohibits spending more than an amount equal to 1 percent of the state budget on welfare. These are the redistributive services discussed previously. Neither tax structure nor the political culture supports such activities. Many students of budgeting have made the point that a budget is a statement of policy in monetary terms. What and how much money a state spends largely expresses its priorities. The budget becomes a statement of the dominant values in the state. A comparison of Texas with other large industrial states on the primary budget items will tell us something about what Texans value.

As shown by examining the 15 most populous states, Texas ranks near the lower-mid range in expenditures for health and human services (Table 12.7). Although Texas spends much money in total dollars, it tends to spend less than the average comparable state in per capita dollars for most items. In recent years, most of the growth in state expenditures has been driven by population increases alone. In terms of per capita expenditures, the state has remained at about the same level over the past decade.

Continuing Issues in State Finance in Texas

Over the past 20 years, Texas has experienced a number of fiscal shortfalls. The legislature has been forced to meet in special sessions to correct these problems. Many of the fixes have been short term. An examination of several tax issues will help us understand the need for a long-term solution.

TABLE 12.7

State Government Expenditures Per Capita, 15 Most Populous States, Fiscal Year 2011

State	Total	Education	Highways	Hospitals	Welfare	Corrections	All Others
Washington	178	80	11	15	14	13	44
New Jersey	166	38	7	20	10	10	81
North Carolina	160	68	11	21	1	22	37
Virginia	154	68	9	18	3	17	38
Michigan	147	77	3	19	10	15	23
Massachusetts	139	47	4	9	10	9	60
Pennsylvania	132	48	12	9	9	15	40
Georgia	126	56	5	7	9	18	31
New York	125	27	6	22	2	16	51
Texas	**124**	**52**	**5**	**10**	**9**	**17**	**32**
Ohio	120	60	6	14	2	13	25
California	108	42	5	12	1	16	32
Arizona	106	46	4	1	7	16	32
Illinois	102	48	5	9	7	9	24
Florida	97	29	4	2	5	16	40
U.S. AVERAGE	**140**	**55**	**7**	**13**	**7**	**15**	**43**
Texas as% of U.S.	88.80%	93.80%	72.40%	77.40%	120.70%	114.10%	74.20%

Source: U.S. Census Bureau in Legislative Budget Board, *Fiscal Size-Up 2014–15*, p. 62, Figure 76.

Tax Structure

In the past 20 years, Texas has experienced various financial problems. During the 1980s, there were 10 special sessions of the legislature to attempt to correct revenue shortfalls. These shortfalls were caused primarily by a decline in the state economy because of a drop in oil prices from a high of $40 per barrel to a low of less than $10. The fiscal crisis was worsened by the state's tax structure. Texas is very dependent on highly **income-elastic taxes** (85 to 90 percent) that rise or fall very quickly relative to changes in economic conditions. This means that when the economy is growing or contracting, tax revenue grows or contracts proportionately with the growth or contraction in the economy. For example, as retail sales grow, the sales tax grows. Texas is very dependent upon sales and excise taxes, which are highly income-elastic. The same is true for the tax on oil and gas extracted in Texas. As the price of oil increased on world markets, the economy of the state boomed, and tax revenue increased. When the oil bust came, the opposite happened, and Texas found itself extremely short of revenue. People quit buying goods and services subject to the sales and excise tax, and revenue fell accordingly. As the price of oil declined, oil revenue fell. Depressed oil prices also caused severe economic problems in Mexico and a devaluation of the peso. Fewer pesos flowed across the border, and some border communities experienced severe economic problems and declining local revenue along with the state revenue decline.

Figure 12.8 and Table 12.8 compare the tax dependency of the 15 most populous states. Texas is far more dependent on sales taxes than most other large states. Only Florida and Washington are about as dependent as Texas on consumer taxes. Washington, like Texas, lacks both a personal and a corporate income tax, and Florida lacks a personal income tax. Heavy dependency on consumer taxes makes for an income-elastic tax structure. In bad economic times, the state will face revenue shortfalls.

income-elastic taxes

Taxes that rise and fall quickly relative to changes in economic conditions; the Texas tax system is very income-elastic

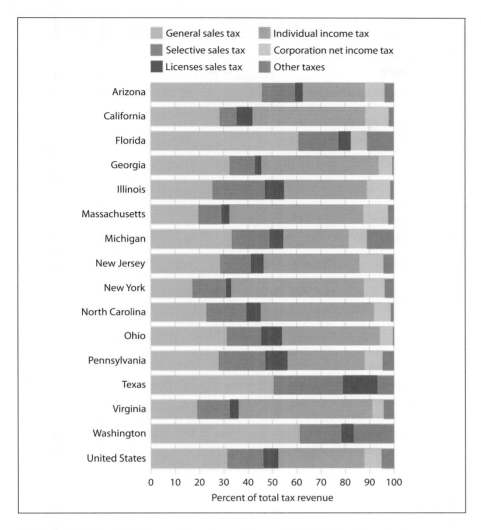

FIGURE 12.8   **State Comparison, Percentage of Total Tax Revenue by Source**

The Texas tax structure is very dependent upon highly income-elastic consumer taxes (such as sales and gasoline taxes), and when, not if, there is an economic downturn, the state will again experience revenue shortfalls. The potential for these problems to occur again is great. In fact, the 2003 session of the legislature faced at least a $10 billion revenue shortfall owing to a downturn in the economy.

Is There a Personal Income Tax in the Future for Texas?

Texas is one of only seven states without any form of personal income tax. The other states are Alaska, Florida, Nevada, South Dakota, Washington, and Wyoming. In addition, New Hampshire and Tennessee have a limited income tax on unearned income (dividends, interest, and capital gains). Being in such a limited company of states without an income tax is not troublesome to most Texans. Politically there is great resistance to imposing such a tax. In 1992, the voters approved a constitutional amendment preventing the legislature from enacting an income tax

TABLE 12.8

Sources of Revenue for 15 Most Populous States (in Percent), 2012

State	Total Sales Tax	General Sales Tax	Selective Sales Tax	License Tax	Individual Income Tax	Corporation Net Income	Other Taxes
Arizona	62.2	47.9	14.3	2.9	23.8	5.0	0.3
California	34.4	25.4	9.0	7.7	49.0	7.1	0.0
Florida	82.6	58.8	23.8	6.7	–	6.1	4.6
Georgia	43.8	32.0	11.8	3.1	49.1	3.6	0.1
Illinois	39.2	22.0	17.2	7.1	43.1	9.6	0.8
Massachusetts	32.1	22.3	9.8	3.9	52.3	8.8	2.8
Michigan	54.7	39.9	14.8	5.9	28.5	2.5	0.8
New Jersey	43.7	29.5	14.2	5.2	40.5	7.0	3.5
New York	32.0	16.6	15.3	2.7	54.2	6.4	4.8
North Carolina	42.0	24.5	17.5	6.5	45.7	5.4	0.4
Ohio	50.6	31.9	18.7	13.8	34.8	0.5	0.3
Pennsylvania	52.1	27.8	24.2	8.0	30.7	5.6	3.6
Texas	**77.0**	**50.4**	**26.6**	**15.5**	–	–	**7.5**
Virginia	32.3	19.2	13.0	4.3	56.3	4.6	2.3
Washington	80.4	60.2	20.2	5.6	–	–	3.2
U.S. Average	**47.2**	**30.5**	**16.6**	**6.8**	**35.3**	**5.3**	**3.9**

Source: U.S. Census Bureau in Legislative Budget Board, *Fiscal Size-Up 2014–15*, p. 54, Figure 67.

without voter approval. Several legislative leaders felt that without voter approval, the tax would never be imposed by the legislature.

Texas will face another fiscal crisis as long as it is so dependent on consumer taxes. What recourses are available to the state? During past crises, the problem of revenue shortfall was often solved by raising sales and gasoline taxes and by increasing fees. Can these taxes be tapped again? Texas has one of the highest sales tax rates, currently sitting at 6.25 percent. Only Indiana, New Jersey, Rhode Island, Mississippi, and Tennessee have reached 7 percent. Raising the rate might not be possible.

CORE OBJECTIVE

Taking Personal Responsibility...

Although few individuals would express a preference for higher taxes, given the information in this chapter about the goods and services the state provides and the revenue data presented in Figure 12.8 and Table 12.7, should Texans advocate for a personal income tax? Why or why not?

One suggestion, made by former Lieutenant Governor Bob Bullock and others, was to expand the base of the sales tax. Currently most services are not subject to a sales tax; most notably excluded are legal and financial services. Politically, given the large number of attorneys in the legislature (35 percent), pushing such a change through the legislature might be difficult. The proposal was killed in the past several sessions of the legislature, including a special session in 2004.

The state tax on gasoline or motor fuel in Texas is currently at 20 cents per gallon, plus 14.5 cents in federal tax. The highest state gasoline tax is in Connecticut, at 29 cents per gallon. There might be room to raise the gas tax a few cents per gallon, but if prices at the pump continue to rise, the prospect of this happening is unlikely.

In the past 10 years, the tax on oil and natural gas production, which is based on the dollar value of the oil and gas extracted from the ground, has increased. Although production has been falling, prices have risen, especially in the past five years. The long-term outlook is for these taxes to rise, with the natural gas tax rising more than the oil tax.[13] In late 1998, the price of oil had fallen to about $11 per barrel, a price not seen since the mid-1980s. In 2008, the price increased to $150 per barrel. The long-term price of a barrel of oil is very much tied to national and international factors. New oil from Russia, continued war in the Middle East, and many other factors can affect the price of oil and the amount of revenue available.

Texas has a form of corporate "income tax" that is called a **franchise fee**. Originally it was assessed only on corporations doing business in the state. It did not apply to limited partnerships, corporations, limited liability companies, business trusts, professional associations, or business associations. Some businesses and corporations changed their structure to avoid the tax. The legislature was forced to eliminate many of these loopholes in 2007 and apply the franchise fee to most businesses in the state. The tax was first collected in 2008. As of 2014, the franchise fee is the second-largest source of tax revenue ($9.3 billion, behind sales and use taxes, which total $48.9 billion).[14] The franchise fee seems to be a much improved source of business tax and may be filling the loopholes in the older franchise fee.

The franchise fee is rather complicated, but basically the tax is applied to the gross receipts of most businesses, with deductions allowed for some expenses such as wages, salaries, and employee benefits. Taxable entities with revenues of $300,000 or less owe no tax; however, all businesses must file a report. The tax rate is 0.5 percent for wholesalers and retailers and 1 percent for most other taxable entities. This tax is applied to most businesses in the state.

franchise fee

Major business tax in Texas that is assessed on income earned by corporations in the state

Conclusion

Although the State of Texas spends much money, measured in total dollars, the state still ranks toward the bottom on per capita expenditures.

Some important conclusions should be drawn from analyzing government financing in Texas. First, although Texas is a resource-rich state, its tax effort is low compared to its tax capacity. Texas has one of the lowest tax burdens of any state, which is in keeping with the political culture of Texas and the emphasis on limited government. Yet, despite Texas's low tax status, Texas has one of the most regressive tax structures. The state government is heavily reliant on the regressive general sales tax, and the state does not have a personal income tax, which tends to be progressive in structure. It should be no surprise that the majority of states with the most regressive tax structures do not have a personal income tax.

Second, it is important to understand that it is difficult to achieve substantial changes in the state's budget. Nearly 83 percent of the state's budget is fixed by constitutional, statutory, or federal mandates. Nearly 40 percent of the state's budget is provided through transfer payments from the federal government and, with that, less budget flexibility.

Finally, Texas will have to decide how best to manage growing fiscal challenges. The Texas legislature slashed the budget in response to a $27 billion shortfall for 2012–2013. Though the state economy is faring much better in comparison to the rest of the country, there is growing concern that state revenues will not keep pace with the demand for services in the coming years. Unlike the federal government, Texas, like all states (Vermont is the only notable exception), is required to balance its budget. It remains to be seen how the state will meet these challenges, although any changes to the tax structure are highly unlikely.

Key Terms

ability to pay	nonrivalrous consumption	regulatory goods
benefit-based taxes	nontax revenue	tax base
collective benefit	per capita tax	tax capacity
consumer taxes	political values	tax effort
discretionary funding	progressive taxes	tax exporting
earmarked revenue	proportional taxes	tax incidence
franchise fee	public goods	tax shifting
income-elastic taxes	redistributive goods	
nonexcludability	regressive taxes	

Notes

[1] U.S. Census Bureau, "State and Local Government Finances Summary: 2011," July 2013, http://www2.census.gov/govs/local/summary_report.pdf.

[2] Tyler Cowen, "Public Goods," *The Concise Encyclopedia of Economics.* 2nd edition, ed. David R. Henderson (Indianapolis: Liberty Fund, Inc., 2007). Also available at http://www.econlib.org/library/Enc/PublicGoods.html. This is a nice general introduction to the concept, and it generally informs the treatment here. The classic work on the subject of public goods is Paul A. Samuelson, "The Pure Theory of Public Expenditure," *Review of Economics and Statistics* 36:4 (November 1954): 387–389.

[3] Some scholars, however, do not think lighthouses meet the nonexcludability criteria. For example, see Nobel Prize-winning economist Ronald H. Coase's classic piece "The Lighthouse in Economics." *The Journal of Law and Economics* Vol. 17, No. 2 (October 1974): 357–376. For more on this debate, see David E. Van Zandt. "The Lessons of the Lighthouse: 'Government' or 'Private' Provision of Goods," *Journal of Legal Studies,* 22:1 (January 1993): 47–72; and William Barnett and Walter Block, "Coase and Van Zandt on Lighthouses," *Public Finance Review* 35 (November 2007): 710–733.

[4] John L. Mikesell, *Fiscal Administration: Analysis and Applications for the Public Sector,* 8th ed. (Boston: Wadsworth, 2011), 3.

[5] Cowen, "Public Goods."

[6] J. Richard Aronson and John L. Hilley, *Financing State and Local Governments,* 4th ed. (Washington, D.C.: Brookings Institution, 1986), 37–40.

[7] U.S. Department of the Treasury, Resource Center, "2012 Total Taxable Resources Estimates," http://www.treasury.gov/resource-center/economic-policy/taxable-resources/Pages/Total-Taxable-Resources.aspx

[8] Texas Research League, "The Rating Game," *Analysis 11* (August 1990): 2.

[9] Institute on Taxation and Economic Policy, "Who Pays? A Distribution Analysis of the Tax Systems in All 50 States," 3rd ed. (Washington, D.C.: 2009), http://www.itepnet.org/whopays3.pdf.

[10] Ibid.

[11] Mikesell, John L., *Fiscal Administration Analysis and Application for the Public Sector,* 8th ed., (Boston: Wadsworth, 2011), 355.

[12] Legislative Budget Board, *Fiscal Size-Up 2014–15,* 42.

[13] Texas Comptroller of Public Accounts, www.cpa.state.tx.us.

[14] Legislative Budget Board, *Fiscal Size-Up* 2014-15, 29, Figure 40.

A

ability to pay   Taxes that are not based on the benefit received but the wealth, or ability to pay, of an individual

absentee voting   A process that allows a person to vote early, before the regular election; applies to all elections in Texas; also called early voting

acting governor   When a governor leaves a state, the position is held by the lieutenant governor, who performs the functions of the office

annual registration   A system that requires citizens to reregister to vote every year

appellate courts   Higher-level courts that decide on points of law and not questions of guilt or innocence

appointive-elective system   In Texas, the system of many judges gaining the initial seat on the court by being appointed and later standing for election

astroturf   A political term for an interest group that appears to have many grassroots members but in fact does not have individual citizens as members; rather, it is sponsored by an organization such as a corporation or business association

at-large election system   System where all voters in the city elect the mayor and city council members

attorney general   Chief counsel to the governor and state agencies; limited criminal jurisdiction

B

Baker v. Carr   Court case that required state legislative districts to contain about the same number of citizens

ballot form   The forms used by voters to cast their ballots; each county, with approval of the secretary of state, determines the form of the ballot.

ballot wording   Description of a proposed amendment as it appears on the ballot; can be intentionally noninstructive and misleading to voters in order to affect voter outcome

benefit-based taxes   Taxes for which there is a relationship between the amount paid in taxes and services received; motor fuel taxes are a good example.

bicameral   Legislative body that consists of two houses

biennial session   Legislature meets every two years.

bill of rights   A list of individual rights and freedoms granted to citizens within a constitution

blanket primary system   A nominating election in which voters could switch parties between elections

block grants   Grants that may be used for broad purposes that allow local governments greater discretion in how funds are spent

boards and commissions   Governing body for many state agencies; members appointed by the governor for fixed term

budget fix   State laws and constitutional amendments that set aside money to be spent on specific items; the best example is the state gasoline tax being committed to state highways.

budgetary powers   The ability of a governor to formulate a budget, present it to the legislature, and execute or control the budget

C

Calendars Committee   Standing committee of the house that decides which bills will be considered for floor debate and to which committee they will be assigned

calendars   Procedures in the house used to consider different kinds of bills; major bills and minor bills are considered under different procedures.

capture   The situation in which a state agency or board falls under the heavy influence of or is controlled by its constituency interest groups

categorical grants   Grants that may be used to fund specific purposes as defined by the federal government

ceremonial duties   The expectation that a governor attends many functions and represents the state; some governors become so active at this role that they get caught in a "ceremonial trap" and neglect other duties.

checks and balances   Power granted by the Constitution to each branch of government giving it authority to restrain other branches

chief legislator   The expectation that a governor has an active agenda of legislation to recommend to the legislature and works to pass that agenda

citizen legislatures   Legislatures characterized by low pay, short sessions, and fewer staff resources

city manager   Person hired by the city council to manage the city; serves as the chief administrative officer of the city

closed primary system   A nominating election that is closed to all voters except those who have registered as a member of that political party

closed rider   Provisions attached to appropriations bills that are not made public until the conference committee meets

collective bargaining   Negotiations between an employer and a group of employees to determine employment conditions, such as those related to wages, working hours, and safety

collective benefit   Goods that are provided with no charge because there is a broader public benefit associated with the good

commission form   A form of local government where voters elect department heads who also serve as members of the city council

commissioner's court   Legislative body that governs a Texas county

comptroller of public accounts   Chief tax collector and investor of state funds; does not perform financial audits

confederal system of government   A system of government that divides power between a weak national government and strong, independently sovereign regional governments

conference committees   Joint committees of the house and senate that work out differences in bills passed in each chamber

constitution   The basic document that provides a framework for government and limits what the government can do

constitutional convention   An assembly of citizens who may propose changes to state constitutions through voter approval

consumer taxes   Taxes that citizens pay when they buy goods and services—sales taxes

conviction   Following adoption of articles of impeachment by the lower legislative house, the senate tries the official under those articles; if convicted, the official is removed from office.

council-manager form   Form of government where voters elect a mayor and city council; the mayor and city council appoint a professional administrator to manage the city.

county chair   Party official elected in each county to organize and support the party

county executive committee   Committee made up of a county chair and all precinct chairs in the county; serves as the official organization for the party in each county

county government   Local unit of government that is primarily the administrative arm of a state government. In most states, it does not provide urban-type services.

county sheriff   Elected head of law enforcement in a Texas county

creatures of the state   Local governments are created by state government, and all powers are derived from the state government; there are no inherent rights for local governments independent of what the state grants to them.

crisis manager   The expectation that the governor will provide strong leadership in times of a natural or man-made disaster.

crossover voting   Occurs when voters leave their party and vote in the other party's primary

cumulative voting   A system where voters can concentrate (accumulate) all their votes on one candidate rather than casting one vote for each office up for election

D

delegate   Representational role of member that states that he or she represents the wishes of the voters

"deregulated" tuition   A decision by the state legislature to allow state colleges and universities to set the rate of tuition charged to students

discretionary funding   Those funds in the state budget that are not earmarked for specific purposes

Due Process of Law Clause   Clause in the Fifth and Fourteenth Amendment of the U.S. Constitution that requires states to treat all citizens equally and that the state must follow certain rules and procedures

E

earmarked revenue   Tax revenue set aside for specific purposes; in Texas about 80 percent of revenue is earmarked.

earmarks   Money dedicated to a specific expenditure; for example, the excise tax on gasoline funds highway infrastructure

economic regions   Divisions of the state based on dominant economic activity

electioneering   Various activities in which interest groups engage to try to influence the outcome of elections

Equal Protection Clause   Clause in the Fourteenth Amendment of the U.S. Constitution that requires states to treat all citizens equally

extra legislative powers   Legislative leaders serve on boards outside of the legislature.

extraordinary session   Legislative session called by the legislature, rather than the governor; not used in Texas

extraterritorial jurisdiction   City powers that extend beyond the city limits to an area adjacent to the city limits

F

federal system of government   The division of powers between a national government and regional governments

filing fee   A fee or payment required to get a candidate's name on the primary or general election ballot

focus groups   Panel of "average citizens" who are used by political consultants to test ideas and words for later use in campaigns

fragmented government structure   A government structure where power is dispersed to many state agencies with little or no central control

franchise fee   Major business tax in Texas that is assessed on income earned by corporations in the state

G

general elections   Regular elections held every two years to elect state officeholders

general law city   Cities governed by city charters created by state statutes

geographic distribution   A characteristic of some interest groups in that they have members in all regions of the state

gerrymandering   Drawing district boundary lines for political advantage

government organizations   Interest groups that represent state and local governments; also called SLIGs, for state and local interest groups

grand juries   Juries of citizens that determine if a person will be charged with a crime

H

Higher Education Assistance Fund (HEAF)   The HEAF is money set aside for use by those universities not benefiting from the PUF.

home rule city   Cities governed by city charters created by the actions of local citizens

Hopwood Decision   Decision by federal courts to end affirmative action in Texas schools; these programs had provided for special treatment for minority students in being accepted to colleges and professional schools.

Hunt v. Cromartie   Court case that ruled while race can be a factor, it could not be the primary factor in determining the makeup of legislative districts.

I

impeachment   The process by which some elected officials, including governors, may be impeached (accused of an impeachable offense) by the lower house adopting articles of impeachment

income-elastic taxes   Taxes that rise and fall quickly relative to changes in economic conditions; the Texas tax system is very income-elastic.

incorporation   Process of creating a city government

independent candidate   A person whose name appears on the ballot without a political party designation

independent school district   School districts that are not attached to any other unit of government and that operate schools in Texas

individualistic subculture   Government that benefits the individual rather than society in general

informal qualifications   Additional qualifications beyond the formal qualifications required for men and women to be elected governor; holding statewide elected office is an example.

informal rules   Set of norms or values that govern legislative bodies

information or administrative hearing   A hearing before a judge who decides if a person must stand trial; used in place of a grand jury

initiative   A process that allows citizens to propose changes to the state constitution through the use of petitions signed by registered voters; Texas does not allow constitutional revision through initiative.

interest group   An organization of individuals sharing common goals that tries to influence governmental decisions

intergovernmental coordinator   The expectation that a governor coordinates activities with other state governments

interim committees   Temporary committees of the legislature that study issues between regular sessions and make recommendations on legislation

Interstate Commerce Clause   Article in U.S. Constitution that gives Congress the exclusive power to regulate commerce between the states; Congress and the courts determine what is interstate commerce.

J

judicial powers   The ability of a governor to issue pardons, executive clemency, and parole of citizens convicted of a crime

L

land commissioner   Elected official responsible for administration and oversight of state-owned lands and coastal lands extending 10.3 miles into the Gulf of Mexico

land-based economy   An economic system in which most wealth is derived from the use of the land

League of United Latin American Citizens (LULAC)   Largest organization representing Latinos in Texas

Legislative Budget Board   State agency that is controlled by the leadership in the state legislature and that writes the state budget

legislative power   The formal power, especially the veto authority, of the governor to force the legislature to enact his or her legislation

legislative professionalism   Legislatures with higher pay, longer sessions, high levels of staff support are considered more professional.

Legislative Redistricting Board (LRB)   State board composed of elected officials that can draw new legislative districts for the house and senate if the legislature fails to act

lieutenant governor   Presiding officer of the Texas Senate; elected by the voters of the state

line-item veto   The ability of a governor to veto part of an appropriations bill without vetoing the whole bill

lobbying   The practice of attempting to influence the legislature, originally by catching members in the lobby of the capitol

Local and Consent Calendars Committee   Committee handling minor and noncontroversial bills that normally apply to only one county

M

magistrate functions   Preliminary hearings for persons charged with a serious criminal offense

majority-minority   Minority groups that make up a majority of the population of the state

membership organizations   Interest groups that have individual citizens or businesses as members, such as the National Rifle Association

merit system, or Missouri system   A system of electing judges that involves appointment by the governor and periodic retention election

military powers   Powers giving the governor the right to use the National Guard in times of natural disaster or civil unrest

minor party   A party other than the Democratic or Republican Party; to be a minor party in Texas, the organization must have received between 5 and 19 percent of the vote in the past election.

moralistic subculture   Government viewed as a positive force to achieve a common good for all citizens

multimember districts   Districts represented by more than one member elected to the legislature

N

name familiarity   Practice in Texas of voting for judges with familiar or popular names

Necessary and Proper Clause (Elastic Clause)   Statement in Article 1, Section 8, paragraph 18 of the U.S. Constitution that says Congress can pass any law necessary and proper to carry out other powers

noncompetitive districts   Districts in which a candidate from either party wins 55 percent or more of the vote

nonexcludability   The inability to practically prevent people from receiving or enjoying a good or service due to nonpayment

nonmembership organizations   Interest groups that represent corporations and businesses and do not have broad-based citizen support

nonpartisan election   Election in which party identification is not formally declared

nonrivalrous consumption   Situation in which the use or enjoyment of a good or service by a person or persons does not diminish the availability of that good or service for others to use or enjoy

nontax revenue   Governmental revenue derived from service charges, fees (tuition), lottery, and other sources

O

objectivity   The appearance that courts make objective decisions and not political ones

office block format   Ballot form where candidates are listed by office with party affiliation listed by their name; most often used with computer ballots

open primary system   A nominating election that is open to all registered voters regardless of party affiliation

ordinances   Laws passed by local governments

P

partial veto   The ability of some governors to veto part of a nonappropriations bill without vetoing the entire bill; a Texas governor does not have this power except on appropriations bills.

partisan election   Method used to select all judges (except municipal court judges) in Texas by using a ballot in which party identification is shown

party caucus   A meeting of members of a political party that is used by minor political parties in Texas to nominate candidates

party chief   The expectation that the governor will be the head of his or her party

party column format   Paper ballot form where candidates are listed by party and by office

party de-alignment   View that a growing number of voters and candidates do not identify with either major political party but are independents

party ideology   Basic belief system that guides the party

party raiding   Occurs when members of one political party vote in another party's primary in an effort to nominate a weaker candidate or split the vote among the top candidates

per capita tax   The total taxes raised in a state divided by the number of residents

permanent party organization   Series of elected officials of a political party that keep the party organization active between elections

permanent registration   A system that keeps citizens on the voter registration list without their having to reregister every year

Permanent University Fund (PUF)   The PUF is money set aside in the state constitution to benefit the University of Texas at Austin and Texas A&M University.

petit juries   Juries of citizens that determine the guilt or innocence of a person during a trial; pronounced *petty* juries

plural executive system   System in which executive power is divided among several statewide elected officials

policy liberalism index   A measure of how liberal or conservative a state is on some state policies

political action committee (PAC)   Spin-offs of interest groups that collect money for campaign contributions and other activity

political culture   A system of beliefs and values that define the role of government and the role of citizens in that government

political gerrymandering   Drawing legislative districts to the advantage of a political party

political participation   All forms of involvement citizens can have that are related to governance

political parties   Organizations that act as an intermediary between the people and government with the goal of getting their members elected to public office

political values   A set of beliefs about political processes and the role that government should play in our society

poll tax   In place from 1902 until 1966 in Texas, a tax citizens were required to pay each year between October and January to be eligible to vote in the next election cycle

popular sovereignty   The idea that power granted in state constitutions rests with the people

precinct chair   Party official elected in each voting precinct to organize and support the party

preferential voting   A system that allows voters to rank order candidates for the city council

presidential preference primary   Elections held every four years by political parties to determine the preferences of voters for presidential candidates

primary election   An election used by major political parties in Texas to nominate candidates for the November general election

professional associations   Organizations promoting the interests of individuals who generally must hold a state-issued license to engage in their profession

progressive taxes   Taxes that take a higher percentage of income from high-income persons

proportional taxes   Taxes that take the same percentage of income from all citizens

public goods   Goods or services characterized by the features of nonexcludability and nonrivalrous consumption; they are often provided by governments.

public policy   "Whatever governments choose to do or not to do."—Thomas Dye

R

racial gerrymandering   Legislative districts that are drawn to the advantage of a minority group

Raza Unida (United Race)   Minor party that supported election of Mexican Americans in Texas in the 1970s

reapportionment   Refers to the process of allocating representatives to districts

recall   The removal of the governor or an elected official by a petition signed by the required number of registered voters and by an election in which a majority votes to remove the person from office

recidivism   The rate at which criminal offenders commit crime after they leave the state's custody

redistributive goods   Those goods where government takes money from one group of citizens and gives it to other citizens; welfare is a good example.

redistricting   The drawing of district boundaries

registered voters   Citizens who have formally gone through the process of getting their names on the voter registration list

regressive taxes   Taxes that take a higher percentage of income from low-income persons

regulatory goods   Good, activity, or resource that the government regulates to prevent overuse; an example is pumping water from a commonly owned aquifer.

rent seeking   The practice of trying to secure benefits for oneself or one's group through political means

retail trade associations   Organizations seeking to protect and promote the interests of member businesses involved in the sales of goods and services

Reynolds v. Sims   Court case that required state legislative districts for both houses to contain about the same number of citizens

rider   Provision attached to a bill that may not be of the same subject matter as the main bill

right-to-work laws   Legislation stipulating that a person cannot be denied employment because of membership or nonmembership in a labor union or other labor organization

Robin Hood Plan   System for funding the state's primary and secondary public school education whereby rich districts send money to the state, which then distributes those funds to poor school districts

Roe v. Wade   Texas court case that limits what states can legally do to prevent abortions

runoff primary   Election that is required if no person receives a majority in the primary election; primarily used in southern and border states

S

same-day voter registration   Voters are allowed to register on election day; no preregistration before the election is required.

secretary of state   Chief election official and keeper of state records; appointed by the governor

semi-closed primary system   A nominating election that is open to all registered voters, but voters are required to declare party affiliation when they vote in the primary election.

semi-open primary system   Voter may choose to vote in the primary of either party on election day; voters are considered "declared" for the party in whose primary they vote.

senatorial courtesy   The courtesy of the governor clearing his or her appointments with state senator from the appointee's home district

separation of powers   Power divided between the legislative, executive, and judicial branches of government

sine die   Legislature must adjourn at end of regular session and cannot continue to meet.

single-member district   A system where the city is divided into election districts, and only the voters living in that district elect the council member from that district

single-member districts   Districts represented by one elected member to the legislature

social contract theory   The idea that all individuals possess inalienable rights and willingly submit to government to protect these rights

Society   An organization that promoted German immigration to Texas in the 1840s

socioeconomic factors   Factors such as income, education, race, and ethnicity that affect voter turnout

"sore loser" law   Law in Texas that prevents a person who lost the primary vote from running as an independent or minor party candidate

speaker of the house   Member of the Texas house, elected by the house members, who serves as presiding officer and generally controls the passage of legislation

special purpose district   Form of local government that provides specific services to citizens, such as water, sewage, fire protection, or public transportation

special sessions   Sessions called by the governor to consider legislation proposed by the governor only

standing committees   Committees of the house and senate that consider legislation during sessions

stare decisis   Court decisions depending on previous rulings of other courts

state and local interest groups (SLIGs)   Interest groups that represent state and local governments, such as the Texas Association of Counties

state executive committee   Committee made up of one man and one woman elected from each state senatorial district that functions as the governing body of the party

state party chair   Heads the state executive committee and provides leadership for the party

statutes   Laws passed by state legislatures

straight ticket voting system   System that allows voters to vote for all candidates of a single political party by making a single mark and that has resulted in an increase in the number of Republican judges

straight ticket voting   Casting all your votes for candidates of one party

strong mayor form   Form of local government where most power rests with the mayor

Sunset Advisory Commission   Agency responsible for making recommendations to the legislature for change in the structure and organization of most state agencies

supremacy clause   A clause that makes constitutional provisions superior to other laws

T

tax base   The items that are subject to tax; for example, the items subject to sales tax

tax capacity   A measure of the wealth of a state or its ability to raise revenues relative to all other states

tax effort   A measure of how close a state comes to using its tax capacity

tax exporting   The shifting of taxes to citizens in other states; a good example is Wyoming coal, which is exported to Texas to generate electricity.

tax incidence   The person actually paying the tax

tax shifting   Passing taxes on to other citizens

temporary party organization   Series of meetings or conventions that occur every two years at the precinct, county, and state levels

Tenth Amendment   Amendment of the U.S. Constitution that delegates or reserves some powers to the state governments or to the people

tenure of office   The ability of governors to be reelected to office

term limits   Limitations on the number of times a person can be elected to the same office in state legislatures

Texas Ethics Commission   State agency responsible for enforcing requirements for interest groups and candidates for public office to report information on money collected and activities

Texas Railroad Commission   State agency with regulation over some aspects of transportation and the oil and gas industry of the state

trade associations   Interest groups that represent more specific business interests

traditionalistic subculture   Government that maintains existing political order for the benefit of a small elite

trial courts   Local courts that hear cases; juries determine the outcome of the cases heard in the court.

trial de novo courts   Courts that do not keep a written record of their proceedings; cases on appeal begin as new cases in the appellate courts.

trustee   Representational role of a member that states that the member will make decisions on his or her own judgment about what is best for voters

turnover   The number of new members of the legislature each session

U

unitary system of government   A system of government where all functions of government are controlled by the central/national government

V

voter registration   The act of qualifying to vote by formally enrolling on an official list of voters

voter turnout   The proportion of people who cast ballots in an election

Voting Rights Act   A federal law aimed at preventing racial discrimination in the operation of voter registration and elections at the state level

voting-age population   The number of people age 18 and over

voting-eligible population   The voting-age population, corrected to exclude groups ineligible to vote, such as noncitizens and convicted felons

W

weak mayor form   Form of government where the mayor shares power with the council and other elected officials

white primary   From 1923 to 1945, Democratic Party primary that excluded African Americans from participating

write-in candidate   A person whose name does not appear on the ballot; voters must write in that person's name, and the person must have led a formal notice that he or she was a write-in candidate before the election.

Design Elements Prairie Chicken: © George Lavendowski/ USFWS; Aqueduct : © National Park Service; State Capitol: © Editorial Image, LLC/Alamy.

Preface Page x(top): © Courtesy of Texas State Library and Archives Commission; p. x(bottom): © National Park Service.

Chapter 1 Page 7: © Courtesy of Texas State Library & Archives Commission; p. 9: Library of Congress Prints and Photographs Division LC-USZ62-26332; 1.2(top left): © iStockphoto.com/Hal Bergman; 1.2(top right): © iStockphoto. com/Andrew Dean; 1.2(bottom left): © iStockphoto.com/Greg Cooksey; 1.2(bottom right): © iStockphoto.com/Eric Foltz.

Chapter 2 Figures 2.1(top, bottom left): © Photov.com/ age fotostock RF; 2.1(bottom right): © Hisham Ibrahim/ Photographer's Choice RF/Getty Images; p. 31: © Universal Images Group Limited/Alamy; p. 32, 34: © Courtesy of Texas State Library and Archives Commission; 2.3: © iStockphoto. com/Greg Cooksey; 2.4: © Harvey Loyd/Stockbyte/Getty Images; p. 53: © Steve C. Wilson/AP Images.

Chapter 3 Page 58: © Mike Norton/Purestock/Superstock RF; p. 70: © Bettmann/Corbis; p. 80: © Eric Gay/AP Images; p. 82: © Richard Carson/AP Images; p. 86: © Jay Janner/AP Images.

Chapter 4 Page 101: Library of Congress Prints and Photographs Division Washington, D.C. 20540 USA http:// hdl.loc.gov/loc.pnp/pp.print; p. 120: © Matthew Bollom.

Chapter 5 Page 129: © Harry Cabluck/AP Images; p. 139: © spxChrome/E+/Getty Images; p. 140: © Erick Schlegel/AP Images; p. 150: © Michael Ainsworth/*Dallas Morning News*/ Corbis.

Chapter 6 Page 161: © Peter Tsai Photography/Alamy; 6.6: © Image Source/Getty Images; p. 180: © Ron T. Ennis/*Fort Worth Star–Telegram*/AP Images.

Chapter 7 Page 187: © Erich Schlegel/AP Images; p. 190: © Hill Street Studios/Getty Images; 7.3: © Jerry Caywood; p. 196: Library of Congress Prints and Photographs Division [LC-USZ62-25338]; 7.4: © Ryan McVay/Photodisc/Getty Images RF; p. 200: © McGraw-Hill Companies, Inc./Jill Braaten, photographer; p. 203: © Tamir Kalifa.

Chapter 8 Page 207: © Rex C. Curry/AP Images; p. 209: © Courtesy of Lubbock County, Texas; p. 211: © Duane A. Laverty/*Waco Herald Tribune*/AP Images; p. 217: © Ashley Landis; p. 218: © YAY Media AS/Alamy.

Chapter 9 Page 228: Library of Congress Prints and Photographs Division [LC-USZ62-110029]; p. 229: Library of Congress Prints and Photographs Division [LC-USZC4-1473]; p. 231(top): © Photo by John Dominis/The LIFE Picture Collection/Getty Images; p. 231(bottom): © Image courtesy of Jimmy Tyler/Senator John G. Tower Archives, Southwestern University, Georgetown, TX; p. 232: © Kenneth Lambert/AP Images; p. 233: © Bettmann/Corbis; p. 235: © LeAnn Mueller; p. 236: © Tony Gutierrez/AP Images; p. 246(top): © Republican Party of Texas; p. 246(bottom): © Texas Democratic Party; p. 250: © LM Otero/AP Images.

Chapter 10 Page 256: © Courtesy National Gallery of Art, Washington; p. 260: © Tom Williams/CQ Roll Call/Getty Images; p. 261: © The McGraw-Hill Companies, Inc./Jill Braaten, photographer; p. 268: © Richard Michael Knittle Sr./ Demotix/Corbis.

Chapter 11 Page 281: © Eric Gay/AP Images; p. 286: © Eric Gay/AP Images; p. 295(left): © Tom Williams/Getty Images; p. 295(right): © Tamir Kalifa/File/AP Images; p. 298: © Guadalupe Williams/AFP/Getty Images.